Kntx
2/95

A MODERN TREATISE
ON THE
LAW OF CRIMINAL COMPLICITY

A Modern Treatise
on the
Law of Criminal Complicity

K. J. M. SMITH

CLARENDON PRESS · OXFORD
1991

Oxford University Press, Walton Street, Oxford OX2 6DP
Oxford New York Toronto
Dehli Bombay Calcutta Madras Karachi
Petaling Jaya Singapore Hong Kong Tokyo
Nairobi Dar es Salaam Cape Town
Melbourne Auckland
and associated companies in
Berlin Ibadan

Oxford is a trade mark of Oxford University Press

Published in the United States
by Oxford University Press, New York

© Keith J. M. Smith 1991

All rights reserved. No part of this publication may be reproduced,
stored in a retrieval system, or transmitted, in any form or by any means,
electronic, mechanical, photocopying, recording, or otherwise, without
the prior permission of Oxford University Press

This book is sold subject to the condition that it shall not, by way
of trade or otherwise, be lent, re-sold, hired out or otherwise circulated
without the publisher's prior consent in any form of binding or cover
other than that in which it is published and without a similar condition
including this condition being imposed on the subsequent purchaser

British Library Cataloguing in Publication Data
Smith, K. J. M.
A modern treatise on the law of criminal complicity. –
(Oxford monographs on criminal law and justice)
1. Criminal law
I. Title
342.5
ISBN 0–19–825238–2

Library of Congress Cataloging in Publication Data
Smith, K. J. M. (Keith John Michael)
A modern treatise on the law of criminal complicity/K.J.M. Smith.
(Oxford monographs on criminal law and criminal justice)
Includes bibliographical references and index.
1. Accomplices—Great Britain.   2. Criminal liability—Great Britain.   I. Title.
II. Series.
KD7910.S65   1991   345.41'03—dc20   [344.1053]   90–46629
ISBN 0–19–825238–2

Set by Pentacor PLC, High Wycombe, Bucks
Printed in Great Britain by
Biddles Ltd
Guildford & King's Lynn

To
ATS, AAS, and CWB

Preface

From their vantage point of the mid-1830s, the first Criminal Law Commissioners[1] felt not the least inclined to mince words over what they saw as the shambling edifice of English criminal law. Looking back over the 'great fluctuations which the Criminal Law has undergone during the lapse of many centuries', they perceived a miserable 'want of general principles and rules defining and limiting' liability, with those principles which were discernible often being patently contradictory. It was a state of affairs in large measure attributable to the common law's accretive nature: of chasing 'subtle refined and useless distinctions . . . in order to reach some case of peculiar aggravation'. The effects of this failure to articulate a clear and consistent body of rules and doctrines were further reinforced by the 'considerable discrepancies . . . met with in books of authority' and the 'imperfect and often erroneous lights afforded by the text writers and reporters upon Criminal Law'.[2]

Less than two decades later the convoluted state into which law can wind itself was captured in *Bleak House*. On this occasion, rather than criminal law, the target is the Court of Chancery, whose painful and appalling condition of institutionalized injustice is evoked by resort to the imagery of fog and mud: 'Never can there come fog too thick, never can there come mud and mire too deep, to assort with the groping and floundering condition which this High Court of Chancery, most pestilent of hoary sinners, holds, this day, in the sight of heaven and earth.'[3] Applying Dickens's unrivalled evocation of legal complexity and opacity of principle to a single area of criminal law may appear far-fetched and well beyond any licence that might be conceded to authors of academic texts. However, to label complicity 'most pestilent of hoary sinners' in obscure and foggy substantive criminal law would be a forgivable exaggeration in that it conveys a solid kernel of truth. For, as will be seen, those undesirable features then generally manifest in the criminal law and identified by the first Criminal Law Commissioners, still appear frequently and in generous proportions in complicity. Consequently, the subject-matter demands particular caution in the treatment of authorities and doctrines whose coherence may have rested more on passing procedural quirks than enduring substantive logic.

[1] First Criminal Law Commissioners appointed by Lord Chancellor Brougham in 1833, and whose members included three distinguished jurists: John Austin, Andrew Amos, and Thomas Starkie.
[2] First Report (1834), 2–4.
[3] Ch. 1, 'In Chancery'. As many have noted, Dickens's representation of the Court of Chancery's grossest excesses was already outdated by the reforms of the 1840s.

The general approach adopted in this examination of the law of criminal complicity is expositional and evaluative. In theoretical respects, at least, it is an attempt at 'disencumbering [complicity] from the superfluities and inconsistencies under which it labours'.[4] Although the primary focus of the study is English law, both American and Commonwealth jurisdictions also figure prominently to facilitate and inform theoretical analysis. This is true to a much lesser degree in the case of Continental codes and theories where, because of more wide-ranging fundamental structural and conceptual distinctions, the risks of misleading comparisons or distortions by fragmentary borrowings are particularly high.

As for matters of organization and content, rather than forming any particular designated sections or chapter, relevant historical material is incorporated and distributed throughout the text and notes. Similarly, except where clearly germane to substantive law or theory, neither procedural nor evidential matters relating to accomplices will be examined. The reasons for the existence of such special rules and procedures are largely peculiar to the demands and limitations of the trial process and do not relate to substantive issues of liability.

Finally, as already noted, treatment of the subject-matter will be expositional and evaluative; no concerted attempt is made to set out detailed concrete proposals for changes in the style or substance of complicity. To a large degree the appeal, or otherwise, of the present parasitic or derivative form of secondary liability turns on the acceptance of a group of fundamental tenets of responsibility; most especially the legitimacy granted to the role of causally attributed harm. The initial stance adopted on such fundamental matters will be crucial to any potential reformer's direction and eventual preferences. For instance, those of a subjectivistic persuasion, strongly inclined to centre criminality on mental culpability, obviously will be more tempted to abandon current complicity structures for inchoate or endangerment based liability than those adhering to more orthodox notions of the place of attributable harm in criminal responsibility. However, despite the inhibiting effects of the cardinal need to settle such initial premises, both broad speculation and reform proposals will be offered in the course of each chapter.

---

[4] These riskily ambitious sentiments appear in the 7th Report of the 1833 Criminal Law Commissioners (1843), 1 n.

Acknowledgements

I have been singularly fortunate in having Professor J. C. Smith's unfailingly helpful and typically penetrating comments on the manuscript. For these and for his general interest in the work I am greatly indebted. Valuable insights on draft chapters were also provided by my colleague Dr Alex Stein. Needless to say, no views expressed hereafter should be taken as necessarily endorsed or accepted by them. The book's remaining inadequacies are solely the author's responsibility.

My thanks are also due to Mrs Donna Baston and Mrs Angela Duncan for exercising secretarial skills considerably beyond the call of duty. I have also enjoyed the polished professionalism of Mr Richard Hart, Ms Jane Williams, Ms Jane Robson, and Mr Peter Momtchiloff from Oxford University Press.

Contents

ABBREVIATIONS	xv
TABLE OF STATUTES	xvii
TABLE OF CASES	xix

1. Introduction	1
1. Theories of Complicity: An Overview	4
2. Neighbouring or Kindred Forms of Liability	7
(1) Accessory after the Fact	7
(2) Vicarious Liability	8
(3) Inchoate Liability	8
3. Structure, Scope, and Principal Issues	10

I THE *ACTUS REUS*

2. Modes of Complicity	20
1. Historical Antecedents: Treason, Felonies, Misdemeanours, and Procedural Paralysis	20
2. The Significance of Presence	24
3. Modes of Complicitous Behaviour	26
(1) Who is a Principal Offender?	27
(2) The Meaning of 'Aid, Abet, Counsel or Procure'	30
(3) Complicity through Inaction	34
(a) 'Mere presence' as a Basis of Complicity	35
(b) Complicity through Omission to Exercise Control	39
(4) Conspiracy as an Auxiliary Mode of Complicity	47
3. Causation's Role in Complicity	55
1. Case Law and Other Authorities	55
(1) English Case Law	55
(2) Institutional Authorities	61
(3) Foreign Authorities	61
(4) The Paucity of Case Law	63
2. Theoretical Possibilities	64
(1) Preliminary Premises	64
(a) Choice and Chance in Criminal Responsibility	64
(b) The Problematic Meaning of 'Cause'	66
(c) Harm, Wrongdoing, and Punishment	70

(2) The Derivative Nature of Complicity and Equality of Punishment	73
(a) Agency, Consensus, and Ratification Theories	74
(b) Inchoate, Endangerment, and Risk Rationales	76
(3) Causation's Role in Complicity	78
(a) Principal and Accessory Distinction	79
(b) Minimum Causal Contribution by an Accessory	82
(c) Substantiality and Proof of Causal Contribution	86
3. Conclusions	88
4. The Derivative Nature of Complicity	**94**
1. The Doctrine of Innocent Agency	95
(1) The Principal's Mental Culpability	97
(a) Must the Principal Be Aware of the Nature of His Agent's Innocence?	97
(b) Must the Principal Intend to Cause the Agent's Actions?	97
(2) In What Sense Does a Principal 'Cause' an Innocent Agent's Actions?	103
(a) Perpetrators Needing Prescribed Qualities or Status	106
(b) Offences Implicitly Requiring Personally Performed Actions	107
2. Complicity and the Non-Conviction of a Principal Offender or Conviction of Parties for Different Offences	110
(1) Evidential and Procedural Matters	110
(2) Substantive Considerations: Limitation of Derivative Liability	114
(3) Where the Perpetrator is Free of Liability	114
(a) The Necessity of a Principal Offence or Only Harm?	114
(b) Objective Harm or Wrongfulness Where the Perpetrator Lacks the Necessary Criminal Fault	118
(c) Objective Harm or Wrongfulness Where the Perpetrator Has a Complete Defence	120
(4) Statutory Development of 'Causing' Offences	124
(5) Where Accessory and Principal are Liable for Different Levels of Criminality: Complicity and 'Semi-Innocent Agency'	127
3. Conclusions	133

II THE MENTAL REQUIREMENT

5. The Accessory's Purpose or Knowledge that His Actions Will Assist or Encourage the Principal	**141**
1. Nature of the Problem	141

Contents

    2. English Case Law — 143
    3. Practical Consequences of Not Requiring Purpose or 'Assent' — 150
    4. Theory and Solutions — 153
    5. Facilitation Offences — 157

6. **Specificity: The Necessary Extent of the Accessory's 'Knowledge' of the Principal Offence** — 161

    1. The Accessory's Need for 'Knowledge' of 'Essential Matters' of the Principal Offence — 161
        (1) Case Law — 161
        (2) Theoretical Implications — 169
    2. The Perceived Likelihood of the Principal Offence Occurring — 173
    3. The Accessory's Knowledge of the Principal's Mens Rea or Culpable State of Mind — 177
    4. The Accessory's Knowledge of the Circumstances and Consequences of the Principal Offence — 179
    5. Unforeseen Consequences of Foreseen Conduct: Complicity in Offences of Negligence — 185
    6. Complicity in Offences of Strict Liability — 191
    7. Conclusions: The Accessory's Mental Culpability and Complicity Theory — 194

7. **Variations in Performance by the Principal from that Contemplated by the Accessory** — 197

    1. The Relationship of Variation and Common Purpose — 197
    2. Mistaken or Accidental Deviation — 198
    3. Deliberate Variation — 200
        (1) Expressed Limited Authority — 202
        (2) The Voluntary and Causally Independent Principal — 203

8. **The Doctrine of Common Purpose** — 209

    1. Nineteenth-Century and Earlier Developments — 210
    2. Modern Case Law Issues — 214
    3. Agreement or Foresight? — 218
    4. Common Purpose and Variation — 222
    5. Convicting the Errant Principal of Murder or Manslaughter and the Accessory of Manslaughter — 225
        (1) Authorized or Foreseen Actions? — 228
        (2) Unforeseen and 'Overwhelming Supervening Events' — 228
        (3) Relevance of Weapons — 230
    6. Common Purpose and Policy Objectives — 231

III EXCLUSION, LIMITATION, AND WITHDRAWAL

9. Exclusion and Limitation of Complicity — 238

1. *Inevitable Incidental Participation* — 238
2. *Secondary Participation Motivated by Law Enforcement Objectives* — 243
3. *Limitations on Complicity in Subsequent Offences* — 245
   (1) Mens Rea — 246
   (2) Causation — 247
   (3) Express Limitation — 247
   (4) Judicial Discretion in Respect of Criminal Proceedings — 247
   (5) Limitation of Punishment — 248
   (6) A Direct Limitation Rule — 248

10. General Defences and Withdrawal — 250

1. *General Defences* — 250
2. *Withdrawal* — 251
   (1) Preliminary Issues — 251
     (a) Claims of no Actus Reus *and Defences* — 252
     (b) Justifying Rationale of a Withdrawal Defence — 253
   (2) Forms of Withdrawal — 254
     (a) Theoretical and Practical Possibilities — 254
     (b) Case Law — 256
   (3) Must Withdrawal be 'Timely'? — 260
   (4) Motivation for Withdrawal — 261

Bibliography — 263

Index — 269

Abbreviations

ALJR	Australian Law Journal Reports
Am. J. Comp. L.	*American Journal of Comparative Law*
Annot. . . . ALR	American Law Reports annotations
An. Survey of Am. Law	*Annual Survey of American Law*
BCLR	British Columbia Law Reports
Blackstone, *Comm.*	W. Blackstone, *Commentaries on the Laws of England* (1767).
Brig. Young ULR	*Brigham Young University Law Review*
Brooklyn LR	*Brooklyn Law Review*
Buffalo LR	*Buffalo Law Review*
Cal. L. Rev.	*California Law Review*
Cal. Rept.	California Reporter
Case West RL Rev.	*Case Western Reserve Law Review*
CCC	Canadian Criminal Cases
CLJ	Cambridge Law Journal
CLP	Current Legal Problems
CLR	Commonwealth Law Reports
Co. Inst.	E. Coke, *Institutes of the Laws of England* (1797).
Col. LR	Columbia Law Review
Crim. LJ	*Criminal Law Journal* (Aust)
Crim LR	Criminal Law Review
DLR	Dominion Law Reports
East, *PC*	E. H. East, *A Treatise of the Pleas of the Crown* (1803).
FLR	Federal Law Reports
Ford. LR	Fordham Law Review
F. Supp.	Federal Supplement
Hale, *PC*	M. Hale, *The History of the Pleas of the Crown* (1736).
Hastings LJ	*Hastings Law Journal*
Hawkins, *PC*	W. Hawkins, *A Treatise of the Pleas of the Crown*, 8th edn. by J. Curwood (1824).
Hist. Jo.	*Historical Journal*
HKLR	Hong Kong Law Reports
HLR	Harvard Law Review
Is. LR	Israel Law Review
JP Jo.	*Justice of the Peace Journal*
Kenny	Kenny's Outlines of Criminal Law, ed. J. W. C. Turner (1952–66).
LA Ann.	Louisiana Annotated Cases
Law and Contemp. Probs.	*Law and Contemporary Problems*
Law and Phil.	*Law and Philosophy*

Loyola LR	Loyola Law Review
LQR	Law Quarterly Review
LS	Journal of Legal Studies
Mel. ULR	Melbourne University Law Review
Memphis SULR	Memphis State University Law Review
Miss. LJ	Mississippi Law Journal
MLR	Modern Law Review
NIJB	Northern Ireland Judgment Bulletin
NYULR	New York University Law Review
NZLJ	New Zealand Law Journal
NZLR	New Zealand Law Reports
Okl. LR	Oklahoma Law Review
Phil. and Pub. Aff.	Philosophy and Public Affairs
Qd. R.	Queensland Reports
Russell	J. W. C. Turner, Russell on Crime, 12th edn. (1964).
Rut. LJ	Rutgers Law Journal
SACJ	South African Journal of Criminal Justice
SALJ	South African Law Journal
Santa Clara LR	Santa Clara Law Review
SASR	South Australian State Reports
S. Cal. LR	Southern California Law Review
Sol. Jo.	Solicitors Journal
SR	Southern Rhodesian Reports
Stan. LR	Stanford Law Review
Stephen, HCL	J. F. Stephen, History of the Criminal Law of England (1883).
Syr. LR	Syracuse Law Review
Temp. LR	Temple Law Review
UCLA LR	University of California Los Angeles Law Review
U. Penn. LR	University of Pennsylvania Law Review
Van. LR	Vanderbilt Law Review
VLR	Victorian Law Reports
VR	Victoria Reports
Williams, CLGP	G. L. Williams, Criminal Law: The General Part, 2nd edn. (1961).
Wis. LR	Wisconsin Law Review
WWR	Western Weekly Reports
YLJ	Yale Law Journal

Table of Statutes

1275 Statute of Westminster
  (33 Ed 1) 22, 111
1531 (23 Hen 8 c.1)
  s. 3 . . . . 24, 31
  s. 4 24
1546 (1 Ed 6 c.12)
  s. 10 24
  s. 13 31
1558 (4 & 5 P & M c.4) . . 31
1589 (32 Eliz 1 c.12)
  s. 5 31
1597 (39 Eliz 1 c.9)
  s. 2 31
1691 (3 & 4 Will & Mar c.9) . 31
1702 (1 Anne St. 2 c.9) . . 23, 31, 112
1826 (7 Geo IV c.64)
  s. 9 112
1831 Game Act (1 & 2 Will 4 c.32) 107
1833 (3 & 4 Will 4 c.44) . . 24
1848 (11 & 12 Vic c.46) . . 112
1848 Summary Jurisdiction Act
  s. 5 22
1861 Accessories and Abettors Act (24 & 25 Vict c.94) . 31, 191
  s. 2 112
  s. 8 . 21, 27, 30, 31, 105, 112, 124
  s. 71 213
  s. 72 213
1861 Offences Against the Person Act (24 & 25 Vict c.100)
  s. 18 129
  s. 20 129
  s. 58 146
  s. 59 146
1875 Falsification of Accounts Act
  s. 1(1) 106
1883 Explosive Substances Act (46 & 47 Vict c.3) . . . 168
  s. 3(*a*), (*b*) 165
  s. 5 165
1906 Prevention of Corruption Act (6 Edw 7 c.34) . . . 243
1911 Perjury Act (1 & 2 Geo 5 c.6)
  s. 7 124
1938 Infanticide Act (1 & 2 Geo 6 c.36)
  s. 1 131
1952 Magistrates' Courts Act (15 & 16 Geo 6 & 1 Eliz 2 c.55)
  s. 35 22
1953 Food and Drugs Act . . 192
1956 Sexual Offences Act (4 & 5 Eliz 2 c.69)
  s. 1(1) 109, 126
  s. 6 . . . . . . 147, 183
    (3) 184
  s. 28(1) 31, 147
    (3) 147
1957 Homicide Act (5 Eliz 2 c.11) 213
  s. 2(3), (4) 131
  s. 3 132
  s. 5(1) (*a*). 25
1961 Suicide Act (9 & 10 Eliz 2 c.60)
  s. 2 46
1967 Criminal Justice Act (c. 80)
  s. 8 84

Table of Cases

A.C.S., *Re* [1969] 4 CCC 284 36
Ackroyd's Air Travel *v.* D.P.P. [1950] 1 All E.R. 933; 48 L.G.R. 398; 83 Ll.L.Rep. 431, DC 161
Agresti *v.* State 234 A 2d 284 (1967) 123
Ahmed [1990] Crim.L.R. 648 . . . . 96, 100, 145
Allen *v.* Ireland [1984] 1 W.L.R. 903 36
Alphacell *v.* Woodward [1972] AC 824; [1972] 2 WLR 1320; 116 S.J. 431; [1972] 2 All E.R. 475; 70 L.G.R. 455; [1972] Crim.L.R. 41, HL; affirming [1972] 1 Q.B. 127; [1971] 3 W.L.R. 445; 115 S.J. 464; [1971] 2 All E.R. 910; 69 L.G.R. 561, DC . . 192
Anderson *v.* Superior Court 78 Cal App 2d 22 (1974) 49
Att-Gen *v.* Able [1984] Q.B. 795; [1983] 3 W.L.R. 845; (1983) 127 S.J. 731; [1984] 1 All E.R. 277; (1984) 78 Cr.App.R. 197; [1984] Crim.L.R. 35 . . . . 1, 23, 33, 57, 59, 148, 176
Att-Gen's Reference (No. 1 of 1975) Q.B. 773; [1975] 3 W.L.R. 11; 119 S.J. 373; [1975] 2 All E.R. 684; 61 Cr.App.R. 118; [1975] R.T.R. 473; [1975] Crim.L.R. 449, CA . . . 31, 32, 46, 47, 58–60, 143, 146, 151
Austin [1981] 1 All ER 374 122

Backun *v.* US 122 F 2d 635 (1940) 142, 152, 154
Bailey *v.* Comm 329 SE 2d 37 (1985) 101
Ball *v.* Loughlin (1966) Cr.App.R. 266 108
Barker *ex p.* (1891) 30 NBR 406 240
Bateman *v.* Evans 108 S.J. 522; [1964] Crim.L.R. 601, DC . . 180, 181
Beatty *v.* Gilbanks (1882) 9 Q.B.D. 308 67
Benchwick *v.* US 297 F 2d 330 (1961) 200
Benford *v.* Sims [1898] 2 Q.B.D. 641 56
Benson *v.* Offley (1686) 2 Show KB 510; 89 E.R. 1071 112
Bentley *v.* Mullen District Council [1986] R.T.R. 7 58
Bibithe's Case (1597) 4 Co Rep 43b; 76 E.R. 991 185
Biggs *v.* Lawrence (1789) 3 TR 454; 100 E.R. 673 156
Bonar *v.* McLeod 1983 SCCR 161 42
Boushea *v.* US 173 F 2d 131 (1949) 104
Bowker *v.* Premier Drug Co [1928] 1 K.B. 217 . . . 31, 161, 162, 191
Bowry *v.* Bennett (1808) 1 Camp 348; 170 E.R. 981 156
Boyne *v.* H.M. Advocate 1980 SLT 56 221
Breaz *v.* State 13 NE 2d 952 (1938) 62

Table of Cases

C v. Hulme [1979] Crim.L.R. 328 36
Cafferata v. Wilson [1936] 3 All E.R. 149 . . . . 145, 156
Cain v. Doyle (1946) 72 C.L.R. 409 115
Caldwell v. Bethell [1913] 1 K.B. 119 239
Callanan v. US 364 US 587 (1961) 52
Callow v. Tillstone (1900) 19 Cox 576 . . . . . 161, 162, 191, 192
Carter v. Mace 113 J.P. 527; [1949] 2 all E.R. 714 161
Carter v. Richardson [1974] R.T.R. 314; [1974] Crim.L.R. 190, DC 41, 180, 181, 191
Carter, Patersons and Pickfords v. Wessel [1947] K.B. 849; 177 L.T. 448; 91 S.J. 446; sub nom Wessel v. Carter Paterson and Pickfords [1947] L.J.R. 1370; 63 T.L.R. 517; 111 J.P. 474; [1947] 2 All E.R. 280, DC 31, 161, 239
Cassady v. Morris (Reg) (Transport) [1975] R.T.R. 470; [1975] Crim.L.R. 398, DC 42
Chan Wing-Siu v. The Queen [1985] A.C. 168; (1984) 3 W.L.R. 677; (1984) 128 S.J. 685; [1984] 3 All E.R. 877; (1984) 80 Cr.App.R. 117; [1984] Crim.L.R. 549; (1984) 81 L.S.Gaz 216, PC 63, 174, 175–7, 195, 203, 218–21, 228, 231
Chief Constable of Hampshire v. Mace (1987) 84 Cr.App.R. 40; (1986) 150 J.P. 470; (1986) 150 J.P.N. 574, DC 53
Chivers v. Hand (1914) 24 Cox 520 . . . . 161, 191
Churchill v. Walton [1967] 2 A.C. 224; [1967] 2 W.L.R. 682; 131 J.P. 277; 111 S.J. 112; [1967] 1 All E.R. 497; 51 Cr.App.R. 212, HL; reversing sub nom R v. Churchill [1967] 1 Q.B. 190; [1966] 2 W.L.R. 1116; 110 S.J. 526; [1966] 2 All E.R. 215; [1966] C.L.Y. 2175, CA 161, 193
Cody v. State 361 P 2d 307 (1961) 115
Collins and Fox v. Chief Constable of Merseyside [1988] Crim LR 247, DC 27
Comm. ex rel Smith v. Myers 261 A 2d 550 (1970) 99
Comm. v. Flowers 387 A 2d 1268 (1978) 63
Comm. v. French 259 NE 2d 195 (1970) 50
Comm. v. Henderson 378 A 2d 393 (1977) 36
Comm. v. Jackson 485 A 2d 1102 (1984) 50
Comm. v. Lee 399 A 2d 104 (1979) 260
Comm. v. Mangula 322 NE 2d 177 (1975) 50, 260
Comm. v. Orlowski 481 A 2d 952 (1984) 50
Comm. v. Richards 293 NE 2d 854 (1972) 50
Comm. v. Root 170 A 2d 310 (1961) 187
Commonwealth v. Almeida 68 2d 595 (1949) 99
Commonwealth v. Moyer 53 AD 736 (1947) 99, 100
Commonwealth v. Redline 137 A 2d 472 (1958) 99, 100
Commonwealth v. Thomas 117 A 2d 204 (1955) 99

Table of Cases

Connelly v. D.P.P. [1964] A.C. 1254; [1964] 2 W.L.R. 1145; 128 J.P. 418; 108 S.J. 356; [1964] 2 All E.R. 401; 48 Cr.App.R. 183, HL; affirming *sub nom* R v. Connelly [1963] 3 W.L.R. 839; 107 S.J. 793; [1963] 3 All E.R. 510, CCA. 247
Cook v. Stockwell 15 Cox 49 . . . . 145, 156
Cornwall's Case (1730) St 881; 93 E.R. 914 210
Crampton v. Fish [1970] Crim.L.R. 235; (1969) Sol Jo 1003. . 41, 180
Curtis [1988] 1 NZLR 734. 159

D v. Parsons [1960] 1 W.L.R. 797; 124 J.P. 375; 104 S.J. 605; [1960] 2 All E.R. 493; 58 L.G.R. 325, DC 36
Davies v. D.P.P. [1954] A.C. 378; [1954] 2 W.L.R. 343; 118 J.P. 222; 98 S.J. 161; [1954] 1 All E.R. 507; 38 Cr.App.R. 11, HL; affirming *sub nom* R v. Davies [1954] 1 W.L.R. 214; 98 S.J. 64 . . . . 219, 230
Davies, Turner & Co v. Brodie [1954] 1 W.L.R. 1364; 118 J.P. 532; 98 S.J. 770; [1954] 3 All E.R. 283; 52 L.G.R. 558, DC . 161, 162, 180, 182
Dennis v. Pight (1968) 11 F.L.R. 458 43
Devlin v. Armstrong (1971) N.I. 13 121
D.P.P. for Northern Ireland v. Lynch [1975] A.C. 653; [1975] 2 W.L.R. 641; 119 S.J. 233; 61 Cr.App.R. 6; *sub nom* Lynch v. D.P.P. for Northern Ireland [1975] 1 All E.R. 1913; [1975] Crim.L.R. 707, HL . . . 56, 73, 116, 122, 145, 148–151, 181, 250
D.P.P. for Northern Ireland v. Maxwell (1978) 122 S.J. 758; [1978] 3 All E.R. 1140; [1978] Crim.L.R. 40; *sub nom* Maxwell v. D.P.P. for Northern Ireland (1978) 68 Cr.App.R. 128; *sub nom* D.P.P. v. Maxwell [1978] 1 W.L.R. 1350, HL; affirming [1978] Crim.L.R. 422, CA (N.I.) 33, 53, 74, 105, 141, 145, 161, 164–70, 174, 175, 177, 180, 181, 194, 201–3, 206–8, 210, 219, 221, 223, 224, 232, 246
D.P.P. v. Beard [1920] A.C. 479 . . . . 215, 216
D.P.P. v. Humphreys; *sub nom* R v. Humphreys [1977] A.C. 1; [1976] 2 W.L.R. 857; 120 S.J. 420; [1976] 2 1497; [1976] R.T.R. 339; 63 Cr.App.R. 95; [1977] Crim.L.R. 421, HL; reversing *sub nom* R v. Humphreys [1976] Q.B. 191; [1975] 3 W.L.R. 81; 119 S.J. 473; [1975] 2 All E.R. 1023; 62 Cr.App.R. 1; [1975] Crim.L.R. 708, CA 247
D.P.P. v. Hyam, *see* Hyam v. D.P.P.
D.P.P. v. Majewski [1977] A.C. 443; [1976] 2 W.L.R. 623; 120 S.J. 299; [1976] 2 All E.R. 142; 62 Cr.App.R. 262; [1976] Crim.L.R. 374, HL; affirming *sub nom* R v. Majewski [1975] 3 W.L.R. 401; 119 S.J. 560; [1975] 3 All E.R. 296; [1975] Crim.L.R. 570, CA 250, 251

D.P.P. *v.* Merriman [1973] A.C. 584; [1972] 3 W.L.R. 545; 116
  S.J. 745; [1972] 3 All E.R. 42; 56 Cr.App.R. 766; [1976]
  Crim.L.R. 784, HL; reversing *sub nom* R *v.* Merriman [1971] 2
  Q.B. 310; [1971] 2 W.L.R. 1453; 115 S.J. 466; [1971] 2 All E.R. 424,
  CA 56, 116, 117
D.P.P. *v.* Newbury; D.P.P. *v.* Jones [1977] A.C. 500; [1976] 2
  W.L.R. 918; [1976] 2 All E.R. 365; (1976) 62 Cr.App.R. 291;
  [1977] Crim.L.R. 359; *sub nom* D.P.P. *v.* Newbury and Jones
  120 S.J. 402, HL 190
D.P.P. *v.* Shannon [1975] A.C. 717; [1974] 3 W.L.R. 155; 118 S.J.
  515; 59 Cr.App.R. 250; *sub nom* R *v.* Shannon [1974] 2 All E.R.
  1009; [1975] Crim.L.R. 703, HL; reversing [1974] Crim.L.R. 177,
  CA 113
D.P.P. *v.* Stonehouse [1978] A.C. 55; [1977] 3 W.L.R. 143; (1977)
  121 S.J. 491; [1977] 2 All E.R. 909; (1977) 65 Cr.App.R. 192; [1977]
  Crim.L.R. 544, HL 96
Drury (1974) 60 Cr.App.R. 195 36
Du Cros *v.* Lambourne [1907] 1 K.B. 40 . 21, 31, 40, 45, 113, 185, 187
Dunning *v.* Graham (1985) Unreported. Smith and Hogan,
  Criminal Law, p. 146 201
Dusenbury *v.* Commonwealth 263 SE 2d 392 (1980) 109
Duxley *v.* Gilmore (1959) 123 JP Jo 331; [1959] Crim.L.R. 454 . 42, 43

Eddy *v.* Niman (1981) 73 Cr.App.R. 237; [1981] Crim.L.R. 502,
  DC 257
Emmund *v.* Florida 458 US 782 (1982) 78
Evans *v.* Pesce and Att-Gen for Alberta [1970] 3 CCC 61 240

Fairburn *v.* Evans [1916] 1 K.B. 218 . . . . 39, 239
Ferguson *v.* Weaving [1951] 1 K.B. 814; [1951] T.L.R. 465; 155
  J.P. 142; 95 S.J. 90; [1951] 1 All E.R. 412; 49 L.G.R. 339,
  DC 32, 42, 143, 161
Foster *v.* Driscoll [1929] 1 K.B. 496 156
Francis and Francis *v.* Central Criminal Court [1988] 3 All E.R.
  775, HL 96
Freeman *v.* State 362 SW 2d 251 (1962) 189
Fritz *v.* State 130 NW 2d 279 104
Fuson *v.* Comm. 251 SW 995 (1923) 86

Gardner *v.* Akeroyd [1952] 2 Q.B. 743; [1952] 2 T.L.R. 169; 116
  J.P. 460; 96 S.J. 483; [1952] 2 All E.R. 306, DC 8
Garret *v.* Arthur Churchill (Glass) [1970] 1 Q.B. 92; [1969] 3
  W.L.R. 6; 133 J.P. 509; 113 S.J. 381; [1969] 2 All E.R. 1141,
  DC 152, 153

Table of Cases

Gibbons *v.* Pepper (1965) 1 Ld Raym 38; 91 E.R. 922 95
Gibson (1984) 80 Cr.App.R. 24 36
Gillick *v.* West Norfolk & Wisbech Area Health Authority and the
   DHSS [1986] A.C. 112; [1985] 3 W.L.R. 830; (1985) 129 S.J.
   738; [1985] 3 All E.R. 402; [1986] Crim.L.R. 113; (1985) 135
   New L.J. 1055; [1986] 1 F.L.R. 224; (1985) 82 L.S. Gaz 3531,
   HL; reversing [1985] 2 W.L.R. 413; (1985) 129 S.J. 42; [1985] 1
   All E.R. 533; (1985) 15 Fam.Law 165; (1985) New L.J. 81;
   (1985) L.S. Gaz 762, CA; reversing [1984] Q.B. 581; [1983] 3
   W.L.R. 859; (1983) 127 S.J. 696; (1983) 147 J.P. 888; [1984] 1
   All E.R. 365; (1984) 14 Fam.Law 207; (1983) 80 L.S. Gaz 2678;
   (1983) 133 New L.J. 888. . . 1, 31, 59, 143, 146, 147, 149, 169, 245
Giorgianni *v.* R [1985] 156 CLR 473 . . . . 180–2, 187
Goose's Case (1597) Moore K.B. 461; 72 E.R. 695 185
Gouth *v.* Rees (1929) 29 Cox 74 . . . . 42, 43, 191
Gould & Co *v.* Houghton [1921] 1 K.B. 509 113
Griffith *v.* State 26 Ga 493 (1858) 28
Griffiths *v.* Studebakers [1924] 1 K.B. 102 115
Gurrieri *v.* Gunn 404 FS 21 (1975) 49

H.M. Advocate *v.* Johnstone (1926) JC 89 159
H.M. Advocate *v.* Semple (1937) JC 41 159
Hall *v.* Norfolk [1900] 2 Ch. 500 36
Halloway's Case (1628) Cro.Car.131; 79 E.R. 715 95
Harawira [1989] 2 NZLR 714 29
Henshall (John) (Quarries) *v.* Harvey [1965] 2 Q.B. 233; [1965] 2
   W.L.R. 758; 129 J.P. 224; 109 S.J. 152; [1965] 1 All E.R. 725,
   DC 161
Hodgson *v.* Temple (1813) 5 Taunt 181; 128 E.R. 656 156
Hollington *v.* Hawthorn [1942] K.B. 587 112
Hotchkins *v.* Hindmarsh [1891] 2 Q.B. 181 239
Howe [1987] 1 All E.R. 771 108
Howell *v.* Doyle [1952] V.L.R. 128 62
Howells *v.* Wynne (1863) 15 CB (NS) 3; 143 E.R. 682 41
Hyam *v.* D.P.P. [1955] A.C. 55; [1974] 2 W.L.R. 607; [1974] 2 All
   E.R. 41; 59 Cr.App.R. 91; *sub nom* R *v.* Hyam 118 S.J. 311;
   [1974] Crim.L.R. 365, HL; affirming *sub nom* R *v.* Hyam [1974]
   Q.B. 99; [1973] 3 W.L.R. 475; 117 S.J. 543; [1973] 3 All E.R.
   842; [1973] Crim.L.R. 638; *sub nom* R *v.* Hyam (Pearl Kathleen)
   57 Cr.App.R. 824, CA 142, 182

Invicta Plastics *v.* Clare (1975) 120 S.J. 62; [1976] R.T.R. 251;
   [1976] Crim.L.R. 131, DC 34

Table of Cases

Jacobs v. State 184 So 2d 711 (1966) 187–8
Jindra v. US 69 F 2d 429 (1934) 86
Johns v. R [1980] 143 C.L.R. 108 . . . . . . 150, 174, 220, 224
Johnson v. State 142 Ala 70 100
Johnson v. US 386 A 2d 710 (1978) 232
Johnson v. Youden [1950] 1 K.B. 544; 66 T.L.R. (Pt.1) 395; 114 J.P. 136; 94 S.J. 115; [1950] 1 All E.R. 300; 48 L.G.R. 276, DC 161, 169, 180, 191, 213
Jones v. State 486 A 2d 184 (1985) 128

Keithler v. Mississippi 10 Sm and M 192 (1848) 85

Ladbrokes (Football) v. Perret [1971] 1 W.L.R. 110; (1970) 114 S.J. 930; [1971] 1 All E.R. 129, DC 145
Lang v. Lang [1954] 3 W.L.R. 762 145
Lee Chun-Cheun, alias Lee Wing-Cheuk v. R [1963] A.C. 220; [1962] 3 W.L.R. 1461; 106 S.J. 1008; [1963] 1 All E.R. 73, PC 132
Lenzi v. Millar [1965] S.A.S.R. 1 62
Lewis [1975] 1 NZLR 222 159
Little v. H.M.A. 1983 S.C.C.R. 56 61
Lloyd v. Johnson (1798) 1 Bos and Pul 340; 126 E.R. 939 . . . 156
Lynch v. D.P.P. for Northern Ireland, see D.P.P. for Northern Ireland v. Lynch

McBryde v. State 352 A 2d 324 (1976) 26
MacDaniel's Case (1755) 19 St Tr 745 112
McGhee v. Comm. 270 SE 2d 729 (1980) 62, 200
McGhee v. National Coal Board [1973] 1 W.L.R. 1; 116 S.J. 967; [1972] 3 All E.R. 1008; 13 K.I.R. 471, HL; reversing 1972 S.L.T. (Notes) 61, Court of Session 88
McGregor v. Benyon [1957] Crim.L.R. 608, DC; reversing [1957] Crim.L.R. 250 116
MacNeil v. H.M. Advocate 1986 SCCR 288 252
Mancini v. D.P.P. [1942] A.C. 1 123
Marsh v. Johnston [1959] Crim.L.R. 444 244
Matusevich v. R (1977) 51 ALJR 657; [1976] VR 470 . . . 98, 108, 116
Melvin v. H.M. Advocate 1984 SCCR 113 . . . . 128, 229
Miller v. R (1980) 55 ALJR 23 174
Mills v. Cooper [1967] 2 Q.B. 459; [1967] 2 W.L.R. 1343; 131 J.P. 349; 111 S.J. 273; [1967] 2 All E.R. 100; 65 L.G.R. 275, DC 247
Mohan v. R, see Ramnath Mohan v. R
Mok Wei Tak and Mok Chiu Yee Man v. R [1990] 2 W.L.R. 897 . 169

Table of Cases

Moore v. Lowe 180 SE 1 (1935) 132, 185
Moreland v. State 139 SE 77 (1927) 40
Morris v. Tolman [1923] 1 K.B. 166. . . . . 113, 115

National Coal Board v. Gamble [1959] 1 Q.B. 11; [1958] 3 W.L.R. 434; 122 J.P. 453; 102 S.J. 621; [1958] 3 All E.R. 203; 42 Cr.App.R. 240, DC . . . 40, 43, 56, 141, 143–8, 150, 151, 153

O'Sullivan v. Truth and Sportsman (1957) 96 C.L.R. 220. 62

Palmer (Sigismund) v. R; Irving (Derrick) v. R [1971] A.C. 814; [1971] 2 W.L.R. 831; *sub nom* Palmer v. R; Irving v. R 115 S.J. 264; *sub nom* Palmer v. R [1971] 1 All E.R. 1077; 55 Cr.App.R. 223, PC 186
Parker v. R [1964] A.C. 1369; [1964] 3 W.L.R. 70; 108 S.J. 459; [1964] 2 All E.R. 641, PC 132
Parker, *ex p.* (1957) S.R. (N.S.W.) 326 26
Parish v. Garfitt [1984] 1 W.L.R. 911 36
Paterson [1976] 2 N.Z.L.R. 394 159
Peak v. State 520 NE 2d 465 (1988) 261
Pellecart v. Angell (1835) 2 CM & R 311; 150 E.R. 135 . . . 156
People v. Allsip 74 Cal Rept 550 (1969) 113
People v. Beeman 674 P 2d 1318 159
People v. Brown 186 NE 2d 321 (1962) 260
People v. Gilbert 47 Cal Rept 909 (1965) 100
People v. Gilmore 134 AD 2d 653 (1987) 261
People v. Gordon 295 NE 2d 777 (1973) 159
People v. Hernandez 96 Cal Rept 7 (1971) 109, 110, 126
People v. Luna 295 P 2d 457 (1976) 36
People v. Monks 24 P 2d 508 (1933) 104
People v. Oritz 219 P 1024 (1973) 252
People v. Pitts 270 NW 2d 482 (1978) 189
People v. Rybka 158 NE 2d 17 (1959) 255
People v. Turner 229 NW 2d 861 (1975) 123
People v. Vedder 98 NY 630 (1885) 240
People v. Washburn 280 NW 132 (1938) 62
People v. Washington 44 Cal Rept 442 (1965) 100
People v. Wyherk 178 NE 890 (1931) 113
Pereira v. US 347 US 1 (1954) 126
Pinkerton v. United States 328 US 640 (1946) 49, 50–3
Piri [1987] 1 NZLR 66 174
Plunkett v. Matchell [1958] Crim.L.R. 252 . . . . 95, 107
Pratt v. Martin (1911) 2 K.B. 90 . . . . 95, 107, 108
Provincial Motor Co v. Dunning [1909] 2 K.B. 599 . . . . 161, 191

R v. Abbott [1955] 2 Q.B. 497; [1955] 3 W.L.R. 369; 119 J.P. 526; 99 S.J. 544; [1955] 2 All E.R. 899; (1955) 39 Cr.App.R. 141, CCA 218
R v. Abbott [1977] A.C. 755 250
R v. Adams (1812) R & R 225; 168 E.R. 773. 96
R v. Adams (1989) 49 CCC (3d) 100 179
R v. Allan (1963) 47 Cr.App.R. 243 . . . . 36, 37
R v. Allan [1966] A.C. 1; [1965] 1 Q.B. 130; [1963] 3 W.L.R. 677; 127 J.P. 511; 107 S.J. 596; [1963] 2 All E.R. 897; 47 Cr.App.R. 243, CCA. 36, 141
R v. Anderson (William Ronald) [1986] A.C. 27; [1985] 3 W.L.R. 268; (1985) 129 S.J. 522; [1985] 2 All E.R. 961; (1985) 81 Cr.App.R. 253; [1985] Crim.L.R. 651; (1985) 135 New L.J. 727; (1985) 82 L.S.Gaz 3172, HL; affirming (1984) 128 S.J. 660; (1984) 80 Cr.App.R. 64; [1984] Crim.L.R. 550; (1984) 81 L.S.Gaz 2141, CA 51, 52, 78
R v. Anderson; R v. Morris [1966] 2 Q.B. 110; [1966] 2 W.L.R. 1195; 130 J.P. 318; 110 S.J. 369; [1966] 2 All E.R. 644; 50 Cr.App.R. 216, CCA 56, 57, 63, 219, 220, 224, 226–9
R v. Andrews-Weatherfoil; R v. Sporle; R v. Day [1972] 1 W.L.R. 118; (1971) 115 S.J. 888; 56 Cr.App.R. 31; *sub nom* R v. Andrews-Weatherfoil [1972] 1 All E.R. 65, CA 113
R v. Annakin (1989) 13 Crim L.J., NSW Ct of App 86
R v. Anthony [1965] 2 Q.B. 189; [1965] 2 W.L.R. 748; 129 J.P. 168; [1965] 1 All E.R. 440; 49 Cr.App.R. 104, CCA . . . 113, 123
R v. Antonelli and Barberi (1905) 70 J.P. 4 162
R v. Appleby (1940) 28 Cr.App.R. 1. . . . . 217, 223
R v. Ardalan [1972] 1 W.L.R. 463; [1972] 2 All E.R. 2567; [1972] Crim.L.R. 370; *sub nom* R v. Ardalan (Siamek); R v. Babet; R v. Nicholson; R v. Sands; R v. Royde 56 Cr.App.R. 320, CA. . . . 53
R v. Ashmall (1840) 9 Car & P 236; 173 E.R. 817 112
R v. Ashton (1698) 12 Mood 256; 88 E.R., 1304 211
R v. Assistant Recorder of Kingston-upon-Hull, *ex p.* Morgan [1969] 2 Q.B. 58; [1969] 2 W.L.R. 246; (1968) 133 J.P. 165; 112 S.J. 1005; [1969] 1 All E.R. 416; 53 Cr.App.R. 96, DC . . . 57
R v. Attwell (1801) East, PC ii 767–9 25
R v. Bainbridge [1960] 1 Q.B. 129; [1959] 3 W.L.R. 656; 123 J.P. 499; [1959] 3 All E.R. 200; 43 Cr.App.R. 194, CCA . 163–71, 177, 181, 194, 200, 202, 203, 206–8, 210, 214, 223, 224, 232, 246, 253, 258
R v. Baker (1909) 28 N.Z.L.R. 536 . . . . 33, 53
R v. Bannen (1844) 1 Car & K 295; 169 E.R. 123 . . . 96, 104, 244
R v. Bannister (No. 2) (1936) 66 CCC 357. 216
R v. Barber (1844) 1 C & K 542; 174 E.R. 884 85
R v. Barker (1844) 1 Car & K 442; 174 E.R. 884 56

R v. Barnard (1979) 132 S.J. 803; (1979) 70 Cr.App.R. 28; [1980]
  Crim.L.R. 235, CA 262
R v. Barr (1989) 88 Cr.App.R. 362 . . . . 195, 228
R v. Barrett (1862) 9 Cox 255 36
R v. Barton [1976] Crim.L.R. 514, CA 259
R v. Baskerville [1916] 2 K.B. 658 240
R v. Beccera; R v. Cooper (1975) 62 Cr.App.R. 212 255–62
R v. Beck (Brian) [1985] 1 W.L.R. 22; (1985) 149 J.P. 276; (1984)
  128 S.J. 871; [1985] 1 All E.R. 571; (1984) 80 Cr.App.R. 355;
  (1985) 82 L.S.Gaz 762, CA 57, 58
R v. Bernard (1858) 1 F & F 240; 175 E.R. 709 . . . . . . 147, 204
R v. Bettles [1966] Crim.L.R. 503, 513, CA 163, 164, 168
R v. Betts and Ridley (1930) 22 Cr.App.R. 148 . . . 26, 214, 216, 223
R v. Betty (1963) 48 Cr.App.R. 6, CCA. . . . 219, 224, 226–8, 230
R v. Bingley (1821) R & RCC 446; 168 E.R. 890 28
R v. Birtles [1969] 1 W.L.R. 1047; 133 J.P. 573; 113 S.J. 424;
  [1969] 2 All E.R. 1131n; *sub nom* R v. Birtles (Frank Alexander)
  53 Cr.App.R. 469, CA 243, 244
R v. Bland (1987) 151 J.P. 857; [1988] Crim.L.R. 41; (1987) 151
  J.P.N. 825, CA. 36
R v. Blaue [1975] 1 W.L.R. 1411; 119 S.J. 589; [1975] 3 All E.R.
  466; *sub nom* R v. Blaue (Robert Konrad) (1975) 61 Cr.App.R.
  271; [1975] Crim.L.R. 648, CA 29, 83
R v. Bleasdale (1848) 2 Car & K 765; 175 E.R. 321. 96
R v. Bodin [1979] Crim.L.R. 176. 54
R v. Bolster (1909) 3 Cr.App.R. 81 . . . . 210, 215
R v. Borthwick (1779) 1 Doug 207; 99 E.R. 136. . . . . . 35, 36
R v. Bourne (1952) 36 Cr.App.R. 125, CCA . . 104, 115, 116, 127, 179
R v. Bowen (1841) Car & M 149; 174 E.R. 448. 211
R v. Brisac and Scott (1803) East, PC iv 164; 102 E.R. 792 . . . 96
R v. Britten and Egger (1988) 36 A.Crim.R. 48 . . . . . 220, 231
R v. Broadfoot [1976] 3 All E.R. 753; (1976) 64 Cr.App.R. 71;
  [1977] Crim.L.R. 690. 59
R v. Brown (1878) 14 Cox 144 116
R v. Browne (1910) 6 Cr.App.R. 24 239
R v. Browne and Kennedy, *The Times*, 28 Apr. 1928 . . . 215, 217
R v. Buck and Buck (1960) 44 Cr.App.R. 187
R v. Bull (1845) 1 Cox 281. 96
R v. Bullock [1955] 1 W.L.R. 1; 119 J.P. 65; 99 S.J. 29; [1955] 1
  All E.R. 15; 38 Cr.App.R. 151, CCA. . . . 144, 151, 162, 163, 168
R v. Burrows [1970] Crim.L.R. 419, CA 113
R v. Burton (1875) 13 Cox 71. 113
R v. Butcher (1858) Bell 6; 169 E.R. 1145 96
R v. Butt (1844) 15 Cox 564 . . . . 96, 104

xxviii   *Table of Cases*

R v. Caird 114 S.J. 652; [1970] Crim.L.R. 656; (1970) 54
  Cr.App.R. 499   36
R v. Calderwood and Moore [1983] 10 NIJB   163
R v. Calhaem [1985] Q.B. 808; [1985] 2 W.L.R. 826; (1985) 129
  S.J. 331; [1985] 2 All E.R., 226; (1985) 81 Cr.App.R. 131;
  [1985] Crim.L.R. 303; (1985) L.S.Gaz 1485, CA. . . .   57, 59, 207
R v. Cato; R v. Morris; R v. Dudley [1976] 1 W.L.R. 110; 119 S.J.
  775; [1976] 1 All E.R. 260; [1976] Crim.L.R. 59; *sub nom* R v.
  Cato (Ronald Philip); R v. Morris (Neil Adrian); R v. Dudley
  (Melvin) (1975) 62 Cr.App.R. 41, CA   86
R v. Caton (1874) 12 Cox 624. . . . . 211, 214, 224, 230
R v. Chandler (1913) 8 Cr.App.R. 82   104
R v. Chapin (1978) 41 CCC (2d) 300   251
R v. Charles (1892) 17 Cox 499   29
R v. Clarke (Dennis) (1984) 80 Cr.App.R. 344; [1985] Crim.L.R.
  209; (1985) 82 L.S.Gaz 682, CA 145, 146, 243, 244
R v. Clarkson; R v. Carroll; R v. Dodd [1971] 1 W.L.R. 1402; 55
  Cr.App.R. 445; *sub nom* R v. Clarkson 115 S.J. 654; [1971] 3
  All E.R. 34; Cts-Martial App Ct 36, 141, 251
R v. Clayton (1843) 1 Car & K 128; 174 E.R. 743   53
R v. Clifford (1845) 2 Car & Kir 202; 175 E.R. 84   96
R v. Cogan; R v. Leak [1976] Q.B. 217; [1975] 3 W.L.R. 316; 119
  S.J. 473; [1975] 2 All E.R. 1059; [1975] Crim.L.R. 584; *sub nom*
  R v. Cogan (John Rodney); R v. Leak (Michael Edward) (1975)
  61 Cr.App.R. 217, CA 32, 58, 104, 106, 108, 109, 116,
                            117, 120, 124–7, 129, 131, 178, 179, 250
R v. Coggins (1873) 12 Cox 517   28
R v. Collingwood (1705) 6 Mood.Rep. 288; 87 E.R. 1029, 1030 . . 56
R v. Collison (1837) 4 Car & P 565; 172 E.R. 565; 172 E.R. 827 . 211
R v. Coney (1882) 8 Q.B.D. 534 . . . . 36, 37, 38, 85, 141
R v. Connor (1913) 8 Cr.App.R. 152   215
R v. Conroy and Conroy [1954] Crim.L.R. 141   131
R v. Coombes (1785) 1 Leach 388; 168 E.R. 296   95
R v. Cooper (1846) Q.B. 533; 115 E.R. 976 . . . .   96, 211
R v. Cooper and Wicks (1833) 5 Car & P 536; 172 E.R. 1087 . 148, 204
R v. Crabbe [1985] 156 CLR 464   180
R v. Craig and Bentley, *The Times*, 10–13 Dec. 1952 . . . 26, 77, 261
R v. Cratchley (1913) 9 Cr.App.R. 232   240
R v. Creamer [1966] 1 Q.B. 72; [1965] 3 W.L.R. 583; 129 J.P. 586;
  109 S.J. 648; [1965] 3 All E.R. 257; 49 Cr.App.R. 368, CCA . . 187
R v. Crisham (1841) C & M 187; 174 E.R. 466   116
R v. Croft [1944] K.B. 29 . . . . 48, 57, 252, 256, 258
R v. Cruse (1838) 8 C & P 541; 173 E.R. 610. . . . . . .   173, 179
R v. Cuddy (1843) 1 C & R 210; 174 E.R. 779   36

R v. Cunningham [1957] 2 Q.B. 396; [1957] 3 W.L.R. 76; 121 J.P. 451; 101 S.J. 503; [1957] 2 All E.R. 412; 41 Cr.App.R. 155, CCA; reversing [1957] Crim.L.R. 326 182
R v. Curr [1968] 2 Q.B. 944; [1967] 2 W.L.R. 595; 131 J.P. 245; 111 S.J. 152; [1967] 1 All E.R. 478; 51 Cr.App.R. 113, CA. 105, 135
R v. Curran (1978) 38 CCC (2d) 151 159
R v. D 1969 (2) SA 591 (RAD) 108, 116
R v. Daily Mirror Newspapers and Glover [1922] 2 K.B. 530 . 113, 115
R v. Dalby [1982] 1 W.L.R. 621; (1982) 126 S.J. 97; [1982] 1 All E.R. 916; [1982] Crim.L.R. 439, CA. 100
R v. Davenport (1826) MSI Archb. Peels Acts 3rd ed, 271. 96
R v. Davis (1805) Russ & Ry 113; 168 E.R. 711. 26
R v. Davis [1977] Crim.L.R. 542, CA 13, 148, 201
R v. De Marney [1907] 1 K.B. 388 . . . . 56, 115, 145
R v. Deutsch (1983) 5 CCC (3d) 41 62
R v. Donnelly and Vaughan (1816) Russ & Ry 310; 168 E.R. 818 . 117
R v. Dowey (1868) 11 Cox 115 96
R v. Draper (1929) 21 Cr.App.R. 147 239
R v. Duffy (1830) 1 Lew 194; 168 E.R. 1009 224
R v. Dunbar [1988] Crim.L.R. 693; *The Times,* 5 Apr. 1988, CA . 220, 228
R v. Dunnington [1984] Q.B. 472; [1984] 2 W.L.R. 125; (1984) 148 J.P. 316; (1983) 127 S.J. 882; (1984) 78 Cr.App.R. 171; [1984] Crim.L.R. 98; (1984) 81 L.S. Gaz 38, CA. 53
R v. Dyer and Disting (1801) East, PCii 767–9 . . . . . . 25, 30
R v. Edmeads (1828) 3 Car & P 390; 172 E.R. 469 . . . 211, 215, 256
R v. Eggington (1801) 2 Leach 913; 168 E.R. 555 . . . . . 104, 244
R v. Flatman (1880) 14 Cox 396 96
R v. Fletcher 106 S.J. 554; [1962] Crim.L.R. 551, CCA 48
R v. Fletcher and Zimnowodski [1962] Crim.L.R. 551. . . . 256, 257
R v. Forman and Ford [1988] Crim.L.R. 677 42
R v. Franz (1861) 2 F & F 580; 175 E.R. 1195 . . . . . . 211, 215
R v. Fraser (1984) 13 CCC (3d) 292. 251
R v. Fretwell (1862) Le & Ca 161; 169 E.R. 1345 . . 56, 146, 148, 149, 245, 258
R v. Froggett [1966] 1 Q.B. 152; [1965] 3 W.L.R. 602; 129 J.P. 474; 109 S.J. 492; [1965] 2 All E.R. 832; 49 Cr.App.R. 334, CCA 26, 36
R v. Garforth [1954] Crim.L.R. 936, CCA 128, 225
R v. Giles (1827) 1 Mood CC 166; 168 E.R. 122 96
R v. Girdwood (1776) 1 Leach 142; 168 E.R. 773 96
R v. Glushek 41 CCC (2d) 380 (1978) 38 CCC (2d) 151 159
R v. Godspeed (1911) 6 Cr.App.R. 133. 256

R v. Goodfellow (1845) 1 Den 81; 169 E.R. 159. 210
R v. Grant and Gilbert (1954) 38 Cr.App.R. 107, CCA 217
R v. Gray (1917) 12 Cr.App.R. 244 36
R v. Greenwood (1825) 2 Den 453; 169 E.R. 578 26
R v. Gregory (1867) 10 Cox 459 115
R v. Grey and Wise 7 Car & P 164; 173 E.R. 72 116
R v. Griffith (1553) 1 Plowd 97; 75 E.R. 152 . . . 23, 25, 26, 109, 111, 117, 211
R v. Griffith (1831) 1 Mood CC 306; 168 E.R. 1283 28
R v. Griffiths [1966] 1 Q.B. 589; [1965] 3 W.L.R. 405; 129 J.P. 380; 109 S.J. 312; [1965] 2 All E.R. 448; *sub nom* R v. Griffiths; R v. Booth; R v. Bishop; R v. Brown; R v. Pinner; R v. Read; R v. Riches; R v. Topham; R v. Tyrell, 49 Cr.App.R. 279, CCA . . . 53
R v. Groombridge (1836) 7 C & P 582 106
R v. Grundy [1977] Crim.L.R. 543, CA 258
R v. Gush [1980] 2 N.Z.L.R. 92 . . . . 174, 220
R v. Hamel (1968) 64 WWR 173 193
R v. Hamilton [1987] 6 NIJB 1 166
R v. Hamilton [1985] 2 N.Z.L.R. 245 . . . . 174, 220
R v. Hancock and Shankland [1986] A.C. 455; [1986] 2 W.L.R. 357; (1986) 130 S.J. 184; (1986) 150 J.P. 203; [1986] 1 All E.R. 646; (1986) 82 Cr.App.R. 264; [1986] Crim.L.R. 400; (1986) New L.J. 214; (1986) 83 L.S. Gaz 967, HL; affirming [1985] 3 W.L.R. 1014; [1986] 1 All E.R. 641; [1986] Crim.L.R. 180; (1986) 150 J.P. 33; (1985) 129 S.J.793; (1985) 135 New L.J. 1208 . . . . 148, 150, 221
R v. Hansill (1849) 3 Cox 577. 112
R v. Hapgood and Wyatt (1870) 11 Cox 471 53
R v. Harding [1976] VR 129 . . . . 159, 174
R v. Hargrave (1831) 5 Car & P 70; 172 E.R. 925 186
R v. Harley (1830) 4 C & P 369; 172 E.R. 744 . . . . 96, 97
R v. Harrington (1815) 5 Cox 231 63
R v. Harrington [1976] 2 N.Z.L.R. 763 113
R v. Harris [1964] Crim.L.R. 54, CCA 41, 45
R v. Hartford and Frigon (1979) 51 CCC (2d) 462 169
R v. Hartley [1978] 1 N.Z.L.R. 199 . . . . 78, 115, 128
R v. Harvey and Caylor (1843) 1 Cox 21 211
R v. Headley (1945) 31 Cr.App.R. 35 217
R v. Hebert (1986) 51 CR (3d) 264 128
R v. Henderson (1949) 2 DLR 121 262
R v. Hennigan (1971) 115 S.J. 268; [1971] 3 All E.R. 133; [1971] R.T.R. 305; *sub nom* R v. Hennigan (James) 55 Cr.App.R. 262, CA 29, 86
R v. Higgins (1801) 2 E H East 10

Table of Cases xxxi

R v. Hodgson (1730) 1 Leach 6; 168 E.R. 105	211
R v. Holbrook (1878) 4 Q.B.D. 42	41
R v. Hollinshead; R v. Dettlaf; R v. Griffiths (Kenneth) [1985] A.C. 975; [1985] 3 W.L.R. 159; (1985) 129 S.J. 447; [1985] 2 All E.R. 769; (1985) 81 Cr.App.R. 365; [1985] Crim.L.R. 653; (1985) 135 New L.J. 631; (1985) 82 L.S.Gaz 2739, HL; reversing (1984) 80 Cr.App.R. 285; [1985] Crim.L.R. 301; (1985) 82 L.S.Gaz 1718, CA; reversing [1985] 2 W.L.R. 761; (1985) 129 S.J. 219; [1985] 1 All E.R. 850	54
R v. Hornby (1844) 1 Car & Kir 305; 174 E.R. 822	25, 28
R v. Howard and Trudel (1983) 3 CCC (3d) 399	169
R v. Howe; R v. Bannister (JD); R v. Burke (CJ); R v. Clarkson [1987] A.C. 417; [1987] 2 W.L.R. 568; (1987) 151 J.P. 265; (1987) 131 S.J. 258; [1987] 1 All E.R. 771; (1987) 85 Cr.App.R. 32; (1987) 151 J.P.N. 206; [1987] Crim.L.R. 480; (1987) 84 L.S.Gaz 900; (1987) 137 New L.J. 197, HL; affirming [1986] Q.B. 626; [1986] 2 W.L.R., 294; (1986) 150 J.P.N. 161; (1986) 130 S.J. 110; [1986] 1 All E.R. 833; (1986) 83 Cr.App.R. 28; [1986] Crim.L.R. 331; (1986) 150 J.P.N. 143; (1985) 82 L.S.Gaz 612, CA	116, 122, 129, 130, 145, 149, 250
R v. Howell (1839) 9 C & P 437; 173 E.R. 901	26
R v. Howells [1977] Q.B. 614; [1977] 2 W.L.R. 716; (1977) 121 S.J. 154; [1977] 3 All E.R. 417; (1977) 65 Cr.App.R. 86; [1977] Crim.L.R. 354, CA	192
R v. Huggins (1730) Ld Raym 1574; 93 E.R. 915	41
R v. Hughes (1860) Bell, CC 242; 169 E.R. 1245	113
R v. Humphreys and Turner 130 J.P. 45; [1965] 3 All E.R. 689	113, 116
R v. Hurse and Dunn (1841) 2 Moo & Rob 360; 174 E.R. 316	29
R v. Hyde (1672) Hale 1 PC i 537	256
R v. Irwin [1966] Crim.L.R. 514, CCA	78
R v. Jackson (1673) Hale PC i 464	261
R v. Jakeman (1983) 76 Cr.App.R. 223; [1983] Crim.L.R. 104	254
R v. James and Ashford (1985) 82 Cr.App.R. 226; [1986] Crim.L.R. 118, CA	34
R v. Jefferies and Bryant (1848) 2 Cox	26
R v. Joachim (1912) 7 Cr.App.R. 222	215
R v. Johnson (1805) 29 St Tr 81; 103 E.R. 25	96
R v. Johnson and Jones (1841) Car & M 218; 174 E.R. 479	104, 244, 261
R v. Jones [1959] 1 Q.B. 291; [1959] 2 W.L.R. 190; 123 J.P. 164; [1959] 1 All E.R. 411; 43 Cr.App.R. 94, CCA	25
R v. Jones and Mirrless (1977) Cr.App.R. 250, CA	141
R v. Jordan (1836) 7 C & P 432; 173 E.R. 192	26

Table of Cases

R v. Joyce [1968] N.Z.L.R. 1070. 257
R v. Jubb; R v. Rigby [1984] Crim.L.R. 616, CA. 175–7
R v. Kay (1857) Dears & B 231; 169 E.R. 988 96
R v. Kearon and Williamson [1955] Crim.L.R. 183 251
R v. Kelly (1820) Russ & Ry 421; 168 E.R. 876 25
R v. Kelly (1847) 2 Car & K 379; 175 E.R. 157 28
R v. Kemp; R v. Else [1964] 2 Q.B. 341; [1964] 2 W.L.R. 648; 108 S.J. 139; [1964] 1 All E.R. 649; 48 Cr.App.R. 131, CCA . . . 116
R v. Kerr (1921) 15 Cr.App.R. 165 215
R v. Kew and Jackson (1872) 12 Cox 355; 154 E.R. 682 42
R v. King (1817) Russ & Ry 332; 168 E.R. 830 . . . . 25, 30
R v. King [1964] 1 Q.B. 285; [1963] 3 W.L.R. 892; 107 S.J. 832; [1963] 3 All E.R. 561; 48 Cr.App.R. 17, CCA. 114
R v. Kirkwood (1831) 1 Mood CC 304; 168 E.R. 1821 28
R v. Kulbacki (1966) 1 CCC 167 (Canada Criminal Ct) 40
R v. Kupferberg (1918) 13 Cr.App.R. 166. . . . . 47, 218
R v. Kwaku Mensah [1946] A.C. 83. 128
R v. Larkin (1976) 62 Cr.App.R. 109 229
R v. Lawrence (1850) 4 Cox 438 104
R v. Leahy [1985] Crim.L.R. 99 201
R v. Lewis [1975] 1 N.Z.L.R. 222 . . . . 115, 128
R v. Lockett (1836) 7 Car & P 300; 173 E.R. 133 210
R v. Logan (1988) 46 CCC (3d) 354. 232
R v. Lomas (1913) 9 Cr.App.R. 220. . . . . . . 58, 146, 151, 162
R v. Longbottom (1849) 3 Cox 439 187
R v. Lord Mohun (1962) Holt K.B. 479; 90 E.R. 1164. . . 117, 128, 211
R v. Lovesey; R v. Peterson [1970] 1 Q.B. 352; [1969] 3 W.L.R. 213; 133 J.P. 571; 113 S.J. 445; [1969] 2 All E.R. 1077; *sub nom* R v. Lovesey (John Dennis); R v. Peterson (Anthony) 53 Cr.App.R. 461, CA 219, 220 227, 228, 230
R v. Low (1850) 3 C & K 123; 173 E.R. 489 102
R v. Luck (1862) 3 F & F 483; 176 E.R. 217 . . . . 211, 215
R v. Lynch, *see* D.P.P. for Northern Ireland v. Lynch
R v. McCann (1971) 56 Cr.App.R. 359; [1972] Crim.L.R. 196, CA. 244
R v. McCarron [1977] Crim.L.R. 559, CA. 132
R v. McCarthy [1964] 1 W.L.R. 196; 128 J.P. 191; 108 S.J. 17; [1964] 1 All E.R. 95; 48 Cr.App.R. 111, CCA. 36
R v. McClafferty [1980] 11 NIJB. 165
R v. McDaid (1974) 19 CCC (2) 572 180
R v. MacDaniel *Crown Law*, p. 137. . . . . 30, 31
R v. McEvilly (Michael James); R v. Lee (Peter John) (1973) 60 Cr.App.R. 150; [1974] Crim.L.R. 239, CA. 243
R v. Mcleod and Georgia Straight Publishing Co (1970) 75 WWR 161. 33–4

Table of Cases

R v. M'makin (1808) Russ & Ry 333, 168 E.R. 830 . . . . . 25, 30
R v. McNulty (1910) 17 CCC 26. 62
R v. MacPhane (1841) 174 E.R. 476. 30
R v. Macklin (1838) 2 Lew 225; 168 E.R. 1136 . . . . 63, 74, 85, 209
R v. Malcolm [1951] N.Z.L.R. 470 257
R v. Manley (1844) 1 Cox 104 96
R v. Mansell (1556) 2 Dyer 1286b; 73 E.R. 279 211
R v. Markus, *see* Secretary of State for Trade v. Markus
R v. Martyn [1967] N.Z.L.R. 396 33
R v. Mastin (1834) 6 Car & P 396; 172 E.R. 1292 186
R v. Mastin (1934) 26 Cr.App.R. 177 217
R v. Maxwell, *see* D.P.P. for Northern Ireland v. Maxwell
R v. Mazeau (1840) 9 C & P 676; 173 E.R. 1006 . . . . 96, 104
R v. Mealey (1974) 60 Cr.App.R. 59 243
R v. Menniti [1985] 1 Qd.R 520 . . . . 252, 257
R v. Meyrick (1929) 21 Cr.App.R. 94 53
R v. Michael (1840) 9 Car & P 356; 173 E.R. 867 . . . . . 96, 102
R v. Millar; R v. Millar (Robert) (Contractors) [1970] 2 Q.B. 54;
   [1970] 2 W.L.R. 541; [1970] 1 All E.R. 577; [1970] R.T.R. 147;
   54 Cr.App.R. 158, CA; affirming *sub nom* R v. Hart; R v. Millar
   and Millar (Robert) (Contractors) [1969] 3 All E.R. 247; *sub
   nom* R v. Hart; R v. Millar 133 J.P. 554. . . . . 187, 189
R v. Millard (1921) 59 DLR 34 128
R v. Miller [1983] A.C. 161; [1983] 2 W.L.R. 539; [1983] 1 All
   E.R. 978; (1983) 77 Cr.App.R. 17; [1983] Crim.L.R. 466, HL;
   affirming [1982] Q.B. 532; [1982] 2 W.L.R. 937; (1982) 126 S.J.
   327; [1982] 2 All E.R. 386; [1982] Crim.L.R. 526; (1982) 75
   Cr.App.R. 109, CA 38, 44, 259
R v. Miller and Cockriell (1976) 31 CCC (2d) 170 . . . . . 256, 260
R v. Mills (1986) 61 ALJR 59 220
R v. Moloney [1985] A.C. 905; [1985] 2 W.L.R. 648; (1985) 149
   J.P. 369; (1985) 129 S.J. 220; [1985] 1 All E.R. 1025; (1985) 81
   Cr.App.R. 93; [1985] Crim.L.R. 378; (1985) 135 New L.J. 315;
   (1985) 82 L.S.Gaz 1637, HL; reversing *The Times*, 22 Dec.
   1983 . . . . 148, 150
R v. Moxon-Tritsch (Leona) [1988] Crim.L.R. 46, Reading Crown
   Ct 248
R v. Munton (1793) 1 Esp 62; 170 E.R. 280 96
R v. Murtagh and Kennedy [1955] Crim.L.R. 315; subsequent
   proceedings (1955) 39 Cr.App.R. 72, CCA. 128, 217, 227
R v. Nedrick [1986] 1 W.L.R. 1025; (1986) 150 J.P. 589; [1986] 3
   All E.R. 1; (1986) 130 S.J. 572; (1986) 83 Cr.App.R. 267;
   (1986) 9 Cr.App.R. (S) 179; [1986] Crim.L.R. 792; (1986) 150
   J.P.N. 637; (1986) 83 L.S.Gaz 2755, CA 148
R v. Oliphant (1905) 2 K.B. 73 . . . . 96, 106

R v. Owen (1825) 11 Mood 96; 168 E.R. 1200 26
R v. Paget and Pembourne (1983) 76 Cr.App.R. 279; (1982) 4
  Cr.App.R. (S) 399; [1983] Crim.L.R. 274, CA . . . 98, 100, 101
R v. Palmer (1804) 2 Leach 978; 127 E.R. 395 96
R v. Palmer and Hudson (1804) 1 B & PNR 96 104
R v. Passey (1836) 7 Car & P 282; 173 E.R. 124 210
R v. Patel [1970] Crim.L.R. 274, CA 168
R v. Paterson [1978–86] N.Z.L.R. 394 96
R v. Payne [1965] Crim.L.R. 543, CCA. 163
R v. Pearce (1929) 21 Cr.App.R. 79 215
R v. Pedley (1834) 1 Ad & E 832; 110 E.R. 1422 36
R v. Penfold and Penfold (1979) 71 Cr.App.R. 4; [1980] Crim.L.R.
  182, CA 56, 219, 225, 228, 231
R v. Phelps (1841) C & M 180; 174 E.R. 463. 112
R v. Piri [1987] 1 N.Z.L.R. 66. 220
R v. Pitham and Hehl (1976) 65 Cr.App.R. 45; [1977] Crim.L.R.
  285, CA 25
R v. Pitman (1826) 2 C & P 423; 172 E.R. 192 96
R v. Po Koon-tai [1980] H.K.L.R. 492 54
R v. Popen (1981) 60 CCC (2d) 232 159
R v. Pratt (1855) 4 El. & Bl. 380; 119 E.R. 319 . . . . . . 95, 107
R v. Preston [1962] Tas.SR 141 239
R v. Price (1858) 8 Cox 96 . . . . 211, 214
R v. Price (1968) 52 Cr.App.R. 295 240
R v. Pridmore (1913) 8 Cr.App.R. 198 . . . . 213, 215
R v. Quick; R v. Paddison [1973] Q.B. 910; [1973] 3 W.L.R. 26;
  [1973] 3 All E.R. 347; sub nom R v. Paddison; R v. Quick 117
  S.J. 371; sub nom R v. Quick (William George Henry); R v.
  Paddison (William) 57 Cr.App.R. 722; sub nom R v. Quick
  [1973] Crim.L.R. 434, CA 56, 98, 116, 117, 179
R v. Reed [1982] Crim.L.R. 819, CA 59
R v. Reid (1975) 62 Cr.App.R., 109; [1976] Crim.L.R. 570,
  CA 29, 56, 224, 225, 228–31
R v. Remillard (1921) 59 DLR 340 . . . . 128, 132
R v. Richards [1974] Q.B. 776; [1973] 3 W.L.R. 888; 117 S.J. 852;
  sub nom R v. Richards (Isabelle) [1973] 3 All E.R. 1088; sub
  nom R v. Richards (Isabelle Christina) (1973) 58 Cr.App.R. 60;
  [1974] Crim.L.R. 96, CA 26, 129–31
R v. Riebold [1964] Crim.L.R. 530, CCA 248
R v. Roan (1985) 17 CCC (3d) 534 159
R v. Rogers (1839) 2 Mood 85; 169 E.R. 34 210
R v. Rowley 112 J.P. 207; 92 S.J. 299; [1984] 1 All E.R. 570; 32
  Cr.App.R. 147; 46 L.G.R. 224, CCA. 113
R v. Royce (1767) 4 Burr 2072; 98 E.R. 81 . . . . 32, 35

Table of Cases xxxv

R v. Rubens (1909) 2 Cr.App.R. 163 214
R v. Russell [1933] VLR 59. 44
R v. Russell (1832) 1 Mood 356; 168 E.R. 1302 112
R v. Russell and Russell (1987) 85 Cr.App.R. 388; [1987] Crim.L.R. 494, CA 27
R v. Salford Health Authority, *ex p.* Janaway [1988] 3 W.L.R. 1350; (1988) 132 S.J. 1731; [1988] 3 All E.R. 1079; (1988) 138 New L.J. 348, HL; affirming [1988] 2 W.L.R. 442; (1988) 132 S.J. 265; (1988) 18 Fam.Law 389; (1988) 85 L.S.Gaz 36, CA; affirming [1988] 1 F.L.R. 17; (1987) 17 Fam.Law 345 . . . . 146, 152
R v. Salmon (1880) 6 Q.B.D. 79 188
R v. Sang [1980] A.C. 402; [1979] 3 W.L.R. 263; (1979) 123 S.J. 552; [1979] 2 All E.R. 1222; (1979) 69 Cr.App.R. 282; [1979] Crim.L.R. 655, HL; affirming R v. Sang; R v. Mangan [1979] 2 W.L.R. 439; (1978) 123 S.J. 232; [1979] 2 All E.R. 46; (1978) 68 Cr.App.R. 240; [1979] Crim.L.R. 389, CA; [1980] Crim.L.R. 129; 143 J.P.N. 558 243
R v. Saunders and Archer (1576) 2 Plowd 473 . 200, 201, 204, 205, 223
251, 256, 261
R v. Saylor [1963] QWN 14 256
R v. Scott (1978) 68 Cr.App.R. 164; (1978) 122 S.J. 523; [1979] Crim.L.R. 456, CA 169
R v. Searle (1971) 115 S.J. 739; [1971] Crim.L.R. 592, CA . . . 36
R v. Serne (1887) 16 Cox 311 213
R v. Seymour [1983] 2 A.C. 493; [1983] 3 W.L.R. 349; (1984) 148 J.P. 530; (1983) 127 S.J. 522; [1983] 2 All E.R. 1058; (1984) 77 Cr.App.R. 215; [1983] R.T.R. 455; [1983] Crim.L.R. 742; (1984) 148 J.P.N. 331, HL; affirming (1983) 76 Cr.App.R. 211; [1983] R.T.R. 202; [1983] Crim.L.R. 260, CA 190
R v. Sharp (David) [1987] Q.B. 853; [1987] 3 W.L.R. 1; (1987) 131 S.J. 624; (1987) 151 J.P. 832; [1987] 3 All E.R. 103; (1987) 85 Cr.App.R. 207; [1987] Crim.L.R. 566; (1987) 151 J.P.N. 825; (1987) 84 L.S.Gaz 1491, CA. 221, 231
R v. Sheppard (1839) 9 C & P 121; 173 E.R. 767 28
R v. Short (1932) 23 Cr.App.R. 170 215
R v. Siracusa [1989] Crim.L.R. 712 . . . . . . 47, 51, 52, 78
R v. Skeet (1866) 4 F & F 931; 176 E.R. 1136 . . . . 209, 210, 211, 215, 230, 233
R v. Skelton and Batting (1853) Car & K 119; 175 E.R. 488 . . . 210
R v. Skerrit (1826) 2 C & P 427; 172 E.R. 193 29
R v. Slack [1989] 3 All E.R. 90; [1989] Crim.L.R. 903 . . 177, 218, 221
R v. Smith [1959] 2 Q.B. 35; [1959] 2 W.L.R. 623; 123 J.P. 295; 103 S.J. 353; [1959] 2 All E.R. 193; 43 Cr.App.R. 121, Cts-Martial App Ct 56, 83, 229

Table of Cases

R v. Smith [1960] 2 Q.B. 423; [1960] 2 W.L.R. 164; 124 J.P. 137;
  [1960] 1 All E.R. 256; 44 Cr.App.R. 55, CCA. 243
R v. Smith (Wesley) [1963] 1 W.L.R. 1200; 128 J.P. 13; 107 S.J.
  873; [1963] 3 All E.R. 597, CA . . . 26, 219, 224, 226, 227, 230
R v. Smith [1988] Crim.L.R. 616 . . . . 195, 228
R v. Smith and Taylor (1847) 2 Cox 233 186
R v. Soares (1802) Russ & Ry 25; 168 E.R. 664 26
R v. Sockett (1908) 1 Cr.App.R. 39 . . . . 240, 241
R v. Solomon [1959] Qd.R 123 216
R v. Soloway [1976] 2 WWR 127 25
R v. Sotton (1844) 5 Q.B. 493; 114 E.R. 1333 210
R v. Spraggett [1960] Crim.L.R. 840, CCA 226
R v. Standley (1816) Russ & Ry 305; 168 E.R. 816 210
R v. Stannard (1863) 9 Cox 405 36
R v. Sterne [1787] 1 Leach 473; 168 E.R. 338 24
R v. Stewart and Lincoln, *The Times*, 21 Jan. 1926 . . . . . 215, 217
R v. Swindall (1846) 2 Car & K 230; 175 E.R. 95 . . . . . 186, 187
R v. Tate (1908) 1 Cr.App.R. 39 240
R v. Tatum (1921) 15 Cr.App.R 132 240
R v. Taylor (1785) 1 Leach 360; 168 E.R. 283 . . . . . . 112, 113
R v. Taylor (1875) LR 2 CCR 147 147
R v. Thompson (1869) 11 Cox 362 . . . . 29, 210
R v. Thomson Holidays [1974] Q.B. 592; [1974] 2 W.L.R. 371;
  [1974] 1 All E.R. 823; (1973) 58 Cr.App.R. 429; sub nom R v.
  Thomson Holidays (1973) 118 S.J. 96; [1974] Crim.L.R. 198,
  CA 247
R v. Tinsley [1963] Crim.L.R. 520, CCA 191
R v. Tomkins [1985] 2 N.Z.L.R. 253 . . . . 174, 220, 228
R v. Tonkin [1975] Qd.R 1 128
R v. Tooley (1709) 2 Ld Raym 1296; 92 E.R. 349 117
R v. Towle (1816) R & R 314; 168 E.R. 820 113
R v. Tracey (1703) 6 Mod 30; 87 E.R. 795 21
R v. Treacy, see Treacy v. D.P.P.
R v. Tuckwell (1841) Cor. & M 215; 174 E.R. 447 26
R v. Tyler and Price (1838) 8 C & P 616; (1838) 1 Mood CC 428;
  173 E.R. 643 . . . . 95–8, 104, 115, 230
R v. Tyrell [1894] 1 Q.B. 710 239
R v. Valler (1844) 1 Cox 84 . . . . 96, 104, 244
R v. Vanderstein (1865) 10 Cox 177 26
R v. Wagner (1979) 8 BCLR 258 . . . . 260, 262
R v. Wakeley [1990] Crim.L.R. 119 221
R v. Walker and Hayles [1990] Crim.L.R. 44; *The Times*, 11 Aug.
  1989, CA 148
R v. Wallace (1841) C & M 200; 174 E.R. 471 112

Table of Cases

R v. Wallis (1703) 1 Salk 334; 91 E.R. 294 . . . . . 112, 113, 211
R v. Ward (JD) (1987) 85 Cr.App.R. 71; [1987] Crim.L.R. 338,
    CA 150, 175, 176
R v. Waterfield (1974) 18 CCC (2d) 140 251
R v. Wauby [1895] 2 Q.B. 482 113
R v. Welham (1845) 1 Cox 192 96
R v. West; R v. Northcott; R Weitzman; R v. White [1948] 1 K.B.
    709; 64 T.L.R. 241; [1948] 1 All E.R. 1718; 32 Cr.App.R. 152;
    sub nom R v. West [1948] L.J.R. 1377; 112 J.P. 222; 92 S.J. 232;
    46 L.G.R. 325, CCA 48
R v. White and Ridley (1978) 140 CLR 342 . . . . . 254, 255, 257
R v. Whitefield [1984] Crim.L.R. 97; (1984) 79 Cr.App.R. 36;
    (1983) 80 L.S.Gaz 3077, CA 257
R v. Whitehouse [1977] Q.B. 868; [1977] 2 W.L.R. 925; 121 S.J.
    171; [1977] 3 All E.R. 737; (1977) 65 Cr.App.R. 33; [1977]
    Crim.L.R. 689, CA 54, 239
R v. Whitehouse [1941] 1 WWR 112 . . . . . , 252, 256, 259–61
R v. Williams (Gladstone) [1987] 3 All E.R. 411; (1984) 78
    Cr.App.R. 276; [1984] Crim.L.R. 163; (1984) 81 L.S.Gaz 278,
    CA 121
R v. Williams and Blackwood (1973) 21 WIR 329 230
R v. Withorne (1828) 3 C & P 394; 172 E.R. 470 26
R v. Wong (No. 2) (1978) 41 CCC (2d) 196 221
R v. Woolworth (FW) & Co (1974) 18 CCC (2d) 23 . . . 159, 193
R v. Yanover and Gerol (1985) 20 CCC (3d) 300 165
R v. Young (1838) 8 C & P 644; 173 E.R. 655 . . . . 36, 37, 85, 256
Ramnath Mohan v. R [1967] 2 A.C. 187; [1967] 2 W.L.R. 676;
    111 S.J. 95; sub nom Mohan v. R [1967] 2 All E.R. 58,
    PC 74, 222
Reismann v. US 409 F 2d 789 (1969) 256
Roberts v. Preston (1860) 9 CB (NS) 208; 142 E.R. 81 42
Roper v. Taylor's Central Garages (Exeter), see Taylor's Central
    Garages (Exeter) v. Roper
Rozell v. State 502 SW 2d 16 (1973) 115
Rubie v. Faulkner [1940] 1 K.B. 571 . . . . 41, 43, 45, 185
Runyowa v. R [1967] A.C. 26; [1966] 2 W.L.R. 877; 110 S.J. 911;
    [1966] 1 All E.R. 633, PC 113

S v. Aaron (1909) Trans LR 937 40
S v. Beukes 1988 (1) SA 511(1) 174
S v. Chenjere 1960 (1) SA 473 (FC) 30
S v. Claasen 1979 (4) SA 460 (ZRAD) 41
S v. Hartman 1975 (3) SA 532 201
S v. Kazi 1963 (4) SA 742(W) 174

Table of Cases

S v. Khoza 1982 (3) SA 1019 (A) 62, 79, 174
S v. Longone 1938 AD 532 . . . . 204, 205
S v. Madlala 1969 (2) SA 637 (AD) 30
S v. Mapolisa 1965 (3) SA 578 (PC) 205
S v. Maxaba 1981 (1) SA 1148 (A) 62
S v. Mgedezi 1989 (1) SA 687 62
S v. Mgxwitti 1954 (1) SA (AD) 383 61
S v. Mkhwanazi 1988 (4) SA 30 101
S v. Mneke 1961 (2) SA 240 (N) 30, 61
S v. Ndebu 1986 (2) SA 133 257
S v. Nhiri 1976 (2) SA 789 (RAD) 233
S v. Njenje 1966 (1) SA 369 (SR) 376 48
S v. O'Brien 1970 (3) SA 405 . . . . 159, 193
S v. Quinta 1974 (1) SA 544 159
S v. Robinson 1968 (1) SA 666 . . . . 201, 204, 206
S v. Safatsa 1988 (1) SA 686 (A) 62, 209
S v. Shikuri 1939 AD 225 40
S v. Thomo 1969 (1) SA 385 (AD) 30
S v. Tshwape 1964 (4) SA 327 159
S v. Williams 1980 (1) SA 60 (A) 33, 62
S v. Zeelie 1952 (1) SA 400 (AD) 48
Salisbury's Case (1553) 1 Plowd 97; 75 E.R. 152 117
Saqui and Lawrence v. Stearns [1911] 2 K.B. 426 26
Sayce v. Coupe [1953] 1 Q.B. 1; [1952] 2 T.L.R. 664; 116 J.P. 552;
    96 S.J. 748; [1952] 2 All E.R. 715, DC 39, 161, 239
Secretary of State for Trade v. Markus [1976] A.C. 35; [1975] 2
    W.L.R. 708; 119 S.J. 271; [1975] 1 All E.R. 958; 61 Cr.App.R.
    58; [1975] Crim.L.R. 716, HL; affirming *sub nom* R v. Markus
    [1974] 3 W.L.R. 645; 118 S.J. 809; [1974] 3 All E.R. 705;
    [1974] Crim.L.R. 603, CA 29
Sheckles v. State 501 NE 2d 1053 (1986) 253
Sherras v. deRutzen [1895] 1 Q.B. 918 191
Simmons v. State 594 SW 2d 760 (1980) 200
Smith v. Baker [1971] R.T.R. 350, DC 36
Smith v. Jenner 112 S.J. 52; [1968] Crim.L.R. 99, DC 41
Smith v. Mellors and Soar (1987) 84 Cr.App.R. 279; [1987]
    Crim.L.R. 421 181
Smith v. Scott [1973] Ch. 314; [1972] 3 W.L.R. 783; 116 S.J. 785;
    [1972] 3 All E.R. 645 36
Smith v. White (1866) LR 1 Eq 626 156
Spiers v. H.M.A. (1980) J.C. 36 36
Stallard v. State 348 SW 2d 489 (1961) 187
Stanley's Case (1663) Kel.J. 86; 84 E.R. (1904) 26, 117

Table of Cases

Stanton (D.) & Sons *v.* Webber (1972) 116 S.J. 667; [1973] R.T.R. 87; [1972] Crim.L.R. 544, DC 180, 181
State, *ex rel* Att-Gen *v.* Tally 102 Ala. 25 (1894) 26, 74
State *v.* Austin 228 SE 2d 507 (1976) 113
State *v.* Bass 120 SE 2d 580 (1961) 62
State *v.* Blackwell 407 P 2d 617 (1965) 108
State *v.* Breese 12 Ohio 146 (1846) 26
State *v.* Canola 374 A 2d 20 (1977) 99
State *v.* Dault 608 P 2d 270 (1980) 128
State *v.* Davies 682 P 2d 883 (1984) 171
State *v.* Dowell 11 SE 525 (1890) 108
State *v.* Duran 526 P 2d 188 (1974) 86
State *v.* Gelb 515 A 2d 1246 . . . . 63, 85
State *v.* Gray 39 P 1050 (1895) 128
State *v.* Guptill 481 A 2d 772 (1984) 255
State *v.* Hamilton 13 Nev. 386 (1878) 26
State *v.* Hayes 351 NW 2d 654 (1984) 240
State *v.* Horner 103 SE 2d 694 (1958) 36
State *v.* Kennedy 1616 P 2d 594 (1980) 115
State *v.* King 74 NW 691 (1898) 85
State *v.* McAllister 366 So 2d 1340 128
State *v.* McVay 132 A 436 (1926) 187
State *v.* Poynier 36 La Ann. 572 (1884) 26
State *v.* Pyle 476 NE 2d 124 (1985) 260
State *v.* Rollie 585 SW 2d 78 (1979) 62
State *v.* Serebin 350 NW 2d 65 (1984) 86
State *v.* Spates 405 A 2d 656 (1978) 86
State *v.* Stein 360 A 2d 347 (1976) 50
State *v.* Tally 102 Ala 25 (1894) 62
State *v.* Tazwell (3rd Ed 1982) p. 740 62
State *v.* Thibodeau 353 A 2d 595 (1976) 26
State *v.* Walden 293 SE 2d 780 (1982) 35, 44
Surujpaul (called Dick) *v.* R [1958] 1 W.L.R. 1050; 102 S.J. 757; [1958] 3 All E.R. 300; 42 Cr.App.R. 266, PC . 113, 114, 130
Sweet *v.* Parsley [1970] A.C. 132; [1969] 2 W.L.R. 470; 133 J.P. 188; 113 S.J. 86; [1969] 1 All E.R. 347; 53 Cr.App.R. 221, HL; reversing [1968] 2 Q.B. 418; [1968] 2 W.L.R. 1360; 112 S.J. 330; [1968] 2 All E.R. 337; [1968] C.L.Y. 3977, DC 191
Sweetman *v.* Industries and Commerce Department [1970] N.Z.L.R. 139 113

Tansley *v.* Painter (1968) 112 S.J. 1005; [1969] Crim.L.R. 139, DC . 36
Taylor *v.* State 41 Tex Ct R 504 100

Taylor's Central Garages (Exeter) *v.* Roper [1951] W.N. 383; 115
J.P. 445; *sub nom* Roper *v.* Taylor's Central Garages (Exeter)
[1951] 2 T.L.R. 284, DC. 182
Tesco Supermarkets *v.* Nattrass [1972] A.C. 153; [1971] 2 W.L.R.
1166; 115 S.J. 285; [1971] 2 All E.R. 127; 69 L.G.R. 403, HL;
reversing [1971] 1 Q.B. 133; [1970] 3 W.L.R. 572; 114 S.J. 664;
[1970] 3 All E.R. 357; 68 L.G.R. 722, DC 193
Thambiah *v.* R [1966] A.C. 37; [1966] 2 W.L.R. 81; 109 S.J. 832;
[1965] 3 All E.R. 661, PC 163
Thomas *v.* Deakin [1952] Ch. 646 58
Thomas *v.* Lindop [1950] W.N. 227; 66 T.L.R. (Pt.1) 1241; 94 S.J.
371; [1950] 1 All E.R. 966; 48 L.G.R. 353, DC . . . 43, 161, 180
Thompson *v.* Mitchell [1940] 1 All E.R. 339 . . . . . 108, 115, 124
Tison *v.* Arizona 107 S.Ct 1676 (1987). 78
Treacy *v.* D.P.P. [1971] A.C. 537; [1971] 2 W.L.R. 112; (1970)
115 S.J. 12; [1971] 1 All E.R. 110; (1970) 55 Cr.App.R. 113,
HL; affirming *sub nom* R *v.* Treacy [1970] 3 W.L.R. 592; 114
S.J. 604; [1970] 3 All E.R. 205, CA 29
Tuck *v.* Robson [1970] 1 W.L.R. 741; 114 S.J. 191; [1970] 1 All
E.R. 1171, DC 42, 43, 45
Tyler *v.* Wharmore [1976] R.T.R. 83; [1976] Crim LR 315, DC . 108

US *v.* Bailey 444 US 394 (1980) 122
US *v.* Chiarella 184 F 2d 903 (1950 125
US *v.* Claybourne 509 F 2d 473 (1974) 232
US *v.* Farrar 281 US 624 (1930) 240
US *v.* Harper 579 F 2d 1235 (1978) 123
US *v.* Lester 363 F 2d 68 (1966) 126
US *v.* Lopez 662 F Supp 1083 (1987) 122
US *v.* Michel 588 F 2d 986 (1979) 50
US *v.* Peoni (1938) 142
US *v.* Ruffin 613 F 2d 408 (1979). 115, 126
US *v.* Scruggs 583 F 2d 238 (1978) 49–50
US *v.* Tilton 610 F 2d 302 (1980). 50
US *v.* Tobon-Builes 706 F 2d 1092 (1983) 126
US *v.* Wiseman 445 F 2d 792 (1971). 126

Vaux's Case (1591) 4 Co Rep 44a; 76 E.R. 992 115

Wakely [1990] Crim.LR 119 231
Walters *v.* Lunt [1951] W.N. 472; 115 J.P. 512; 95 S.J. 625; [1951]
2 All E.R. 625; 35 Cr.App.R. 94; 49 L.G.R. 89, DC. 116
Weaver *v.* State 42 SE 745 (1902) 260

Wessel *v*. Carter Paterson and Pickfords, *see* Carter Paterson and Pickfords *v*. Wessel

Westminster City Council *v*. Croyalgrange [1986] 1 W.L.R. 674; (1986) 130 S.J. 409; (1986) 150 J.P. 449; [1986] 2 All E.R. 353; (1986) 83 Cr.App.R. 155; (1986) 84 L.G.R. 801; [1986] Crim.L.R. 693; (1986) 136 New L.J. 491; (1986) 83 L.S.Gaz 2089, HL; affirming (1985) 149 J.P. 161; [1985] 1 All E.R. 740; (1985) 84 L.G.R. 68; (1985) 149 J.P.N. 149, DC. 182

Weymell *v*. Reed (1794) TR 599; 101 E.R. 335 156

White *v*. Richardson (1806) Russ & Ry 99; 168 E.R. 704. . . . 211

White *v*. Ridley (1978) Hale PC i 618 260

Wilcox *v*. Jeffery [1951] W.N. 77; [1951] 1 T.L.R. 706; 115 J.P. 151; 95 S.J. 157; [1951] 1 All E.R. 464; 49 L.G.R. 363, DC. 37, 38, 39, 179, 242

Williamson *v*. Norris [1989] 1 Q.B. 7 239

Wilsher *v*. Essex Area Health Authority [1988] A.C. 1074; [1988] 2 W.L.R. 557; (1988) 132 S.J. 418; [1988] All E.R. 871; (1988) 138 New L.J. 78, HL; affirming [1987] Q.B. 730; [1987] 2 W.L.R. 425; [1986] 3 All E.R. 801; (1986) 130 S.J. 749; (1986) 136 New L.J. 1061; (1986) 83 L.S.Gaz 2661, CA 88

Wilson *v*. State 188 Ark 846 100

Wilf *v*. State 260 So. 2d 325 (1972) 29

Workman *v*. State 21 NE 2d 712 (1939) 62

Woby *v*. B. and O. [1986] Crim.LR 183 108

1
Introduction

In broad terms, the criminal law may be viewed as a structure and system for describing, proscribing, and punishing certain forms of socially unacceptable behaviour. Whether common law or statutory, an individual offence's liability elements will be found in its particular definition. But definitions alone reveal neither the meanings of specific terms employed nor the governing effect of many more general concepts operating throughout the system, such as, for example, defences or causal notions. This is similarly true for complicity where, rather than being expressly set out in every individual offence's definition,[1] the conditions for and possible range of participation in any particular crime are to be discovered by resorting to a general body of concepts and rules. Complicity's function is to determine the circumstances when one party (an accessory)[2] by virtue of prior or simultaneous activity or association will be held criminally responsible for

---

[1] One prominent example of this approach in respect of attempt is Macaulay's (1837) Indian Penal Code (enacted 1860), which although containing a general attempt provision (s. 511) covered most major offences with specific provisions. To a much lesser degree this practice was also used in relation to complicity. See the commentary by W. Stokes, *Anglo-Indian Codes* (1887), i. 67-8 and 64-7. Many exceptions exist where particular offences either include complicity provisions within general definitions, or the offence is of an exclusively complicitous nature. For example, 'to cause or encourage . . . unlawful sexual intercourse' under s. 28 (1) of the Sexual Offences Act 1956, and complicity in suicide under s. 2 (1) of the Suicide Act 1961. However, when applying and interpreting such specific instances courts employ general rules and notions of complicity. See e.g. *Gillick* [1986] 1 AC 112 and *Attorney General* v. *Able* [1984] QB 795. Cf. instances where secondary forms of behaviour are incorporated into the definition of principal liability; e.g. handling goods under s. 22 of the Theft Act 1968 ('undertakes or assists in their retention, removal' etc.) covers activity which might otherwise constitute complicity in either theft or handling.

[2] 'Accessory' will be used for participants helping or inciting the principal or perpetrator, a course adopted in Law Commission Working Paper 43 (1972), 5-6; and also in Law Commission Report 177 (1989), cls. 25-8. For stylistic variety 'secondary party' will also be used in the same sense. 'Accomplice' is a participant who may be either a principal or accessory. Perpetrators were formerly principals in the first degree, abettors or principals in the second degree being those present assisting or inciting the perpetrator, accessories before the fact being those inciting or assisting but not present. The Criminal Law Act 1967 shed the law of the ancient terminology employed to distinguish participants in felonies by abolishing the distinction between felonies and misdemeanours and making all parties principals. The term 'complicity' itself, although now in widespread use (e.g. the Model Penal Code (1962), s. 2.06; Law Commission Working Paper 43; G. L. Williams, *Textbook of Criminal Law* (1983)) is not universally employed, sometimes giving way to 'parties', 'secondary parties', or 'secondary participation': e.g. Law Commission Report 177, pt. 9; J. C. Smith and B. Hogan, *Criminal Law* (1988); R. M. Perkins, *Criminal Law* (1982), W. R. La Fave and A. W. Scott, *Criminal Law* (1986).

another's (the perpetrator's)[3] wrongful behaviour. Because of this general function throughout criminal law, the opportunities, if not the need, for extreme complexity have been considerable; it has been a potential for complexity and uncertainty which courts, with almost perverse satisfaction, have over many centuries done much to realize.

The need to supplement penal laws formulated for, and most immediately aimed at, the culpable perpetrator and to bring in and incriminate other less directly involved participants has been obvious to law makers for as long as criminal law has existed.[4] As the 1833 Criminal Law Commissioners observed in their Seventh Report (1843):

> It can make no difference either in respect of the mischief resulting from an injury done or for its prevention whether the offender do it directly with his own hand or indirectly by [another party or by] mechanical means, or whether he effect it by proximate or remote means, or whether he be present or absent at the time when any hurtful effect or consequence results.

This attitude runs into common consciousness, with complicity being a familiar form of unlawful behaviour regularly depended on by authors as a plot device and well represented in imaginative literature by characters as far apart as Lady Macbeth and Thérèse Raquin. Yet while the criminal nature of such indirect participation is intuitively obvious, this does not extend to its underlying theoretical basis. Criminalizing indirect participation can be approached in two fundamentally different ways: by regarding

---

[3] 'Principal' (along with 'actor' and 'perpetrator') will be used to denote the immediate perpetrator of the substantive offence. It is accepted that following strict linguistic logic 'perpetrator' alone should be employed. See Williams, *Textbook*, 329.

[4] Anglo-Saxon law provides examples of various modes of participation, but, as with the bulk of the law from this period, the gloss on the basic law has not survived along with those general propositions which have. Some of the earliest references to complicity law are found in the laws of Ine dating from the end of the 7th cent.: 'A ten year old child can be regarded as accessory to a theft', c. 7 (2); 'If stolen property in the hands of a trader is attached, and he has not bought it in the presence of trustworthy witness, he shall declare with an oath equal to the penalty [involved] that he has been neither an accessory nor an accomplice [to the theft]', c. 25 (1). See *The Laws of the Earliest English Kings*, ed. and trans. by F. L. Attenborough (1922). Later illustrations from the 10th cent. are contained in the laws of Aethelstan, II Aethelstan c. 3 (1): 'And if a lord is accessory to a theft by one of his slaves . . . (2) And in like manner also, [any] of the royal treasurers or [any] of our reaves who have been accessories of thieves . . .', VI Aethelstan c. 1 (1). 11th-cent. examples can be discovered in the laws of Aethelred and Canute (VIII Aethelred cc. 23 and 27 and II Canute c. 21). See *The Laws of the Kings of England from Edmund to Henry I*, ed. and trans. by A. J. Robertson (1925). The general vagueness and absence of detailed provisions eliminates the possibility of worthwhile deductions as to whether accomplices were usually treated with greater leniency than principal offenders. The slim evidence available suggests generally not. Although e.g. under c. 23 of VIII Aethelstan, the punishment for instigating homicide would appear less severe than that specified for perpetrating homicide as stated in c. 26. It is not until the time of Henry I that the written law becomes a little more explicit in its attitude towards the punishment of accomplices: Henry I, c. 85 (1)–(3). Note the similarity of treatment for one who 'counsels or himself' slays another specified in 85 (3); and further, the provisions of c. 86 (3). In c. 87 (1) (*a*) and (*b*) the case of assisting by providing the means for the commission of an offence is dealt with. See *Leges Henrici Primi*, ed. and trans. by E. J. Downer (1972).

the substance of liability as the secondary actor's mental association with or commitment to a criminal objective, as manifested in and evidenced by his overt action; or, shifting the focus, through his culpable activities, making the secondary party share responsibility for the occurrence of the principal offence. The former approach is characterizable as inchoate or, possibly, endangerment based, with criminality residing in either the accessory's demonstrated anti-social proclivities, or in his risking the commission of a principal offence. In contrast, the latter approach, parasitic or derivative in nature, makes the accessory's liability contingent upon the actual occurrence of a principal offence,[5] requiring a variety of participation or sharing in the principal offender's criminality.

English common law moved in this latter direction, adopting and developing a derivative form of complicity. The reasons for following this course almost certainly centre around the early common law's overwhelming concern with resting criminal liability on a causal association between action and proscribed harm.[6] And along with this derivativeness of liability came the early but by no means inevitable rule of equality of punishment for accessories. More sophisticated and subtle notions relating to inchoate or threatened criminal conduct took root only many centuries after derivative based complicity had become well entrenched. But whether or not principal and accessory are to be subject to similar punishment, there remains the need for appropriate rules to settle just how much or how little a party must do in relation to the principal offence to incur accessorial liability. As will be consistently seen, it is the contestability of the appropriate level of this responsibility threshold, both in respect of the nature of accessorial action and accompanying mental culpability, which has long fuelled judicial confusion and conflict.

The primary reasons for such variations of attitude are not hard to find. Most obviously, devising a mechanism of universal application throughout a widely diverse range of offences inevitably generates linguistic and conceptual tensions; a formula tailor-made to punish secondary activity in, say, homicide will not necessarily easily accommodate complicity in theft offences. The products of this formulatory and conceptual compromise, forced by the generality of complicity provisions, are often ill-adapted, badly fitting, and, most frequently, ill-defined or elastic terms of liability.

Beyond inherent difficulties of this nature is a clutch of contentious policy questions. In dealing with activities often some way removed in distance and time from the core of proscribed principal harm, complicity is well placed to

---

[5] As will be seen, the nature of the criminality upon which parasitic or derivative liability may be fixed is problematic. It will be maintained that doctrinal development in complicity legitimately permits secondary liability to rest on less than a principal offence. However, for simplicity's sake, until the issue becomes directly relevant, reference will be made to a 'principal offence'.

[6] Cf. F. Pollock and F. W. Maitland, *History of English Law*, 2nd edn. (1898), i. 509.

raise awkward policy dilemmas as to the appropriate limits of criminality.[7] They are prime examples of penumbral issues, where the law is operating on the outer edge of justifiable criminalization, and, for example, in some respects paralleling problems of proximity long experienced in attempt liability.

Difficulties and tensions of this sort need to be held permanently in view when approaching complicity law, whether in respect of interpretational or evaluative questions. Moreover, the absence in so many areas of developed complicity theory throws up the intriguing conundrum of whether this is the cause or consequence of universality and penumbral problems. As will be seen, circularity of argument and explanation is both tempting and easily fallen into. But, however cause and effect are distributed between these factors, to some extent they each feed on and reinforce the uncertain natures of the other.

With such contingent difficulties in mind a preliminary review of theoretical possibilities will serve to demonstrate the extent of the uncertainty ahead, as well as laying the foundations of more detailed and directed analysis in subsequent chapters.

1. Theories of Complicity: An Overview

Surveying complicity's hazy theoretical landscape can, depending on the commentator's nerve, temperament, and resilience, induce feelings running from hand-rubbing relish to hand-on-the-brow gloom. Despite a pedigree tailing off into Anglo-Saxon times, certain theoretical features of complicity have never been openly nor authoritatively articulated. Complicity's derivative basis coupled with the principle of eligibility for equal punishment of all parties have been the only clear and enduring foundational requirements of liability. Over the centuries, a formidably complex superstructure of rules has been constructed, adapted, and refashioned by wider developments within the criminal law; these in themselves reflect evolving views on the proper basis of criminal responsibility generally. Recognizing and prescribing appropriate forms of complicity with coherent culpability requirements has been an especially problematic and pragmatic exercise, lacking reasonably clear notions of complicity's underlying principles and operating on unspoken premises as to the nature of its relationship with principal liability.

---

[7] The broad-brush legislative drafting and subsequent (il)liberal judicial construction of 'The Waltham Black Act' (1723) is a notorious illustration of perceived political need compromising distinctions between individual criminal roles and appropriate levels of punishment. See L. Radzinowicz, *A History of English Criminal Law and its Administration from 1750* (1948–) i. 611–98, for an exhaustive analysis of the general penal significance of the Act. For the political dimensions, cf. E. P. Thompson, *Whigs and Hunters* (1975) with P. Rogers 'The Waltham Blacks and the Black Act' (1974) 17 *Hist. Jo.* 465.

This relationship may be posited on one of a number of apparently feasible, if not ultimately convincing, theories; some of which (with varying degrees of emphasis) have extensive implications for all aspects of the demands of complicity liability. Such theories, which need not be seen as mutually exclusive, include and may be labelled 'equivalence', 'agency', 'participation', 'causal', and 'control'. Although subject to detailed scrutiny in subsequent chapters, the broad natures of such competing theories can usefully be sketched out at this stage.

Despite being by no means a necessary corollary of equal eligibility to similar levels of punishment, it is tempting to view complicity as a shadow variety of principal liability, following, as far as possible, both its *actus reus* and *mens rea* contours. As a starting-point, paradigmatic principal liability could be taken as involving a voluntary actor, with any appropriate fault, engaging in harmful conduct or causing harm. An equivalence or parallel liability theory of complicity would demand a variable level of culpability as dictated by the principal offence's fault requirements. Such a shadowing process would, though, require the accessory's mental state to be an amalgam of purpose, perception, etc., in respect of both his own and the principal's actions. Paralleling the requirements of principal liability becomes even more difficult in respect of the principal's *actus reus*. While there is some plausibility in maintaining that an accessory must have a similar level of mental culpability to the perpetrator, this is not possible in respect of *actus reus* demands. Whether the principal offence is one based on the actor's conduct or the result of such conduct, the accessory's involvement (depending on the offence) cannot always be that stipulated by the offence's definition.

Equivalence theories will, therefore, inevitably often fall some way short of replicating principal criminality in an indirect form. Rather than *paralleling* all the requirements of principal liability there may be an *overall equivalence* of culpability entailing a skewing towards and raising of mental culpability to compensate for the accessory's more restricted causal role. Theories of parallelism or equivalence have strongest appeal when, as in ancient times, the only punishment for principals (felons) and other participating parties was inflexibly fixed as the same (death). The theory's attraction diminished with the law's adoption of the more flexible position of equal eligibility to similar punishment of all parties, whereby an accessory may suffer a more or less severe sentence, depending on the overall weight given to his culpability and nature of participation. Yet still in the theory's favour is its far greater sensitivity to the culpability gradations of each offence by demanding, so far as possible, similar culpability levels from the accessory and principal. The greatest divergence between this approach and the current English law of a (broadly) universal culpability standard for all secondary liability occurs in the case of strict liability offences. Here, unlike the present English law, applying an equivalence theory and not requiring at least foresight of the nature of the principal's actions or their consequences would widen the incidence of liability. Conversely, for offences demanding intention (such as murder and wounding with intent) an equivalence theory would raise the level of accessorial culpability and produce a narrowing of the incidence of complicity in these offences.

Regarding perpetrators of crimes as agents of accessories provides a second possible theoretical account of complicity. Certainly primitive civil law notions of agency originate from a very early point in legal history, although not as far back as complicity.[8] Much of the terminology of both forms of responsibility is shared, with judicial pronouncements frequently incorporating references to perpetrators being 'authorized' or 'commanded' to carry out or execute the accessory's purpose, or accessories having 'consented' to or 'ratified' criminal behaviour. But, at best, agency doctrine, grounded on some sort of consensus between the parties, is capable of explaining only part of complicity's coverage, for liability without consensus has long been a recognized form of complicity. Moreover, as will be suggested below, a rationale appropriate for civil responsibility is far from a fitting basis for incriminating a party where a range of quite different policy considerations hold sway.

A further possible theoretical explanation looks to culpable acts of participation as sufficient without any necessary causal effect on the principal's actions or their outcome. Participation alone serves as potent evidence of an accessory allying or associating himself with the principal's criminal venture. Such a doctrine, though, has at least two underlying alternative or even complementary rationales hardly very different from those sometimes employed to justify inchoate offences: association with or involvement in another's crime may be seen as deserving punishment because it increases the likelihood of the principal offence occurring — a risk or endangerment rationale; or participation may be taken as a sufficiently strong manifestation of the accessory's criminal proclivities to warrant punishment. Additionally, there is a variant form of participation account which does not rely on inchoate type rationales. Instead, liability is premised on a likely but not always demonstrable causal contribution made by the accessory's actions towards the criminal effect created by the principal's behaviour.

Theories more openly and directly revolving around the notion of cause and control provide a final area of feasible explanation of complicity liability. The idea of 'causing' another human agent to behave in a particular way presents philosophical as well as evidential problems. This is less true of 'controlling' another's actions in the sense of exercising some acknowledged (by the actor) authority to bring about a particular objective. But control in *this* sense is exceedingly narrow; consequently its explanatory

---

[8] Pollock and Maitland, *History*, ii. 228 and 531.

Introduction 7

value and relevance to most complicity situations is limited. Control in the sense of engineering a set of conditions to bring about a particular result, or manipulation of the agent's sensibilities or anticipated reactions towards a desired end, although of wider potential, is still of very restricted explanatory value for complicity. Rather than control, it will be maintained here that a broad causal account of complicity offers the most internal coherence alongside the greatest consistency with general principles of criminal responsibility that touch and concern complicity.

2. Neighbouring or Kindred Forms of Liability

At this stage in identifying complicity's nature it is useful briefly to distinguish the theoretical natures of three areas of neighbouring liability, further references to which will appear in succeeding chapters. These forms of cognate criminality are (1) assisting an offender to avoid detection or apprehension (formerly[9] an 'accessory after the fact'), (2) vicarious liability, and most importantly (3) inchoate liability.

(1) *Accessory after the Fact*

An accessory after the fact was one who 'knowing a felony to have been committed by another, receives, relieves, comforts or assists the felon'.[10] The role performed by a common law accessory after the fact was associated with the principal's substantive offence yet distinct and separate from it. Using the term 'accessory' set up a linguistic association, tying the party in with true participants. Anciently this was acceptable in so far as harbouring or assisting a felon was regarded as seriously as participation in the commission of the substantive offence and, consequently, carried the same punishment.[11] Moreover, such liability was formally dependent on establishing the commission of a principal offence. However, despite these links, it has long been understood that accessories after the fact, as a 'different species of guilt',[12] stood outside complicity. Rather than resting culpability on participation in the bringing about of the substantive offence, an accessory after the fact's criminality centres on the distinct behaviour of preventing an existing offender's detection or apprehension—essentially interference in the process of bringing offenders to book.[13] Current English

---

[9] Until changes under the Criminal Law Act 1967, substituting (s. 4) new offences of 'assisting'.
[10] Turner, *Russell on Crime*, 12th edn. (1964), i. 163 (hereafter '*Russell*'). M. Hale, *The History of the Pleas of the Crown* (1736), i. 618 (hereafter *PC*); W. Blackstone, *Commentaries on the Laws of England* (1767), iv. 37 (hereafter *Comm.*).
[11] Pollock and Maitland, *History*, ii. 510, 'receiving outlaws or thieves was among the oldest [crimes] and was severely handled by ancient law'.
[12] Blackstone, *Comm.* iv. 40.
[13] See Model Penal Code TD1 (1953), 13.

law makes 'assisting' the subject of separate liability under section 4 of the Criminal Law Act 1967.

(2) Vicarious Liability

Other than both using the behaviour of one party as a basis for holding another party criminally responsible, vicarious and complicity liability are diverse and distinct doctrines. With a few common law exceptions,[14] vicarious liability is a creature of nineteenth-century statutory construction founded on reasoning borrowed from the notion of *respondeat superior*[15] by which employers are liable for their employees' torts committed in the course of employment. In great contrast with complicity, vicarious responsibility cuts across or represents an abandonment of common law axioms that place responsibility on the twin bases of personal culpability and cause. In Hobbes's words, legal attribution is through the 'fiction' of employees — 'Persons Artificiall' — having their 'words and actions Owned by those whom they represent'.[16] Vicarious liability is perceived as a 'necessary doctrine for the proper enforcement of modern legislation';[17] the general social benefits gained by this incriminating technique are seen to outweigh any consequential personal injustice. It embodies a superintendence rationale whereby employers are held responsible for their employees' criminal transgressions through a deemed failure to exercise proper control and authority over their employees. Although largely of relevance to regulatory offences requiring no fault, even where it is necessary the employee's actual culpability is imputed to the employer. This process of imputation of fault is quite alien to complicity[18] requirements which do not rest on the nature of the parties' prior relationship and operate across the full span of substantive offences.

(3) Inchoate Liability

As a matter of genealogy, operation, and appearance, complicity and inchoate offences are related forms of liability. Yet, in terms of maturity, compared with complicity the general[19] common law inchoate offences of

---

[14] See G. L. Williams, *Criminal Law: The General Part*, 2nd edn. (1961) (hereafter *CLGP*), 267–9.

[15] See generally F. B. Sayre, 'Criminal Responsibility for the Acts of Another' (1930) 43 HLR, 689.

[16] *Leviathan*, pt. i, ch. 16, 'Of Persons, Authors, And Things Personated'.

[17] Goddard LCJ, *Gardner v. Akeroyd* [1952] 2 QB 743, 751.

[18] Corporate responsibility may apply to the full range of offences, subject to punishability by fine. Conviction also of the company's 'controlling officers' for the criminal actions of others will almost invariably rest on complicity principles.

[19] For specific instances of earlier conspiracy offences see R. S. Wright, *Law of Criminal Conspiracies and Agreements* (1873), 5–18, and P. H. Winfield, *History of Conspiracy and Abuse of Legal Procedure* (1921), ch. 1. For earlier particular examples of attempts see J. F. Stephen, *History of the Criminal Law of England* (1883), ii. 222–3 (hereafter *HCL*). Clear recognition of a general offence of attempt did not occur until the beginning of the 19th cent.

conspiracy, attempt, and incitement are striplings, with origins in the seventeenth century and the Star Chamber's political needs. Although not a parent[20] of inchoate liability in any direct sense, complicity was, at least, an inspirational source or comparative model. Very broadly, inchoate modes of liability which, through another party's actions, culminate in a substantive offence will incur secondary liability. Crudely, in some limited respects, complicity could be seen as occupying the intermediate ground between inchoate and principal liability.

The logic justifying the creation of inchoate forms of criminality was fairly plain and compelling: if instigated or concerted action when substantively successful could incriminate the secondary party the obvious further stage in the development of criminal jurisprudence was to ground liability on preliminary actions without needing or waiting for their substantive ripening. The great intellectual and political obstacle standing in the way of such a development was the common law's entrenched attachment to punishing involvement in the causing of demonstrable harm. Not until the seventeenth century was the notion of anticipatory or threatened harm sufficiently widely acknowledged as an acceptable foundation from which to launch more generalized forms of inchoate liability; an acceptability reinforced by greater consciousness and strengthening of the role in criminal responsibility of mental culpability, with its roughly contemporary embodiment in the great maxim 'actus non facit reum nisi mens sit rea', generally attributed to Coke's authoritative early seventeenth-century *Third Institute*.[21]

The most distinctive feature separating inchoate and complicity liability is the autonomous or free-standing nature of the former — unlike the latter, responsibility is not derivative. Individual inchoate offences offer further contrasts. The language of conspiracy often supports a complicity charge where there has been a confederacy or common purpose between parties; but agreement is not an essential ingredient of complicity, merely one possible (albeit uncertain) mode. This link between complicity and conspiracy is seen in a very strong form in Macaulay's Indian Penal Code, originally drafted in 1837. Here no distinct offence of conspiracy is recognized; rather it is viewed as an example of incomplete complicity.[22] A similar drafting pattern also appears in Wright's draft Jamaican Criminal Code (1877), vetted by Stephen at the Colonial Office's request.[23] Although not a course which recommended itself for home consumption in the 1879

---

[20] Cf. Turner in *Russell* who saw inchoate offences as 'emerging out of the law of principal and accessory' (174).
[21] Attribution of this maxim is of course debatable. For an irreverent comment on its origins, see Stephen, *HCL* ii. 94 n. 1.
[22] Ss. 107 and 108. Neither the early English Criminal Law Commissioners' draft codes nor Stephen's later 1879 code follow this course. Surprisingly, Stephen in his commentary on Macaulay's code saw nothing in ss. 107 and 108 as worth remarking upon; *HCL* ii. 307–8. But see Stokes's commentary in *Anglo-Indian Codes*, i. 64–7.
[23] *Parliamentary Papers*, LXI; ss. 32 and 35 and introduction.

Draft Criminal Code, Stephen found nothing fundamentally objectionable in Wright's approach. Attempt[24] will most likely operate in conjunction with complicity where the chosen perpetrator of an offence is 'innocent' and fails to complete the *actus reus*. Here the 'accessory' may be deemed to have attempted to commit the substantive offence through the doctrine of innocent agency. However, beyond these similarities and contrasts it will be seen that underlying notions of inchoate liability also have the important capacity to illuminate the theoretical function of attributable harm when determining appropriate levels of punishment for secondary parties.

3. STRUCTURE, SCOPE, AND PRINCIPAL ISSUES

Examination of what is broadly comprehended within complicity's *actus reus* requirements is carried out in Part I. More particularly, three aspects are explored: the range of complicity modes (Chapter 2), the role of causation in complicity (Chapter 3), and the meaning and implications of complicity's derivative nature (Chapter 4).

Analysis of complicity's scope, as governed by what modes of behaviour may incur liability (Chapter 2), commences with an attempt to unpick the convoluted logic of medieval common law's restriction to felonies of the differentiation of party roles, with no such designation occurring for treasons and misdemeanours. Beyond such historical developments survives the active question of the span of behaviour which may form the basis of complicity. Still open to a degree of dispute in English law is whether the terms 'aid, abet, counsel or procure' fix the possible range of complicity by embodying common law concepts or by their literal or 'natural' meanings. This, in turn, leads to consideration of three contentious areas of behaviour where complicity liability *may* be held to exist. The first two of these possible modes of liability—mere presence at the commission of the principal offence and omission to exercise a power to control or regulate the perpetrator's actions—currently occupy positions on opposite sides of the line of responsibility: mere inactive presence at the scene of an offence being insufficient, whereas omitting to exercise a power of control may sometimes provide a basis for liability. Cases of large-scale attendance at illegal functions pose the policy dilemma of there being no performances without spectator attendance, yet the impracticability of mass prosecutions of those attending (as well as distinct latent causal issues) has tended to stifle liability for what otherwise wears the appearance of complicitous activity. Grounding secondary liability on a party's omission to exercise a right to control or supervise the perpetrator raises questions of *when* and *why* it is appropriate

---

[24] The modern basis of attempt and incitement is *Higgins* (1801), E. H. East, *A Treatise of the Pleas of the Crown*, ii. 5 (hereafter PC) 5, 102 ER 269. The language of the judgment shows how closely attempt and incitement were conceived of. See *Russell*, 176.

to convert a civil power to control into a duty to do so. Furthermore, just how extensive is such a duty? What must be done to satisfy it? How far is the general entitlement to remain passive in the presence of criminality eroded by employing such a basis for complicity?

Conspiracy is the third and final contentious potential mode of liability considered in Chapter 2. Despite entailing the abbreviation of standard complicity demands, both in respect of *mens rea* and cause, should (and does) conspiracy act as an auxiliary complicity mode, as in some American jurisdictions, with the practical need of controlling 'organized crime' taken as legitimizing this approach?

Following on from initial issues on possible complicity modes, attention is turned to the nature of the linkage or necessary nexus between the accessory's actions and the occurrence of the principal offence (Chapter 3). A range of alternative theoretical models is reviewed. This exploration of viable theoretical bases is preceded by the establishing of preliminary working premises of general relevance to criminal responsibility: most particularly, the acceptable operating levels of choice and chance, the function of harm, and the meaning of 'cause'. Settling the width of the notion of cause presents clear practical and conceptual difficulties, especially whether freely acting human agents may reasonably be claimed to have their actions 'caused' by another. But whether 'caused' or not in any linguistically or philosophically appropriate sense, the question is still reducible to whether the accessory's behaviour in some way affected the bringing about of the principal offence — this being true for both instigation and assistance forms of complicity.

The nature and extent of complicity's dependent or derivative structure is the third discussion area concerning what might be described as *actus reus* elements (Chapter 4). Having already considered possible complicity modes, and how they must be related to or connected with the perpetrator's actions or their effects, discussion moves on to the nature of the *perpetrator's* actions and their ability to be sources of derivative liability. Traditional or orthodox doctrine operates on a model of the perpetrator's offence feeding the accessory's liability; the perpetrator's responsibility is principal, the accessory's secondary; without a principal *offender* (even if unknown or still at large) there can be no principal offence; without a principal *offence* there can be no secondary liability. The general issue is how closely is the accessory's liability tied to the principal's? How firmly and formally is the accessory's liability regulated by the principal's? Does derivativeness inhibit the proper representation and fair labelling of the criminality of each participating party?

It is when circumstances depart from the standard model that the nature and scope of complicity's derivative quality need more thorough probing. In response to situations where the perpetrator is for some reason completely without responsibility, the common law at a relatively early period recognized the doctrine of innocent agency to ensure that a culpable 'accessory' did not evade punishment for wrongdoing. Rather than an offshoot of complicity, innocent agency is a form of principal liability based on equating a non-responsible human agent with a non-human agent. Though simple in broad conception, the limits of the doctrine are yet to be authoritatively determined; most especially, does innocent agency rest on a theory of imputed or attributed *actions* or on a theory of causal responsibility? Linked to this is the live question of whether actions of a particularly personal kind are excluded from innocent agency responsibility on the grounds of linguistic inappropriateness—that there is a class of 'non-proxyable' behaviour. A further disputed area affecting the doctrine's scope relates to whether innocent agency is tied to *intended* manipulative use of the agent.

Beyond innocent agency, situations occur where the perpetrator is in some degree criminally responsible for his actions but there is a mismatch or disparity between the perpetrator's and the accessory's individual culpability. On such occasions uncertainty arises as to how both parties may be incriminated for different offences or for different levels of the same type of offence, and on what theoretical basis.

The four chapters making up Part II of the text are devoted to matters which, in one way or another, qualify as aspects of the mental requirement in complicity. The first (Chapter 5) considers the appropriate attitude for an accessory towards the outcome of his actions: must the accessory's actions in some way be purposeful in respect of the principal offence? This is followed by the multi-faceted question of the necessary extent or specificity of the accessory's 'knowledge' of the principal's possible offence (Chapter 6). The effects on complicity liability where variation occurs between anticipated and actual principal behaviour is the third topic (Chapter 7). The distinctiveness or otherwise of *mens rea* requirements possibly implicit in the ancient doctrine of common purpose is the final area of consideration (Chapter 8).

Whether an accessory's liability requires a purposeful or positive attitude towards the principal's criminal venture is both contentious and of obvious practical relevance to the scope of complicity. The less committed an accessory needs to be to a criminal enterprise the greater the potential reach of liability for facilitatory yet undirected or disinterested action. It is an issue arising most acutely with sales, in the normal course of trading, of materials suspected to be destined for future use in criminal activity. To approach a measured response to this question of accessorial attitude a group of distinct but interlinked matters must be reviewed: the extensiveness of other culpability demands and how, in aggregate, they match up to principal requirements; the policy dilemma created by setting a universal attitudinal standard across a complete range of crimes; the ability of a complementary facilitation offence to ease such strategic problems; and the capability of sentencing discretion satisfactorily to reflect and accommodate culpability differences between hostile, indifferent, and purposeful secondary participants.

While an accessory's attitude towards the principal offence is one (potential) major measure of mental culpability, the other focuses on the necessary specificity of the accessory's knowledge or foresight of the principal's possible course of action and its circumstances. Many degrees of knowledge, belief, or foresight may exist as to what a principal may be intending to do. The shortfall between the putative principal's criminal objectives and quite how much is known of them or foreseen by the accessory may be large or small. The general question of specificity of the accessory's knowledge or foresight only seriously arises in cases of assistance and not where the basis of complicity is instigation.[25] Moreover, difficulties over the necessary level of knowledge or foresight are largely (though not exclusively) a consequence of the (likely) immateriality of accessorial attitude to the principal offence under current English law.

Construction of the modern broad requirement of 'knowledge of essential matters' of the principal offence has inevitably led to progressive judicial refinements aimed at producing a more detailed account of what an accessory must know or foresee. The separately formulated specificity tests, knowledge of 'type' (*Bainbridge*) or 'contemplation' (*Maxwell*) of an inclusive range of offences, present both interpretational questions as to their individual effect and potential problems of compatibility. Each test raises the same issue of the desirable extent of the subjective nexus between the accessory and principal action: how mobile or transferable is (and should be) an accessory's mental culpability? Taking the most extreme manifestation of free-floating, yet subjective, culpability, does complicity law recognize 'blank cheque' responsibility—where an accessory has indicated a willingness to support any unspecified form of criminality which the principal may chose to engage in?

A further distinct factor affecting the accessory's culpability level is his assessment of the likelihood of the principal offence being carried out. If perceived as no more than a remote possibility, the provision of assistance should not be regarded as so blameworthy as where the perpetrator appears determined to act in a particular fashion. This suggests two questions: what level of perceived likelihood of principal action is necessary to incriminate a secondary party and is it a fixed standard for all offences, regardless of seriousness, or is it variable, depending on the principal offence involved?

A final area of examination relating to the necessary extent of the accessory's foresight of 'essential matters' is the position of offences for which the principal requires no subjective culpability: offences of negligence

---

[25] Except in so far as problems of the principal's deviation or variation from agreed conduct are regarded as involving 'specificity' matters.

and strict liability. The common question is whether, in addition to foresight of the principal's behaviour and surrounding circumstances, an accessory must foresee (even though the perpetrator need not) the possibility of certain criminal consequences which in fact materialize? As a matter of penal policy, how far should (respectively) the objective and no fault bases of negligence and strict liability be reflected in complicity requirements for such offences?

Variations may occur in the principal's actions as to the object, subject, or mode of offence foreseen by the accessory. Problems of variation, in contrast with common purpose difficulties, generally, though not exclusively, relate to situations where the accessory is absent from the scene of the principal offence. But a more material distinction is that, although both common purpose and deviation cases may involve deliberate changes by the perpetrator from agreed or foreseen behaviour, it is only in non common purpose circumstances that mistaken or accidental deviation is likely to arise, although remaining a distinct hypothetical possibility in cases when the accessory is present at the offence.[26] Where deviation is accidental principal liability offers the mechanism of transferred malice as a model solution, along with its arguable theoretical defects. However, no such loosely comparable case and solution is available where variation is deliberate. When deliberate, the most frequent treatment of variation questions is limited to a *mens rea* grounded analysis, with 'substantiality' of variation as the working criterion. What is 'substantial' and why should a 'substantial' deviation free the 'accessory' of responsibility? Is resolution of variation cases best approached through a combined *mens rea* and causal analysis?

Of considerable antiquity, the 'doctrine' of common purpose has provided a specially adapted terminology and possibly distinct culpability standard for dealing with cases where a member of a group, acting in concerted action, exceeds the original scope of the criminal venture and commits a further or collateral offence. The doctrine's function, of providing an apparently straightforward and convenient means for incriminating partners in crime when the settling of the respective roles performed by each was inaccessible to usual techniques of proof, was later infiltrated and complicated by the workings and evolution of the felony-murder rule. Such is the interweaving of these two doctrines over later periods of complicity's development that confident pronouncements on many features of common purpose's operation are made impossible.

The central question requiring detailed review is whether the doctrine of common purpose is simply a linguistic variant of a single general culpability standard, or whether it embodies a substantive culpability distinction. Two

---

[26] When the accessory is present, unilateral mistakes made by the principal would be more open to correction or intervention by the accessory. This would be less true, though not without some validity, in cases of accidental deviation.

aspects carry at least implicit challenges to the leading general authorities on the *mens rea* of complicity. The first concerns the dispute over the need for an accessory to possess a positive or purposeful attitude towards the principal's actions. It is in common purpose cases that the language and concept of community or commonality of purpose appears most regularly; the frequent implication is that, although he may have foreseen the risk of criminal action beyond that agreed, an accessory's liability is limited to that within the common purpose. A second area of possible inconsistency with general *mens rea* demands relates to a reduced culpability requirement for collateral offences; more particularly, that *mens rea* for the primary criminal objective acts as a variety of qualifying culpability for the collateral offence.

Part III, in addition to reviewing the applicability of general defences, considers four factors of special relevance to cutting back potential complicity liability: offences entailing inevitable incidental secondary participation, complicity motivated by law enforcement objectives, limitation of an accessory's possible liability for a succession of similar offences beyond that initially counselled or assisted (Chapter 9), and the ability of an 'accessory' effectively to renounce or withdraw from a criminal enterprise (Chapter 10).

Where an offence's definitional requirements inevitably involve secondary participation courts have on occasions excluded from liability an 'accessory' who has been a 'victim' of the offence, on the grounds of the imposition of liability being contrary to implied statutory objectives. 'Victims' and other examples of inevitably incidental participation raise questions as to what particular rules of statutory interpretation are being employed, how deserving and undeserving cases are distinguished, and the general acceptability of using courts to carry out this discriminatory process. A second possible restriction on complicity liability is when an 'accessory's' actions have been motivated by law enforcement objectives. What are the limits to this defence? Are all such motivated actions excusable? Repeated principal offences is a third area where the possibility of some limitation mechanism arises. Because of its dependency on another's free actions, complicity raises the special problem of repeated principal offences beyond that initially encouraged or assisted. The nub of the concern here is not incriminating the accessory for multiple subsequent offences, but his *unfair* incrimination: 'unfair' in the sense of being inadequately underpinned by or linked to the original complicitous act.

Withdrawal or renunciation is a variety of limitation of a quite different nature in that it relates to putative complicity in the original substantive offence[27] and looks to positive remedial or counter action by the 'accessory'. In criminal responsibility complicity offers a unique

[27] Although it is also one way of curtailing liability for subsequent offences.

opportunity, in the interval between the 'accessory's' act and his liability crystallizing through the commission of the principal offence, for the 'accessory' to renounce or withdraw in some way from his prior actions. Despite being well established in general terms, both the defence's theoretical basis and the qualifying requirements are obscure. Most especially: what credible policy reasons can be offered to justify granting the defence? How far must the accessory go in his efforts to withdraw? Must they be aimed at erasure of the effects of his prior activities or directed at preventing the principal offence? Does it matter if withdrawal is motivated merely by the accessory's desire to save his own skin, or is something more altruistic necessary?

I

The *Actus Reus*

The forms of behaviour which may constitute a basis for complicity and the nature of the relationship between such behaviour and the principal offence is the subject-matter of Part II of the text.

An initial determinant of complicity's scope is the range of possible modes of behaviour capable of generating liability, examined in Chapter 2. Procedural, substantive, and evidential complexities which for centuries plagued complicity prosecutions have been largely exorcised, although a few pockets of resistant doctrinal anomaly survive. However, with the most arcane of these features relating to complicity modes now gone, attention is focused on issues currently affecting the potential span of secondary liability. In particular, consideration is given to two contentious areas: the extent to which different varieties of inactivity may incriminate a party as an accessory, and whether conspiracy is an auxiliary mode of incurring liability not subject to complicity's general requirements.

Causation's substantially submerged role is the second major *actus reus* component to be analysed (in Chapter 3). Although open to dispute, a causal element is seen here to be an essential ingredient of every form of complicity. Requiring a causal contribution to link the accessory's actions with those of the principal offender's serves two separate functions: it partly demarcates principal and accessory roles (complicity's upper boundary) and it fixes the minimum level of involvement necessary for complicity (the lower boundary). Yet, because of practical problems of proof of causal contribution in many common complicity situations, rather than a positive causal requirement the law has evolved what might be described as a covert doctrine of presumed cause arising once encouragement or assistance is shown to have been communicated or given to the perpetrator, but subject to rebuttal by evidence suggesting causal ineffectiveness.

The third principal feature of complicity examined as an *actus reus* element is the derivative quality of liability (in Chapter 4). Essentially, the general question reduces to how far the level of an accessory's liability is governed or moderated by the perpetrator's. It will be seen that complicity's anciently conceived derivative or parasitic structure does not comfortably lend itself to punishing deserving but unorthodox modes of participation. Permutating the separate elements of principal liability or activity with those of the accessory to achieve a fair representation of the true level of accessorial culpability sets up clear doctrinal stresses — some might suggest fractures. Even the long established complementary notion of innocent agency, which absorbs many problematic examples of secondary participation by transmuting 'accessories' into principals, cannot always convincingly accommodate complicity's leftovers. It is largely through such marginal, hybrid, or non-orthodox examples of participation that the substance and limits of complicity's derivative nature will be explored and tested.

2

Modes of Complicity

1. Historical Antecedents: Treason, Felonies, Misdemeanours, and Procedural Paralysis

As already suggested, the evolution of English complicity law is of considerable complexity, born out of piecemeal acceptance of and response to changes both in the perceived legitimate scope of criminality and parallel developments in the laws of procedure and evidence. Within complicity significant distinctions evolved between offences designated treasons, felonies, and misdemeanours; and in the case of felony, between different degrees of participation. Only for felonies did the common law recognize separate levels of participation. The apparent rationale amounted to misdemeanours being regarded as not serious enough and treasons being too serious to justify the distinction between parties.[1]

In the case of misdemeanours, by the beginning of the fourteenth century all participants were accepted as principals[2] because[3]

> trespass had . . . their civil side as well as their criminal side, and, seeing that all concerned in a trespass[4] were equally liable to pay damages if sued . . . in a civil action, it was only logical to make them equally liable to punishment if prosecuted by the crown.

Indeed, the (initial) relative lack of seriousness[5] with which this form of liability was regarded is indicated by the absence of any liability for being 'an accessory after the fact'.[6] Furthermore, as a consequence of the penalty for misdemeanour being less severe,[7] there was no risk of the law suffering

---

[1] This is also Stephen's view, *HCL* ii. 234.
[2] YB 30, 31 Ed. I (RS) 106–8; cf. YB 20, 21 Ed. I (RS) 392. See also *Co. Inst.* iii. 138. Hale, *PC* i. 233 and 613.
[3] W. Holdsworth, *A History of English Law* (1922), iii. 208. Also Blackstone, *Comm.* iv. 36.
[4] Even as late as Hawkins's time the term trespass is used: W. Hawkins, *A Treatise of the Pleas of the Crown* (1795), ii. c. 29, s. 2 (hereafter *PC*). For an account of the process of development see Pollock and Maitland, *History*, ii. 511–12; S. F. C. Milsom, *Historical Foundations of the Common Law* (1969), 353–6, and T. F. T. Plucknett, *A Concise History of the Common Law* (London, 1956), 5th edn., 455–9.
[5] The law 'does not descend to distinguish the different shades of guilt in petty misdemeanours': Blackstone, *Comm.* iv. 36.
[6] Hale, *PC* i. 613.
[7] Originally, unlike felony, there was no automatic forfeiture of property and, most important, death was not the standard penalty. Pollock and Maitland, *History*, i. 284–6, ii. 463–8.

Modes of Complicity

the extreme embarrassment of executing a party as an accomplice only *later* to acquit the alleged principal.

For treason, the governing, somewhat hyperbolic, justification for lack of discrimination between participants was the overwhelming 'heinousness of the crime',[8] making 'the bare intent to commit treason . . . many times actual treason'.[9] Foster,[10] for one, was less than swept away by the force of such reasoning. Although hardly oblivious of the offence's strong political resonances, he not unreasonably questioned why the grounds supporting the differentiation of roles in felony were not equally valid in respect of treason.[11] The great practical beneficial consequence of the law's refusal to recognize degrees of participation in treason and misdemeanours was avoidance of ensnarement in the web of procedural requirements established for felonies, whereby the ability to try and convict a secondary party was closely tied to the principal offender's convictability and conviction. However, whilst the full formality of degrees of participation did not develop for treason and misdemeanours, the actual nature of non-perpetrating liability in such offences was frequently acknowledged by casual resort to the language of parties when demarcating the roles performed by defendants.[12] Despite these important procedural contrasts with the position of felonies, the substantive law in relation to the physical and mental ingredients of 'secondary liability' in all offences (subject to individual modifications) was similar.[13]

[8] Blackstone, *Comm.* iv. 35; *Tracey* (1703) 6 Mod. 30, 87 ER 795. '[T]he courts wished as a rule, to make the law as severe and to spread as wide a net for offenders, as they could': Stephen, *HCL* ii. 233.

[9] This view reflected the law from at least 1440: YB 19 Hy. VI Mich. pl. 103.

[10] According to M. Foster, *A Report on Crown Cases and Discourses on the Crown Law* (1762 edn.), 342, 'LCJ Coke, who while he was in the service of the Crown, seemeth to have had no bowels in state prosecutions when he layethe down and applieth the rule . . . that all are principals in treason.'

[11] Along with Hale (*PC* i. 613; and also Hawkins, *PC* ii. c. 29, who made the same criticisms of *all* accessorial conduct) Foster found difficulty in understanding how accessories *after* the fact could be described as principals despite their liability being dependent on the guilt of the principal party. ('[K]nowing receivers and comforters of traitors, are all principals': Hale, *PC* i. 613). However, Foster did not acknowledge such a problem with accessories *before* the fact, for he reasoned any act of incitement (an unlikely reference to inchoate liability as it was not finally established until 1801) is a complete overt act of treason without dependence on the future behaviour of another. Yet it might be argued that similar reasoning was applicable to accessories after the fact, as any overt act of willingness to harbour enemies of the Crown was in itself a mischief aimed at by the law of treason. The practical effect of the change for a party during the period, when benefit of clergy was an important mitigator of the severity of punishment, could have been substantial, for high treason was, in the main, non-clergyable. Hale, *PC* ii. 332; Foster, *Crown Law*, 190–3. Interestingly, later the First Criminal Law Commissioners, in their 7th Report (1843 at 34), imply quite strongly that there might have been some value in the context of treasons and misdemeanours of acknowledging the distinctions between accessories before the fact and principals in the second and first degree.

[12] e.g. in *Du Cros* v. *Lambourne* [1902] 1 KB 40 the accomplice was described as an 'aider and abettor' (at 43). The Accessories and Abettors Act 1861, s. 8, refers to '[w]hosoever shall aid, abet, counsel, or procure the commission of any misdemeanour . . .'.

[13] Accessories and Abettors Act 1861, s. 8, as amended by s.1of the Criminal Law Act 1967 and schedule 12 of the Criminal Law Act 1977, provides: 'Whosoever shall aid, abet, counsel

The Actus Reus

Complicity's tortured procedural history, so heavily laced up with 'Cobweb Lawes',[14] centres largely on felonies where four degrees of criminal participation became established: principal in the first degree,[15] principal in the second degree, accessory before the fact, and accessory after the fact.[16] When *Bracton* was published around 1250, it was already a clear requirement that the principal offender be convicted before any question of accessorial liability could arise.[17] According to Coke,[18] the Statute of

or procure the commission of any indictable offence whether the same be an offence at common law or by virtue of any Act passed or to be passed shall be liable to be tried, indicted and punished as a principal offender.' Summary proceedings are governed by similar provisions under s. 44 of the Magistrates' Courts Act 1980; superseding s. 35 of the Magistrates' Courts Act 1952 and s. 5 of the Summary Jurisdiction Act 1848.

[14] T. Hobbes, *Leviathan*, pt. 2, ch. 27, 'Of Crimes, Excuses and Extenuations'.

[15] 'The actor or absolute perpetrator of the crime': Blackstone, *Comm.* iv. 34.

[16] This fourway classification represents the third stage in the development of participation in felonies, with the changes occurring in relation to accessories. Originally no distinction was registered between those secondary participants who were present or absent at the commission of the offence. The second stage was the emergence of the distinction between an accessory *before* and *at* the fact. At the time *Bracton* was published (*c.*1250) there was no significant recognition of the difference between an 'accessory at the fact' (later principal in the second degree) and an 'accessory before the fact'. Controversy and doubt surround the period from which this distinction originated. Coke maintains (*Co. Inst.* i. 182) in his commentary on the Statute of Westminster (1275, 33 Ed. I) that an accessory may incite, procure, or provide the means ('furnishing of a weapon of force to do the act'), indeed practically anything so long as such a person is 'not present when the act is done; for if the party commanding, furnishing with weapon or aiding, be present when the act is done then he is principal'. Foster (*Crown Law*, 348) suggests that such a view was in advance of the law at the time and only later became accepted. Plowden (Comm. i. 97a) sets the period for the establishment of the distinction much later, citing a case of 40 Ed. III (1366) as illustrative of the old law, and proposes that the change occurred early in the 15th cent. (Comm. i. 99a, also Hale, *PC* i. 437 and 440). As *Bracton* was completed before 1275 no change could be expected to be reflected within that text, but the contrary might be expected from *Britton*, published around 1291. The limited amount of evidence (F. M. Nichols, ed. 1865, at 110 reference is made to *Bracton*, F. 139, which is a passage where no distinction is drawn and is cited as representing the law of the time) points to the conclusion that even after the Statute of Westminster, to which *Britton* refers in connection with other matters, no generally recognized distinction existed between accessories *at* and *before* the fact. Quite why the distinction was drawn between an accessory *at* and *before* the fact is without firm explanation. All were felons and therefore subject to the death penalty and no distinction existed between them in respect of the availability of any defence, especially benefit of clergy; it was available regardless of the nature of the accessoryship. It is possible that the forms of incriminatory *conduct* at that time differed according to whether the accessory was present at the offence's commission. Another possibility is that the practice of distinguishing made clearer the nature of the evidence and charge against the accessory (cf. Blackstone, *Comm.* iv. 39–40).

[17] *Bracton on the Laws and Customs of England*, trans. S. E. Thorne, ii. (1968); e.g. at F. 128 (360–1). Exactly when this rule first became established is unknown, but only a few years before the publication of *Bracton* the position was otherwise; a case from 1221 appears to accept that an accomplice may be tried despite the acquittal of the perpetrator: No. 832, *Rolls of Justices in Eyre*, Selden Society, v. 59, 369. Note also YB 33–5 Ed. I (RS) 54 (1305). At least as late as 1345 examples may be found where the rule is not recognized as absolute: YB 19 Ed. III (RS) 174; cf. 176. Moreover, the possibility is recognized that an accomplice may have a defence which is independent of the guilt of the principal offender: 'When both are present and the principal has been convicted, the accessory though present is not to be convicted on that accord since he may have his independent defence'. Also at F. 142 (400–1) and F. 144 (407).

[18] *Co. Inst.* ii. 183–4, and Hale, *PC* i. 623 and 625. Note also Hawkins, *PC* i. 451.

Westminster I reflected the common law rule that an accessory could not be forced to go to trial until the principal had been convicted or outlawed. But even the principal's *conviction* was insufficient as

> if the principall be convict by verdict and prayeth his clergie; or if the principall upon his arraingement confesse the felonies, and before judgement obtaine a pardone the accessarie is thereby discharged . . . and so it is if the principall dies before judgement, or upon his arraingement stand mute.[19]

The rule, then, demanded more than proof of principal guilt but the formal requirement of 'attainder', sentence of death.[20] The administrative quagmire caused by this rule eventually 'induced the judges from a principle of true political justice, to come into the rule now settled, *That all persons present aiding and abetting are principals.*'[21] *Griffith*[22] was one of the earliest, if not the first, declared examples of where 'true political justice' was done, the expressed basis of the reasoning being

> Notwithstanding there is but one wound given by one only, yet it shall be adjudged in law the Wound of every one, that is, it shall be looked upon as given by him who gave it, by himself and given by the rest by him as their Minister and Instrument. And it is as much the Deed of the others as if they had all jointly holden with their hands the Club or other Instrument with which the Wound was given as if they had all together struck the Person that was killed. So that it cannot be well termed that they who have the Wound, are Principals in Deed, and the others Principal in Law, but they are all Principals in Deed, and in one the same degree.[23]

This change in status and classification of accessories at the fact (still occasionally described as such in modern times)[24] to principals in the second degree, besides affecting eligibility for trial, carried incidental consequences for punishment. Up to the end of the fifteenth century benefit

---

[19] *Co. Inst.* ii. 183. 'If the principal be attained and has his clergy, or be pardoned after attainder, the accessory shall be put to answer': Hale, *PC* i. 625. The position was made a little less absurd by Anne, st. c. 9 (1702), which made the accessory open to conviction provided a principal offender could have been convicted 'notwithstanding that such principal felon shall be admitted to the benefit of clergy, pardoned or otherwise delivered before attainder'.

[20] The accessory was given the option of waiving his right not to be tried before conviction of his principal. If he chose this and was convicted, judgment against him had to be postponed until the later conviction (if any) of the principal: Hale, *PC* i. 623. A further complication concerned jurisdiction to try the accessory. At one time, by statute, the accessory was not triable where the principal offence took place but only within the local jurisdiction appropriate to the accessorial conduct. See W. Staunford, *Pleas of Ye Crown* (1607), c. 45, 41–2; and also 2 & 3 Ed. VI, c. 24, ss. 3 and 4 and Hale, *PC* i. 623.

[21] Foster, *Crown Law*, 348. Cf. Bromley CJ in *Griffith* (1553) 1 Plowd. 97, 75 ER 152: 'For if we should give judgment that the prisoners at the Bar (if it should so happen that they were arraigned, and found guilty) should be hanged, and afterwards they should be executed, and then the others, viz. the principals in deed, who are indicted of killing the man, should be acquitted, I would ask you whether we should not have done a great injury to the prisoners now of the Bar.' See below for Bromley CJ's rationalization of why this reasoning should not hold good for principals in the second degree. Note also Stephen's caustic observations, *HCL* ii. 232–3.

[22] (1553) 1 Plowd. 97, 75 ER 152.

[23] Ibid. 98. Plowden saw *Griffith* as being *the* case responsible for change. Cf. *Co. Inst.* ix. 67b.

[24] See e.g. Woolf J. in *Attorney General* v. *Able* [1984] QB 795, 808.

24 *The* Actus Reus

of clergy[25] was similarly available to all participants in a felony. But thereafter[26] this notorious mitigatory device was by a series of statutes cut back, and with the creation of new felonies the courts began a long process of nit-picking statutory interpretation. As Foster observed: 'Cases without number may be cited to show in general how extremely tender the Judges have been in the construction of statutes which take away clergy, sometimes even to a degree of scrupulosity excusable only in favour of life'.[27] Differences in the availability of benefit of clergy between principals and accessories before the fact was more marked and of greater duration than those between principals in the first and second degree. But courts appeared to take little cognizance of the nature of the participation; essentially, it was an indiscriminate pragmatic exercise aimed at mitigating the criminal law's severity. Consequently, according to Hawkins,

> A statute excluding the principals from benefit of clergy doth not thereby exclude the accessories before or after. Neither doth a statute excluding the accessories thereby exclude the principals.[28]

No part of the history of benefit of clergy suggests differentiation in moral or fault terms between parties.[29]

Since the Criminal Law Act 1967 abolished the distinction between felonies and misdemeanours, the old position relating to misdemeanours, effectively, represents current English law.[30]

2. The Significance of Presence

As previously noted, redesignation of accessories at the fact as principals in the second degree was a judicial manoeuvre aimed at extricating the law

---

[25] See Stephen, *HCL* i. 459, for an account of the nature and use of this device.

[26] e.g. (for forms of murder and robbery) 23 Hen. VIII, c. 1, ss. 3 and 4 (1531); (for forms of murder, burglary, robbery, etc.) 1 Ed. VI, c. 12, s. 10 (1563); (rape and burglary) 18 EC 7 (1576).

[27] *Crown Law*, 355. Stephen comments (*HCL* i. 466): 'if a statute taking away clergy did not expressly mention all the possible cases [i.e. various ways a trial might be conducted] and take away clergy in all of them both from principal and from his accessories both before and after, clergy remained in every omitted case. Hence questions arose on the special wording of every statute as to whether it ousted an offender of clergy not only if he was convicted but if he pleaded guilty, if he stood mute, etc., and similarly his accessories. Hardly any branch of the law was so technical and so full of petty quibbles as this.'

[28] *PC* ii. 476; cf. Hale, *PC* ii. 347.

[29] Specific instances existed of where the law deliberately punished the perpetrator more severely than the secondary party, e.g. 3 & 4 Will. IV, c. 44 (1833) and *Sterne* [1787] 1 Leach 473, 168 ER 338.

[30] See s. 3, art. 1, n. 4 of the 2nd Criminal Law Commissioners' 2nd report (1846) draft code proposing abolition of the distinction between treason, felony, and misdemeanours in respect of accessories, which appeared to introduce the notion of accessories into treasons and misdemeanours. It was also proposed that the distinction between the two degrees of principal be abolished (art. 2). Under the 1879 Draft Code Bill, s. 71 was 'so framed as to put an end to the nice distinction between accessories before the fact and principals in the second degree' by making all parties to an indictable offence.

from a crippling doctrinal stalemate whereby accessories could not be dealt with until the principal offender was convicted and sentenced. Quite why accessories before the fact were not also designated principals escapes clear explanation. The close identification by Bromley CJ (in *Griffith*) of principals in the second degree with the perpetrator's role and 'deed' might be compared with the broader sweep of Bracton's considerably earlier comment that 'the wound, the assistance and the instigation together form a single deed: there would be no wound had there been no assistance, and neither wound nor assistance without the instigation';[31] cause rather than presence is used as a unifying concept between all those 'at the fact'. The distinction between the nature of the conduct and necessary mental culpability for types of accessories appears to have rested solely on the notion of presence.

Presence of a party at the time of the offence certainly provided a crude and simple distinguishing criterion which in rough terms may have approximated to existing notions of culpability and causation. Presence was possibly associated with influence, or at least the potential to assist or encourage;[32] but why should it have been limited to broadly simultaneous involvement in the crime's commission? The difference between Bracton's view and Bromley CJ's may have represented the slight refinement and narrowing over 300 years of notions of causal attribution. However, the concept of the principal in the second degree's presence[33] was from the outset very liberally interpreted:

When the law requireth the presence of the accomplice at the perpetration of the fact, in order to render him a principal, it doth not require a strict, actual, immediate presence, such a presence as would make him an eye or ear witness of what passeth.[34]

---

[31] *Trans. Thorne*, ii. 392.

[32] '[F]or the presence of the others is a terror to him that is assaulted, so that he dare not defend himself, for if a man sees his enemy and 20 of his servants coming to assault him, and they all draw their swords and surround him, and only one strikes him, so that he dies thereof, now the others shall with good reason be adjudged as great offenders as he that struck him, for if they had not been present he might probably have defended himself and so have escaped: but the number of the others being present and ready to strike him also, shall be adjudged a great terror to him, so as to make him lose his courage, and despair of defending himself, and by this means they are the occasion of his death.' Per Bromley CJ in *Griffith* (1553) cited n. 21. This justification would hardly account for situations where the victim is unaware of the presence of an accomplice of the perpetrator. Cf. Hawkins, *PC* ii. 312.

[33] The question *when* an offence occurred was approached by the courts in a broad and commonsense fashion. Larceny, being the most important in practical terms, was regarded as either a continuing offence or the acts of the principal and the abettor were viewed as part of the same transaction. See e.g. *King* (1817) Russ. & Ry. 332, 168 ER 830; *M'Makin* (1808) Russ. & Ry. 333, 168 ER 830; *Kelly* (1820) Russ. & Ry. 421, 168 ER 876; *Dyer* (1801) and *Attwell* (1801), both East, *PC* ii. 767–9; *Hornby* (1844) 1 Car. Hir. 305, 174 ER 832. Cf. *Pitham and Hehl* (1977) 65 Cr. App. Rep. 45. A modern illustration concerning the meaning of 'in the course of theft' for the purposes of s. 5 (1) (*a*) of the Homicide Act 1957 is *Jones* [1959] 1 QB 291; similarly *HMA* v. *Graham* 1958 SLT 167. Cf. *Soloway* [1976] 2 WWR 127.

[34] Foster, *Crown Law*, at 349–50. Cf. the definition of 'presence' in the 7th report of the First Criminal Law Commissioners (1843), art. 8: 'who shall be near enough to lend any help

In other words, presence was a legal notion; it could be actual or 'constructive'.[35] Presence was not 'determined by mere contiguity of space',[36] although sometimes courts required a physical proximity sufficient to provide support if necessary.[37] The extreme tenuousness as to the nature of assistance or encouragement and proximity which would suffice for 'presence' exposes the high artificiality of Bromley CJ's declaration in *Griffith* of the distinctiveness of principals in the second degree and accessories before the fact, and the affinity between both degrees of principal. It may be credible to describe closely acting (and reacting) participants in a typical common purpose homicide example as 'Principals in Deed, and in one the same degree', but when applied to the broad span of cases where the secondary party was present it reveals itself as mere judicial rhetoric dressed up as doctrinal revelation, brought on by acute administrative embarrassment. The procedural and pragmatic nature of this manœuvre of redesignating accessories at the fact principals in the second degree has, as will be seen, implications for some modern concerns over tampering with the accumulated wisdom of ages, if not with what are seen as complicity's immutable principles.

3. Modes of Complicitous Behaviour

So far consideration has been limited to the early structural development and division of criminal participation into principals and accessories,

or assistance to the person who does or persons who do the act or to encourage such person or persons with the expectation of help or assistance'. Similar provisions are also found in the Second Commissioners' 2nd report (1846), art. 6, and 4th report (1848), art. 6.

[35] Blackstone, *Comm.* iv. 34. See e.g. *Soares* (1802) Russ. & Ry. 25, 168 ER 664; *Davis* (1806) Russ. & Ry. 113, 168 ER 711; *Owen* (1825) 11 Mood 96, 168 ER 1200; *Howell* (1839) 9 C. & P. 437, 173 ER 901, Cf. *Vanderstein* (1865) 10 Cox 177 with *Greenwood* (1825) 2 Den. 453, 169 ER 578; *Betts and Ridley* (1930) 22 Cr. App. Rep. 148; and *Smith* [1963] 1 WLR 1200. Cf. *State v. Poynier* 36 La Ann. 572 (1884), in which it was held that if a person whose duty it is to remain in a particular area stays away in order to facilitate the commission of an offence by another, then, although absent, he is an abettor. This is consistent with the earlier English case of *Jordan* (1836) 7 C. & P. 432, 173 ER 192. However, in *Jefferies and Bryant* (1848) 2 Cox, it was decided that, where a servant left a door unlocked so as to provide access for a thief, the servant was not liable as an abettor if he was not physically present; so also in *Tuckwell* (1841) Cor. & M. 215, 174 ER 447. But see *Saqui and Lawrence v. Stearns* [1911] 1 KB 426, a civil case, which takes a view similar to that in *Jordan*. Note also *Ex p. Parker* (1957) SR (NSW) 326; and see *State ex. rel. Att. Gen. v. Tally* 102 Ala. 25, (1894).

[36] *Wharton's Criminal Law and Procedure*, ed. Anderson (1957) i. s. 107, 232–3; cited in the judgment of *State v. Thibodeau* 353 A. 2d 595 (1976), based on *State v. Hamilton* 13 Nev. 386 (1878). Cf. *State v. Breese* 12 Ohio 146 (1861). See also *McBryde v. State* 352 A. 2d 324 (1976). Being under arrest did not prevent a party abetting an offence. *Withorne* (1828) 3 C. & P. 394, 172 ER 470. Cf. *Craig and Bentley* (10–13 Dec. 1952) *The Times*; *Stanleys Case* (1663) Kel. J. 86, 84 ER 1094.

[37] As e.g. in *Betts and Ridley* (1930) 22 Cr. App. Rep. 148, at 154: 'It is clear law that it is not necessary that the party . . . should be . . . an eye witness or ear witness . . . He is present if with the intention of giving assistance, he is near enough to afford it, should the occasion arise'; similarly *Froggett* [1965] 2 All ER 832. Although see *Richards* [1974] 3 All ER 1088, in Ch. 4 below.

followed by the redesignation of accessories *present* at the fact as principals in the second degree. These preliminaries aside, several distinct yet related issues require examination in order to establish the span of accepted or recognized modes of complicitous behaviour. First, how is the principal party identified? Obviously, behaviour regarded as principal in nature cannot be secondary.[38] The upper limits or boundaries of complicity abut those of principal liability, and to that extent they are demarcated by what is found to constitute principal liability. Secondly, what is the status of the verbs 'aid, abet, counsel or procure'? Is the scope or reach of complicity fixed by resort to their 'natural' connotations or are they terms of art whose meanings have over time been judicially settled? Thirdly, to what extent may inaction constitute complicity? And fourthly, what is the relationship between inchoate liability and complicity, and, most particularly, is conspiracy an auxiliary mode of complicity?

So far as feasible, consideration of *mens rea* and broad causal implications thrown up by these questions will be postponed until a later stage.

(1) Who is a Principal Offender?[39]

Most cases offer little room for dispute over who is the principal offender. It is the party whose actions satisfy the relevant offence's definitional requirements: he who has, for example, 'permitted', 'suffered', 'caused', or 'allowed' the proscribed circumstances or consequences.[40] However, more than one party may be sufficiently proximately connected with the occurrence of the *actus reus* to put into question the nature of his (or their) responsibility, if any. This liability may be secondary or that of a joint principal. However, not only can there be frequent evidential difficulty[41] in identifying the precise role of each participant, but there is also a degree of

---

[38] Although cf. *Cogan*.
[39] Excluding principal liability whether vicariously or through the doctrine of innocent agency.
[40] See generally J. L. J. Edwards, *Mens Rea in Statutory Offences* (1955), 98–163; and Williams CLGP, para. 119. Cf. Proposition 2 (1) of the Law Commission's Working Paper No. 43, *Codification of the Criminal Law: Parties Complicity and Liability for the Act of Another*, 1972, hereafter Working Paper 43: 'A principal in an offence is one who, with any necessary fault element, does the acts constituting the external elements of the offence.' Under Law Commission Report 177, Draft Criminal Code, cl. 26 (1) a party is a principal if: 'with the fault required for the offence—(a) he does the act specified for the offence'. See cl. 26 (1) (b) and (c) for joint principal and innocent agency provisions. The Accessories and Abettors Act 1861, s. 8, recognizes but does not attempt to define what constitutes a principal. See also the 1843 draft code, s. 4, art. 2, the 1846 draft code s. 3, art. 2, and the 1879 Draft Code, s. 71 (a).
[41] The practical problem of identifying offenders' individual roles is circumvented by all participants being subject to the same punishment. But there must be evidence of a common purpose. Where such evidence is absent direct proof must be adduced of individual culpability. See e.g. *Russell* (1987) 85 Cr. App. Rep. 388 and *Collins and Fox* v. *Chief Constable of Merseyside* [1988] Crim. LR 247. For a review of the procedural and evidential difficulties, see E. Griew, 'It Must Have Been One of Them' [1989] Crim. LR 129; and Williams, 'Which of You Did It' (1989) 52 *MLR* 179.

uncertainty over the substantive criteria for its determination.[42] If an offence's definitional requirements include a perpetrator with certain characteristics or qualities their absence will necessarily eliminate the possibility of principal liability.[43] But beyond this preliminary issue several other factors have potential relevance to the distinction between joint principals and secondary liability.

Mens rea aside, the standard or traditional basis on which a participant's liability in a crime is designated as principal or secondary is whether their actions are the most direct or immediate cause of the *actus reus*: 'direct' in the sense of not acting through a responsible human agent. Therefore, if

one holds a victim while a second inflicts a fatal injury with a knife, only the stabber is a principal in the first degree, because the stabbing caused the death and holding was merely aiding, thus rendering the holder guilty as a principal in the second degree.[44]

Similarly, one who hands an actual killer the murder weapon is performing an act essential to that killing but with no immediate or direct effect in bringing about the death.[45] However, assuming for the present[46] that directness of cause is an invariably reliable and predictable determinant of participatory roles, there is also scope for joint principal liability either where the *actus reus* is made up of distinct elements or where a single element is in some way satisfied by joint activity.

An illustration of the first joint principal situation would be where, during a robbery, one party holds a gun or the victim whilst his confederate grabs the victim's property,[47] the use of force and stealing being two separate definitional components of robbery. An example of the second type of case is provided by *Bingley* where forgery of a document entailed three distinct processes carried out at separate times by different people, not all of whom had met. None the less, all were convictable as joint principals in forgery of the completed document for it was the product of their several individual contributions.[48] Offences involving illegal possession of specific substances

---

[42] Cf. e.g. the decisions in *Hornby* (1844) 1 Car. & K. 305, 174 ER 822, and *Kelly* (1847) 2 Car. & K. 379, 175 ER 157, where joint principal liability was found to exist, with *Coggins* (1873) 12 Cox 517, in which it was held there had been abetting. As is understated in *Russell*, ed. Turner, i. 131 n. 24, 'Cases such as these of course turn on fine distinctions of fact.' See proposition 5 of the Working Paper 43.

[43] But see 'Innocent Agency', in Ch. 4 below.

[44] R. M. Perkins, *Criminal Law* (1982), 736, and Hale, *PC* i. 437. Similarly Smith and Hogan, *Criminal Law*, 1st edn., 69, and 6th edn., 131: 'the principal offender is the one who is the most immediate cause of the *actus reus*'; and Williams, *Textbook*, 330.

[45] Cf. *Agresti v. State* 234 A. 2d 284 (1967).

[46] See below, Ch. 3, 'Causation' and the notion of directness.

[47] Working Paper 43, illustration *b*, 33, and Law Commission Report 177, cl. 26 (1) (*b*), ex. 26 (i). See also the 1846 draft code 3, art. 4, Macaulay's Indian Penal Codes 37, and the 1879 English Draft Code, s. 71a.

[48] *Bingley* (1821) R. & RCC 446, 168 ER 890. Cf. *Sheppard* (1839) 9 C. & P. 121, 173 ER 767, multi-party fraud. Note also *Kirkwood* (1831) 1 Mood CC 304, 168 ER 1281, and *Griffith* (1831) 1 Mood CC 306, 168 ER 1283. An American equivalent of this period is *Griffin v. State* 26 Ga. 493 (1858) at 498. In relation to the offence of uttering counterfeit

may be principally committed despite another party having physical possession. In *Charles*[49] each of the six members of 'a socialist club' was held (potentially) liable for possession of an explosive substance as 'each member of the confederacy is responsible in respect of such articles as were in the possession of others, connected . . . in the carrying out of their common design'.[50] Again, in homicide the defendant's conduct need only be a 'substantial',[51] not sole, cause of the victim's death. Consequently, there may be two or more causes (and causers) of death, each alone not fatal but combining to result in death.

A further question is whether to qualify as a joint principal a party, although not directly responsible for causing part of the *actus reus*, must, nevertheless, satisfy the necessary fault requirements for every element of the *actus reus*. Most especially, if part of the *actus reus* has been completed before another (*P2*) joins in, can that party be convicted as a joint principal for the whole offence? For 'consequence'[52] offences (such as homicide) there is no definitional need for *P2* to be in any way associated with the *prior* conduct of *P1*, for the independent action and bodily harm caused by *P2* — although alone insufficient to kill — is accompanied by the complete *mens rea* requirement of the offence. By contrast, in cases of 'conduct'[53] offences the previous behaviour of *P1* will be outside the ambit of *P2*'s *mens rea* unless an earlier agreement existed. Therefore, if *P1* attacks *V* in order to steal his valuables — rendering him unconscious in the process — and immediately after the attack *P2* happens along and, at *P1*'s invitation, helps himself to valuables of *V*, it would seem that *P2* could not be liable for robbery, even though aware of what previously occurred, as he in no way participated in that particular element of the offence. Effectively, a joint principal must be at least a 'secondary party' in respect of the other elements of the offence which he does not directly cause.[54] In this respect a joint

coins see *Hurse and Dunn* (1841) 2 Moo. & Rob. 360, 174 ER 316, and *Skerrit* (1826) 2 C. & P. 427, 172 ER 193; in both cases the utterers were physically apart when the other was committing his offences, but were (probably) convicted as joint principals in the other's offences. Because of the reports' brevity it is impossible to be completely certain if the references to 'principal' mean in the first or second degree.

[49] (1892) 17 Cox 499 at 502. Cf. *Thompson* (1869) 11 Cox 362.

[50] Cf. *Reid* (1975) 62 Cr. App. Rep. 109 at 112, and *Wolf v. State* 260 So. 2d 325 (1972) at 332, 'Possession of contraband may be actual or constructive and may be joint or individual. Two or more persons may be in possession where they have joint power of control and an inferable intent to control jointly.'

[51] e.g. *Hennigan* [1971] 3 All ER 133, and *Blaue* (1975) 61 Cr. App. Rep. 271 at 274. Cf. the confusion between a joint principal and accessory apparent in the assault case of *Harawira* [1989] 2 NZLR 714 at 726.

[52] Any offence whose definition simply prescribes an end result or consequence without stipulating the method by which this is achieved. Cf. *Treacy* [1971] AC 537 at 560; *Markus* [1976] AC 35 at 61.

[53] Any offence the *actus reus* of which is made up exclusively or partially of prescribed forms of conduct.

[54] In contrast with Report 143, cl. 30 (1) (*b*)), Law Commission Report 177, cl. 26 (1) (*b*) expressly adopts this view: 'he does at least one [definitional] act and procures, assists or encourages any other such acts done by another'; commentary para. 9. 9. And see Kadish's

principal's liability is made up of a combination of both direct and indirect responsibility for the causing of the substantive offence's *actus reus*.[55] Quite rightly, ratification theory is not and has never been accepted by English criminal law.[56]

(2) *The Meaning of 'Aid, Abet, Counsel or Procure'*

Like many aspects of complicity, the language describing and delimiting its various modes is ancient, reflecting an unsystematic process of organic growth with occasional statutory intervention spread over more than 700 years. Two related matters arise from this historical process. Is the scope of behaviour which may constitute complicity to be deduced from a natural or literal reading of the verbs set out in section 8 of the 1861 Act, or from the vast body of common law cases? Secondly, what are the behavioural or modal limits of complicity?

As to the first question, the curious position developed where, although it was undisputed[57] that the existence or creation of any offence normally entailed the corollary of potential complicity liability, it was nevertheless common for statutes to incorporate express complicity provisions. Whether or not the extent of secondary liability for any particular (statutory) offence was to be discovered by construction of statutory terms was considered in *MacDaniel*.[58] Delivering a 'Special Verdict' for 'all the Judges of England', Foster's judgment leaves little room for doubt as to the answer:

wide-ranging and penetrating analysis, 'Complicity, Cause and Blame: A Study in the Interpretation of Doctrine' (1985) 73 *Cal. LR* 324, 345 n. 36. (All refs. are to this version.) Professor Kadish's article is reproduced in *Blame and Punishment* (1987) and, in an abbreviated form, as 'A Theory of Complicity', in Gavison, ed., *Issues in Contemporary Legal Philosophy; The Influence of H. L. A. Hart* (1987).

[55] See a theoretical extrapolation of the significance of this feature of the principal-accessory boundary, in M. Gur-Arye, 'A Theory of Complicity — Comment', in Gavison, ed., *Issues in Contemporary Legal Philosophy*, 304.

[56] See below Ch. 3. Cf. *MacPhane* (1841) 174 ER 476; *M'Makin* (1808) Russ. & Ry. 333 n., 168 ER 830; *King* (1817) Russ. & Ry. 332, 168 ER 830; *Dyer and Disting* (1801) East, PC ii. 767. Until relatively recently the doctrine of ratification, or variations of it, had some currency in South Africa and Rhodesia. See *S.* v. *Chenjere* 1960 (1) SA 473 (FC) and *S.* v. *Mneke* 1961 (2) SA 240 (N). However, the doctrine has since found disfavour; see *S.* v. *Thomo* 1969 (1) SA 385 AD and *S.* v. *Madlala* 1969 (2) SA 637 (AD); and note Hugo (1969) 86 SALJ 391. Liability as an accessory *after* the fact (and superseding offences of harbouring or assisting) or for the old crimes of misprision or compounding a felony does not rest on any notion of ratification.

[57] e.g. Hale, *PC* i. 613–4; Co. *Inst.* iii. 59.

[58] *Crown Law*, 137. Very early authority that the complicity terms were not to be considered literally but represented legal concepts is found in Coke's commentary (Co. *Inst.* ii. 182) on the Statute of Westminster I, which described accessories before the fact as comprising 'three branches', 'commandement', 'force', and 'aide': '[*Commandement*] *Praeceptum*. Under this is understood all those that incite, procure, set on, or stir up any other to do the fact, and are not present when the fact is done. [*Force*] *Fortia* is a word of art, and properly signifieth the furnishing of a weapon of force to do the fact, and by force whereof the fact is committed, and he that furnisheth it is not present when the fact is done . . . [*Aide*] *Auxilium*. Under this word is comprehended all persons counselling, abetting, plotting, assenting, consenting, and encouraging to do the act, and are not present when the act is done; for if the party is commanding,

Modes of Complicity 31

The principle is true that in prosecutions on penal statutes the words of the statute are to be pursued. But it is equally true, that we are not to be governed by sound, but by the well-known, true legal import of the words [pp. 126–7] . . . the legislation, in statutes made from time to time concerning accessories before the fact hath not confined itself to any certain mode of expression; but hath rather chosen to make use of a variety of words, all terminating in the same general idea. [p. 130]

Some statutes [31 Eliz. I, c. 12, s. 5 (1589)] make use of the word accessories, simply without any other words descriptive of the offence. Others [23 Hen. VIII, c. 1, s. 3 (1532)] have the words, abetment, procurement, helping, maintaining and counselling, or [1 Ed. VI, c. 12, s. 13 (1547)] aiders, abettors, procurers, and counsellors. One [4 & 5 P. & M., c. 4 (1558)] describeth the offence by the words, command, counsel or hire; another [39 Eliz. I, c. 9, s. 2 (1597)] calleth the offenders, procurers or accessories. One [3 & 4 W. & M., c. 9 (1691)] having made use of the words, comfort, aid, abet, assist, counsel, hire or command, immediately afterwards in describing the same offence in another case useth the words counsel, hire or command only. One statute [1 Anne st. 2, c. 9 (1702)] calleth them counsellors and contrivers of felonies; and many others make use of the terms counsellors, aiders and abettors, or barely aiders and abettors . . . [pp. 130–1] [W]e are not to be governed by the bare sound, but by the true legal import of the words; and also that every person who cometh within the description of these statutes, various as they are in point of expression, is in the judgment of the legislation an accessory before the fact; unless he is present at the fact, and in that case he is undoubtedly a principal. [p. 131]

Modern judicial affirmation of *MacDaniel* appears in various later judgments including Lord Goddard CJ's in *Carter Patersons and Pickfords Carriers Ltd. v. Wessel*[59] where it was accepted that the 1861 Act was 'declaratory of the common law'. Yet, despite this considerable weight of authority extending back beyond Foster, the Court of Appeal in *Attorney-General's Reference (No. 1 of 1975)*[60] chose to

approach section 8 of the Act of 1861 on the basis that the words should be given their ordinary meaning, if possible [for] the probability is that there is a difference between each of those four words and the other three, because, if there were no such difference, then Parliament would be wasting time in using four words where two or three would do.

---

furnishing with weapon, or aiding be present when the act is done, then he is principal.' It is clear that considerable overlap occurred between the coverage of these expressions. Cf. J. C. Smith, 'Aid, Abet, Counsel, or Procure' in Glazebrook, ed., *Reshaping the Criminal Law*, 120, 123–4.

[59] [1947] 1 KB 849 at 852. See also e.g. *Du Cros v. Lambourne* [1907] 1 KB 40. The same opinion is given by C. S. Greaves, draughtsman of the 1861 Act: *Russell*, 4th edn., i. 70, cited by J. C. Smith, 'Aid, Abet, Counsel, or Procure', 125.

[60] [1975] QB 773 at 779. Inferentially *Gillick* [1986] AC 112 is to the contrary. The relevant special provision under s. 28 (1) of the Sexual Offences Act 1956 provides a particular form of complicity by using the expression 'cause or encourage'. At first instance, in the Court of Appeal and in the House of Lords the wording was given no special meaning and interpreted under the general principles of complicity — often being referred to as 'aiding and abetting' in all three courts.

Of course it does not follow from the employment of the four terms with possibly different meanings that those meanings are to be discovered by literal construction rather treated as conceptual labels. Further, English statute-books are littered with post-1861 Acts where no consistent or (apparently) focused use is made of verbs to describe particular modes of complicity.[61] Laxity in legislative drafting (as the Court of Appeal is frequently reminded in its work) was and is commonplace. Nevertheless it is to be doubted whether this difference of opinion could be of much consequence in a case where the conduct charged as complicity was apparently novel. Both the extensive 'ordinary' meaning of the terms and considerable conceptual width promoted by countless judgments are likely to produce the same outcome.[62]

An aspect of this distinction relating to the scope or range of complicity modes is whether the presence of the secondary party operates as any sort of governor on what behaviour is capable of qualifying as complicity. Most especially, 'aiding and abetting' has often been taken to connote presence.[63] But supplying materials used later in the commission of an offence without accessorial presence or any behaviour which could be described as 'counselling' or 'procuring' is undoubtedly complicity, as made plain by case law, institutional works, and code reformulations.[64] Although customary to reserve 'aiding and abetting' for secondary parties present at the offence, and 'counselling and procuring'[65] for those absent, there is no substantive rule delimiting modes of complicity on the basis of presence. As Foster suggests,

[61] e.g. in s. 8 of the Sexual Offences Act 1967, for no obvious reason and with no obvious effect, 'commanding' supplements 'aid, abet, counsel or procure'.

[62] Working Paper 43 proposed (proposition 6) the full range of complicity should be covered by the 'one who incites or helps the commission of an offence by a principal . . . Incitement includes encouragement and authorisation . . . Help includes . . . help given of which the principal was unaware; and conduct of a person which leads the principal to believe when committing the offence that he is being helped, or will be helped if necessary, by that person in its commission.' Report 177 uses the terms 'procures, assists or encourages', (cl. 27 (1) (*a*)) in 'their ordinary meanings'. These terms were chosen on the basis of being 'familiar and avoid the difficulties of interpretation of the traditional language of aiding, abetting and counselling'. Furthermore, it was thought that 'inciting' as used in Working Paper 43 was 'too narrow to encompass satisfactorily all the cases envisaged by the concepts of procuring and encouraging' (commentary paras. 9. 18–19). For the problematic nature of 'procure' see below, Ch. 3 (1) (1). Cf. the Model Penal Code which uses the terms 'solicits . . . aids or agrees or attempts to aid', s. 2.06 (3) (*a*).

[63] Particularly *Bowker* v. *Premier Drug Co. Ltd.* [1928] 1 KB 217 and e.g. Blackstone, *Comm.* iv. 34 and *Royce* (1767) 4 Burr. 2072, 98 ER 81. In *Cogan*, where on one interpretation the secondary party was present, the defendant was described as a 'procurer': [1975] 2 All ER 1059 at 1062.

[64] In *Bainbridge* the defendant, not being present at the bank robbery, was described as an 'accessory before the fact'. Supplying equipment, on a literal interpretation, could not easily be regarded as counselling or procuring.

[65] Until *Attorney-General's Reference (No. 1 of 1975)*, 'procure' was generally taken to be a synonym of 'counsel' (e.g. *Ferguson* v. *Weaving* at 818–9). The causal and *mens rea* implications of the judgment in *Attorney-General's Reference* are considered below in relation to *causation* and to *mens rea*.

It is a principle in law which can never be controverted that he would procureth a felony to be done is a felon. If present he is a principal if absent an accessory before the fact.[66]

Similarly Hale:[67]

An accessory before is he that being absent at the time of the felony committed doth yet procure, counsel or abet another to commit a felony . . . for if he be present he is a principal.

This is unsurprising in view of the common ancestry of principals in the second degree and accessories before the fact.[68] Procedurally, the 1861 Act enables all parties to be 'tried, indicted and punished as a principal offender'. However, despite the lack of any strict need to specify in a charge whether a party participated as a principal or by aiding, abetting, counselling, or procuring, the House of Lords in *Maxwell* strongly and appropriately emphasized the desirability of indictments indicating the true factual nature of the case to be presented against any defendant.[69]

Overall, the range of general complicity liability should not be, and is not, determined by strict literal construction of the terms employed for, as Bentham reminds us, a verb 'slips through your fingers like an eel'.[70] All forms of behaviour having the potential to either encourage or influence the perpetrator or help him carry out the offence can form the basis of complicity, something to be borne firmly in mind when selecting or devising verbal formulae for any codifying effort. Help may, of course, be encouraging as well as facilitative. Encouragement or influence can stretch from mere advice[71] to persuading or directing a party to act. A secondary

---

[66] *Crown Law*, 125 and 131.

[67] PC 615–16 and 438; and *Co. Inst.* ii. 182.

[68] The 1st edn. of *Russell* defined principals in the second degree as 'those who were present aiding and abetting at the commission of the fact. They are generally termed "aiders and abettors".' (19) An accessory before the fact (30) is described as 'he who being absent at the time of the offence committed doth yet procure, counsel, command or abet another . . .' Similarly in the 1st edn. of *Chitty* (1816), i. 256. Although very widely drawn for secondary liability, the Criminal Law Commissioners' Reports of 1843 and 1846, draft codes, make the association between aiding or abetting and presence as 'to encourage [the perpetrator] with expectation of help, and who shall by consent or any other means help or encourage [the perpetrator]' (1846, art. 6; 1843, art. 8). An accessory before the fact was one who not being present 'by commandment, advice, consent, aid, encouragement, or otherwise, continued, directly or indirectly, or immediately or mediately procured or promoted' the offence. (1846, art. 8; 1843, arts. 10 and 11).

[69] [1978] 1 WLR 1350 at 1352, 1357, and 1360.

[70] *Works*, x. 569. South African and German law e.g., have been more concerned with causality than seeking to label types of behaviour in settling the limits of secondary liability. See *S. v. Williams* 1980 (1) SA 60 (A) at 63 and see below, Ch. 3.

[71] As a matter of principle there is no reason to regard advice or information differently from other modes of complicity, provided that general *mens rea* and causal requirements are satisfied. On the supply of information see *Attorney General* v. *Able* [1984] QB 795 and *Baker* (1909) 28 NZLR 536; although in *Baker* two of the five appeal judges (Chapman and Cooper JJ) appear to have found the presence of 'encouragement' as well as the mere supply of information. See also *Martyn* [1967] NZLR 396, and *McLeod and Georgia Straight Publishing*

role may be initiatory or supportive, dominant or subordinate, in character. Rather than terminological, complicity's limits, as will be seen, are conceptual and mainly embodied in causal expectations and *mens rea* requirements. However, two further important aspects of the scope of complicity that are not substantially causal or *mens rea* in nature and which raise matters of broad penal policy merit examination at this stage. These are the extent to which inaction can serve as a basis for complicity, and the relationship of inchoate and complicity liability.

(3) *Complicity through Inaction*

The association of inactivity and complicity may come about in a variety of ways with varying legal consequences. Clearest in legal outcome is where *A* encourages (or assists) *P* not to act in a particular way when *P* is legally bound to do so: for example, inciting a father to starve his child. Here the matter is one of *A*'s complicity by positive action in *P*'s principal liability through his criminal failure to perform a legal duty. However, rather than the relationship of complicity and inaction in cases where it is the principal offender's inactivity at issue, the present discussion concerns the circumstances under which an 'accessory' might incur liability without positive action. The question may arise in two distinct forms. Can a party's mere inactive presence at the commission of another's offence ground complicity? And may a party's failure to exercise or assert a contractual, property, or other right also incriminate?

Both issues share inaction as a common focus, raising similar policy

Co. Ltd. (1970) 75 WWR 161. 'Advice' covers several different forms of behaviour, ranging from full-blooded instigation to dispassionate or disinterested advice on the best way of achieving a particular objective — such as removing a safe door. It is possible for information to be given with the purpose of inciting the receiver to commit the offence foreseen by the giver. If *A* reveals to *P* the latter's wife's infidelity, believing that *P* is likely to kill his wife, which he subsequently does, the fact that *A*'s information is true should be immaterial to his guilt as an accessory for he has both foreseen and facilitated the murder. Is his moral position significantly distinct from the situation where *P*, having himself discovered his wife's unfaithfulness, asks *A* for a revolver which *A* gladly supplies whilst fully alive to its probable use? See 'procure' in Chs. 3 and 4; and cf. Kadish's discussion of Iago's mischief-making ('Complicity, Cause and Blame', 364) and Stephen, *HCL* iii, 8. The position of Henry II in relation to Becket's murder is subject to much the same analysis. If 'Will no one rid me of this meddlesome priest!' was uttered with Henry's awareness of its possible effect on his henchmen, then his complicity in Becket's killing appears arguable under modern English law. Such cases of what amounts to reckless instigation suggest a further distinction between the inchoate offence of incitement and encouragement as a mode of complicity. For incitement requires at least deliberate encouragement, not simply foresight of encouragement to commit the substantive offence. Cf. *Invicta Plastics Ltd.* v. *Clare* [1976] RTR 251 with *James and Ashford* (1985) 82 Cr. App. Rep. 226. And note K. Greenawalt, 'A Vice of its Virtues' (1988) 19 *Rut. LJ* 929, 942–3. According to Hume, there is neither instigation nor complicity simply by 'proclaiming of it as a meritorious thing to destroy the hateful object; no words of mere permission or allowance to do the deed; no intimation of thanks or approbation if it shall be done; not the strongest expressions of enmity to the person, or the most earnest wishes for his death'. Quoted by G. H. Gordon, *The Criminal Law of Scotland*, 2nd edn. (1978), 139.

questions, such as the proper minimal qualifying activity for complicity and the limits of the general entitlement of individuals to abstain from intervening to prevent criminal activity. But, unlike 'mere presence' cases where the 'accessory's' behaviour is uniformly simple inaction, for those involving omission to assert a power to control there is a range of different rights of control and the possible consequential need to draw distinctions between the legal effect of failure to exercise such disparate rights. Although more often occurring separately, the two issues may arise in combination from a single event if the controlling 'accessory' is present at the commission of the principal's offence. This would be so when a car's owner-passenger has forewarning of the driver's road traffic offence, or where a mother fails to intervene to prevent an elder son's assault on his very young brother.[72] Despite clear common and overlapping policy concerns, the sources of potential liability in omission and mere presence cases are sufficiently distinct to warrant separate consideration.

(a) *'Mere Presence' as a Basis of Complicity* One aspect of a person's general entitlement not to involve himself in preventing an offence which fate may cause him to witness is freedom from complicity in the offence by virtue of simple inaction. The generality of this extends even to serious offences such as murder:

[T]herefore if A. happeneth to be present at a Murder for instance, and taketh no part in it, nor endeavoreth to prevent it, nor apprehendeth the murderer, nor levyeth hue and cry against him, this strange behaviour of his though highly criminal [in a moral sense], will not of itself render him either principal or accessory.[73]

However, this broad principle requires refinement for, arguably, different considerations of policy and practicality may apply according to the nature of the offence. More particularly, a possible distinction might be set up between occasions where an offence takes place in the incidental presence of a non-active third party and 'public performance' offences contingent upon the non-participating presence of third parties.

Where, as in riot or affray, an offence is substantially made up of, or dependent upon, inter-party association, the temptation to see simple presence and likely encouragement as sufficient for liability is obvious but, so far, a move resisted by English courts. In *Royce*[74] Lord Mansfield accepted that: 'aiding and assisting is a matter of fact, and ought to be expressly found by the jury; and that a verdict which only finds that the defendants were present, but finds no particular act of force committed by them is not full enough for the court to judge upon.' Even a direction

---

[72] Cf. *State* v. *Walden* 293 SE 2d 780 (1982).
[73] Foster, *Crown Law*, 350, and Hale, *PC* i. 439, *Borthwick* (1779) 1 Doug. 207, 99 ER 136.
[74] (1767) 4 Burr. 2073, 98 ER 81.

testing liability on presence at the scene of an affray, ready to intervene if necessary but without indicating this to others, had been held to be defective.[75] Rather, actual encouragement, in one form or another, of the principal is the minimum requirement for complicity in any offence. Although presence following some sort of prior association can be taken as evidence of encouragement, this will not be inevitable. Thus cohabitation alone may not be evidence of encouragement or assistance.[76] However, if presence is in consequence of an agreement to be on hand to render any necessary assistance, then encouragement will be presumed.[77] Similarly, in possession offences, although complicity follows if gaining or maintaining possession is actively encouraged,[78] mere close proximity to the principal with knowledge of his unlawful possession will not constitute assistance or encouragement.[79]

Rape cases are illustrative of crimes where the *actus reus* is of a more positive type. In such cases courts[80] see a passive spectator's liability as turning on whether there was evidence that his presence was perceived by the principal as not just acquiescence but an 'act' of encouragement, and that whilst aware of this perception the spectator remained present.

Coney[81] is a prime example of a 'public performance' offence. Here the Court for Crown Cases Reserved made up of eleven judges was (effectively) required to settle whether simple attendance at an illegal prize fight

---

[75] *Allan* [1965] 1 QB 130. See also *Caird* (1970) 54 Cr. App. Rep. 499 at 503. *Parrish* v. *Garfitt* [1984] 1 WLR 911, *Allen* v. *Ireland* [1984] 1 WLR 903 at 910. Similarly in American jurisdictions, e.g. *State* v. *Horner* 103 SE 2d 694 (1958); *People* v. *Luna* 295 P. 2d 457 (1976); *Comm.* v. *Henderson* 378 A. 2d 393 (1977). Cf. the Canadian student occupation case of *Re ACS.* [1969] 4 CCC 284.

[76] In *Bland* [1988] Crim. LR 41, on a charge of unlawful possession of drugs, the defendant's cohabitee's knowledge of the possession was held by the Court of Appeal not in itself to be 'evidence of assistance, active or passive'. Cf. *Barrett* (1862) 9 Cox 255, *Stannard* (1863) 9 Cox 405, and *Smith* v. *Scott* [1973] 1 Ch. 314 suggesting that, where not present, a landlord is not party to tenants' offences even though he has knowledge of them and the ability to prevent them. In *Stannard* Pollock CB saw the landlord's lack of any direct right to control the premises as crucial. The entitlement to give notice to quit was not equated to a right to control. Cf. *Pedley* (1834) 1 Ad. & E. 832, 110 ER 1422, and *Hall* v. *Norfolk* [1900] 2 Ch. 500. Cf. cases where a legal duty to act in a particular way is cast on *all* parties. See e.g. *Drury* (1974) 60 Cr. App. Rep. 195 and *Gibson* (1984) 80 Cr. App. Rep. 24.

[77] Cf. *Spiers* v. *HMA* 1980 JC 36. Williams, CLGP, 353, appears to accept that as a matter of law a conspirator who is present at the time of the offence will be an abettor, but no supporting authority is cited beyond *Young* (1838) 8 C. & P. 644, 173 ER 655; *Cuddy* (1843) 1 C. & R. 210, 174 ER 779, and *Borthwick* (1779) 1 Doug. 207, 99 ER 136, all of which are equivocal on this point. There is at least one modern English authority contrary to this view: *Froggett* [1965] 2 All ER 832, where the Court of Criminal Appeal stated 'It follows that unless a party to a conspiracy to steal becomes *by virtue of his participation in the overt acts of stealing* done in pursuance of the conspiracy a principal either in the first or second degree' etc. at 835, emphasis added. Cf. *Russell*, i. 147, where the question whether actual encouragement was given is treated as one fact.

[78] *McCarthy* (1964) 48 Cr. App. Rep. 11.

[79] *Tansley* v. *Painter* (1968) 112 *Sol. Jo.* 1005; *Bland* [1988] Crim. LR 41; *D.* v. *Parsons* [1960] 2 All ER 493; *Searle* [1971] Crim. LR 592; *Smith* v. *Baker* [1971] RTR 350. Cf. *C.* v. *Hume* [1979] Crim LR 328.

[80] *Clarkson* (1971) 55 Cr. App. Rep. 445, and *Allan* (1963) 47 Cr. App. Rep. 243. Cf. *Gray* (1917) 12 Cr. App. Rep. 244.

[81] (1882) 8 QBD 534.

necessarily amounted to complicity in the same. The greater weight of relevant earlier decisions reviewed in the judgments inclined towards the opinion that:

[S]ome active steps must be taken by word or action with intent to instigate the principal or principals. Encouragement does not of necessity amount to aiding and abetting, it may be intentional or unintentional, a man may unwittingly encourage another in fact by his presence by misinterpreted words or gestures, or by his silence or non-interference or he may encourage intentionally by expressions, gestures or actions intended to signify approval. In the latter case he aids and abets.[82]

This view of Hawkins J., was taken by eight[83] members of the court in *Coney*: that presence is no more than prima-facie evidence from which a jury *could* infer encouragement by the party present at the principal offence. Therefore, finding, as a matter of fact, that a spectator's silent presence encouraged the prize fight permitted a conviction for complicity, provided that person 'intended' to encourage. However, ambiguity runs throughout the judgments as to whether more than awareness of the natural encouraging effect of attendance was sufficient. Clearly those attending an illegal fight want the event to take place. But the casual passer-by, stopping out of 'mere curiosity' to view the spectacle, would not have 'intended' encouragement in a sufficiently positive manner as to incriminate.[84]

Underlying both 'mere presence' and 'public performance' cases is justified judicial hesitation over whether the threshold of complicitous association or involvement should be low enough to incriminate someone for actual encouragement produced by simple presence. Given that awareness of possible encouragement is probably sufficient *mens rea*, then requiring a positively directed accessorial act beyond being at the scene of the crime raises[85] the overall culpability threshold beyond that generally

---

[82] Ibid. Hawkins J. at 557. Presumably applause would be regarded as an 'expression . . . intended to signify approval'.

[83] e.g. Lord Coleridge CJ (at 568–9). The minority attitude in *Coney* was that a jury, subject to cogent evidence to the contrary, was bound to presume intended encouragement as a consequence of intended presence at a prize fight.

[84] The apparent view of Stephen J., at 550. Cf. *Young* (1838) 8 Car. & P. 644, 173 ER 655 at 658, where much the same is suggested. *Wilcox* v. *Jeffery* [1951] 1 All ER 464, raised a question similar to *Coney*, regarding attendance as a member of an audience at an illegal performance of saxophone playing. The involvement of Wilcox was stronger than that of Coney. Wilcox, a well-known music critic, met the saxophonist on his arrival in England, thus providing evidence of professional interest in and likely encouragement of the performance; something reinforced by payment of an entrance charge: Wilcox 'had gone to hear him, and his presence and his payment to go there was an encouragement'. As hinted at in *Coney*, more than awareness of possible encouragement by presence may explain Devlin J's suggestion that: 'It may well be that if a spectator goes to a concert he may explain his presence during an illegal item by saying that he hardly felt it necessary to get up and go out and then return when the performance resumed its legality . . .', [1951] 1 All ER 464 at 467. Edmund Davies J. noted in *Allan* (1963) 47 Cr. App. Rep. 243 at 249, that *Wilcox* v. *Jeffery* 'turned on special facts very different from the present, and is [a case] from which we think no general principle can be deduced'.

[85] Unless it is said that the initial action of going to the scene of the crime must be with the 'intention' of viewing the activity; see below, Ch. 5.

necessary of accessories. However, although sharing this common feature, the two types of case also raise distinguishable problems which may be considered sufficient to support different rules or outcomes for each.

In 'mere presence' examples, once a party becomes aware that encouragement is being derived from his being present then to avoid liability he must either disabuse[86] the principal of this belief or, possibly, immediately quit the scene.[87] Realistically, requiring communication of disapproval to a person about to (or in the process of) perpetrating a violent crime would be casting a hazardous duty on a party possibly faced with the dilemma through no fault of his own. Such situations represent some of the most marginal of potential complicity cases. The policy argument centres around the importance and scope attributed to the right of abstaining from intervening to prevent an offence; for it could be reasonably maintained that this entrenched principle ought only to extend to ignoring or avoiding involvement in criminal activity. Where presence *also* provides encouragement the entitlement of non-intervention is overridden by the greater social priority of not permitting behaviour which encourages crime, satisfying curiosity by witnessing a crime being socially too costly where encouragement occurs. The two most feasible courses open to English law are imposing a duty to leave[88] or requiring a higher level of mental culpability than is presently probably the case — more particularly, requiring something approaching an approving presence.

Policy conflicts of this nature are not raised by 'public performances' because, usually, attendance will be a consequence of a voluntary and informed decision. Instead, difficulties relate to matters of causal contribution and prosecutorial practicalities. Causal problems will be considered at length below but a few specific observations are apt here. Part of the minority view in *Coney* rested on the belief that, as the presence of spectators was a prerequisite of performance (or continued performance), attendance in a very real sense encouraged or facilitated the unlawful fight. Pollock B.[89] denied any

> true analogy between a crowd of persons voluntarily collected round a fight, and those who in a public street or elsewhere are present whilst an illegal act (the sight of which in itself cannot reasonably be supposed to give pleasure to any one) is going on. In the one case it is usually the bystanders collected around who create and who are responsible for the fight as a matter of interest and amusement to themselves. In the other, unless there be some overt act by gesture or word which denotes assistance

---

[86] Cf. *Miller* [1983] 2 AC 161, recognizing the duty to take reasonable measures to abate a danger of harm created unintentionally (and without fault) by the defendant. See the restatement in Law Commission Report 177, cl. 23.

[87] See below, Ch. 10, for the general law on withdrawal. Under these rules simply leaving the scene would probably be insufficient to exculpate.

[88] As envisaged by Devlin J. in *Wilcox* v. *Jeffery* [1951] 1 All ER 464 at 467.

[89] (1882) 8 QBD 534 at 564.

or encouragement, it would be contrary to all reason to infer that the bystanders were taking any part in the illegal act.

But, even accepting this, could a measurable (and sufficient) causal contribution be individually attributed to each spectator? Objections of this kind were recognized and met (in a fashion) by Lord Coleridge CJ's[90] comment that

> Practical wisdom, rather than scientific exactness, seems to me to be the thing to aim at in a branch of the law which is concerned with the affairs of men generally speaking in their simplest and least complicated forms. In such a case as this the spectators really make the fight; without them, and in the absence of any one to look on and encourage, no two men, having no cause of personal quarrel, would meet together in solitude to knock one another about for an hour or two.

Causal difficulties aside, there is the further question of the scale of possible proceedings where the audience numbers run into hundreds or more. Sample prosecutions would be one practical, if not entirely satisfactory, solution. However, despite real theoretical and practical constraints, to argue for the exclusion[91] of possible complicity liability from 'public performance' cases (without compensating specific measures) would be to leave certain areas of passive but supportive presence thoroughly deserving punishment beyond the law's reach.[92]

(b) Complicity through Omission to Exercise Control Broadly, as in principal liability, complicity also recognizes that in certain circumstances a party may be incriminated by his failure to act. Again, as with principal liability and partly for similar reasons, both the basis and scope of complicity through omission are subject to a fair measure of uncertainty. For principals, the uniform feature of liability incurred through omission is the defendant's failure to perform particular acts where the criminal law deems such performance a duty. In complicity, the common thread linking

---

[90] Ibid. at 569.
[91] Cf. Williams, *Textbook*, 350. Law Commission Working Paper 43, proposition 8, would exclude from accessorial liability those who attend illegal performances. See ex. (b) 67, and commentary. The expressed justification for the approach is that 'a criminal offence should not be created by implication' (69). As the report concedes, the rule and logic extends to buyers and sellers of unlawful articles, such as obscene books where a buyer is exempted from liability but those encouraging the transaction are liable as accessories (69). See *Fairburn* v. *Evans* [1916] 1 KB 218 and *Sayce* v. *Coupe* [1953] 1 QB 1 for the current law; and Model Penal Code s. 2.06 (6) (b). There is also an arguable possibility of incriminating soliciting prostitutes' clients as accessories: Criminal Law Revision Committee 16th Report, 14, 32, and 33. Contrastingly, the Law Commission (Report 177) Draft Code team thought it 'right that the spectator or buyer who incites the commission of the offence should not be protected from prosecution', but surprisingly felt it unnecessary to restate the existing law in any express provision (para. 9.40). No direct indication is offered as to the status of *Wilcox* v. *Jeffery*. See also Ch. 9 'Inevitable Incidental Secondary Participation'.
[92] e.g. relatively small gatherings to witness various forms of illegal animal fighting where the spectators use the event for wagering.

these areas of accepted potential liability is the 'accessory's' entitlement to exercise some sort of civil right to control the principal's behaviour or the use he makes of the 'accessory's' property. Such distinct areas of omission-based liability include the ownership or control of premises or motor vehicles, and an employer's authority over his employees. Running through these cases is the central unspoken question: when (and why) for accessorial purposes is a *right* or power to control treated as a *duty* to do so? Furthermore, do the recognized bases[93] creating duties to act in principal liability have relevance in settling the legitimate range of situations for complicity by omission?

The most frequent reported occurrences where secondary liability by omission has been imposed concern various aspects of motor vehicle control or possession. An early example is *Du Cros* v. *Lambourne*[94] where an owner-passenger was convicted of abetting dangerous driving. Although normally taken[95] to indicate that an owner's simple failure to exercise control over a driver may be sufficient to incriminate, the Court of Criminal Appeal's judgments contain ambivalent elements.[96] Lord Alverstone CJ,[97] after referring to the finding of the defendant having driven with the owner's 'consent and approval', would not

Attempt to lay down any general rule or principle, but having regard to these findings of fact it is in my opinion impossible to say that there was in this case no evidence of aiding and abetting.

Crucially unclear is whether Lord Alverstone regarded absence of any expressed disapproval as necessarily constituting 'consent and approval'.

However, any equivocality in *Du Cros* v. *Lambourne* disappears with

---

[93] In English law, probably in cases of imposed or assumed dependency, contractual duty, and creating a dangerous state of affairs.

[94] [1907] 1 KB 40. Expressly followed in the Canadian case of *Kulbacki* (1966) 1 CCC 167. Cf. *Moreland* v. *State* 139 SE 77 (1927), in which a chauffeur driving (with his employer as passenger) in a dangerous manner killed a woman; the employer was convicted of her manslaughter, the court holding: 'It would be the owner's duty, when he saw that the law was being violated and his machine was being operated in such a way as to be dangerous to the life and property of others . . . to curb and restrain one in his employment and under his control . . .' In the South African case of *Aaron* (1909) Trans. LR 937, the Supreme Court ruled that a vehicle's owner was not liable for a driving offence committed by his driver whilst the owner was a passenger unless the offending conduct was directed or authorized by him. Cf. *Shikuri* 1939 AD 225 at 239.

[95] e.g. P. Gillies, *The Law of Criminal Complicity* (1980), p. 132; and D. Lanham, 'Drivers, Control and Accomplices' [1982] Crim. LR 419 at 420.

[96] Darling J. appears to have based liability purely on the owner's failure to exercise his right of control [1907] 1 KB 40 at 46. And see also Slade J. in *NCB* v. *Gamble* [1959], 1 QB 11 at 25: '[M]ere passive acquiescence is sufficient only, I think, where the alleged aider and abettor has the power to control the offender and is actually present where the offence is committed: for example, the owner of a car sitting alongside his chauffeur when the latter commits an offence.'

[97] [1907] 1 KB 40 at 45–6. The third member of the court, Ridley J., agreed with Lord Alverstone's judgment.

Rubie v. *Faulkner*[98] and a cluster of later decisions.[99] Rather than from ownership, here the duty to exercise proper control was imposed by driving regulations under which a provisional licence holder could only lawfully drive when supervised by a full licence holder. For Lord Hewart CJ and the court, the matter was one of statutory interpretation[100] which revealed a duty extending to

> Whatever can reasonably be expected to be done by a person supervising the acts of another to prevent that other from acting unskilfully or carelessly or in a manner likely to cause danger to others, and to this extent to participate in the driving ... For him to refrain from doing anything when he could see that an unlawful act was about to be done, and his duty was to prevent an unlawful act if he could, was for him to aid and abet.[101]

Moreover, liability for failure to control runs beyond the principal's immediate crime to responsibility for consequential offences such as death by reckless[102] driving: a policy consistent with complicity where the accessory's *actus reus* is of a positive nature.

Whether mere failure to exercise a right of control may constitute complicity in employment[103] situations is more difficult to answer. Authorities are few, and mostly equivocal.[104] Modern support for the view

---

[98] [1940] 1 KB 571. The defendant was convicted of abetting the offence of driving without due care and attention committed by a learner-driver whom he was supervising at the time.

[99] *Harris* [1964] Crim. LR 54, following *Rubie* v. *Faulkner* on the question of the existence of a supervisor's duty. This duty (not to permit a learner-driver to drive with an excess blood-alcohol level) was assumed, *sub silentio*, in *Crampton* v. *Fish* [1970] Crim. LR 235 and *Carter* v. *Richardson* [1974] RTR 314. In *Smith* v. *Jenner* [1968] Crim. LR 99, a driving instructor's duty was held not to extend to ensuring his pupil's provisional licence was unexpired as that standard would be 'putting it too high'. Cf. *S.* v. *Claasen* 1979 (4) SA 460 (ZRAD).

[100] [1940] 1 KB 571 at 573–4. 'The regulation contemplate[d] a duty and the presence of the person, properly called a supervisor, who is to perform that duty, and the duty is obviously comprised in the task of supervision ... The duty being clear on the face of the regulation it was a pure question of fact for the justices to decide whether that duty had been performed.'

[101] Hilbery, J. [1940] 1 KB 571 at 575.

[102] In *Harris* [1964] Crim. LR 54 it was causing death by dangerous driving.

[103] Vicarious liability also relies on the existence of an employer/employee relationship but, unlike complicity through omission, it does not require knowledge of 'essential matters' of the likely offence. It has long been clear that there is no general criminal vicarious liability: *Huggins* (1730) Ld. Raym. 1574, 93 ER 915; *Holbrook* (1878) 4 QBD 42. Where there is such necessary knowledge, employment situations may occur where both vicarious liability and complicity through omission arise.

[104] In *Howells* v. *Wynne* (1863) 15 CB (NS) 3, 143 ER 682, failure by a pit owner (A) to prevent an employee (E) from carrying out his work in breach of safety regulations was the basis of conviction of A for abetting E's offence. But the reasoning underlying the court's collective judgment lacks consistency. Taken overall, Williams and Byles JJ appear to suggest that abstaining from intervention to prevent E's offence was (non-conclusive) evidence that A had 'afforded active encouragement to the actual offender' (688). Sufficient emphasis was placed (in the examination of witnesses and in the judgments) on the importance of A being close enough to E for the latter to be aware of A's presence to suggest the need for E to derive actual encouragement from A's non-intervention. In contrast the third member of the court, Willes J., appeared to support conviction solely on the basis of A having effectively consented

that actual encouragement must be derived by an employee from his employer's non-intervention is found in *Cassady* v. *Reg Morris (Transport) Ltd*.[105] where an employer's failure to enforce an employee's compliance with certain road traffic regulations was held to be evidence which might lead only to the conclusion that the employer knowingly encouraged the employee's offence. Such an approach substantively resembles that adopted in 'mere presence' cases, although evidentially a party with a right to control is more likely to be seen as consciously allowing his non-intervention to be interpreted as encouragement.

However, the main body of English case law opinion runs counter to this view, favouring the proposition that a power to control is to be equated with a duty to do so, and failure to (attempt to) carry out the duty will incur accessorial liability. Confirmation of this stance is provided by the Divisional Court's relatively lengthy review of the subject in *Tuck* v. *Robson*. Although most immediately concerning a licensee's duty to act, *Tuck* v. *Robson* deals with the issue in the broad context of 'how far inaction, passive tolerance, can amount to assistance so as to make the accused guilty of aiding and abetting'.[106] Here, as the controller of the premises, the

---

to the offence: by knowingly permitting it to occur 'whether active[ly] or passive[ly] by a person having the authority to prevent the act being done, is . . . consent'. Cf. Williams, CLGP 361, suggesting this case supports the proposition that a 'particular duty' existed to intervene and failure to do so necessarily means the aware employer is 'deemed to authorise' the criminal act. See also Gillies, *Criminal Complicity*, 130. *Roberts* v. *Preston* (1860) 9 CB (NS) 208, 142 ER 81, contains no discursive judgment and for that reason alone is of rather limited value. In *Gough* v. *Rees* (1929) 29 Cox 74, a bus owner was convicted of having 'counselled and procured' the conductor to carry unlawfully an excess number of passengers by failing to take adequate precautions to avoid what he knew would otherwise be bound to occur. It is clear from the judgment of Lord Heward CJ that he based his confirmation of conviction on the grounds that the employer 'knew what would happen unless he took precautions'. The fact that this practice of overloading was well established could have been taken as evidence that acquiescence by the owner had been *communicated* to the conductor. Cf. the extreme view of Byles J. in *Kew and Jackson* (1872) 12 Cox 355, 154 ER 682 at 687; following the authority of *Co. Inst.* ii. 182 that 'consenting and encouragement' constituted aiding.

[105] [1975] RTR 470. The principal offence was the driver failing to provide his employer with the necessary records of journey times. The employer's alleged complicity was in his failure to *require* the driver to produce such records. Cf. the Scottish decision of *Bonar* v. *McLeod* 1983 SCCR 161, where it was held that failure by a senior police officer to intervene and prevent a junior officer assaulting a prisoner in their joint custody could be sufficient to incriminate the senior officer as an accessory to the assault. And see *Forman and Ford* [1988] Crim. LR 677.

[106] [1970] 1 All ER 1171. The charge was aiding and abetting the consumption of intoxicating liquor out of hours. The defendant, a public house licensee, in his efforts to prevent the drinking out of hours called 'time', switched off the main lights, and requested 'glasses please'. The evidence showed he knew that drinking was continuing after this until the police subsequently arrived. Cf. ex. 27 (vi) in Law Commission Report 177. A similar earlier Divisional Court case is *Duxley* v. *Gilmore* (1959) 123 JP Jo. 331, [1959] Crim. LR 454, in which it was said that aiding and abetting could be established if the licensee's 'conduct encouraged it and that conduct might be active encouragement or marked passive tolerance' and if there was also evidence of the licensee's 'knowledge *and* connivance'. Cf. *obiter* of Lord Goddard CJ in *Ferguson* v. *Weaving* [1951] 1 KB 814 at 819, 'there can be no doubt that, if a

defendant was found to be at least under a positive duty to 'revoke [his patrons'] licence[s] to be on the premises',[107] by not doing so the defendant had passively assisted in the commission of the principal offence of drinking after hours.

Assuming, as the general run of English cases suggest, that a right to control the actions of another may in certain circumstances be translated[108] into a duty to act, then quite what must a party do to satisfy such a duty and fend off complicity? *Rubie* v. *Faulkner* spoke of 'whatever can reasonably be expected to be done'. Similarly, the Australian decision of *Dennis* v. *Pight* suggests liability where the defendant 'having a reasonable opportunity to act to discontinue or prevent such use, fails to take reasonable steps within his power to do so'.[109] But *Tuck* v. *Robson* illustrates that only very demonstrative action may suffice. Here, after spending much time assessing the forcefulness of the defendant's action in attempting to terminate his patrons' drinking, Lord Parker CJ found that calling 'time', 'glasses please', and switching off the bar's main lights was insufficient to 'revoke their licence to be on the premises'. Exactly what would have constituted an effective act of revocation is impossible to glean from the judgment. There is an obvious parallel between what constitutes fulfilling a duty to act and the positive acts necessary for withdrawal from complicity. Notions of reasonableness and possible correlations between the level of the accessory's assistance or encouragement and the required degree of countermanding effort, which logically also have relevance to omissions, will be examined in Chapter 10.

Moving to the question of the theoretical legitimacy of this form of complicity, the comparison with principal liability through omission, although useful, is not totally appropriate. First, many instances exist throughout complicity where the degree of criminality, whether expressed through *mens rea* or *actus reus*, does not correspond with that required for the principal. Strict liability is a simple example. Reasons of policy and practicality (as has been and will be seen) are adducible to justify the

---

licensee consciously permits consumption after hours, it would amount to aiding and abetting the offence'; and also in *Thomas* v. *Lindop* [1950] 1 All ER 906 at 968, 'it is necessary to show either that the licensee in a case of this sort knew what was being done *or* connived at what was being done'; and repeated a little later in the judgment. Unlike in *Duxley* v. *Gilmore*, Lord Goddard appears to suggest mere knowledge is a sufficient basis of complicity.

[107] Noting with approval the comment of Slade J. in *NCB* v. *Gamble* quoted in n. 96 above.

[108] The case law mostly involves situations where the controller was present at the commission of the principal's offence. (The employer/controller was absent, e.g. in *Gough* v. *Rees* (1929) 29 Cox 74.) According to Slade J. in *NCB* v. *Gamble*, quoted in n. 96, liability for failure to control is limited to where another is 'actually present when the offence is committed'. In addition to the further complexity introduced by the flexible nature of presence, there seems to be little point in such a limitation if the notion of control and duty is accepted. Where there is the necessary awareness by the controller of a threatened (further) offence, whether he is present or not only affects the range of possible measures he might take to acquit himself of his duty to act.

[109] (1968) 11 FLR 458.

distinctions. In the present context it could be maintained that the general suspicion[110] which liability by omission has long attracted is reinforced by the more remote position occupied by a secondary party from the commission of the principal offence. Secondly, causal needs in complicity create their own peculiar problems when combined with omissions.[111] For instance, in the case of complicity by omission the proscribed harm is brought about by an informed voluntary agent. Contrastingly, omissions in principal responsibility raise causal questions relating to the ascription of blame for consequential harm through the unfettered run of natural events or undirected forces.[112]

However, such qualifications aside, some theoretical support can be extracted from principal liability for omissions; and in particular from what may be termed 'supervening fault' liability which occurs where

> D does an act which puts in peril P's person, his property, his liberty or any other interest protected by the criminal law and D is aware that he has created the peril, he has a duty to take reasonable steps to prevent the harm in question resulting. The act may be done without any kind of fault but, if D fails to intervene, it is undoubtedly his act which is the cause of the harm.[113]

Once again, *causal* attributability is quite different in 'supervening fault' and complicity situations. But similarities exist in that the essence of both forms of responsibility is the creation of a duty to take avoiding or neutralizing action, when a risk of harm has been generated. In both cases it is irrelevant that the dangerous potential is created without fault and is unforeseen. For complicity the risk potential is produced by putting another party in a (better) position to carry out an offence, whether by furnishing a car, providing access to licensed premises and alcohol, or whatever. In both cases the extent of the duty appears to be the taking of reasonable measures to extinguish the harm-threatening potential. In this respect the omitter is in

---

[110] Generally e.g. J. Feinberg, *Harm to Others* (1984), 118–25, 165–86; A. J. Ashworth, 'The Scope of Criminal Liability for Omissions' (1989) 105 *LQR* 424.

[111] In principal liability duty is, arguably, treated as equivalent to or as a substitute for cause (e.g. P. H. Robinson, 'Imputed Criminal Liability' (1984) 93 *YLJ* 609, 674). *If* principal and secondary liability were fundamentally distinguished by the test of the presence or absence of legal cause of harm, then also basing complicity liability on duty would be theoretically impermissible—or the general view that duty is equivalent to cause is faulty. See H. Benyon, 'Causation, Omissions and Complicity' [1987] Crim. LR 539. However, the logic of such arguments turns on the implied premise that complicity liability does *not* rely on the presence of a causal contribution. See Ch. 3, for the contrary view and the causal problem of omissions generally.

[112] Examples can be imagined where the two are combined. If *M* the mother of *S1* aged 12 and *S2* aged 3 did nothing to stop *S1* stabbing *S2*, then, depending on *S1*'s state of mind, *M* could be either the principal offender in the stabbing through the innocent agency of *S1* (if he lacked mischievous discretion) or an accessory if *S1* was liable (by having mischievous discretion). It is assumed that *M* has a duty of care to look after her children and the power to control *S1*. Cf. *Russell* [1933] VLR 59 and *State* v. *Walden* 293 SE 2d 780 (1982).

[113] Smith and Hogan, *Criminal Law*, p. 53, derived from *Miller* [1983] 2 AC 161. See also the formulation in Law Commission Report 177, cl. 23 (i) and G. L. Williams, 'What Should the Code Do About Omissions' (1987) 7 LS 92 at 111.

a different position from anyone else not responsible for furnishing some sort of assistance. For instance, a passenger in a car recklessly driven by another has the general legal right to take reasonable interventionary measures to prevent continuation of the offence. If the passenger is also the owner, his general interventionary entitlement is reinforced by particular civil rights derived from ownership.

Even granting that some sort of theoretical pedigree for complicity through omission is capable of being traced out, it remains debatable whether or not, as a matter of policy, it is also an acceptable form of criminality.[114] Clearly it is socially desirable that the likelihood of principal offences being committed is diminished by those with a civil power to control the exercise of such power. At the same time it would hardly be extravagant to suggest that such people owed some degree of moral responsibility to take reasonable measures to ensure that criminal behaviour was not encouraged or facilitated by their inaction. It has already been argued, in relation to 'mere presence' cases, that it is an acceptable erosion of the general right to remain inactive in the face of an offence's commission to require a witness to take reasonable disabusing action once he becomes aware that his presence is actually encouraging the perpetrator. *A fortiori* this holds true where a controller knows his acquiescence is being interpreted as encouragement or condonation by the perpetrator. What is contentious is whether, where there is no evidence (or a reasonable

---

[114] Working Paper 43 proposed that 'A person who is in a position to prevent an offence because he is in control of property or for some other reason, is not to be taken to be an accessory merely because he fails to prevent an offence' (proposition 6 (4)). As the proposed principle's illustrations (*a* and *c*) suggest, situations as in *Du Cros* v. *Lambourne* and *Tuck* v. *Robson* would no longer result in convictions. The basis for the change was the desire not to erode the 'general principle, that a party does not become a party to a crime by mere omission' and that 'before a person can be . . . an accessory for failing to prevent a crime he must be involved in some way other than by his failure to prevent an offence when he is in a position to do so. It is not possible to spell out what additional factors should be present . . . as they can be many and varied.' (43 and 8.) Such 'additional factors' may explain why, as is shown by illustration (*b*), *Rubie* v. *Faulkner* and *Harris* would survive the proposed change of law. The illustration, though, entails three types of potentially 'additional factors': (i) driving supervisors having actual detailed minute-by-minute control, (ii) a duty to control under a specific statutory provision, (iii) the supervisor's failure to intervene actually 'encouraged the driver'. On this provision Law Commission Report 177, notes: 'most commentators on the Working Paper and on the Bill found nothing objectionable in the principle' (para. 9. 23). The Draft Criminal Code formulation of the existing law is contained in cl. 27 (3): 'Assistance or encouragement includes assistance or encouragement arising from a failure by a person to take reasonable steps to exercise any authority or to discharge any duty he has to control the relevant acts of the principal in order to prevent the commission of the offence'. The code team believed 'that it is not possible to express it more narrowly by any formula limiting the range of cases in which a relevant authority or duty arises.' (commentary, para. 9. 23). The Model Penal Code, s. 2.06 (3) (*a*) (iii), provides a party may be an accomplice if 'having a legal duty to prevent the commission of the offense, fails to make proper effort to do so'. No attempt is made to elaborate on the expression 'legal duty', but the scope of the provision is, in any case, immediately narrower than English law because of the general requirement of the accessory (not) acting with the 'purpose of promoting or facilitating'. (s. 2.06 (3) (*a*)). A similar approach is seen in the proposed Draft Federal Criminal Code 1971, art. 401 (1) (iii).

presumption) of encouragement taken by the principal and known to the controller, this special legal burden of intervention is fairly laid upon individuals associated with the principal offender in this way — in one sense a policy of conscripting 'controllers' into the ranks of crime prevention authorities. Effectively, it is the facilitatory aspect of a controller's inaction which marks him off from the non-controlling witness of a crime and which, in turn, raises the additional moral and social policy issues.

Instances where courts have recognized duties to act are, so far, not extensive and, as a matter of individual justification, nowhere near approach being unrealistic in what the controller could reasonably be expected to do in the circumstances. However, unexceptionable as these examples are, their acceptance makes the drawing of principled policy boundaries exceedingly difficult. Two hypothetical cases illustrate the nature of the problem:

(i) Would Ralph Nickleby have been an accessory to the rape of his niece Kate at his house if he had not intervened and thwarted Sir Mulberry Hawk?

(ii) Well aware that his terminally ill wife intends to kill herself with a drugs overdose, a doctor continues to allow her access to his drugs cabinet for the purposes of dispensing certain prescriptions. Will the husband be an accessory to the wife's suicide if she acts as he anticipated?[115]

In both situations the owner/controller was in a position to take interventionary measures. Morally, most would heavily condemn Ralph Nickleby's inaction whereas few are likely to be critical of the doctor's conduct. Yet simple application of the control-equals-duty principle could not easily separate the two examples.[116] Discriminating between what might be considered deserving and undeserving cases for criminalization may, it has been suggested, be approached in two ways: by declaring that failure to exercise a civil right to control, in itself, is an insufficient basis for liability, though it may be sufficient when coupled with an 'additional factor';[117] or by affirming that simple failure to exercise 'authority or discharge a duty' may incriminate. But for both judicial creativity would determine what the 'additional factor' or cases of 'authority or duty' were.[118] Yet whichever approach is adopted, whether the discriminatory device is designated an 'additional factor' or 'authority or duty', the need remains for a conceptual basis capable of selecting appropriate cases for punishment. This severe difficulty[119] is probably the most convincing single

---

[115] Effectively, the wife would have access and part control of the drugs cabinet for legitimate purposes. As the owner such access and control would be granted and capable of being withdrawn at will by the husband.

[116] As a matter of procedure the consent of the Director of Public Prosecutions is necessary before proceedings can be brought under s. 2 of the Suicide Act 1961.

[117] The approach in Working Paper 43, cit. in n. 114.

[118] Cf. Law Commission Report 177, cl. 27 (3), cit. in n. 114.

[119] The position of the generous social host combines an awkward moral and social dilemma with the broad problem of omissions. *Giving* guests alcohol before driving, knowing it will increase their blood/alcohol level beyond permissible limits, raises the question of

argument for confining passive complicity to those situations recognized by particular legislative measures.[120]

But, whether judicial or legislative in origin, it might be suggested that the basis of liability should acknowledge the necessity of *either* a relationship between parties where the 'accessory' is clearly accepted as dominant, and the principal, by virtue of dependency or otherwise, is subordinate *or*, a substantial risk of personal harm. The presence of either of these two factors — formal relational dominance or the likelihood of personal harm — could be claimed properly to override (or at least mollify) a fair portion of the concern associated with the imposition of omission liability. The first class would extend to (inter alia) driving and employment cases; the second to where, say, a gun is innocently loaned to another party who is then discovered to be of a dangerous disposition. Additionally, whichever of these two limbs of liability operates, it should be reasonable in all the circumstances to have expected the 'accessory' to have acted (reasonably). This final objective requirement offers a tolerably flexible and certain facility for filtering out undeserving examples, such as that of the doctor's suicidal wife.

(4) *Conspiracy as an Auxiliary Mode of Complicity*

Although in certain respects conspiracy and complicity share several common features and functions, their ancestry,[121] nature, and current scope are quite distinct. Like all inchoate offences, conspiracy is free-standing, liability being fixed the moment the agreement is concluded, without regard to achievement of the criminal objective. At the same time, agreement or

potential complicity liability of hosts to which no real solution was offered in the drinks 'lacing' case of *Attorney-General's Reference (No. 1 of 1975)* [1975] 1 QB 773, discussed in Ch. 3. An added dimension of difficulty arises where the host provides alcohol on a 'help yourself' basis and then fails to intervene to prevent the guest/driver consuming excessive quantities. Some American jurisdictions have recognized civil liability for injury and death resulting from supplying alcohol; criminal responsibility remains a possibility. See e.g. H. R. Weinert, 'Social Hosts and Drunken Drivers: A Duty to Intervene?' (1985) 133 *U. Penn. LR* 867; and R. D. Kelly, 'Social Host's Criminal Liability' (1986) 39 *Okl. LR* 689. The possibility of a new offence of 'sale of alcohol to drivers' was considered and rejected in HMSO, *Road Traffic Law Review Report* (1988), ch. 7.

[120] Broadly favoured by Williams, *Textbook*, 349, and (1987) 7 LS 92, at 117–18; and Ashworth, 'The Scope of Criminal Liability for Omissions'. Cf. Edwards, *Mens Rea*, 147–50. The New Zealand Crimes Bill 1989, cl. 57 (2) (b) adopts a wide unspecific approach: liability based on presence and failure 'to exercise any authority that he . . . has in the circumstances to prevent the . . . offence'. See K. E. Dawkins 'Parties, conspiracies and attempts' (1990) 20 VUWLR Monograph 3, 117, 124.

[121] Even though statutory conspiracy provisions stretching back to the 14th cent. are known of (Ordinance of Conspirators, 1305), conspiracy was not firmly established until the 16th cent., more than 300 years after complicity's well-documented origins. Moreover, after a relatively brief period during the Middle Ages of complementary (but hardly unified) development the separate natures of inchoate (autonomous) and complicity (derivative) liability were fully recognized. Cf. Stephen *HCL* ii. 223–4 in relation to attempt. For a brief overview of this process, see Law Reform Commission of Canada, Working Paper 45 (1985), 9–14.

consensus — of the essence of conspiracy — is unessential to complicity.[122] However, there are clear points of intersection between the two forms of criminality where a degree of theoretical ambivalence generates the potential for imposing complicity in circumstances which would represent a dilution of or deviation from the standard conditions of secondary liability.

More particularly, uncertainty exists as to whether conspiracy is an independent or auxiliary mode of complicity — whereby a conspirator will necessarily be a party to any offence committed in execution of collective criminal objectives. Or posing the question from the directly opposite stance: where do the boundaries of conspiracy lie and how is conspiracy liability to be kept within generally acceptable limits? Whichever way the question is set, where an offence is committed in pursuance of a conspiracy by a conspirator, it is very likely to be inferred that he received encouragement, thus providing a basis for incriminating other conspirators as parties to the substantive offence. Yet, although likely, encouragement capable of supporting complicity is not an inevitable by-product of every conspiracy,[123] especially where it is sizeable with a fluid membership often unknown to each other. And neither will each party necessarily have sufficient knowledge of the substantive offence(s) capable of incriminating under normal complicity requirements.

Direct English authority on the question of conspiracy's possible 'auxiliary status' is scant; though, for instance, Halsbury's *Laws of England*[124] maintains:

A person who conspires to commit or who incites the commission of a crime is, without more, a secondary party to that crime if and when it is committed, unless before its commission he has effectively countermanded or nullified the incitement.

[122] *Kupferberg* (1918) 13 Cr. App. Rep. 166; *Attorney-General's Reference (No. 1 of 1975)* [1975] QB 773. Although cf. *Anderson* [1986] AC 27 and *Siracusa* [1989] Crim. LR 712 for the nature of agreement in conspiracy.
[123] As Schreiner JA noted in *Zeelie* 1952 (1) SA 400 (AD) at 402: 'a crime may be agreed upon without either party inciting the other, for the party who first opened negotiations may have proceeded so tentatively, and the other may have been so predisposed to concurrence that there may, in fact, not merely as a matter of difficulty of proof have been nothing amounting to an offer or proposal which I take to be the minimum required for an incitement.' 'Incitement' is used here in the broad sense, and not as a reference to the inchoate offence. See also *S.* v. *Njenje* 1966 (1) SA 369 (SR) 376 where *Zeelie* is approvingly cited.
[124] 1975, 4th edn. vol. xi, para. 44, on the basis of *Croft* [1944] KB 295 at 297 and 298. In *Croft* the Court of Criminal Appeal ruled that if two people agree to commit suicide and one survives, the survivor by virtue of the prior agreement shall be liable as an accessory before the fact unless he expressly countermanded the encouragement. As authority the court relied *inter alia* on a series of earlier cases involving aiding and abetting suicide, together with the authority of Hawkins. It seems reasonably clear that the court in *Croft* intended to express an opinion of application beyond suicide cases. *Fletcher* [1962] Crim. LR 551 at 552, was a case of murder where it was disputed whether one of the defendants had been present when the fatal acts were committed. The Court of Criminal Appeal accepted that 'You may well be satisfied that he was a conspirator and that he got cold feet at the last moment and did not come near the scene of the firing, but unless he withdrew from the conspiracy he remains equally guilty "of participation in the murder"'. *West* [1948] 1 All ER 718 is a statutory example of where membership of a conspiracy was deemed sufficient to incriminate the parties of the offences conspired at. There the defendants were charged with conspiracy to contravene regulation 55

Modes of Complicity

In so far as this is intended to suggest that conspiracy *per se* will incriminate all parties of any offence carried out in its execution, it is indirectly at odds with a substantial body of authorities relating to the 'doctrine' of common purpose.[125] As will be seen, a strong preponderance of modern common purpose cases establishes the need for proof of the standard *mens rea* requirements of complicity. However, although of relevance, common purpose case law has centred around the issue of the extent of foresight which one party to the common purpose (conspiracy) must have to be convicted of offences, outside the main purpose of the agreement,[126] committed by a co-conspirator. The further question concerning (excessive) causal remoteness that may arise in large-scale and loose-knit conspiracies is not addressed in the typically single objective common purpose authorities. For although, if the circumstances are such as to satisfy any fault requirements, subsequent offences are likely to be causally sufficiently proximate, it will not invariably follow.[127] Therefore, to *that* limited extent the relevance of conspiracy to complicity under English law remains open.[128]

In considerable contrast with the position in England, the subject has received extensive attention in American state and federal courts, with the most extreme manifestation of the effects of prior conspiracy on complicity liability embodied in the widely known 'Pinkerton doctrine'. According to the Supreme Court, in *Pinkerton* v. *United States*,[129] each member of a conspiracy is liable as a party to all offences carried out by co-conspirators in furtherance of the conspiracy, even though there is no evidence of their direct or indirect participation in, or knowledge of, such offences. By recognizing conspiracy as a special basis of complicity, complicity's reach extends to merely remotely associated parties of whose existence co-conspirators may not even know.[130] Effectively, each member of the conspiracy is viewed as the incriminating agent of every other member.

of the Defence (General) Regulations 1939. Regulation 90 provided 'that any person who conspires with any other person to commit an offence against any of the regulations shall be guilty of an offence against that regulation'.

[125] Generally, see Ch. 8, and Ch. 9, 'Limitation'.

[126] Under English law the potential does exist, in the notion of 'blank cheque' assistance or encouragement, for a co-conspirator to have sufficient mental culpability for complicity in subsequent offences, where the 'essential matters' of such were unknown to him. See Ch. 6, 'Knowledge of Essential Matters'.

[127] e.g. C, an accountant for Murder Incorporated, is aware that the organization has contracted to have *V* (amongst many others) killed. Murder Incorporated, a national organization, employs hundreds of people in various menial and supporting roles. Although C, in common with many others, knew sufficient details of *V*'s murder before it was carried out to satisfy standard complicity *mens rea* needs, has he, by membership of the conspiracy to kill, aided, abetted, counselled, or procured the killing in a sufficiently proximate sense to make him an accomplice? See Ch. 3, and cf. P. E. Johnson, 'The Unnecessary Crime of Conspiracy' (1973) 61 *Cal. LR* 1137, 1146.

[128] Cf. Lanham 'Complicity, Concert and Conspiracy', 289–90.

[129] 328 US 640 (1946).

[130] As in *Anderson* v. *Superior Court* 78 Cal. App. 2d 22 (1947) where by simply referring women to an abortionist the defendant was held to be a party to a conspiracy under which she

In seeking to hold the doctrine within what are seen as appropriate bounds, courts sometimes resort to insisting that not only must the substantive offence be committed in *furtherance* of the common objective, but that it was 'reasonably foresee[able] as a necessary or natural consequence of the unlawful agreement'.[131] More restricted formulations of this nature place liability on a footing resembling some nineteenth-century code provisions, including the 1879 English Draft Code:[132]

If several persons form a common intention to prosecute any unlawful purpose, and to assist each other therein, each of them is a party to every offence committed by any one of them in the prosecution of such common purpose, the commission of which offence was or ought to have been known to be a probable consequence of the prosecution of such common purpose.

By requiring the intention 'to assist each other' (as well as 'probable consequence') this provision is narrower than is possible under *Pinkerton* and its derivatives in that it appears to assert the need for a clearly identifiable *causal* relationship between all parties. The Pinkerton doctrine implicitly treats each co-conspirator as the causal agent of the other, regardless of the extreme remoteness or tenuousness of the actual relationship.

Pinkerton's potential to subvert standard complicity demands also turns on what behaviour is deemed sufficient to make someone a party to a conspiracy and, further, whether under *Pinkerton* membership of the conspiracy entails principal or secondary liability in pursuant offences.

As for the first question, it has been maintained[133] that aiding or

---

was convictable for a number of other illegal abortions on women not known to her referred to the abortionist by other parties. See also *Gurrieri* v. *Gunn* 404 FS 21 (1975); *US* v. *Scruggs* 583 F. 2d 238 (1978); *US* v. *Michel* 588 F. 2d 986 (1979); *Comm.* v. *Orlowski* 481 A. 2d 952 (1984); *Comm.* v. *Jackson* 485 A. 2d 1102 (1984). The Pinkerton doctrine is not accepted in all state courts, see e.g. *Comm.* v. *French* 259 NE 2d 195 (1970); *Comm.* v. *Richards* 293 NE 2d 854 (1972); *Comm.* v. *Mangula* 322 NE 2d 177 (1975); and see Model Penal Code revised commentary (1985), 307–10, noting the general move in state code revisions to exclude conspiracy as an auxiliary complicity mode.

[131] *Dicta* in *Pinkerton*. Applied e.g. in *State* v. *Stein* 360 A. 2d 347 (1976); *US* v. *Tilton* 610 F. 2d 302 (1980); *Comm.* v. *Orlowski* 481 A. 2d 952 (1984). Such a limitation is incorporated in some state codes, e.g. Minn. Stat. Ann. s. 609.05 (2) (1964); Tex. Penal Code Ann. s. 7.02 (b) (1974); Wis. Stat. Ann. s. 939.05 (2) (C) (1982) on which see G. R. Ostos-Irwin, 'Wisconsin's Party to a Crime Statute' (1984) *Wis. LR* 769.

[132] S. 71, produced by the Criminal Code Bill Commission of which Stephen was a member and principal draughtsman. S. 71 of the Draft Code was incorporated, without change, in the 1892 Canadian Criminal Code; currently s. 21 (2) of the 1970 Criminal Code. See Chs. 7 and 8 for consideration of the relevant case law and other code provisions.

[133] G. P. Fletcher, *Rethinking Criminal Law* (1978), 660: 'Rendering aid to an existing conspiracy may make one a party to the group, but never as an accessory, only as a full member of the conspiracy. The logic is that contribution betokens an agreement; an agreement implies a conspiracy; and a conspiracy entails liability as a perpetrator. If the Anglo-American law were ever to admit of a more refined classification of actors as accessories and perpetrators, the system would have to abandon the doctrine of conspiratorial complicity, which effectively prevents treating a member of a conspiracy as an accessory rather than a perpetrator.' The vulnerable kernel of Fletcher's observation is that 'contribution betokens an agreement' and therefore (i) there can be no complicity in conspiracy, so making all assisters and encouragers

encouraging existing conspirators inevitably constitutes principal liability in the conspiracy. However, this would be true if such behaviour necessarily entailed agreement, but it does not. The point is of some consequence in that an even larger spread of liability would be possible under the Pinkerton doctrine if the qualifying threshold for principal membership of the conspiracy were so low: making *accessories* to the conspiracy also parties to offences committed in its execution would entail an additional corruption of complicity theory.

On the second related matter, some commentators have suggested that 'conspiratorial membership functions not as a category of accessorial liability but as a test for what it means to be a co-perpetrator'.[134] Such a position would mark a greater departure from general principles than the Pinkerton doctrine is usually credited with. It is one thing to deem that a conspirator, simply by being a conspirator, supported or encouraged the perpetrator in any pursuant offence; it is quite another (implicitly) to jettison not only *mens rea* requirements but the strict causal demands necessitated by principal liability. Nor do the justifications adducible in support of *Pinkerton* require adoption of such a position.

It might be imagined that a good deal of the Pinkerton doctrine's appeal, and a prime justification for it, was the relatively long-established American problem of large-scale organized crime. Yet this is only partly borne out by the expressed rationales of reported case law. As in *Pinkerton*, the principle has been invoked where the number of parties and offences has been small. Even so, it is the problem of meeting organized criminal activity that promises the most convincing defence of *Pinkerton*:

If a defendant can be convicted as an accomplice for advising or counselling the perpetrator, it likewise seems fair to impose . . . liability upon one who, in alliance with others, has declared his allegiance to a particular common object, has implicitly assented to the commission of foreseeable crimes in furtherance of this object, and

principals; and (ii) such behaviour will also incriminate the actor as a (principal) party to substantive offences carried out in pursuance of the conspiracy. But contribution does not *inevitably* betoken an agreement: e.g. knowingly facilitating the detailed planning for something already agreed upon by renting a room to others should constitute secondary not principal liability in the conspiracy. (Cf. J. C. Smith, 'Secondary Participation and Inchoate Offences' (see n. 145).) Although 'contribution' in a narrower sense may betoken agreement according to *Anderson* [1986] AC 27, whereby agreeing to provide material assistance in the execution of a conspiratorial objective was regarded as sufficient to incur *principal* liability in the conspiracy. However, in this case the defendant may also have been involved in the formation of the conspiracy: [1985] Crim. LR 651. But see to the contrary, *Siracusa* [1989] Crim. LR 712 and Report 177, cl. 48, requiring an 'intention that an offence be committed' for principal conspiracy liability. Therefore the first of Fletcher's twin consequences does not automatically follow.

[134] Fletcher, *Rethinking Criminal Law*, 647; no authority is cited. Here Fletcher is not arguing in support of this conclusion, rather that it is a consequence of the current '[un]refined' rules of complicity (660). As Fletcher recognizes (674), such a view 'collapses the distinction between accessories and perpetrators'. To the contrary see Lanham, 'Complicity, Concert and Conspiracy', 286–7; Foster, *Crown Law*, 126; *Co. Inst.* ii. 182; and Hawkins, *PC* ii, ch. 29, s.16 and, generally, authorities cited in Ch. 8 below.

has himself collaborated or agreed to collaborate with his associates, since these acts necessarily give support to the other members of the conspiracy. Perhaps the underlying theme of this argument is that the strict concepts of causality and intent embodied in the traditional doctrine of complicity are inadequate to cope with the phenomenon of modern-day organised crime.[135]

However, while possibly defensible as an alternative to (more) severe or aggravated[136] penalties for membership of the conspiracy, the Pinkerton doctrine still facilitates substantive conviction of inconsequential parties in large organizations, as well as the 'higher ups' responsible for establishing and running the criminal operation.[137]

Essentially, the extent to which complicity principles are compromised in any particular jurisdiction by accommodating a conspiracy/complicity provision turns on the distance between what (within that jurisdiction) constitutes a conspiratorial 'agreement' and the *mens rea/actus reus* demands of complicity. In England although indifference as to the carrying out of the principal offence *may* suffice for both conspiracy[138] and

---

[135] Arguments reviewed but not seen as conclusive in 'Developments in the Law — Criminal Conspiracy' (1959) 72 *HLR* 920, 999, quoted by La Fave and Scott, *Criminal Law*, 514. Similarly Frankfurter J. in *Callanan* v. *US* 364 US 587 (1961) 593–4. Cf. Fletcher, *Rethinking Criminal Law*, 664; and note the concept of 'blank cheque' authorization, below, Ch. 6.

[136] The initial position adopted by the National Commission on Reform of Federal Criminal Laws in its 'Study Draft' (1970) was in support of a special 'Organized Crime Leadership' offence devised to tackle large (10 or more parties) criminal syndicates; (art. 1005): 'Aiding should mean something more than the attenuated connection resulting solely from membership in a conspiracy and the objective standard of what is reasonably foreseeable. The analytical problems which have arisen from the effort to fit the Pinkerton doctrine into existing statutory formulations have little significance for us in drafting new laws. The pertinent question therefore is one of policy: should the *Pinkerton* grounds be a basis of vicarious liability? The draft takes the position that such an extension is unwarranted. The persons in a conspiracy who ought to be liable will become so under complicity principles or under the proposed organized crime offense. Those who are "higher ups" in any organization for commission of crime will, if the group is small, be close enough to have commanded, induced, procured or aided its commission. If the organization is so large that such facts are difficult to establish, the "higher ups" will be subject to aggravated penalties under the proposed organized crime offense.' However, in its 'Final Draft' (1971) the Commission notes that the proposed offence was 'shelved' in favour of more generalized provisions permitting the imposing of '"upper ranges" of imprisonment for dangerous special offenders, including leaders of organised crime'. (72). Cf. the less hostile view taken of the Pinkerton doctrine in the Report of the Committee on the Judiciary United States Senate (1980), 73.

[137] Cf. Model Penal Code, TD 1 (1953), commentary 21–2, where the Pinkerton doctrine was excluded as a basis of complicity liability; and s. 2.06 (3), official draft (1962). Similarly in the proposed Federal Criminal Code (1971), arts. 401 and 1004 (5); and Working Papers 155–7, National Commission on Reform of Federal Criminal Laws for consequential procedural and evidential problems raised by *Pinkerton*: '(a) is the co-conspirator liable for crimes committed before he joined the conspiracy, as he is for overt acts (a principle which serves another purpose)? (b) do different rules of evidence apply to his liability for conspiracy and his liability for the specific offense? (c) can he be acquitted for conspiracy and re-tried for the specific offense? (d) should the test of withdrawal from the conspiracy be the same as for terminating liability for the specific offense?'

[138] See *Anderson* [1986] AC 27 and commentary [1985] Crim. LR 651; but cf. *Siracusa* [1989] Crim. LR 712.

complicity[139], differences remain elsewhere in other requirements. In particular, the nature of agreement[140] in conspiracy appears wider than 'common purpose' in complicity; and certainly the complicity requirement of knowledge of the 'essential matters' of the principal offences is not met by simple membership of a conspiracy.[141] Neither is the causal contribution implicitly required[142] in complicity necessarily present between conspirator and perpetrator. Overall, the running together of conspiracy and complicity in the *Pinkerton* fashion (by recognizing conspiracy as a separate head of complicity) tends to act, as some jurisdictions have found,[143] as a generally subversive and confusing influence within the body of secondary liability rules as a whole, and especially in diluting *mens rea* requirements in non-conspiracy complicity. Moreover, compensating law enforcement advantages that might be identified as promoted by *Pinkerton* could be more effectively achieved by distinct or targeted measures.[144]

Beyond the question of whether conspirators are necessarily parties to offences carried out in execution of a conspiracy is the separate but related matter of the scope for complicity in inchoate offences.[145]

The general dearth of authority confirms the limited range of practical possibility for such liability, particularly for incitement and conspiracy. Case law[146] and logic support the existence of complicity in attempt. In the

---

[139] See below, Ch. 5. In this respect the Pinkerton doctrine, because of the general requirement of purposive assistance in complicity, constitutes a greater departure from complicity requirements in American jurisdictions.

[140] The broad approach in *Meyrick* (1929) 21 Cr. App. Rep. 94 is doubtful after *Griffiths* [1966] 1 QB 589 and *Ardalan* [1972] 2 All ER 257 where, rather than a single conspiracy with many parties unaware of the identities of all except certain co-ordinating members, the court inclined towards regarding the circumstances as involving a number of separate conspiracies.

[141] e.g. A, B, C, and D plan to rob X Bank. C and D are assigned the task of obtaining the necessary car and guns by whatever illegal means necessary. If C and D use blackmail to get hold of the equipment, A and B will not be implicated in that offence unless they have the necessary level of knowledge prescribed by *DPP for Northern Ireland* v. *Maxwell*. The simple fact that the blackmailing offence was carried out in pursuance of the main conspiracy would be insufficient. But cf. the notion of 'blank cheque', Ch. 6.

[142] See below, Ch. 3, 'Causation'.

[143] See particularly the account of the problematic evolutionary cycle of the conspiracy/complicity provision in Ostos-Irwin (1984) *Wis. LR* 769.

[144] See e.g. the proposed Draft US Federal Code, Working Papers, 156.

[145] Generally, J. C. Smith 'Secondary Participation and Inchoate Offences', in C. F. H. Tapper, ed., *Crime, Proof and Punishment* (1981), 21, to which I am indebted.

[146] *Clayton* (1843) 1 Car. & K. 128, 174 ER 743, *Hapgood and Wyatt* (1870) 11 Cox 471, and *Baker* (1909) 28 NZLR 536. The converse situation, attempting to be an 'accessory', is not criminal under the Criminal Attempts Act 1981, s. 1 (4) (*b*). *Dunnington* [1984] QB 472; cf. *Chief Constable of Hampshire* v. *Mace* (1986) 84 Cr. App. Rep. 40. Strong arguments may be deployed in favour of such liability; see e.g. J. R. Spencer, 'Trying to Help Another Person Commit a Crime', in P. F. Smith, ed., *Criminal Law: Essays in honour of J. C. Smith* (1989) 148. The Model Penal Code caters for two varieties of attempt liability relating to 'accessories': (i) where a principal crime takes place but, for some reason, the 'accessory' is causally completely ineffective in his would-be complicitous act; s. 2.06 (3) (*a*) (ii) confirms that such ineffectiveness still constitutes complicity; (ii) where the 'accessory' is effective but 'principal' offence is not even attempted then s. 5.O.1 (3) of the Code converts the action into a form of (principal) attempt. Cf. Macaulay's Indian Penal Code, s. 108, which made the latter type of

same way as an accessory may share in another's liability for a substantive offence, so also when the principal offence is of an inchoate nature, once its culpability elements are satisfied — there being, so to speak, substance in the 'complete' inchoate activity from which secondary liability may be derived. This is equally true of incitement[147] and conspiracy[148]. However, as already suggested, in the case of complicity in a conspiracy, complicitous actions will very often make the 'accessory' a principal party to the conspiracy. In settling the potential range of activities capable of constituting secondary but not principal participation in a conspiracy, the width ascribed to the meaning of 'agreement' in conspiracy assumes key importance. Therefore, if A, aware that P1 and P2 have agreed to carry out a robbery, expresses his warm approval of their plan, A although offering encouragement is hardly a principal party to the criminal agreement. Again, knowingly facilitating the concluding of an agreement by renting out a room to others should constitute complicity and not principal liability in the conspiracy.[149]

attempt abetting. Of course, liability for either form of attempted complicity dealt with by the Model Penal Code would be difficult to swallow linguistically so long as indifference as to the commission of the principal offence remains sufficient for accessorial liability under English law.

[147] It is likely that even after the Criminal Attempts Act 1981 there may be attempted incitement and, consequently, complicity in attempted incitement; see Williams, *Textbook*, 443. Incitement to attempt is incitement to commit the full offence. In English law it is an open question whether there can be incited complicity. Interpretational uncertainty surrounds the effects of the Criminal Law Act 1977, s. 30 (4), and the decisions in *Whitehouse* [1977] 1 QB 868 and *Bodin* [1979] Crim. LR 176. For the view that there is 'probably' no such liability see Smith, loc. cit., 29–30 and Smith and Hogan, *Criminal Law*, 255; and restated in Law Commission Report 177, cl. 47 (5). For the contrary case, see Williams, *Textbook*, 443–4. The policy issue is the desirability of extending back liability to activity which is two stages removed from the substantive offence. The acceptability of the practice, arguably, varies with the precise permutation of inchoate conduct involved; e.g., incitement or attempt to conspire no longer exists since the enactment of s. 5 (7) of the Criminal Law Act 1977, although conspiracy to incite does. In the case of incitement to be an accessory a similar question arises as to the desirability of criminalizing behaviour so far removed from the substantive offence. But, in addition, the liability of the *most* remote party is subject to an undesirable two-fold contingency: e.g. *I* incites *A* to sell safe-breaking equipment to *P*, both *I* and *A* being aware that *P* will use it in the course of a bank robbery. Here, *I*'s liability is contingent upon (*a*) *A* acting appropriately and (*b*) *P* at least attempting the robbery. If either (*a*) or (*b*) does not occur then *I* will be free of liability. If (*a*) and (*b*) do occur, *I*'s liability could be that of incitement to complicity (if such exists) or simply as an accessory to *P*'s offence. The latter possibility may well be open to challenge on the grounds of being too remote to satisfy causal needs in complicity (see Ch. 3 'Causation'). Incitement to incite is not subject to this double contingency delay before liability of *I* crystallizes.

[148] As with incitement to complicity, similarly with conspiracy to promote complicitous acts, English law lacks any authoritative ruling. In relation to statutory conspiracy, the House of Lords in *Hollinshead* [1985] AC 975 left open the point, but may have implicitly decided against such liability. See [1985] Crim. LR 653 at 656. The Court of Appeal in *Hollinshead* expressly ruled against conspiracy to promote complicity. *Po Koon-tai* [1980] HKLR 492 provides some support for the existence of such liability in the case of common law conspiracy. For the constructional difficulties with s. 1(1) of the Criminal Law Act 1977 see Smith and Hogan, *Criminal Law*, 265 and J. C. Smith, 'Secondary Participation', 40–1. *Hollinshead* is restated in Law Commission Report 177, cl. 48 (7) and commentary para. 13.34. Arguments against liability on the grounds of excessive remoteness and double contingency, suggested in respect of incitement to complicity, have similar relevance here.

[149] Cf. examples of Smith, loc. cit., 28–9, contrary Fletcher, cit. in n. 133.

3

Causation's Role in Complicity

In the theoretical overview of complicity the problematic nature and extent of the causal relationship between an accessory's actions and the principal offender or offence was seen as of central importance. Also noted to be of general relevance to causation's role were complicity's two most clearly enduring features: its derivative nature and equality of potential punishment for all parties, regardless of the exact form of their participation.

Following on from these brief introductory comments, it will be maintained here that non-causal explanations, either singularly or jointly, fail to produce an adequate theoretical account of complicity's derivative structure. Furthermore, it will be suggested that in specifying complicity's *actus reus* elements a causal requirement offers a combination of internal conceptual coherence and the most convincing analysis of complicity's relationship with other forms of criminality and general principles of criminal liability and punishment. In seeking to establish these propositions an account of equivocal English, Commonwealth, and American case law, along with other authority, will be followed by consideration of the theoretical credentials of causal and other apparently plausible rival explanatory models.

1. Case Law and Other Authorities

(1) *English Case Law*

English case law dealing with the issue of cause in secondary liability is distinctly thin on the ground, being largely restricted to a number of isolated and relatively recent judicial references which make no attempt to provide anything remotely approaching a thorough exposition of the subject. Such limited authority as there is offers both support for and opposition to the view that some causal requirement exists for all forms of complicity. This needs to be set alongside more recent judicial opinion in favour of a discriminatory approach between different modes, suggesting the need for cause only in 'procuring'; a consequence of determining the nature and scope of complicity by (mistakenly) resorting to the so-called 'natural meaning' of terms, rather than seeing them as conceptual expressions. These modal distinctions will be noted, but, as will be later maintained, whatever the mode of complicity the underlying question of causal relevance is the same.

Collingwood[1] is a rare early English authority implying that in complicity the instigated offence must be carried out in 'pursuance' of an accessory's instigation. The nineteenth-century cases of *Fretwell*[2] and *Benford* v. *Sims*[3] provide more support for a causal requirement. In the former, on a charge of complicity in murder, it was suggested that the 'acts of the procurer were too remote from the death to make him guilty of murder'.[4] Similarly, in *Benford* v. *Sims*, reference was also made to whether the accessory's actions were not too 'remote' to be a sufficiently 'proximate' cause of the principal offence.[5]

More recently, in *National Coal Board* v. *Gamble*,[6] Devlin J. seemed to see an accessory's causal contribution as a *sine qua non* of the commission of the principal offence: 'A person who supplies the instrument for a crime or anything [else] *essential* to its commission aids in the commission of it, and if he does so knowingly and with intent to aid he abets it' (emphasis added). Though open to other constructions, reference to 'essential' could be taken to suggest that a prerequisite of liability by assistance is the provision of aid without which the principal offence would not have occurred when or in the actual manner it did.

In *Anderson and Morris*,[7] when discussing an accessory's liability for a principal's actions which had gone beyond the parties' common purpose, Lord Parker CJ saw the matter as also having a causal complexion, rather than being just a problem of *mens rea*:

Considered as a matter of causation there may well be an overwhelming supervening event which is of such a character that it will relegate into history matters which would otherwise be looked upon as causative factors. ('Matters' here meaning the accessory's actions.)[8]

---

[1] (1705) 6 Mod. Rep. 288, 87 ER 1029, 1030.
[2] (1862) Le. & Ca. 161, 169 ER 1345.
[3] [1898] 2 QBD 641, Cf. *Barker* (1844) 1 Car. & K. 442; 174 ER 884.
[4] Martin B., 169 ER 1347.
[5] In *De Marny* [1907] 1 KB 388, a newspaper editor was charged with 'causing and procuring' obscene materials to be sold by having authorized facilitatory advertisements in his newspaper. Defence counsel argued that though the advertisements assisted the sales they were 'legally too remote from the commission of the offence' to constitute complicity (390). Lord Alverstone CJ for the CCCR felt able to affirm the conviction on the basis of the advertisements having 'brought about' the sale of obscene publications (391).
[6] [1959] 1 QB 11, 20. Cf. Slade J. at 25–6. Cited with approval by Lord Simon in *Lynch* v. *DPP for N. Ireland* [1976] AC 563, 598.
[7] [1966] 2 QB 110, 120. See also *Quick* [1973] QB 910, 912, and 914; and Lords Morris and Diplock in *DPP* v. *Merriman* [1973] AC 584, 592, and 607.
[8] This approach was also expressly applied by the Court of Appeal in *Reid* (1976) 62 Cr. App. Rep. 109, 112. See the very similar test laid down by Lord Parker on matters of cause in the non-complicity case of *Smith* [1959] 2 QB 35, 42–3; and also *Penfold* (1979) 71 Cr. App. Rep. 4, where the certified point of appeal framed by the Court of Appeal included reference to 'supervening causative events'.

Although not completely unambiguous, the burden of these comments is reasonably clear: actions performed by the principal in furtherance of the common purpose incriminate the accessory because his association with the principal is a cause of or a reason for the principal's conduct or its criminal consequences. If this causal relationship were not essential it would be a logical irrelevance to exculpate the accessory on the grounds of lack of causation where the principal acted beyond the scope of the common purpose. Three years after *Anderson and Morris*, Lord Parker returned to the issue of cause in the context of instigation. In *Assistant Recorder of Kingston-upon-Hull ex p. Morgan*,[9] when distinguishing the offence of incitement from complicity, he observed:

It is of the essence of the offence established by counselling procuring or commanding *that as a result* of the counselling, procuring or commanding, something should have happened which constituted either the full offence or the attempt... [Emphasis added.]

Rather more equivocal are comments in *Attorney-General v. Able*,[10] a case involving complicity in suicide through the provision of information on suicide techniques. Addressing the question of the necessary connection between a booklet detailing methods of suicide and a recipient's use of it, Woolf J. remarked that it did not have to be shown that the suicide (or attempt) 'would not have occurred but for the booklet'. However, it would not be enough if the booklet 'has nothing to do with the suicide', as for example where a 'long period of time may have elapsed between sending the booklet and the attempt'. And, in contrast with 'procure', 'the same close causal connection is not required when what is being done is the provision of assistance'.[11] It is not easy to follow why a lapse of time should prevent liability if the information provided is still employed by the suicide. However, the nature of the necessary connection envisaged appears to have been less than a *sine qua non* cause but something which 'assisted or encouraged' the suicide.

---

[9] [1969] 2 QB 58, 62. When considering the justification for the offence of incitement the Law Commission Working Party seemed to take as self-evident the need for a causal connection between instigation and principal action in complicity; see Working Paper 50 (1973), para. 94. Rather bafflingly the Court of Appeal in *Calhaem* [1985] 2 All ER 266, 271, saw the comments in *ex p. Morgan* as unhelpful when considering the need for cause in 'counselling'. This was so, it was said in the court's view, because it was used in the company of 'procuring or counselling'. But it appears clear that Lord Parker intended the causal requirement to apply to each of the three terms; indirectly confirmed by his comments in *Anderson and Morris*, see Ch. 8. Similarly unconvincing was the attempt in *Calhaem* (at 270) to deny any value in comments from *Croft* [1944] KB 295, 297–8, which seemed to suggest the need for a causal contribution in suicide pacts.

[10] [1984] QB 795. Although concerned with the substantive offence of abetting suicide under s. 2 (1) of the Suicide Act 1961, the general principles of complicity were used to fix the ingredients of the offence. Similarly in connection with 'procuring' under s. 20 of the Theft Act 1968 in *Beck* [1985] 1 All ER 571.

[11] [1984] QB 795 at 812.

The special causal connotation attributed to 'procure' follows from the Court of Appeal's judgment in *Attorney-General's Reference (No. 1 of 1975).*[12] Here the accessory's liability was based on his having surreptitiously 'laced' the drink of a friend who later drove with an excessive blood/alcohol level as a consequence of the lacing. The accessory was held to have procured the driving offence, it being Lord Widgery's view that, giving 'procure' its 'ordinary meaning', 'you cannot procure an offence unless there is a causal link between what you do and the commission of the offence'. Such a causal link apparently occurs when an effect is 'produce[d] by endeavour.[13] You procure a thing by setting out to see that it happens and taking appropriate steps to produce that happening.'[14] Some incompletely formed notion of control or manipulation may well have been in Lord Widgery's mind, otherwise the simple producing-of-an-effect-by-endeavour test would cover many examples of assistance or instigation. Much the same view of 'procuring' appears in the reasoning of *Beck*[15] which involved the substantive offence of procuring the execution of a 'valuable security' by deception. When construing 'procure' the Court of Appeal expressly followed Lord Widgery's *dicta*, emphasizing that the defendant had 'by his dishonesty set off a chain of events with inevitable consequences'. Apparently vital features of this 'inevitable' process were the issuing bank's and the credit card agency's 'obligations' 'to pay for their valuable securities'; they had 'no alternative for legal and/or commercial reasons'.[16]

The implied manipulative or controlling nature of 'procure' also appeared to be in Lawton LJ's mind in *Cogan*:

The act of sexual intercourse without the wife's consent was the actus reus; it had been procured by Leak who had the appropriate mens rea, namely his intention that Cogan should have sexual intercourse with her without her consent. In our judgment it is irrelevant that the man whom Leak had procured to do the physical act himself did not intend to have sexual intercourse with the wife without her consent. Leak was using him as the means to procure a criminal purpose.[17]

Here, as will be seen, the court suggested that Leak was capable of being convicted either as an accessory or as a principal through Cogan's innocent agency, a doctrine by which causal responsibility for another's actions or their consequences is attributed to the non-perpetrator.

---

[12] [1975] QB 773. *Bentley* v. *Mullen* [1986] RTR 7 is a further example of complicity in a road traffic offence produced by giving complicity terms their 'natural meaning'.

[13] Cf. the tort of interference with contractual rights where the defendant *induces* a contractual party to break the contract. According to Morris LJ to 'Bring about or procure or induce a breach', *Thomas* v. *Deakin* [1952] Ch. 646, 702.

[14] [1975] QB 773, 780, and 779. Cf. the use of 'procuring' in *Russell*, 3rd edn. by Greaves. Here the term is used as apposite to cases where the procurer uses an intermediate party to instigate the ultimate perpetrator of an offence (32).

[15] [1985] 1 All ER 571.

[16] Ibid. 576. Cf. *Lomas* (1913) 9 Cr. App. Rep. 220; see below, Part II.

[17] [1975] 2 All ER 1059, 1062.

However, neither an inevitable cause and effect nor manipulation rationale is employed in *Broadfoot* or *Reed*,[18] two further decisions considering the meaning of 'procure'. Though purporting to apply the Widgery *dicta*, both cases suggest that the causal requirement is satisfied by instigation or the provision of means. Both judgments also emphasize the 'produced by endeavour' element as being central to 'procure', indicating that the distinction between procure and other forms of complicity may, in the court's mind, be more in the area of *mens rea* than *actus reus*.[19] Although this cluster of authorities sees cause as an essential feature of 'procure', beyond requiring 'endeavour' it is impossible to be reasonably sure what other element is necessary. Except in *Attorney-General* v. *Able*,[20] the judgments make no clear allusion to whether the accessory's actions need to be a *sine qua non* (or less) of the principal offence.

Overall, according a special meaning to 'procure' by setting down additional requirements attracts objections on two fronts. First, rather than any substantive distinction, the 'produced by endeavour' formula involves no more than a particular form of encouragement or assisting where, linguistically, 'procure' is the most appropriate verb — as in *Attorney-General's Reference* where to say the accessory 'aided' the principal by clandestinely 'lacing' his drink would be inapposite.[21] Secondly, giving special causal status to 'procure', because of the term's manipulative connotation, generates additional conceptual difficulties when attempting to distinguish innocent agency liability from complicity (see Chapter 4).

Aside from the position of 'procuring', in *Calhaem*[22] the Court of Appeal came closer than any previous English court to a full consideration of whether 'counsel' requires a causal connection between the act of counselling and the principal's action. *Calhaem* involved a very strong form of counselling in that the defendant had hired Zajac, a private detective, to kill R. Zajac claimed that he had visited R with the intention of faking an attempted murder, but that R's reaction had completely unnerved him and

---

[18] [1976] 3 All ER 753; [1982] Crim. LR 819 respectively.

[19] See below, Ch. 5. If a procurer must both act with the purpose of bringing about the principal offence *and* be a 'cause' of its commission then the distinction between principal and secondary parties would need further refinement. The distinction is maintained in Law Commission Report 177, cl. 17 (3), by declaring that a 'person who procures, assists or encourages another to cause a result that is an element of an offence' does not cause the result so as to make him a principal, unless within an excepted category. On the general question of distinguishing parties if cause is taken as a necessary element of complicity, see below, 3 (*a*) 'Principal and Accessory Distinction'.

[20] Cf. Woolf J. in *Gillick* v. *West Norfolk and Wisbech AHA* [1984] QB 581, who noted when considering whether a doctor prescribing contraceptive pills to an under-age woman could be an accessory to unlawful sexual intercourse (590): 'I would regard the pill prescribed to the woman as not so much "the instrument for a crime or anything *essential* to its commission" but a palliative against the consequences of the crime' (emphasis added).

[21] Cf. the 'Othello situation' where Iago's objective is hidden and not comfortably describable as 'encouragement' or 'instigation'; see Ch. 2 n. 71.

[22] [1985] 2 All ER 266.

in this state he had fatally attacked her. Calhaem appealed against a conviction for complicity in R's murder on the grounds that counselling required a 'substantial causal connection between the acts of the secondary offender and the commission of the offence and . . . on [Zajac's] evidence there was no causal connection, or at any rate no substantial causal connection'.[23]

After declaring the 'point . . . a novel one, on which there is no direct authority', the court adopted the general course established in *Attorney-General's Reference (No. 1 of 1975)* and gave 'counsel its ordinary meaning' which is

'advise', 'solicit', or something of that sort. There is no implication in the word itself that there should be any causal connection between counselling and the offence. [However] there must clearly be, first, contact between the parties, and, second, a connection between the counselling and the murder . . .[24] So long as there is counselling . . . so long as the principal offence is committed by the one counselled and so long as the one counselled is acting within the scope of his authority . . . we are of the view that the offence is made out.[25]

Although resisting easy comprehension, the judgment appears to suggest that it is sufficient if the principal's actions *coincided* with what was counselled. This seems to be the extent of the 'connection' spoken of by the court. By implication, if, for some other reason, Zajac had already been minded to visit R and carry out similar actions, Calhaem would still have been a party, the demonstrably superfluous character of the communicated act of counselling being immaterial to secondary responsibility. The principal must simply act 'within the scope of his authority', and apparently not in any way *because* of it. However, on the facts and the evidence the Court of Appeal regarded the particular counselling, in any case, as constituting a 'substantial cause of the death',[26] and therefore even sufficient for procuring. As will be seen, this final point is not without significance in relation to the meaning of 'cause' in complicity, for it implicitly admits that there is no conceptual obstacle to accepting that the informed voluntary actions of a principal can be regarded as 'caused',[27] as is also implied by at least most authorities on the meaning of 'procure'.

---

[23] The last phrase was probably intended to meet the possible argument that if the defendant had not originally hired Zajac, he would not have gone to R's home, even to fake a murder attempt. In other words, that the defendant's actions were too remote from R's death.

[24] [1985] 2 All ER at 269.

[25] Ibid. at 272; expressly following Smith and Hogan, *Criminal Law*, p. 122, and Williams, *CLGP* 381.

[26] [1985] 2 All ER at 268.

[27] The court did not demur from the trial judge's definition of 'procure': to 'set in train a series of events which she intended would produce the death of Mrs. Rendell and that Mrs. Rendell was killed as a result, in the sense that her actions were a substantial cause of the death' (ibid.).

(2) Institutional Authorities

Beyond conflicting case law exist a few scattered observations from established authorities on the relevance of cause to complicity.

Foster's[28] treatise on accessories appears to imply that proof of cause is a necessary ingredient of complicity, at least in cases of encouragement. When discussing the problem of a principal's variation from that counselled by the accessory, Foster contrasts liability for criminal conduct within the confines of the accessory's instigation with that which was 'no more than a fruitless ineffectual temptation [and therefore] the fact cannot with any propriety be said to have been committed under the influence of that temptation'. Similarly, Stephen also asserts that one 'who counsels, commands or procures any person to commit [an offence is liable only for that] which is committed in consequence of such counselling, procuring or commandment'.[29] However, as with Foster, no reference is made to the position of 'aid' and 'abet'.

(3) Foreign Authorities

The question has also received judicial attention outside England[30] in other common law based (or influenced) jurisdictions. This has been most notably so in the South African courts, which, after initially flirting with notions of ratification or authorization, have turned towards openly recognizing a causal requirement.[31] But, as recent appellate decisions such as *S* v.

---

[28] *Crown Law*, 369. Cf. Hawkins, *PC* ii, ch. 29, s. 16, and *Co. Inst.* iii. 169.

[29] J. F. Stephen *Digest of the Criminal Law* (1877), ed. L. F. Sturge (1950), art. 39 and art. 18. Turner in successive edns. of *Kenny* and *Russell*, only succeeds in muddying the waters—appearing to base aiding and abetting on neither consensus nor cause, and instigation on some indistinct form of effective encouragement. For aiding and abetting see the similar examples used by Turner in *Kenny's Outlines of Criminal Law*, 18th edn. (1962), 23, and *Russell on Crime*, 12th ed. (1964), i. 31. In this case of counselling or instigation Turner initially seemed to dismiss any requirement of effective encouragement, but later moved without explanation to recognition of the need for it: compare the 10th edn. (1950), 1867, and 11th edn. (1958), 161, of *Russell*. See also Williams, *CLGP* 382. For punishment purposes, Macaulay's Indian Penal Code makes a point of distinguishing cases where the accessory's actions causally contribute to the occurrence of the principal offence from when they do not. See arts. 108, 109, and 115, *Anglo-Indian Codes* (1887), ed. Stokes, i, ch. v.

[30] Gordon suggests 'it must be shown that the instigation was such as to be capable of influencing the perpetrator, and that it did in fact influence him . . . If [the crime] was committed independently of the suggestion or inducement, there is no connection between the instigation and the crime, and so no art and part guilt': *Criminal Law of Scotland*, 140. Cf. *Little* v. *HMA* 1983 SCCR 56.

[31] In respect of ratification, see particularly Schreiner JA in *Mgxwitti* 1954 (1) SA (AD) 383. Also in *Mneke* 1961 (2) SA 240 (N). For a discussion of the South African controversy on complicity and causation see Burchell and Hunt, *SA Criminal Law*, i. 421–4, and Snyman, *Criminal Law*, 213–14.

Williams[32] and *S v. Safatsa*,[33] well demonstrate, a sizeable division in both judicial and academic opinion remains over the precise nature of the causal element and when it is necessary.

Conflicting attitudes also emerge from the limited number of Commonwealth authorities. For example, the Victorian case of *Howell v. Doyle*[34] expressly denies the need for demonstrated causality. An opposing view is found in the South Australian decision of *Lenzi v. Millar*[35] where it was noted that between the accessory's actions and the principal offence 'a nexus sufficient in character and degree' must be shown which is not 'too tenuous because it is too remote in the chain of causation'.

American case law reveals similar divisions on the question of cause, both between states and within states, although the predominant opinion is hostile to any requirement. For example, in *Breaz v. State*[36] the court stipulated 'it is necessary that there be an immediate causal connection between instigation and the [principal's] act'. Against this view are cases such as *State v. Tally*[37] where courts have emphatically denied any need to demonstrate cause and effect between the accessory's and the principal's actions or their consequences.

[32] 1980 (1) SA 60 (A) 63. 'According to general principles there must be a causal connection between the accomplice's assistance and the commission of the crime by the perpetrator': Joubert JA, trans. cited by Burchell and Hunt, *SA Criminal Law*, 415. And also *S. v. Khoza* 1982 (3) SA 1019 (A) and *S. v. Maxaba* 1981 (1) SA 1148 (A).

[33] 1988 (1) SA 868 (A) affirmed in *S. v. Mgedezi* 1989 (1) SA 687. *Safatsa* restricts the need for a causal contribution to complicity cases where there is no common purpose. In common purpose situations, besides the necessary *mens rea*, cause is 'imputed' so long as there has been 'active association' by the accessory: *Safatsa*, at 901, *Mgedezi*, at 705–6. These two decisions leave unsettled quite what constitutes 'common purpose' and 'active association'. See discussions of N. A. Matzukis, 'The Nature and Scope of Common Purpose' (1988) 2 *SACJ* 226, and D. Unterhalter, 'The Doctrine of Common Purpose' (1988) 105 *SALJ* 671. On the general problem of group complicity see below, s. 2 (3) (b).

[34] [1952] VLR 128, 134. See also *O'Sullivan v. Truth and Sportsman* (1957) 96 CLR 220.

[35] [1965] SASR 1, 14. On the Australian code provisions see Gillies, *Criminal Complicity*. In the Canadian case of *McNulty* (1910) 17 CCC 26 it was noted that there could be no complicity if the defendant's 'counsel had in fact no effect in inducing the actual perpetration'. Liability required it to be shown 'by inference or otherwise, that counsel had some effect in bringing [the crime] about, as well as some motive for [the perpetrator's] conduct'(34). See also *Deutsch* (1983) 5 CCC (3d) 41 — no liability if the incitement was clearly unsuccessful.

[36] 13 NE 2d 952 (1938) 953. See also *McGhee v. Comm.* 270 SE 2d 733 (1980); *Workman v. State* 21 NE 2d 712 (1939); *State v. Bass* 120 SE 2d 580 (1961) 586–7; *State v. Tazwell* 30 La. Ann. 844 (1878). Perkins, Criminal Law, 740, notes 'Guilt or innocence of the abettor is not determined by the quantum of his advice or encouragement. If it is rendered to induce another to commit the crime *and actually has this effect*, no more is required' (emphasis added), citing *People v. Washburn* 280 NW 132 (1938) and *State v. Rollie* 585 SW 2d 78 (1979).

[37] 102 Ala 25 (1894). According to the court 'the assistance given, however, need not contribute to the criminal result in the sense that but for it the result would not have ensued. It is quite sufficient if it facilitated a result that would have transpired without it. It is quite enough if the aid merely renders it easier for the principal actor to accomplish the end intended by him and the aider and abettor, though in all human probability the end would have been attained without it. If the aid in homicide can be shown to have put the deceased at a disadvantage, to have deprived him of a single chance of life, which but for it he would have had, he who furnishes such aid is guilty though it can not be known or shown that the dead man, in the absence thereof, would have availed himself of that chance. More recently see e.g.

(4) The Paucity of Case Law

As weighty negative evidence against the general need for cause in all modes of complicity it has been argued that 'if it were incumbent on the prosecution to prove that the offence would not have been committed but for . . . encouragement [or aiding] it seems safe to say that the point would figure much more prominently in the law reports'.[38] This argument carries some force. Providing a plausible explanation of why a causal requirement, if existing, has received such scant attention is not easy. However, a number of possibly decisive factors can be put forward as having combined to produce this state of affairs.

Of considerable relevance is the existence and operation of the so-called 'common purpose' doctrine under which each party in a criminal venture will be liable as an accessory to the agreed or anticipated acts of others carried out in pursuance of the common design. The broadness of concept and imprecision of the doctrine's language, certainly until relatively recently, have obscured and perhaps obviated the need for direct reference to the question of causality. Typical examples of these characteristics are found in the nineteenth-century reports of *Macklin*[39] and *Harrington*.[40] Such decisions go little beyond simply declaring that 'every act done . . . by each of them is, in law, done by all'. Not only the terminology of the doctrine of common purpose but also the usual brevity of reports, coupled with the factual circumstances of cases (which generally indicate the presence of a causal contribution from the accessory), would have removed much of the need to refer expressly to such a causal requirement. Moreover, unlike most modern decisions,[41] earlier authorities are capable of being construed in a way which suggests that once a common illegal purpose was found then that constituted the accessory's *actus reus*; consequently, there would be no need to prove a distinct causal contribution from the accessory.

Secondly, as a matter of prosecutorial policy, it could be expected that those cases where the effect of an alleged secondary party's activities was not reasonably clear (or could not be easily assumed) were least likely to be prosecuted; again reducing the possible occasions when causal questions are likely to surface at trial.

Finally, also relevant to the lack of prominence of causal issues in the

---

Comm. v. *Flowers* 387 A. 2d 1268 (1978) 1271, and *State* v. *Gelb* 515 A. 2d 1246 (1986) citing at 1252 the comment of the New Jersey Code's Revision Committee that the complicity provisions dealt with enhancing 'the probability that another will commit a crime'.

[38] J. C. Smith, 'Aid, Abet, Counsel, or Procure', 120, 133.

[39] (1838) 2 Lew. 225, 168 ER 1136. If *A* joins in an existing agreed upon common purpose between other parties, then, as in all cases of multi-secondary party complicity, there may be considerable problems in attribution of causal contribution and causal superfluousness of any particular party's actions. And see further below.

[40] (1815) 5 Cox 231.

[41] e.g. *Anderson and Morris* [1966] 2 QB 110 and *Chan Wing-Siu* v. *R* [1984] 3 All ER 877, and below, Ch. 8.

mass of the reported decisions is the embarrassing intractability of evidential problems involving proof of cause in many common complicity situations, something likely to have operated as a strong disincentive against judicial probing into the question of causality.[42] These evidential problems and how they may have been accommodated by courts are discussed in the last sub-section of this chapter.

2. Theoretical Possibilities

Seeking the most internally and externally convincing account of the link between an accessory's and principal's actions forces a return to the basic premises on which criminal responsibility is reckoned to be constructed — in so far as anything approaching a consensus or recognizably predominant view exists on such matters. Perhaps more than any other form of criminality, complicitous activity raises, in large measures and in complex combinations, questions relating to practically every aspect and stage of the imposition of criminal liability, most particularly: the moral basis of responsibility, with in-built issues concerning freedom of choice of action; the acceptability and operation of chance and risk; the meaning of 'cause'; the nature and legitimate function of harm or wrongdoing; the relevance and relationship of such issues to the justifying aims of punishment.

To this list must be added the obvious qualification that even though logical or moral coherency may indicate a preference for one or other theoretical explanation, distinct and larger overriding policy considerations may, ultimately, win the day. Furthermore, analysis of any of complicity's distinct *mens rea* and *actus reus* elements needs to be carried out within the complete framework of responsibility demands: each being permeated with or informed by the requirements and justifying philosophies of the others. Attempting to examine and weigh the significance of any single constituent of liability completely abstracted from the company of co-requirements is to invite distorted perceptions and misleading conclusions.

(1) *Preliminary Premises*

(a) *Choice and Chance in Criminal Responsibility* The paradigm of criminal responsibility might be said to entail the free acting and fully informed agent choosing[43] either to behave in a proscribed way or to bring about an

---

[42] Cf. e.g. Lord Coleridge CJ in *Coney* (1882) 8 QBD 534, at 569.
[43] See e.g. H. L. A. Hart, *Punishment and Responsibility* (1968), ch. 1; Kadish 'Complicity, Cause and Blame', 330; and A. J. Ashworth, 'Belief, Intent, and Criminal Liability', in J. S. Bell and J. M. Eekelaar, eds., *Oxford Essays in Jurisprudence* (1987), 1, 2, and 13. Cf. Moore, 'Causation and Excuses' (1985) *Cal. LR* 1091, 1148; similarly Hart and Honoré, *Causation*, 41, defining voluntariness.

unlawful state of affairs. Departures from this model generate expectations of compensatory justifications; the greater the departure, as for instance with strict liability, the stronger the expectation and the more convincing an explanation is expected. For offences with proscribed results as part of the *actus reus* the contingencies of chance and cause reduce, to a greater or lesser degree, an actor's ability to exercise control over the incurring of responsibility. Whether the defendant who shot another will face a charge of wounding or some form of homicide will turn on his mental culpability and the outcome of the shooting,[44] the latter possibly depending on the victim's robustness and the skills of his surgeon.

Opportunities for chance to play a significant role in determining responsibility are boosted where, as in complicity, one party's liability turns on the uncontrollable and unpredictable behaviour of another. Indeed, in complicity pure chance may settle the potential accessory's fate at several stages: it may prevent the encouragement or assistance even reaching the principal; for some reason the principal may manifestly reject it; the 'principal' may initially accept it but later decide to abandon the whole venture; he may fail in trying to carry out the principal offence, or in some way deviate from the course hoped for or expected by the 'accessory'. Chance's unrivalled potential in complicity's incriminating mechanism can be either reduced or aggravated by culpability demands: if the intentional or purposeful bringing about of an offence is a requirement of liability (as, for example, in complicity in most American jurisdictions) the extensiveness of the role which chance may play will be less than where knowledge or subjective recklessness suffices (as is probably the case in English law). This relationship of *actus reus* and *mens rea* needs to be borne in mind when considering any feature of either of these two major elements of complicity; something which runs true throughout criminal liability.

The broader question posed by considerations of an actor's ability to exercise control over the determining factors of his criminality is whether the thread of responsibility linking the accessory with the principal's *actus reus* may be too finely spun to be regarded as a morally satisfactory basis for imposing criminal liability: although chance does play a frequent and substantial role in ascribing criminal responsibility, there is a stage at which it assumes too great a part to be acceptable in the process of settling liability. In such cases there is a pronounced risk of detaching liability from that aspect of the moral basis of responsibility represented by the requirement of freely chosen and informed actions and properly attributable results.[45]

[44] See J. C. Smith, 'The Element of Chance in Criminal Liability' [1971] Crim. LR 63.

[45] In one sense the role of chance in criminal responsibility undeniably extends back to preliminary matters including capacity and opportunity to act. On this see T. Nagel, 'Moral Luck' (1976) 50 *Proc. of the Aristotelian Soc.* supp. 137. However, recognizing this is not to accept that chance should be given a completely free run in fixing criminal liability. Arguments favouring its restricted role are necessarily relativistic, but not invalid because of this. Cf. the exchange between Professors Moore, Ashworth, and Greenawalt to this effect. 'Model Penal Code Conference Transcript—Discussion Four' (1987) reproduced in (1988) 19 *Rut. LJ* 797-8.

Objections of this nature tend to suggest resort to either inchoate or risk/endangerment rationales as a preferable or more defensible basis of liability. These matters will be addressed later.

(b) The Problematic Meaning of 'Cause' Settling responsibility for offences which incorporate a harm element in the form of a specified result or consequence necessarily draws on notions of causal attribution. If the alleged principal cannot be said to have 'caused' the result he will at least be free of full responsibility. In criminal law when determining principal liability both factual and legal cause must be established. To be a factual cause the conduct must be a *sine qua non* of the result. To be legally imputable such a factual cause must be reasonably 'proximate'. However, there is no universally accepted formula which may be applied to determine proximity.[46] A succinct compression of English general principles, so far as they exist, appears in the Law Commission Draft Criminal Code Bill:

A person causes a result which is an element of an offence when — he does an act which makes a more than negligible contribution to its occurrence; A person does not cause a result where, after he does such an act . . . , an act or event occurs — (a) which is the immediate and sufficient cause of the result; (b) which he could not foresee, and (c) which could not in the circumstances reasonably have been foreseen.[47]

---

[46] For accounts of the causal issues raised by criminal law see e.g. Williams, *Textbook*, ch. 16, and an American view in La Fave and Scott, *Criminal Law*, 277–301.

[47] Report 177, cl. 17 (1) and (2), and commentary at paras. 7.14–22. See critical comments of G. L. Williams, 'Finis for *Novus Actus*?' (1989) CLJ 391. Complicity doctrine relies on the *novus actus* principle in the sense that the principal's (so to speak, *novus actus*) role, rather than eliminating the secondary party from causal attribution changes the nature of it from a direct to an indirect causal contribution. To maintain, in causal terms at least, the distinction between principals and accessories (and so eliminate any concession to a unified structure of participation) cl. 17 (3) provides: 'A person who procures, assists or encourages another to cause a result that is an element of an offence does not himself cause that result so as to be guilty of the offence as a principal except when — (a) [the other is his innocent agent], or (b) the offence consists in the procuring, assisting or encouraging another to cause the result.' More concise than the *general* English Law Commission's provisions under cl. 17 (1) and (2) is the Canadian Law Commission's Report 31 (s. 2 (6)): 'Everyone causes a result when his conduct substantially contributes to its occurrence and no other unforeseen and unforeseeable cause supersedes it.' Cf. the Model Penal Code's expansive proposal; s. 2.03 provides: '(1) Conduct is the cause of a result when: (a) it is an antecedent but for which the result in question would not have occurred; and (b) the relationship between the conduct and the result satisfies any additional causal requirements imposed by the Code or by the law defining the offence. (2) When purposely or knowingly causing a particular result is an element of an offense, the element is not established if the actual result is not within the purpose or the contemplation of the actor unless: (a) the actual result differs from that designed or contemplated, as the case may be, only in the respect that a different person or different property is injured or affected or that the injury or harm designed or contemplated would have been more serious or more extensive than that caused; or (b) the actual result involves the same kind of injury or harm as that designed or contemplated and is not too remote or accidental in its occurrence to have a

Crucially neither this nor any other general formulation attempts to elaborate the extent to which human actions may be treated as intermediate causal agencies capable of receiving and transmitting the causal impulse or force of another's actions without relieving that other person of causal responsibility for any ultimate result. The relevance and importance of this to complicity is readily apparent: if one culpable party can intelligibly be said to have 'caused' another culpable party's actions, then such actions and any consequences may be attributable to the first party in a fashion which (amongst other things) supports equality of eligibility for punishment.

Causal conclusions of this order do have, for example, clear implications for both the derivative basis of complicity and *mens rea* requirements. If an accessory can be said to be capable of 'causing' the principal's criminal actions then, without some method of qualitatively or quantitatively distinguishing the parties' causal roles, complicity's derivative basis assumes a rather hollow guise, for attributing cause of the substantive offence's *actus reus* to the accessory would appear largely to eliminate any claimed dependency. In respect of *mens rea*, one explanation for limiting complicity to the accessory's intended actions is that the wider range of principal culpability (from purposive acts to strictly liable ones) is more acceptable if an actor has caused a proscribed result. The grounds for pegging the minimum culpability level of complicity to intended accessorial actions become vulnerable (or at least weakened) if cause is also ascribable to an accessory.[48] For these and other reasons considered later, the nature of causal attribution in relation to 'interpersonal transactions'[49] requires further exploration.

Broadly, common law complicity rests on some indistinct notion that identifies as the perpetrator or principal the party most immediately connected with bringing about the substantive offence's *actus reus*. What is

just bearing on the actor's liability or on the gravity of his offence'. Possible limitations or inadequacies of these code provisions will only be considered in so far as they relate to complicity.

[48] Although for 'procuring', where English courts have expressly recognized the need for causality, there is a reversal of this logic in that 'procure' is said to require 'endeavour', a higher culpability level than other modes of complicity. This may be trying to meet the risk of undesirably wide-ranging liability flowing from lawful behaviour which incidentally 'causes' an offence. Williams cites the breach of the peace case of *Beatty* v. *Gilbanks* ((1882) 9 QBD 308) as authority for the proposition that a person is not a party to a crime merely by causing it without 'designing to bring about a crime or helping another to commit a crime': *Textbook*, 338–9, and (1989) *CLJ* 394 and 401. *Beatty* v. *Gilbanks* involved lawful action carried out with the foresight that it might provoke or provide an excuse for an unlawful reaction. Clearly the line between giving the (principal) other party the means for committing an offence and the *opportunity* to do so (as in *Beatty* v. *Gilbanks*) can be very fine and difficult to draw. How different in terms of fault and cause is lawfully marching, with the expection of provoking an unlawful attack, from the case of a retailer, otherwise lawfully selling a gun, aware of its possible use for wounding? And cf. the *Miller* 'supervening fault' principle of causing a result without initial fault. (Restated in Report 177, cl. 23.)

[49] Used by Hart and Honoré, *Causation*, 51–2.

it in this notion that distinguishes principals from accessories? In approaching this question an almost inevitable starting-point is Hart and Honoré's treatise on legal causation, whose expressed guiding principle of exposition is 'the delineation of the causal concepts which pervade ordinary thought'.[50] Pertinent to present purposes is their belief in the 'special place' which voluntary[51] human action has in causal enquiries:

> A deliberate human act is . . . most often a barrier and a goal in tracing back causes . . . it is often something *through* which we do not trace the cause of a later event and something *to* which we do trace the cause through intervening causes of other kinds. In these respects a human action which is not voluntary is on a par with other abnormal occurrences: sometimes but not always we trace causes through them, and sometimes but not always we trace effects to them through other causes.[52]

Therefore in the 'field of relationship between two human actions we have to deal with the concept of *reasons* for action rather than *causes* of events . . .'[53]

Distinctions can certainly be drawn between bringing about an event by the 'invariable and unconditional sequence'[54] of direct physical causes and complicity where the human agency of the principal is interposed between the accessory and the proscribed event or consequence. For instance, in a given set of circumstances gravity ensures that when a car's handbrake is released the car will run down hill; whereas if A offers P a large sum of money to assassinate V, P may or may not oblige. In the latter case, unlike the former, there is no invariable or regular sequence of one event following another. It is also undeniable that human action *is* viewed differently from physical actions and reaction.[55] What is disputable is whether the distinction is of a nature and order such as to justify the categorization advocated by Hart and Honoré or the denial of *any* sort of comprehensible causal attribution to secondary parties. In confining the range of observations to matters of clearest relevance to complicity, at least four difficulties arise.

First, why do voluntary human actions, because they are 'logically independent of generalisation', warrant a separate and special status? Whether an agent is 'voluntary' or 'involuntary' his actions are still not

---

[50] Ibid. 2.

[51] When the agent is 'placed in circumstances which give him a fair opportunity to exercise normal mental and physical powers and he does exercise them without pressure from others': ibid. 41 n. 12. For consideration of some general philosophical problems raised by this view see P. Foot, 'Review' (1963) 72 *Phil.* 505, 514, and J. H. Mansfield, 'Causation in the Law—A Comment' (1963) 17 *Van. LR* 487, 510–14.

[52] See n. 44.

[53] See n. 51, continuing: 'yet there are many transitional cases for, while the contrast between these concepts is important, it shades off in many directions'. See Edwards, *Mens Rea*, ch. 6 for support through a study of judgments in statutory offences and the interpretation of 'cause' in such offences.

[54] J. S. Mill, *A System of Logic Ratiocinative and Inductive* (1843), bk. 3, ch. 5.

[55] Kadish, 'Complicity, Cause and Blame', 334.

subject to an invariable sequence. On this basis even 'involuntary' actions ought not to be regarded as capable of being caused. This, though, is contrary to the usual explanation of the doctrine of innocent agency.

Secondly, although the general run of imaginable cases supports Hart and Honoré's thesis, it is possible to construct counter-examples where actions, while voluntary within the meaning accorded by Hart and Honoré, are in 'common speech' reasonably describable as 'caused' by another. Such counter-examples are constructed largely on the basis of one party making use of or manipulating another party's predictable but still voluntary reactions—the Iago stratagem.[56] In these cases the manipulating party is able to 'trigger' a voluntary response in another.[57] Moreover, as has been seen, the attributes given by English courts to 'procure' in complicity reinforces the credentials of such examples.

Thirdly, much of the limited case law support employed by Hart and Honoré is equivocal[58] in that it is open to alternative interpretations antithetical to a voluntary intervention principle. Looking at human interventions in general, they are less foreseeable or predictable than the course of natural events and, consequently, more likely to be recognized as a cut-off point in the process of causal attribution. Further, it would be reasonable to expect this effect to be consolidated by the natural inclination of courts to seek a responsible party to whom blame may be attached. Causally exonerating the original actor (or changing the nature of his causal contribution) may be a more attractive proposition if the *novus actus*

---

[56] The truth or otherwise of his allegations is immaterial; the perpetrator's emotions in both cases were manipulated to a particular end. Cf. K. Greenawalt 'A Vice of its Virtues' (1988) 19 *Rut. LJ* 929, 942–3. See above, Ch. 2.

[57] See D. Gasking, 'Causation and Recipes' (1955) 64 *Mind* 478 and particularly J. Feinberg's colourful examples, 'Causing Voluntary Actions', *Doing and Deserving* (1970), 155–8. For instance, 'Counter example 2: the ingenious suicide. Mr. Blue, tired of life but too squeamish to kill himself, decides to use a more robust kind of person as an unwitting means. He hears about Manley Firmview, who has often announced to his friends that, if he ever encountered a person who would say so-and-so to him, he would kill the rascal. Mr. Blue seeks out Mr. Firmview and says so-and-so to him. Firmview pauses for a moment, calmly considers the consequences, and then shoots the grateful Mr. Blue dead. Would common sense balk at the claim that Mr. Blue caused his own death *by means* of Firmview's free and deliberate "intervention"? That he killed himself or literally committed suicide by going too far, but that his remarks to Firmview were the cause of his demise could scarcely be denied'. Feinberg accepts in his 'Rejoinder' that he makes no explicit distinction between 'explanatory and attributive' causal statements; Feinberg being primarily concerned with explaining causal statements. However, he maintains that the force of his counter examples 'tell just as effectively' in relation to attributive causal statements (183). See also Kadish's treatment of Feinberg, 'Complicity, Cause and Blame', 335 n.11. But it is arguable, in any case, that there is no real distinction in the processes of explanatory accounts (why something happened) and attributive inquiries (who is responsible)—both employ similar criteria. Cf. W. H. Dray, 'Causal Judgment in Attributive and Explanatory Contexts' (1986) 49 *Law and Contemp. Probs.* 13.

[58] Cf. Fletcher, *Rethinking Criminal Law*, 367. Although not hazarding a full analysis, Fletcher finds Hart and Honoré's principle 'conceptually appealing'. 'Stated abstractly, the principle makes some sense, purely voluntary conduct is not caused by antecedent events' (365).

agency is human and culpable. This will be especially true where serious harm has occurred.[59] Again, the contention here is not that voluntary human intervention lacks a strong predictive quality in identifying causal agency, but rather that it carries no invariable efficacy in performing this function.

Connected to this is a final area of difficulty with Hart and Honoré's principle concerning the relationship of the 'abnormal and normal conditions' and the 'voluntary action' principles.[60] It is claimed that the 'notions in this pair of contrasts lie at the root of most of the metaphors which cluster around the notion of a cause'; and, further, that a 'human action which is not voluntary is on a par with other abnormal occurrences'.[61] To pose the obvious question, what is the causal judgment where the intervening act is not only that of a voluntary human agent, but also *foreseen or foreseeable*?

For example, A in the presence of P, his long-standing companion in violence, stabs V. As half expected by A, P, who only hits a man when he is down, then also stabs V through the heart causing death within a few seconds. Evidence suggests that V would otherwise have died from A's initial stabbing within a quarter of an hour.

It could be claimed that, in one sense, as A's act was a precondition of P's, he was (with P) causally responsible for the death,[62] with A being an *indirect* and P being the *direct* cause. More generally, why should the 'voluntary action' principle not be regarded as subsumed within an overreaching abnormality rule? This would make the standard in respect of intervening human agencies: 'the more expectable human behaviour is, whether voluntary or not, the less likely it is a "negative causal connection"'.[63] The ramifications of such conclusions for the common law concept of complicity will be considered later.

(c) *Harm, Wrongdoing,*[64] *and Punishment*   Put at its strongest, it could be maintained that harm is the 'focal point' or 'fulcrum between criminal conduct and the punitive sanction'.[65] Whether fully rational or not, [66] it is

---

[59] Cf. D. J. Karp, 'Causation in the Model Penal Code' (1978) 78 *Col. LR* 1249, 1277.
[60] Hart and Honoré, *Causation*, 33.
[61] Ibid. 44.
[62] Cf. H. Gross, *A Theory of Criminal Justice* (1979), 249–50.
[63] Argued by Feinberg, '*Causing Voluntary Actions*', 166; and cf. J. L. Mackie, *Cement of the Universe* (1980), ch. 5, 'Common Sense and the Law'.
[64] Where the offence is *conduct* based, for complicity purposes that conduct is the equivalent of harm.
[65] J. Hall, *General Principles of Criminal Law* (1960), 213.
[66] For a strongly argued subjectivist case see e.g. S. J. Schulhofer, 'Harm and Punishment: A Critique of Emphasis on the Results of Conduct in the Criminal Law' (1974) 122 *U.Pa. LR* 1497–1607; and Ashworth, 'Sharpening the Subjective Element in Criminal Liability' in N. Simmonds, ed., *Philosophy and the Criminal Law* (1984), 79–89. An ingenious, if not wholly persuasive, justification of the roles of chance and harm in criminal responsibility is provided by D. M. Mandil, 'Chance, Freedom and Criminal Liability' (1987) 87 *Col. LR* 125–41.

undeniable that 'we react quite differently when an act causes harm from when the same act does not'.[67] Linking and apportioning causally attributable harm to responsibility and punishment is a deeply entrenched and virtually universal practice. As Hobbes confidently asserts:

> The Degrees of Crime are taken on divers Scales, and measured, First, by the malignity of the Source, or Cause: Secondly, by the contagion of the Example: Thirdly, by the mischiefe of the Effect...[68]

So well established is the practice that some of broad utilitarian or consequentialist persuasion are ready to defer to this 'obstinate sense of difference'[69] on the grounds that to ignore it would be to diminish the 'plain man's sense of justice', thereby weakening popular support for the system of criminal justice and its effective functioning. But, in general, subscribing to a particular variant of either retributivistic or utilitarian justifications of punishment will have implications for the extent to which resultant harm is seen as performing a legitimate role in determining liability and punishment.[70] However, for present purposes except where particularly noted, an election between rival justifications need not be made, for the objective here is to provide a theoretically coherent account of complicity within and alongside the current system of principal liability which may, in whole or in part, rest on retributive or utilitarian reasoning. Moreover, no assumption[71] can be made that a single theory or cluster of theories with a common home base is capable of completely explaining the whole institution of criminal liability and punishment. The same can be said of competing social policy objectives which may be more or less pressing, depending on the particular types of and the incidence of criminality under consideration.

This multiple-theory or multi-policy possibility of accounting for liability and punishment is one explanation for the existence of inchoate liability where a harm element in any obvious sense is lacking. Even here moderate ingenuity has produced several explanations whereby intangible harm is identified as existing in inchoate or allied endangerment based offences. On one such view 'any conduct which actualises a *mens rea* alters the external world' and the 'quality of daily life is impaired'.[72] Verging less on the metaphysical is the claim that such offences entail 'a disturbance of the social order' and a 'sufficient social harm to be deemed criminal'.[73] Yet

---

[67] J. C. Smith, 'Reform of the Law of Offences Against the Person' [1978] CLP 15, 17; and to similar effect, Fletcher, *Rethinking Criminal Law*, 483.
[68] *Leviathan*, pt. 1, ch. 27.
[69] Hart and Honoré, *Causation* (1985), 396–7.
[70] It is arguable that the presence of caused harm performs a necessary function whether punishment is posited on a utilitarian or retributive basis; e.g. see P. H. Robinson, 'A Theory of Justification: Societal Harm as a Prerequisite for Criminal Liability' (1975) 23 UCLA LR 266–92.
[71] Recognized by many including, for instance, Fletcher, *Rethinking Criminal Law*, 481; and Hall, *General Principles*, 220.
[72] Hall, *General Principles*, 220 and 219.
[73] Cf. L. C. Becker, 'Criminal Attempts and the Theory of the Law of Crimes', who

whichever justifying basis is accepted for inchoate offences — harm or no harm — at least the major portion of responsibility flows from the actor's mental culpability coupled with his overtly demonstrated dangerousness.[74]

The practical root of the long-running dispute over the nature of the criminality represented by inchoate offences is the propriety of punishing them (particularly attempts)[75] as severely as the substantive criminal objective involved. Although there is considerable variation in the formal punishment provisions for inchoate offences in different jurisdictions, with some providing for equality of sentence[76] and others insisting on a mitigated penalty,[77] the perceived overwhelming *practice* of courts in general is to punish such offences less severely.[78] This link between harm caused and punishment for both choate and inchoate liability is a background feature against which the Anglo-American tradition of complicity punishment should be considered.

The eligibility of accessories for punishment as severe as principals may promote inferences, if not solid conclusions, as to the nature of an accessory's relationship to criminal harm. Although accessories are punishable less or more severely than principals, there is neither a general formal[79] lower tariff nor is it a recognized automatic practice in sentencing. One reason for punishing accessories at a level closer to that of principals may be that the accessory is regarded as being partly responsible for bringing about the principal harm. Where the accessory receives the same punishment as

---

characterizes part of the harm in attempts as upsetting the social equilibrium. Cf. Bentham's notion of 'secondary mischief' *Introduction to the Principles of Morals and Legislation*, ch. XII, 'Of the Consequences of a Mischievous Act' (1970 edn.).

[74] 'Dangerousness' in the sense of someone with criminal propensities, and also of one who endangers others by engaging in risky or harm-threatening activity.

[75] From the very extensive literature on the subject see the equality of punishment approach advocated by Becker, 'Criminal Attempts', 262–94; and, representing a less-punishment-for-attempts position, M. Davis, 'Why Attempts Deserve Less Punishment than Complete Crimes' (1986) 5 *Law and Phil.* 1–32. There are, naturally, many refinements possible of the arguments adopted by each; see particularly A. J. Ashworth, 'Criminal Attempts and the Role of Resulting Harm under the Code and in Common Law' (1988) 19 *Rut. LJ* 725.

[76] Using attempt as an index of inchoate offences common to all jurisdictions, this is true of attempt in England, and e.g. the Model Penal Code, s. 5.05 (1) (although attempt to commit a first degree felony is a felony in the second degree). Cf. the Model Penal Code's attitude towards 'reckless' acts: those which only endanger (s. 211.2) are regarded as far less serious offences than those 'reckless' acts which cause harm (manslaughter — s. 210.3).

[77] Most American state codes punish attempt less severely; see those listed by J. Dressler in 'Reassessing the Theoretical Underpinnings of Accomplice Liability: New Solutions to an Old Problem' (1985) 37 *Hastings LJ* 100 n. 44. Broadly, like the current Canadian Criminal Code (s. 421), cl. 4 (3) of the Canadian Law Commission Proposed Code (1987) provides for attempts to be punished with no more than 'half the penalty' of the relevant substantive offence.

[78] For England, see Smith and Hogan, *Criminal Law*, 8, and R. Cross, *The English Sentencing System* (1981 edn.) 152.

[79] Cf. e.g. the 2nd Report of the Second Criminal Law Commissioners: 'We have not deemed the injury to society [between parties] to be so different either in nature or degree, at least in general cases, as to require any inequality in the punishments', s. 3, art. 1 n. 4.

the principal this may indicate a very clear case of sharing causal responsibility. If nothing more, it at least suggests that courts see accessories as capable of substantially contributing towards causing the principal harm element. However, it is conceded that this is distinct from claiming that a causal contribution is always essential for complicity liability.

In the light of these general preliminary premises and observations on the imposition of criminal responsibility (relating to freedom of choice, chance, cause, and harm) the particular basis of complicity liability can now be considered.

(2) *The Derivative Nature of Complicity and Equality of Punishment*

The two most prominent and longest enduring elements of common law complicity have been its derivative nature and equality of potential punishment[80] for all parties. And although throughout complicity's recorded history each has been subject to modification, they remain the closest to bedrock principles to be found in common law complicity doctrine. Both carry wider implications for the theoretical structure of complicity. The precise quality of derivativeness is contentious: in English law the requirement has evolved from a cripplingly strict standard (demanding conviction and execution of the principal) through administratively more convenient stages to one where it may be sufficient if some 'principal' harm has been brought about by an innocent or unconvictable actor. Despite this dilution of complicity's derivative quality, the requirement, none the less, persists. Even in its current abbreviated form there is still the undisputed need to establish some recognized harmful conduct or result which has been most immediately brought about by someone other than the accessory. Therefore the question remains: what function is served by this harm in the process of incriminating the accessory? What is the nature of the linkage between the accessory's behaviour and such harm? Clearly it functions as a vital triggering device for settling the accessory's liability; but the question persists, *what* in the preceding events and relationship between accessory and principal must exist to operate this trigger? Further, is the linking requirement identical for all forms of complicity or does it vary and turn upon the particular mode of complicity or the type of offence[81] — whether it is based on the perpetrator's act or proscribed consequences of it?

---

[80] Indirect affirmation of the absence of any *necessary* distinction in the overall culpability and punishability of principal and secondary parties is found in the three duress cases of *Lynch*, *Abbott*, and *Howe*. Of their lordships, only Lord Morris in *Lynch* ([1975] AC 653 at 671) showed any attraction to the idea of differentiating eligibility for the defence of duress on the basis of whether the party was a principal or accessory.

[81] A position advanced by J. C. Smith in 'Aid, Abet, Counsel or Procure', 131–7; see also Smith and Hogan, *Criminal Law*, 134–5: 'the law probably is that: (i) "procuring" implies causation but not consensus; (ii) "abetting" and "counselling" imply consensus but not

Broadly, other than some form of causal relationship between accessorial action and principal action, two basic varieties of theoretical explanation of these aspects of complicity are sufficiently feasible to warrant attention: the first sees liability as resting on consensual, agency, or ratificatory notions; the second is an inchoate or risk based account, with the principal offence primarily serving an evidential function. Against the background of identified 'preliminary premises' or general expectations of criminal responsibility, both groups of possibilities will be examined for their ability to account for the full spread of complicity modes and power to coexist with other leading features of complicity.

(a) *Agency, Consensus, and Ratification Theories* Attribution of responsibility for the acts of one party to another is the underlying notion of the civil law of principal and agent. It is, therefore, neither strange nor unreasonable for criminal lawyers to see parallels and draw possible conclusions about complicity's nature from what is in some respects complicity's civil sister. Certainly the language (if not the substance)[82] of common purpose or conspiracy tends to be that of authorization: typically, 'every act done in furtherance of [a common] intent by each of them is, in law, done by all'.[83] In agency, as in complicity, responsibility may extend beyond expressly authorized actions to those approved of by implication.

But extensive dissimilarities of both form and character exist between agency and complicity. Consensus is central to agency, in the sense of the principal assenting to the agent's actions and the agent consenting to be the agent of the principal. By contrast, accessories may operate without the principal's consent[84] or even knowledge.[85] Although consensual or authorized actions may often form the basis of complicity, under English law consent is not essential, as knowing or reckless facilitation cases such as *DPP for Northern Ireland* v. *Maxwell*[86] demonstrate. However, in jurisdictions, like most American states, where complicity requires purpose, or for the accessory to have a 'stake in the outcome' of the principal's venture, the agency analogy is more convincing. In such cases it is arguable that the accessory 'identifies himself with the principal party' thereby 'consent[ing] to be bound'.[87]

---

causation; (iii) "aiding" requires actual assistance but neither consensus nor causation'. Cf. I. H. Dennis, 'The Mental Element for Accessories', in P. F. Smith, ed., *Criminal Law* (1987), 40, 58–61.

[82] See below, Ch. 8.
[83] Alderson B. in *Macklin* (1838) 2 Lew. CC 225, 168 ER 1136.
[84] *Mohan* v. *R.* [1967] 2 AC 187.
[85] *State* v. *Tally* (1894) 102 Ala. 25.
[86] [1978]3 All ER 1140.
[87] Kadish, 'Complicity, Cause and Blame', 354. Kadish offers as *one* explanation of the intention requirement in complicity the 'notion of agreement as the paradigm mode by which a principal in agency law . . . becomes liable for the acts of another person . . . we become accountable for the liability created by the actions of others . . . when we join in and identify

Against this, agency theories of ostensible or apparent authority are not replicated in complicity; and, with rare exceptions, neither is the civil concept of *ex post facto* ratification.[88] Moreover, the fact that the 'principal' in civil and criminal law occupies the reverse position of the other, *vis-à-vis* the responsibility-producing action, is significant; most particularly, in one sense the civil agent's liability is derivative of the principal's initially empowering acts which confer authority on the agent, the opposite of the situation in complicity. Also, in true agency, unlike criminal law, the main focus of responsibility is not the actor, but rather the inactive party. Incrimination of a party as a principal through the medium of another's 'innocent agency' is an exception. However, this apparent support for the broader agency theory is of little if any value, for the doctrine of innocent agency may operate not only in circumstances where there has been prior confederacy between principal and agent but also where there has been none.[89] And, as already suggested, cases where there is no prior collaboration between parties cannot sensibly be explained on an agency or consensus basis.

Another major aspect of agency theory is the idea of control or dominance residing in the principal, in so far as the principal authorizes or empowers the agent to act on the principal's account. In some respects the notion of control as a feature of agency is the bridge between agency generally and causation. Anyone who has the ability, so to speak, to activate an agent is in one sense an indirect cause (or necessary condition) of the agent's actions. In German law such 'hegemony over the act' is the basis of distinguishing principals and accessories, with its consequent punishment implications.[90] Under the hegemony theory, control is viewed as an essential ingredient of cause: the principal is he who decisively controls the occurrence of the criminal act. Using control as a determinant of *accessorial* liability would obviously confine the incidence to a level much below that currently recognized, excluding (from complicity) cases where punishment is well justified.

Beyond matters of form, the dissimilarities between agency and complicity prompted Sayre's comment that between the 'two fields of law there seems utter disparity of thought', with the consequence that 'developments

---

with those actions by intentionally helping or inducing them to do those actions' (355). See below, Part II. The accessory 'identifying with' or ratifying the principal's action is relevant to mental culpability. If A shouts words of encouragement to P who is about to attack V, but P fails to hear A, it is true that A still identifies with P's attack but without actual communication there can be no help or inducement. But, in agency, failure to communicate authority can be compensated for by *ex post facto* ratification.

[88] See the South African examples cited above.
[89] e.g. unknown to A, P secretes a bomb in A's luggage which P expects to be, and is, placed on board an aircraft carrying a rival captain of industry.
[90] See H. L. Schreiber, 'Problems of Justification and Excuse in the Setting of Accessorial Conduct' (1986) *Brig. Young ULR* 611, 625–7, and Fletcher, *Rethinking Criminal Law*, 656.

in the one field have not easily penetrated the other'.[91] Whilst perhaps understating the areas of commonality between the two, the sentiment is essentially well founded. Agency law is fashioned by and looks to business and financial considerations and coherence — the commercially fair apportioning and ascribing of financial burdens and benefits. Although not absent from such civil calculations, in criminal liability the role of personal justice and culpability figure much more substantially; and the grounds for allocating financial loss or gain will not necessarily support imposition of punishment and social stigma. Taking an extreme instance: because general commercial coherence demands that P should be held liable to pay for the hotel expenses of A (his appointed agent) there is no obvious moral or social corollary supporting the case that P be held responsible for complicity in murder because he encouraged A to do it.[92]

(b) Inchoate, Endangerment, and Risk Rationales[93] Explicit approval of the criminal activity of another, whether before[94] or after the commission of the offence, is not in itself criminal. Further, encouragement which is not communicated is not, at common law, complicity, even if the would-be accessory has gone as far as acting upon and demonstrating his criminal proclivities. Why does complicity law apparently insist on *communicated* help or encouragement? What does it add to the nature of the 'accessory's' criminality to make it *then* worthy of punishment? The defendant's mental culpability is no greater, but effective communication makes commission of the principal offence either more likely or a possible cause of it. In other words, *either* some variety of inchoate/endangerment *or* causal principle of liability and punishment is operating.

At first glance inchoate and allied forms of liability may appear to promise little explanatory potential for complicity. However, certain features of inchoate and similar responsibility do offer negative insights that indirectly prepare the way for and point to a causal account of complicity.

In relation to inchoate and kindred liability two broad propositions have already been accepted as 'preliminary premises'. First, whether or not the

---

[91] 'Criminal Responsibility for the Acts of Another' (1930) 43 *HLR* 695 n. 27 and text. The 'fundamental difference in conception and in terminology has served to insulate the two fields of thought' (695).

[92] Dressler, 'Reassessing', p. 111, has characterized the process of basing criminal liability on agency theory as one of 'forfeited personal identity': 'she who chooses to aid in a crime forfeits her right to be treated as an individual. Thus, moral distinctions between parties are rendered irrelevant'.

[93] In broad terms, inchoate, endangerment, and risk based offences share a similar core of criminality, being a combination of conduct revealing the actor's anti-social or dangerous tendencies as well as risking the causing of some form of harm. For present purposes, the differences in emphasis between these two elements in the separate types of offence is of limited significance. On the rationale of endangerment liability see K. J. M. Smith, 'Liability for Endangerment: English Ad Hoc Pragmatism and American Innovation' [1983] Crim. LR 127.

[94] Unless incitement.

claims of intangible harm generated by inchoate (or endangering) acts are convincing, the main supporting rationale of liability is a combination of the actor's mental culpability and the social risk or threat posed by his culpable actions. Secondly, inchoate responsibility, although formally often punishable as severely as the substantive offence, is as a matter of practice punished less severely. This phenomenon is seen as a consequence of the prominent place accorded to attributable harm in the common perception of just deserts and the calculation of fair punishments.

As already noted, in complicity the common law insists on encouragement or help being communicated to the principal. If basically similar forms of incriminating activity to those for inchoate offences are required in complicity then why demand effective communication? One possible explanation is that just how far the defendant's actions must have progressed towards bringing about the substantive offence has been an inherent problem for inchoate offences, particularly in attempt. Therefore in complicity it could be suggested that, bearing in mind the increased contingent nature of liability when an additional actor's actions are necessary, anything less than communicated involvement would be too flimsy and too remote to serve as a proper basis for responsibility; only at this fairly advanced stage is the risk or threat of substantive harm sufficiently strong.

But, even accepting such a line of reasoning, unlike inchoate and endangering offences, complicity also requires the occurrence of the principal offence or harm. How is the substance of, say, an instigator's criminality altered (or increased) by another party carrying out the offence instigated? It could be that this is solid confirmatory evidence of the dangerousness of both the accessory and his actions. However, if the principal offence served no more than an evidential function it is not credible that the complex derivative quality of complicity would have been quite so persistent and rigid. This is especially true of the rule limiting the accessory's level of liability by reference to that of the principal. Indeed the whole language of derivativeness is hostile to such an interpretation. An evidential account would also have encouraged far less definite conceptual and definitional boundaries between inchoate offences and complicity. As a matter of historical development, the relatively late and piecemeal arrival of inchoate liability, many centuries after complicity, again suggests a distinct basis of responsibility. Furthermore, as already observed, in contrast with inchoate offences, the formal punishment provisions of accessories do not in common law influenced jurisdictions prescribe a lower tariff. Nor is there evidence of a comparably entrenched practice of mitigating the accessory's punishment regardless of the circumstances of participation.[95]

---

[95] In exceptional circumstances because of the difference in age between parties the accessory may be punished more seriously; a notorious example being *Craig and Bentley* (1952) *Times* 10–13 December. The nature and extent of the accessory's role will affect his

In sum, an inchoate or endangering rationale of liability and punishment is unable either to accommodate complicity's derivative nature or to account for the common law approach to punishment of accessories.[96]

(3) *Causation's Role in Complicity*

It has been suggested here that neither agency nor inchoate based theories, separately or in combination, offer an adequate explanation of the structure and substance of complicity. This could be called the negative, or argument by default, case supporting some form of causal contribution rationale. In providing a positive and convincing causal account two general issues present themselves: what is meant by 'cause' — are there significantly (for distinguishing principals and accessories) different *types* of cause? How much causal assistance or involvement is necessary for complicity?

The meaning of cause has already been considered in relation to the claimed special causal qualities or status given to voluntary action. The thesis that a 'deliberate human act' is 'most often a barrier and a goal in tracing back causes' was seen as subject to the counter-argument that, instead of having a special status, human agency was a distinction between the abnormality or normality of a result. However, whatever logical strength such arguments may carry, common law complicity ignores the predictability or otherwise of actions when assigning principal and secondary roles; as a matter of doctrine the principal's status is not determined by predictability of actions. In this respect complicity runs contrary to general rules governing the effects of a *novus actus* in causal attribution. The crucial consequence of not assigning[97] categoric signific-

---

sentence. See e.g. *Irwin* [1966] Crim. LR 514 and *Hartley* [1978] 2 NZLR 199. See also the Australian authorities cited by Gillies, *Criminal Complicity*, 214–15. On the relevance of the degree of an accessory's participation in capital crime and eligibility for the death penalty, see the US Supreme Court decision in *Enmund* v. *Florida* (1982) 458 U.S. 782 discussed by Dressler, 'Reassessing', 134–7. However, the scope of *Enmund* is curtailed by *Tison* v. *Arizona* 107 S.Ct. 1676 (1987). See L. Kling, 'Constitutionalizing the Death Penalty for Accomplices to Felony Murder' (1988) 26 Am. Crim. LR 463.

[96] In respect of *mens rea*, English law has long required an intention to bring about the substantive offence incited, attempted, or conspired at. Although the House of Lords in *Anderson* [1986] AC 27, held that a conspirator need not intend that the criminal objective of the conspiracy be brought about, but only to participate in the venture. This ruling moves the culpability requirement closer to that of complicity. But cf. *Siracusa* [1989] Crim. LR 712 and Law Commission Report 177, cl. 48 (1).

[97] As e.g. in the Model Penal Code's causal provisions, s. 2.03. This is expressly noted by the code's reporter: in settling attribution where there is divergence between a result designed or contemplated and the actual result 'the draft makes no attempt to catalogue the [possibly relevant factors] e.g. to deal with the intervening or concurrent causes, natural or human; unexpected physical conditions . . . It deals only with the ultimate criterion by which the significance of such possibilities ought to be judged': Commentary on Tentative Draft 4 (1953), 133. The 'ultimate criterion' finally adopted was that of 'just bearing' (s. 2.03 (2) (*b*) and (3) (*b*)). Law Commission Report 177, Draft Criminal Code, also makes no distinction between types of intervening acts or events in its causation provision. Rather, the causal effect of *all* forms of intervening acts or events turns on foreseeability — actual or objective. Foreseeable

ance to voluntary human intervention is the loss of an intuitively appealing and relatively clear-cut causal demarcation point between accessories and principals. Such a loss opens up the problem of how actions of principals and accessories are causally distinct in relation to the substantive offence's *actus reus* if *both* must be causal contributors; for, if they are not *regularly* causally distinguishable, a good portion of established common law complicity doctrine would be seriously undermined, if not destroyed. This would be the outcome of using a 'normality' or foreseeability of result basis for causal attribution, which would turn many parties currently designated 'accessories' into principals because the party they encouraged or assisted acted in a foreseeable fashion. Therefore, how are parties' causal roles regularly distinguishable?

This prompts the first of two separate questions on the causal nature of complicity: how are cases involving the *upper* levels of causality, where the accessory's causal contribution may be high and rivalling that of the principal, separable from principal liability? The second question looks to settling the *lower* boundary of complicity, between being an accessory and having no liability at all because of insufficient causal involvement in the perpetrator's criminal activities. In essence, the Hart and Honoré thesis[98] rests on there being at least a decisive *qualitative* distinction between human and non-human cause and effect; so that only in a very *broad* sense may secondary parties be said to contribute causally. The main alternatives to this are either some other qualitative distinction based on directness, or a quantitative test turning on the degree or extent of causal contribution.

(a) *Principal and Accessory Distinction* If both complicity and principal liability rest on showing that each party in some way helped to cause the principal offence, then wherein lies the distinction between an accessory and a joint principal? This question was directly confronted by the South African Appellate Division in *S v. Khoza*,[99] with Botha AJA concluding that, in the case of murder, conviction of an accessory required proof of 'a causal connection between the conduct of the accomplice and the conduct of the perpetrator' rather than 'the death of the deceased'. At the same time, he recognized that this formulation might not provide a solution to every case. Its relevance to so-called 'result' or 'consequence' offences is obvious, but where a principal's actions themselves constitute the *actus reus* of an offence then the Botha test is inadequate. For example, if A successfully encourages P to steal, then in one sense both have caused P's actions and at the same time the *actus reus* of stealing.

intervening acts or events do not prevent causal attribution. The principal/accessory distinction is maintained by an express provision declaring a person who 'procures, assists or encourages another to cause' at least part of the *actus reus* of an offence is not, subject to exceptions, a principal (cl. 17 (3)).

[98] As refined by Kadish, 'Complicity, Cause and Blame', generally.
[99] 1982 (3) SA 1019A.

The most straightforward way of coping with such cases is by using the notion of directness or immediacy of cause: 'where there are several participants in a crime the principal . . . is the one whose act is the most immediate cause of the actus reus'.[100] Thus where A encourages P to steal, or where A assists P by driving him to and from the place where P commits a robbery, or where A holds the victim of an assault carried out by P, then P is the principal offender. For he has clearly the most direct or immediate connection with the *actus reus* of the offence in each situation. A's causal contribution is *through* the perpetrator by either encouragement or assistance in providing materials or facilitatory conditions. The test's value in offering a simple working standard in most complicity situations is undeniable.

However, limitations show through in exceptional cases when the causal force or contribution of a non-direct action is so substantial that the test suggests results at odds with common sense or intuition. For example,

X and Y have decided to murder V by poisoning. Before V joins them for lunch, X and Y together measure out a fatal dose of strychnine which X sprinkles over V's soup.

Employing the directness standard, as the last act was that of X he would be regarded as the principal with Y his accessory. If, however, in order to introduce the fatal dose into V's soup, Y had lifted the soup bowl across the table and then, after X had acted, replaced it, would application of the directness test clearly point to one or other of the parties as being the principal? The last act was Y's, yet to say that he had been abetted by X would seem inappropriate for the introduction of the poison into the soup has all the normal appearances of the fatal act. What if Y's sole contribution was (without request) to pass a soup spoon to V? Again, although it is the last act of any party other than the victim, it is even more difficult to accept it as being principal in nature. The factual cause of death is most immediately identifiable with X's act of seasoning the soup with poison, but the most immediate precondition of V's death is replacing the bowl or providing a spoon.[101] The common law's simple undeveloped approach to

---

[100] Smith and Hogan, *Criminal Law*, 131. Cf. Williams, *Textbook*, 329–30: 'The "perpetrator" . . . means, and means exclusively, the person who in law performs the offence.' And La Fave and Scott, *Criminal Law*, 569. Under Law Commission Report 177, a principal is one who 'does the act or acts specified for the offence', cl. 26 (1). A person 'does an act not only when he does it himself' but also when attributed to him vicariously or by the doctrine of innocent agency: cl. 26 (1) (c) and 26 (2).

[101] *Joint* principal responsibility occurs where each joint principal has himself made a *direct* causal contribution to an element of the *actus reus* (see above, Ch. 2). This does not occur in the text illustration or in the following example. As previously agreed, X pushes V into the path of a car driven by Y who accelerates and runs down V. The most immediate cause of V's death is being run down and therefore Y would be regarded as principal. It is analogous to where a victim is held by one party whilst assaulted by another. But if Y had leapt from the car after starting it in motion, would he still be the principal? It is the car which is the instrument of V's death, whether Y is still aboard at the moment of impact is causally immaterial — he has

distinguishing principals and accessories is in part the result of the law's greater doctrinal concern with the modes and nature of complicity and neglect of the basis of principal liability. It is the question of who qualifies as an accessory that has been approached in the most positive fashion. By contrast, under German law, for example, the traditional emphasis towards settling accessoryship has been (and is) more indirect or negative:

the so-called concepts of primary perpetration and secondary complicity provide that complicity is a *residual* category consisting only of those who are not perpetrators . . . Only through establishing a range of perpetration is the extent of complicity fundamentally co-determined[102] [emphasis added].

However, considerably more important than such rather exceptional counter-examples which may wrong-foot the 'immediate cause' test is the reason why the perpetrator of the *actus reus* should be distinguished from other causal contributors, whether on the grounds of directness or on the Hart and Honoré 'deliberate human act' thesis. It is true that when the causal agency is 'nature' there will be an invariable sequence[103] and consequence. Whereas (for the accessory) with a voluntary human agency every 'volitional actor is a wild card: he need never act in a certain way'.[104] But to accept the undeniable does not explain why the distinction should be made. Is there a discernible underlying and inevitable moral distinction? Returning to earlier 'preliminary premises' on the relevance and importance attached to control, it might be claimed that the perpetrator, by virtue of exercising the *final* or most direct (human) control over whether the offence is carried out, is in an inherently special position; therefore, whatever the scale of the accessory's contribution the perpetrator's role always assumes a particular and distinct moral importance. Final control by the perpetrator might also be said always to regulate, or hold in check, the causal potency of whatever the accessory contributes to the perpetrator's position or actions.

Thus if squeamish *A*, anxious to kill *B*, there and then asks *P*, his criminal underling, to shoot *V* with *A*'s gun, under common law complicity[105] *A* would be the accessory and *P* the principal to *V*'s killing.

unleashed the instrument in both cases and caused it to run down *V*. The presence of *V* in the path of the car is an essential precondition of its effectiveness, and if the car had not been driven by a confederate of *X* then his actions would be viewed as qualifying him as a principal. Why should this be so? If it is agreed that the party who delivers the fatal blow, stab, etc. must be the principal, as *that* is the cause of death, then immediacy will not be essential. Therefore, *Y* would be the principal offender whether or not he stayed aboard the car, as it was the car, projected by him, that factually caused *V*'s death. This would be so even though the *final* connecting act or link in killing *V* was the push he received from *X*. To apply a test of directness would be to suggest principal liability would rest with *X*.

[102] Schreiber, 'Problems', 626.
[103] Though, in a stricter philosophical sense, even this is challengeable. See e.g. G. E. M. Anscombe, 'Causality and Determination', in E. Sosa, ed., *Causation and Conditionals* (1975), 63.
[104] Kadish's very apposite expression: 'Complicity, Cause and Blame', 360.
[105] Arguably the Model Penal Code's general causation rules would make *A* a principal

This is so even though supplying the gun could be seen as a clear *sine qua non* of the shooting and that A was the instigator of the whole venture; and even though A's immorality might be assessed as materially indistinguishable from P's, or possibly greater.

Complicity's immediate or direct cause test or technique bears the appearance of a pragmatically induced reliable legal rule of thumb required to establish the first vital link between harm and a human causal agent, thereby enabling the more sensitive process of moral attribution and allocation of appropriate punishment to take place. Contrastingly, in tort the notion of joint tortfeasors draws no distinction between parties whose roles would mark them out as either joint principals or accessories in criminal activity. Although needing a more discriminatory method of reflecting likely moral distinctions amongst participants, criminal law's causal attribution nevertheless requires a 'relative degree of certainty, regularity, uniformity, and predictability'[106] to maintain a reasonably apparent link between the punishment and its objectives. A voluntary human action discriminating principle of causal attribution offers an alternative feasible account to a directness of cause test resting on possibly similar underlying notions of the (prima-facie) special moral position occupied by the perpetrator.

(b) Minimum Causal Contribution by an Accessory Turning from the conceptual division between principals and accessories, the second question concerned how limited the accessory's causal contribution may be and yet still incriminate. What is the minimum qualifying level of causal involvement?

As with any other causal question, the problem is identifying a connection between what the actor did and the relevant final outcome. If the actor did not in some demonstrable and attributable way influence that outcome he cannot be causally tied to it; rather, any liability must then rest upon mental culpability with some variant of harm risked or threatened. In relation to the principal's actions or any consequences of them, the nub of the question is: did the accessory's actions matter, did they make a difference?[107] Parallel issues in settling principal liability — whether something 'mattered' causally — are initially pursued through asking whether an action was a *sine qua non* in more than a negligible[108] sense. In relation to proximity disputes, and particularly those of a *novus actus interveniens* variety, an obvious parallel in complicity concerns variation by the principal from those actions

offender ('but for' cause and desired manner of death) and the code's complicity rules would make him an accessory. See Karp, 'Causation', 1277 n. 84. Such duality of roles occurs under *Cogan* (see below, Ch. 4).

[106] G. Mueller, 'Causing Criminal Harm', in Mueller, ed., *Essays in Criminal Science* (1961), 169, 170.

[107] A key point noted by Kadish, 'Complicity, Cause and Blame', 357.

[108] Law Commission Report 177, cl. 17 (1) (a). Model Penal Code, s. 2 12 (2): 'harm or evil too trivial to warrant the condemnation of conviction'.

anticipated by the accessory, whether as to victim, type of offence, or mode of committing it. Variation in principal behaviour and liability for incidental offences is an area of complicity more often analysed in *mens rea* terms, with the causal dimension either neglected or ignored. Its relevance to both *mens rea* and cause will be discussed after the main features of *mens rea* have been examined.[109] More immediate and basic causal matters of *sine qua non* and substantiality are reviewed now.

As already noted, the absence of an invariable sequence of cause and effect in interpersonal relations does make it distinguishable from the operation of cause and effect in the natural world. But what, if any, are the implications of interpersonal activity's lack of causal predictability for the use of the *sine qua non* notion?

The role of invariable sequence of natural phenomena does not exclude the functioning of chance in fixing principal liability. If *P* shoots *V*, whether or not *V* dies may hinge on a number of factors including *V*'s physical robustness, willingness to accept medical care,[110] and the standard of treatment[111] given to him. Of course, in certain given sets of circumstances the result will be predictable: a bullet which stops the heart beating will always result in death, at least without medical intervention; a wound elsewhere may or may not kill. Yet if death follows the wound will be taken as a *sine qua non* of death. In other words, there are also other types of 'wild card', although of a different suit and lower value in the causal pack used to settle principal responsibility. The point is that chance and the lack of complete and predictable control by a *perpetrator* over the effect of his actions does not prevent them being designated a *sine qua non*.

Secondly, difficulties as to the proof of factual cause can arise in principal liability.[112] Establishing cause when inter-party activity is involved may often be even more problematic, although that is not to accept that the idea of *sine qua non* is necessarily inapposite. Employing a *sine qua non* test in complicity undeniably presents peculiar evidential problems most of which centre around non-physical assistance where there has been some form of encouragement. However, the relatively more simple position of help or assistance will be considered first.

Even Hart and Honoré now accept that the provision of 'means . . . used by another to carry out his plan . . . may in a broad sense be said to give rise to a causal relationship'.[113] Therefore 'A person who supplies a burglar

---

[109] See below, Chs. 7 and 8.
[110] *Blaue* [1975] 3 All ER 446.
[111] *Smith* [1959] 2 QB 35.
[112] See Dressler, 'Reassessing', 127, for an example illustrating the point.
[113] *Causation*, 388. The same illustration of 'aiding' was previously offered by J. C. Smith ('Aid, Abet, Counsel or Procure', 120, 134) who concludes 'aiding requires actual assistance but neither consensus nor causation'. Hart and Honoré's view does not appear in the 1st edn. of their work; but its appearance in the 2nd is pre-empted by Kadish, 'Complicity, Cause and Blame', 361.

with a ladder which the latter uses to break in would be said to have contributed to the success of the break-in'. But that is not to concede the need for and feasibility of establishing cause in other instances of assistance. Proving something was the *sine qua non* of a consequence entails showing (beyond reasonable doubt) that it was an essential precondition of that *particular* consequence — as would be demonstrable in the ladder example. However, less accommodating cases are imaginable, such as where while pinioned by *A* and *B* holding an arm each, *V* is clubbed by *P*. Whilst the participation of *A* and *B* indisputably makes *P*'s task easier, can it be claimed that each is performing a *necessary* function without which that attack would not have taken place? In approaching an answer it should be borne in mind that the *sine qua non* condition is concerned with an event's exact occurrence, including time, place, extent and type of harm, and so on.[114] Therefore, someone charged with perpetrating a murder would not excuse himself by showing that his victim was already within minutes of death when the defendant acted. Similarly, neither should it avail an accessory to claim that, if *P* had not used the accessory's knife to kill *V*, *P* could just have easily have used his own revolver. Thus in the case of the clubbing attack it could be reasonably maintained that the carrying out of *that* attack in *that* manner on *that* occasion with those consequences was contingent upon the victim being restrained in precisely that manner by *A* and *B*.

Where complicity takes the form of encouragement, rather than assistance, the credibility of accounting for liability on a positively proved *sine qua non* basis becomes strained.[115] If one party commits an offence soon after being encouraged to do so by another,[116] it would be an acceptable inference that at least part of the perpetrator's motivation was the instigation. As a matter of proof, is the process of establishing the principal's reason(s) for acting really substantially different from or more difficult than determining whether he intended or foresaw the consequence of his actions? Both enquiries entail ascertaining the defendant's state of mind by 'reference to all the evidence drawing such inferences from the evidence as appear proper in the circumstances'.[117] Moreover, the motivating forces behind the defendant's actions are sometimes of direct

[114] The provision of aid may also function as encouragement: e.g. providing the principal with a gun to use should he need to 'persuade' an uncooperative victim to hand over property or for escape from the scene of the crime by shooting his way out. Even if the gun is never used its provision and presence could properly be regarded as effective encouragement.

[115] Although creating greater problems of proof, it is arguable that instigation may be causally stronger than aiding an existing plan, for the likelihood of the offence being committed without such instigation might in some cases be slight. Cf. Fletcher, *Rethinking Criminal Law*, 681. This view of instigation partly explains German law's punishment of instigation ('Anstiftung', s. 26, 1975 Penal Code) more severely than facilitation ('Beihilfe', s. 27).

[116] For a review of suicide cases where the instigator has been convicted as a *principal* for causing death see D. Lanham, 'Murder by Instigating Suicide' [1980] Crim. LR 215.

[117] Extracted from s. 8 of the Criminal Justice Act 1967, the central evidential provision in English law governing how intention or foresight must be proved when specified in an offence's definition.

relevance in fixing principal responsibility.[118] However, simple illustrations aside, many imaginable cases are not so easily dispatched.

One type of awkward example is where the principal has already settled on committing the incited offence. Encouragement to persist in a planned course of action may either be causally superfluous or it may vitally strengthen the principal's (possibly flagging) resolve. Determining whether encouragement has the former or latter effect in many situations could be virtually impossible.[119] In some cases the evidence may point to the 'accessory's' actions having had no influence on the perpetrator. For instance, P, having over many weeks minutely planned the murder of V, receives a letter from A encouraging him to kill V which arrives the day before the date on which P had already decided to carry out the murder. If at P's trial the evidence clearly revealed his pattern of behaviour up to the killing, the implication that A's conduct was quite immaterial to the murder might be such that convicting him of being an accessory, rather than for just inciting the offence, would patently seriously misdescribe the nature of A's criminality.

A different variety of problem is created when the principal has been instigated to act by more than one party, as where both A and B encourage P to steal.[120] Whether instigating parties act jointly or independently the difficulty reduces to much the same: demonstrating the causal imprint of each instigator's encouragement on the principal's action.[121] It is a difficulty which grows in proportion to the number of participants. Perhaps mindful of such causal issues, Lord Coleridge CJ, in the illegal prize fighting case of *Coney* [122] observed

Practical wisdom, rather than scientific exactness, seems to me to be the thing to aim at in a branch of law which is concerned with the affairs of man generally speaking in their simplest and least complicated forms.

The essence of the problem is that, even though it may be clear that an audience is a prerequisite of an unlawful performance, it will normally be impossible to demonstrate individual causal contributions. In cases of this nature proof of some form of collective causation appears to mark the inevitable limit of attributing causal responsibility.

[118] See the examples listed in Smith and Hogan, *Criminal Law*, 79.
[119] Cf. *State* v. *King* 74 NW 691 (1898) and *Keithler* v. *Mississippi* 10 Sm. and M. 192. (1848) at 194. In *State* v. *Gelb* 515 A. 2d 1246 (1986) it was held that encouragement given by the accessory after the principal had begun to act could still constitute complicity.
[120] If instigation is carried out at the same time the causal problem resembles the classic conundrum of simultaneous cause where the victim is shot at the same moment by two assassins, each wound being independently sufficient to cause death.
[121] Cf. *Barber* (1844) 1 C. & K. 542, 174 ER 884.
[122] (1882) 8 QBD 534 at 569. Spectators were charged with being accessories to an illegal prize fight. Cf. Alderson B. in *Macklin*. The majority in *Coney* were in disagreement with the minority in respect of the *mens rea* requirement, but not over the question of causation. See also Pollock B. at 564–5 and Matthew J. at 548. Cf. *Young* (1838) 8 Car. P. 644, 175 ER 655 at 658.

(c) *Substantiality and Proof of Causal Contribution* In addition to problems of proving an accessory's causal effectiveness (whether psychological or physical) on the principal's actions, there is the matter of substantiality of contribution. Although of uncertain scope,[123] in principal liability the law recognizes a *de minimis* principle. For complicity it has been maintained that as 'a matter of common sense a person who gives very minor assistance ought not to be held liable as an accessory'.[124] Direct judicial authority on the point is almost totally absent,[125] but intractable examples readily suggest themselves:

1. Knowing P was on his way to burgle a house, good natured A lends him his bicycle simply to make the ageing burglar's life a little less grim. A's good turn enables P to carry out the offence a few minutes before he would otherwise have done had he arrived on foot.

2. Or, knowing of her husband's burglarious activities, caring Mrs P provides P with clean new gloves to make the work more comfortable.

In the first case the burglary occurred earlier so, arguably, the bicycle was a *sine qua non* of the offence when committed. Similarly the gloves might enable P's work to be carried out marginally more efficiently (faster) as well as in greater comfort.[126] But even if (somewhat artificially) qualifying as necessary conditions of the offences as and when they occurred, *should* such tenuous involvement be capable of constituting complicity? Does it fall below some complicity equivalent of the *de minimis* principle?

Although prompted by other concerns, the original draft of the Model Penal Code contained substantiality provisions as an alternative to complicity based on purposefully aided or encouraged offences. However, both this and the equivalent in the code's general causation proposals were eventually rejected on the grounds of unacceptable uncertainty.[127] While

---

[123] In *Cato* (1976) 62 Cr. App. Rep. 41, the Court of Appeal commented when considering homicide, 'as a matter of law, it is sufficient if the prosecution could establish that it was a cause, provided a cause outside the *de minimis* range, and effectively bearing on the acceleration of the moment of the victim's death'. See also *Hennigan* [1971] 3 All ER 133; *State v. Serebin* 350 NW 2d 65 (1984) and *State v. Spates* 405 A. 2d 656 (1978).

[124] Williams, *CLGP* 294.

[125] In *Jindra v. U.S.* 69 F. 2d 429 (1934), a case of complicity through arranging the sale and purchase of unlawfully imported drugs, the court spoke of requiring causation 'to a material extent [which] excludes trivial or immaterial participation' (431). But cf. *State v. Duran* 526 P. 2d 188 (1974) where briefly minding the principal's child was held to be enough for complicity. In *Annakin* (1989) 13 *Crim. LJ* the New South Wales Court of Criminal Appeal appeared to accept that in the case of homicide an accessory 'must contribute significantly, as distinct from minimally, to the death'. See also *Fuson v. Comm.* 251 SW 995 (1923).

[126] Cf. the 19th-cent. German decision where lending a smock to an assailant to keep his clothes clean during the offence was held to be sufficient for complicity. However, liability turned on the belief that lending the smock had strengthened the assailant's resolve. Fletcher, *Rethinking Criminal Law*, 678.

[127] S. 2.04 (3) (b) 'alternative' incriminated a party who 'knowingly provided means or opportunity for the commission of the crime, substantially facilitating its commission'. See TD 1 (1953) commentary 27–31 and the *Proceedings of the American Law Institute* 1953. The original version of the code's general causal provisions (TD 4 (1955) s. 2.03 (2) (b) and (3) (b))

not proving especially troublesome, substantiality has figured relatively frequently in respect of principal liability, whereas its appearance in complicity has been an inconclusive rarity. If nothing else, this is evidence of its very limited practical importance, partly explicable by the fact that many cases involving the provision of materials are also interpretable as encouragement. However, as a matter of theory, once cause is admitted as a determinant of liability (whether cause must be established as having been actual or just potentially effective) it would be illogical and of doubtful social utility to deny that there must be a *de minimis* level below which the accessory's contribution becomes too insignificant to be used by the law as a peg on which to hang liability. To claim that anything suffices is tantamount to accepting that causality has no substantive role in complicity.

So far it has been argued that complicity's structure, internal logic, and general notions of criminal responsibility all signal the need for accessorial participation which *actually* causally contributes to bringing about the principal criminal harm. If an accessory's involvement is *patently* causally superfluous, whether because his help or encouragement fails to reach the principal or is in some other way ineffectual, no liability follows. But what of situations when this is not so; how does complicity law deal with matters of proof of the theoretically necessary causal contribution? The predominating inference to be drawn from the weight of common law authorities is that the demands of complicity law represent a pragmatic compromise or accommodation of theoretical causal expectations necessitated by inevitable limitations of proof. Rather than a positively established causal contribution, assumed cause[128] is the inevitable operating basis of complicity. It is 'inevitable' in the sense of being the product of tension between what may be feasibly proved and the width of conduct which policy dictates suggest should be covered by complicity law. Similar conflicts are to be seen at work in respect of *mens rea*. Consequently, the most disputed areas of complicity are those where theoretical expectations of both causal and mental culpability are seen to suffer the distorting effects of broader policy demands; variation rules and conspiracy based complicity are two prominent examples of this effect.

Although not unique in criminal responsibility, complicity[129] offers the

---

dealing with variation matters, offered as an alternative to the 'just bearing' proximity test one of substantial probability. A 'substantial factor' test as an alternative to the code's *sine qua non* requirement was unsuccessfully proposed at the ALI's 1962 proceedings. See Karp, 'Causation', 1264–6. Cf. the criteria employed by s. 876 (*b*) for 'substantial assistance' in aiding and abetting under the American *Restatement (Second) of Torts* (1977), discussed by J. L. Rosenthal, 'Aiding and Abetting Liability for Civil Violations of RICU' (1988) 61 *Temp. LR* 1481.

[128] Cf. Kadish's 'possibility of success' test; 'Complicity, Cause and Blame', 359. Professor Kadish's broadly similar conclusions are arrived at through a more elaborate process rooted in a qualitative distinction between voluntary human cause and cause in nature—the 'nature— will distinction' (407).

[129] For the notion of 'presumed evidence' in imputing criminal responsibility, see P. H.

single most important illustration of assumed causal contribution.[130] To appreciate its nature notions of substantial participation and risk or endangerment theories of responsibility must be distinguished. Basing liability simply on any participating act, however insignificant and causally ineffectual, would be little different from inchoate liability. This objection could be at least partly met by requiring *substantial* participation, although courts have shown little inclination to discriminate in this fashion between levels of participation. Furthermore, as already suggested, resting liability on purposeful or knowing participation in the principal offence without a causal requirement renders complicity's derivative structure largely redundant. Much the same may be said of any risk or endangerment thesis. Additionally, on a risk or endangerment explanation, demonstrable failure of the risk to materialize and boost the chances of the principal offence would not eliminate complicity responsibility because it could still be maintained there had been an element of endangerment or risk. However, in complicity, despite slight contrary authority, it is open to an alleged accessory to avoid incrimination by adducing evidence that his involvement failed to affect the occurrence of the offence; in other words, by rebutting the presumption of causal contribution from his communicated encouragement or help.

3. Conclusions

Common law authorities offer little beyond contradictory and, at best, half-articulated theoretical explanations of the nature of the connection between the accessory's conduct and the principal offence. In identifying a tenable account of this aspect of complicity three areas of relevance and influence have been reviewed. The first of these concerned preliminary premises of criminal liability in general, and particularly the connecting roles of choice, chance, cause, harm, and punishment; it was concluded that although several forms of inchoate or risk based offences exist, attributing the causing

---

Robinson, 'Imputed Criminal Liability' (1984) 93 *YLJ* 609, 652–8. In relation to complicity, rather than seeing it as underlying liability generally, Robinson limits 'presumed evidence' to features of complicity such as the Pinkerton doctrine and the natural and probable consequence rule for incidental liability.

[130] In tort actions where there is an evidentiary shortfall between a believed cause and the harm suffered, courts are, in some circumstances, prepared to make up this shortfall by converting proof that certain behaviour generated a 'materially increased' risk of causing the harm into the assumption that the behaviour 'materially contributed' to causing the harm. However, quite when this process is appropriate is open to considerable uncertainty. Cf. the House of Lords decisions in *McGhee* v. *NCB* [1972] 3 All ER 1008 and *Wilsher* v. *Essex Area Health Authority* [1988] 2 WLR 557. Of course, considerations influencing the willingness of civil courts to allocate the burden of loss on such a basis do not enjoy automatic currency in criminal courts.

of tangible harm[131] is a clear factor both in the imposing of liability and in grading punishment for most offences. The second area of consideration focused on the implications of complicity's derivative nature and the principle of eligibility for equal punishment for all parties. Both features were viewed as incapable of satisfactory explanation, whether complicity was seen as either having an agency/consensus nature or being inchoate or risk based. The inability of these theories to account for complicity's derivative structure constitutes the negative case favouring a causal explanation. The positive arguments are that an accessory's liability always requires proof of communicated encouragement or help; and that such a requirement has no reasonably explicable function other than indicating probable influence on the principal or his actions. Principal and accessory causal roles are distinguishable on the basis of immediacy or directness[132] of causal contribution towards the *actus reus*; the accessory must causally contribute indirectly in the sense of encouraging or assisting the principal's actions. However, policy demands for a wide-ranging coverage by complicity combined with inevitable limitations of proof of causal influence or effect necessitates the criminal law's adoption of an implicit rule of presumed cause. And, consistent with principal liability, the actual level of presumed contribution need only be more than trivial or *de minimis* to constitute an indirect 'cause' of the criminal harm through the perpetrator's direct actions. Moreover, it is implicit in this notion of presumed cause that, given appropriate evidence, the 'accessory' may avoid conviction by establishing that his actions were causally ineffectual.

These partly implied and partly declared features of complicity are suggested to represent the common law's evolved approach to participation in crime. As already argued, its internal coherence and relational consistency with general principles of liability and punishment are, in one sense, compromised by the distorting pressures of satisfying more general policy needs. Complicity's growing pains over the centuries, as will be seen, have been experienced in a variety of forms and in most limbs of its considerable and ancient body of doctrine. This doctrinal discomfort has been (and is) the consequence of shifting patterns and notions of liability in other abutting areas of the criminal law. And being of general relevance to all forms of criminal responsibility, such movements have set up stresses in complicity's own body of rules when forced to accommodate such changes.

The common law's history is littered with a great many examples of uncomfortably slow mutation of forms of liability, only finally completed by the ultimately irresistible pressure of overwhelmingly apparent substantive anomaly or administrative inconvenience. Complicity's often elephantine

---

[131] Whether 'consequence' or 'conduct' offences such as theft, where harm is interference with or violation of recognized property interests.

[132] See Kadish, 'Complicity, Cause and Blame', for the arguable alternative qualitative distinction between the two types of cause based on the voluntary human cause theory.

progress exemplifies this somewhat imperfect process of adaptation. Changes and refinements in attitudes towards appropriate levels of culpability, punishment, evidence, and cause have all needed recognition and absorption by complicity doctrine. The tension and doctrinal clumsiness in relation to cause may be seen as one major product of this imperfect accretive process. Common law's almost infinite capacity eventually to adapt and (usually) muddle through, with occasional statutory intervention when judicial inventiveness falters, has implicitly established in complicity a theoretical *modus vivendi* that demonstrably works to a reasonable level of satisfaction but which leaves the theorist unsatisfied. It is a dissatisfaction capable of being relieved by more than one strategy. Exactly which ought to be adopted, and quite how much change would thereby be entailed, turns most especially on the function complicity is expected to fulfil, the roles that other components of complicity are allocated, and the coverage of auxiliary or complementary forms of criminal liability.

Narrowing complicity's coverage to cases of provable causal contribution, besides (re)introducing internal doctrinal integrity, would offer a basis of liability which was more intuitively appealing and morally consistent (with that of a principal). This follows from a closer adherence to the entrenched general practice of partly fixing punishment by reference to harm caused and from a common-sensical perception that 'accessories' who clearly influence events are materially distinguishable from those who do not. How this perception might be translated into effect hinges on the competing attractions of formally[133] designated classes of 'accessory' (causal and non-causal) with fixed punishment differentials and the practice of complete judicial discretion—the latter representing the common law tradition. Grading accessories' punishment according to the degree of *both* mental and causal participation necessarily demands *informal* judicial assessment of each, something which has proved more enduring in common law jurisdictions.[134] But so far the trend in Anglo-American complicity law has been to distinguish criminal participation by means of different levels of mental culpability rather than by resort to causal norms. This emphasis is represented by a few American jurisdictions that have supplemented complicity with facilitation offences punishable less severely than complicity. Unlike the overwhelming American standard culpability requirement of purposeful help, facilitation liability is satisfied by knowingly providing assistance.[135] However, a principal offence carried out with such assistance

---

[133] Cf. Dressler's proposals for distinguishing causal and non-causal accessories, 'Reassessing', 130–1.

[134] For observations on the German aversion to this degree of judicial discretion, see Schreiber, 'Problems', 623.

[135] For the *mens rea* aspects of facilitation offences, see Ch. 5, section 5. Article 115 of the revised New York Penal Code was a pioneering example of a facilitation offence. See also article 1002 (1) of the proposed New Federal Code. The draft Federal provision, by requiring 'substantial' assistance, attempted to lay down in quantitative terms the extent of the facilitation necessary to incur liability. The New York Code stipulates any conduct which

still remains a condition of liability. And other *actus reus* requirements (such as substantiality of contribution) if anything reinforce an attempt to make the facilitator's participation clearer and more substantial than may be necessary for accessories.

A far more radical departure from common law complicity is found in proposals from the Canadian Law Reform Commission. Sweeping away traditional complicity provisions, the proposed offence of 'furthering' would rest liability more heavily on mental culpability by requiring a 'substantial' act with the 'purpose' of furthering an offence. However, although there need not even be communicated help or encouragement, the commission of a principal offence is, curiously, still a requirement of responsibility. At the heart of such proposals is a declared[136] attempt to produce a unified system of inchoate and risk based liability. In contrast, English law, with its (probable) culpability requirement of deliberate action plus foresight of the possibility of a principal offence coupled with presumed cause, sets up a low qualifying complicity threshold. Together with unfettered sentencing ability, the English system represents an infinitely flexible instrument of judicial assessment and discretion for making the punishment fit the *informally* assessed degree of mental and physical participation.

Judgments on the acceptability of the current English position force a return to large general questions on the desirable link between harm and punishment, and the proper rationale of punishment. Such an assessment also demands consideration of the particular issues of complicity's

---

provides the 'means or opportunity for' an offence to be committed. Here there is no attempt to quantify the degree of assistance. The use in the Federal Code of the word 'substantial' carries the obvious difficulty of vagueness; but no more so than the general causal requirement in criminal law of substantiality. Further, the availability from other sources of that which the facilitator provided is a factor relevant to the question of substantiality — how *much* help was the aid, bearing in mind the circumstances. Quite why this should have a bearing on the culpability of the facilitator is not easy to follow. If the offence is concerned with the actuality of assistance this is not changed by the availability of the same. Beyond the United States, e.g. in Israel, an offence of facilitation was enacted (s. 33A of the Criminal Code Ordinance, 1973) to supplement the existing (parasitic) law of complicity. S. 33A states: '(*a*) Whoever gives a person tools, materials, money, information or any other means, knowing the same may be directly or indirectly used for the commission of a felony or to facilitate its commission is liable to punishment for 3 years imprisonment.' Unlike the New York and proposed Federal offences, the commission of the Israeli offence is not contingent upon a principal offence being carried out using the assistance provided. See D. Bein, 'Recent Developments in Israeli Criminal Law' (1977) 12 *Is. LR* 180.

[136] See Law Reform Commission of Canada, Working Paper 45, ch. 4; and Report 31, cl. 4 (2): 'Everyone is liable for furthering a crime, . . . if he helps, advises, encourages, urges, incites or uses another person to commit that crime and that person completely performs the conduct specified by its definition.' Under cl. 2 (4) (*d*) 'furthering' must be carried out purposefully. Variation matters are dealt with by cl. 4 (6) under which differences in the victim's identity or degree of harm will not prevent liability; liability is imposed for all collateral offences foreseen as probable. The function served by the requirement of a principal offence is unclear if help or encouragement need not be communicated. In what way should punishment be determined by the occurrence of a patently causally unconnected act of the 'furtherer'?

appropriate mental culpability requirement, and, as already noted, the coverage of complementary forms of liability, especially inchoate offences. However, the fundamental point is whether complicity is conceived of as being a form of liability, which in common with substantive liability carries causal expectations, or whether it is broadly one of inchoate or risk character with no causal element. If it is the former, then the punishment practices employed there are appropriate — complicity and substantive principal liability largely stand or fall together. The same conclusion follows in respect of an inchoate or risk approach. This is an argument for consistency in the treatment of such forms of liability, not an attempt to justify the relevance of harm[137] to liability and punishment, nor to seek to indicate the most acceptable basis of punishment.[138] What is clearly within the proper scope of the present analysis is whether, given the criminal law's existing policies and practices relating to harm and punishment, complicity's role is most appropriately performed through a causal or non-causal based form of liability.

As observed before, in consequence of relatively low *mens rea* and causal demands, the current law of complicity in England covers an extraordinarily extensive range of conduct. In many cases the causal contribution will be patently strong, in others it will be marginal or even doubtful. To these opposites (and intermediate examples) can be added the permutations provided when the actual level of mental involvement is drawn into the overall calculation of the accessory's culpability and punishability. Thus, there may be a high level of causal and mental commitment or weak causality but purposeful accessorial action, and so on. More concretely, should, for instance, the retailer of a shotgun who correctly suspects that it may be used to murder be regarded as categorically distinct from the shouter of encouragement during a stabbing attack? The first example entails low mental culpability coupled with high causal involvement; the second illustrates the reverse position. Arguably the shotgun supplier, because of his more apparent involvement, fits more comfortably under complicity liability than the encourager whose culpability primarily turns on his active desire for the substantive harm — inchoate in complexion.[139]

---

[137] 'Harm' in complicity in the sense of the *actus reus* of the principal offence, whether a conduct or consequence offence.

[138] Although bearing in mind the range of arguments that can be deployed supporting the relevance of harm for *both* utilitarian/deterrent as well as retributivistic accounts of punishment, the actual difference in effect on the shape and structure of complicity might not be great. See e.g. Karp, 'Causation', and Robinson 'A Theory of Justification'.

[139] Being a participant (rather than simply an inciter) in an offence arguably carries normative implications for *mens rea* requirements. If the gun supplier had no suspicions of the gun's intended use, it would require a strained use of language to describe him as a party to the killing, even though the shotgun was essential for *that* killing. In other words, in complicity causal attribution is influenced by common sense notions as to the appropriate accompanying mental states: it might be said, where there is no suspicion, that supplying the gun was still a factual cause, but not that the supplier was a party to the killing. However (see Chs. 7 and 8) use is sometimes made of an objective probable consequence rule for further incidental offences.

Causation's Role in Complicity

Yet in practically all American states the uninvolved supply of materials believed to be for use in an offence would be insufficient for complicity. The attraction of distinct facilitation offences is clear when complicity is limited to purposeful accessorial conduct: it enables behaviour less culpable than complicity but still sufficiently unacceptable to be punished.[140]

Creating a new offence with lower penalties, rather than enlarging secondary involvement, implies that facilitation is regarded as a sufficiently distinct form of lesser criminality because of the difference between purposeful and knowing assistance. Making a further *formal* distinction between causal and non-causal participation, to demarcate and articulate more subtly the nature of the criminality being punished, has a certain intellectual appeal.[141] Refinements of this order would, to a fair degree, regularize the informal judicial process already gone through in determining an accessory's overall level of criminality and appropriate punishment. Structure is, of course, partly a reflection of a legal system's historic and institutional preference for law in one shape rather than another. However, English complicity law's characteristics of widespread loose and indistinct rule formulations, great reach, and coverage of an enormous diversity of levels of criminality from the most trivial to the most serious, all combine to suggest the desirability of a tighter more compartmentalized approach. Clearly one route to easing these inherent problems of a monolithic structure of liability would be a differentiation of liability based not only on mental culpability but also on causal grounds. Because of overlapping operational areas and a degree of theoretical kinship, inchoate liability's functions and rationale must also be drawn into any reassessment and restructuring of complicity.

Such broad speculations aside, cause-related issues arise extensively, as will be seen in succeeding chapters, in matters concerning *mens rea* and variation through to questions of withdrawal. Bearing in mind its implicit or latent function throughout much of complicity's structure, any serious untrammelled reformulation of complicity which wished to reveal fully the basis of its criminality could hardly fail to address the long submerged role of cause.

---

[140] 'The justification for an offence of facilitation is that provision of such assistance has been held sufficient for complicity in crimes actually committed, and logically, therefore, it ought to be penalised on occasions where no crime is committed. Our provisional conclusion is that despite the attraction presented by the opportunity of filling this apparent gap in the law, no new offence should be created. We take this view because there has not hitherto been any demand for the creation of such an offence and because in principle inchoate offences ought not to be proliferated unless the need for them has been demonstrated.' Law Commission Working Paper 50, para 4. And see Ch. 5.

[141] Not the least important part of which is closer adherence to notions of fair representation or 'labelling' of the nature of the criminality involved. On the proper acknowledgement of this concept in the criminal law generally, see G. L. Williams, 'Convictions and Fair Labelling' (1983) 42 *CLJ* 85; and Ashworth, 'Elasticity of Mens Rea', 53–6. See also above Ch. 2 in relation to omissions.

4

The Derivative Nature of Complicity

An immediate and obvious corollary of complicity's derivative or parasitic nature is the existence of criminal behaviour on which an accessory's liability can be based. Simplistically, if no crime is committed there is no criminality from which another's complicity can be derived. However, there are occasions where although the perpetrator's conduct is not itself criminal or subject to criminal proceedings, the 'accessory' may still in some way be criminally responsible for the perpetrator's conduct. Such an outcome is possible in a variety of ways, some involving aspects of orthodox complicity and others resorting to incriminating mechanisms that are either a particular form of principal liability or quasi-complicitous.

The first and best known technique developed to incriminate a culpable 'accessory'[1] where the actor or perpetrator is free of liability is the doctrine of innocent agency which employs modified rules of principal liability to convert, in effect, an apparent 'accessory' into a principal offender.[2]

A second route, within complicity proper, is the consequence of long-standing rules of evidence and procedure whereby an accessory's liability must be established, so to speak, autonomously and independently of the principal's. Therefore, for example, a principal's acquittal for an offence in which another is alleged to be an accessory does not necessarily mean—for accessorial purposes—that no principal offence occurred.

The third and most contentious approach to the problem, convicting a morally culpable 'accessory' when there is no principal criminality, is achieved by a process of grafting onto the 'accessory's' culpable behaviour the perpetrator's 'objectively' criminal actions—or *actus reus*. This relat-

---

[1] Common law language provides no satisfactory compendious term for the different possibilities where there is no direct principal offender. This is true of the guilty party both in innocent agency situations and cases where the perpetrator's non-criminal actions are the basis of another's complicity liability. The need is satisfied in German criminal jurisprudence by the expression 'hintermann'—literally the person behind the actions. See Schreiber, 'Problems of Justification', 611 n. 1.

[2] It is debatable whether innocent agency doctrine is best viewed as a true variety of principal liability or as a severely modified example of complicity. It is not complicity in any normal sense as liability is not derivative. Yet it *may* not be wholly principal because of the arguable limitations in respect of types of conduct ascribable under the doctrine, and because of the restricted range of mental culpability or fault sometimes claimed as applicable.

ively newly developed (and developing) variety of complicity represents an attempt (both judicially and legislatively) to incriminate a morally deserving party for actions not comfortably reached by either classical complicity theory, with its derivative expectations, or through the doctrine of innocent agency. It is an innovation aimed at (as Foster put it)[3] the 'special cases founded in necessity and political justice ... which is due to the public'.

Although each of these three aspects or forms of potential 'complicity' without 'principal' liability is judicially recognized, their operating conditions and limits remain vague. Moreover, doubts or unease exist as to the conceptual integrity and collective ability of these techniques to punish all deserving 'accessories' on the most appropriate and coherent basis.

1. THE DOCTRINE OF INNOCENT AGENCY

There is a clear need for a formula to incriminate a party (P) who has been instrumental in another (A) carrying out the *actus reus* of an offence where A, for some reason or other, lacked responsibility. The common law identified and satisfied this need by creating the doctrine of innocent agency which probably incorporates the notion that a human agent may be equated with some non-human causal agency,[4] either animate[5] or inanimate; akin to 'a mere machine whose movements are regulated by the offender'.[6] The concept enjoys an appealing simplicity, complementing complicity with few expressed doubts or problems from at least the seventeenth century throughout an extensive range of offences,[7] with commentators largely

---

[3] *Crown Law*, 349, in relation to innocent agency.

[4] Cf. Law Commission Working Paper 43, proposition 3, which speaks of where the defendant 'causes' an innocent agent to act; and Law Commission Report 177, cl. 26 (1) (c), which expresses the connection in terms of the defendant who 'procures, assists or encourages' an innocent agent; see further below.

[5] See e.g. *Halloway's Case* (1628) Cro. Car. 131, 79 ER 715, and *Gibbons* v. *Pepper* (1695) 1 Ld. Raym. 38, 91 ER 922. Note the limitations expressed in *Pratt* (1855) 4 El. & Bl. 380, 119 ER 319, *Pratt* v. *Martin* (1911) 2 KB 90, and *Plunkett* v. *Matchell* [1958] Crim. LR 252.

[6] Williams, *CLGP* 350; and the 7th Report of the First Criminal Law Commissioners (1843), 30.

[7] Murder: e.g. anon. report *c*. 1665, Kel. J. 53, 84 ER 1079: 'if A give poison to JS to give to JD and JS knowing it to be poison give it to JD who taketh it in the absence of JS and dieth of it. In this case JS who gave it to JD is principal. And A who gave the poison to JS and was absent when it was taken, is but accessory before the fact: but if A buyeth poison for JS and JS in the absence of A taketh it and dieth of it; in this case A though he be absent, yet he is principal; so it is if A giveth poison to B to give to C and B not knowing it to be poison, but believing it to be a good medicine, giveth it to C who dieth of it; in this case A who is absent is principal . . . So if A puts a sword into the hand of a mad man, and bids him kill B with it . . . and the mad man kills B with the sword . . . this is murder in A tho' absent, and he is principal'. Murder through perjured testimony is recognized by Hawkins (PC i, ch. 13, s. 7): 'a man shall be said, in the judgment of the law, to kill one who is in truth actually killed by another [members of the judicial process and executioner] as where one by duress or imprisonment compels a man to accuse an innocent person, who on his evidence is condemned and executed.' And cf. Co. *Inst.* iii. 48, 91. Also for murder: *Coombes* (1785) 1 Leach 388, 168 ER 296, *Tyler and Price* (1838)

content with the provision of little more than a few basic illustrations of the doctrine.[8] Yet ease of operation in most circumstances has concealed or, in practical terms, obviated any need to provide a fuller conceptual account of the doctrine. Moreover, the precise characteristics and limitations of the doctrine's ambit lack reasonably firm authority.

The overall question is whether *P* is to be regarded as exactly equivalent to a normal (direct) principal in terms of the forms of liability for which he may be responsible and the appropriate culpability demands usually attached to such forms of liability? In relation to the necessary mental culpability of *P* several issues arise. Must he be aware of the nature of the agent's innocence? Is anything less than intention to bring about the actions of *A* sufficient? Can the doctrine operate where *P* is reckless or negligent as to causing *A* to act? Beyond matters of *mens rea*, in what sense must *P* have brought about or *caused A* to act? Must it be by instigation or encouragement, or is the provision of assistance sufficient to be regarded as 'causing'? Is the doctrine's operation restricted to agency conduct which does not by its intrinsic nature imply actual personal performance by a

---

[1] Mood CC 428, 173 ER 643, *Michael* (1840) 9 C. & P. 356, 173 ER 867. Various forms of forgery e.g. *Palmer* (1804) 2 Leach 978, 127 ER 395, *Giles* (1827) 1 Mood CC 166, 168 ER 1227, *Mazeau* (1840) 9 C. & P. 676, 173 ER 1006, *Clifford* (1845) 2 Car. & K. 202, 175 ER 84, *Bull* (1845) 1 Cox 281, *Valler* (1844) 1 Cox 84, *Bannen* (1844) 1 Car. & K. 295, 169 ER 123. Larceny e.g. *Pitman* (1826) 2 C. & P. 423, 172 ER 192, *Manley* (1844) 1 Cox 104, *Welham* (1845) 1 Cox 192, *Bleasdale* (1848) 2 Car. & K. 765, 175 ER 321, *Flatman* (1880) 14 Cox 396, *Davenport* (1826) MSI Archb. Peel's Acts, 3rd edn., 271, *Adams* (1812) R. & R. 225, 168 ER 773, *Kay* (1857) Dears & B. 231, 169 ER 988, *Paterson* [1976] NZLR 394. Offences involving fraud: (potential use of the doctrine for attempt) *DPP* v. *Stonehouse* [1978] AC 55 and the commentary [1977] Crim. LR 544 at 546–8; *Girdwood* (1776) 1 Leach 142, 168 ER 773, *Munton* (1793) 1 Esp. 62, 170 ER 280, *Brisac and Scott* (1803) East, *PC* iv. 164, 102 ER 792, *Butcher* (1858) Bell 6, 169 ER 1145, *Dowey* (1868) 11 Cox 115, *Butt* (1884) 15 Cox 564, *Oliphant* (1905) 2 KB 73. Libel: *Johnson* (1805) 29 St. Tr. 81, 103 ER 25, *Cooper* (1846) 8 QB 533, 115 ER 974. Poisoning: *Harley* (1830) 4 C. & P. 369, 172 ER 744. For a very recent employment of the doctrine relating to legal privilege under s. 10 (1) of the Police and Criminal Evidence Act 1984, see *Francis and Francis* v. *Central Criminal Court* [1988] 3 All ER 775 (HL). And cf. *Ahmed* [1990] Crim. LR 648.

[8] See e.g. *Co. Inst.* iii. 138; Hale, *PC* i. 514, 555, 616, 617; East, *PC* i. 228; Foster, *Crown Law*, 349; Hawkins, *PC* ii. 440; Blackstone, *Comm.* iv. 35. See also the limited consideration in the 7th Report of the Criminal Law Commissioners (1843), 29–30 and s. 4, arts. 2 and 3, and the 2nd Report (1846), s. 3, arts. 2 and 3. In both reports 'Everyone is a principal in respect of a criminal act who either does it or causes it to be done otherwise than by a guilty agent' (art. 2, 1846). Furthermore, 'A party shall be deemed to cause a criminal act to be done . . . who wilfully causes it to be done by means of any mechanical device . . . or by any innocent person (whether such innocent person act unconsciously or under compulsion, or be or be not the person to whom injury is done)' (art. 3, 1846). Contrastingly, Macaulay's Indian Penal Code broke away from using a theory of innocent agency to convict the instigator as a principal. Instead the code regarded such a party as an 'abettor', whether present or not: 'A person abets an offence who abets either the commission of an offence, or the commission of an act which would be an offence, if committed by a person capable by law of committing an offence, with the same intention or knowledge as that of the abettor' (s. 108). And 'It is not necessary that the person abetted should be capable by law of committing an offence, or that he should have the same guilt intention or knowledge as that of the abetter, or any guilty intention or knowledge' ('Explanation 3').

principal? Must P be endowed with those characteristics and qualities necessary for normal direct principal liability? And in respect of the agent, quite what constitutes innocence?

(1) *The Principal's Mental Culpability*

(a) Must the Principal be Aware of the Nature of his Agent's Innocence? It appears unnecessary[9] for a principal to believe or know that his agent is in some way 'innocent'. Where, as is usual, P acts to achieve a particular objective through the medium of A's behaviour, it should make no difference that P, for example, mistakenly believes A to fully comprehend the nature of the situation. P's misconception of the quality of his own liability as being secondary should not inhibit his conviction as a principal. This being so, *a fortiori*, P's mistake or ignorance as to the nature of A's 'innocence' should, similarly, not affect his liability as a principal. Therefore, if P believes he is using a 15-year-old lunatic to steal, whereas, in reality, the agent is a physically precocious 9-year-old, then P's liability should remain unaffected. However, the reason for the agent's lack of criminality is not always irrelevant. Where 'innocence' involves clandestine collaboration between the authorities and A, P will not be principally liable for A's actions, not because of his lack of knowledge of A's innocence, but for wider overriding policy reasons relating to notions of fairness in the criminal justice system (see below, generally).

(b) Must the Principal Intend to Cause the Agent's Actions? Typically P's use of A will be with the object of achieving some purpose, as where, for instance, P gets innocent A to poison V.[10] Consequently, there is little judicial consideration of whether something less than purposeful activity will suffice. To be able to say that P has 'caused' A's actions is not to accept that P must have acted with the purpose of bringing about such behaviour. Attribution of causal responsibility is not necessarily contingent upon P's purposeful mental state and might, in principle, extend to actions of A foreseen by P as a possibility or even to actions that were no more than objectively foreseeable.

Such points all concern P's state of mind in relation to A's behaviour. Quite distinct is whether P intends his own actions towards A. It will be seen when considering the mental element in complicity that, whether or not an accessory must encourage or assist purposefully, he must at least act

---

[9] Cf. *Tyler and Price* (1838) 8 C. & P. 616, 172 ER 643.
[10] *Harley* (1830) 4 C. & P. 369, 172 ER 744. Stephen's illustrations of the doctrine e.g. are limited to such cases, *Digest*, art. 37; as are Foster's, *Crown Law*, 349. Similarly *Russell*, only speaks of agents being 'employed' or 'incited': 3rd edn., 28, and 12th edn., 129–30. The draft codes of 1843 and 1846 both limit innocent agency to circumstances where the defendant 'wilfully causes' the agent to act.

intentionally with the awareness that his actions can encourage or assist. Therefore if the owner of a shotgun forgetfully left it loaded on the kitchen table, whereupon his 7-year-old son accidentally shot and killed the postman, the shotgun owner would not be an *accessory* for two reasons: first, there is no principal offender nor, probably, an offence; and secondly, he did not intentionally provide his son with the shotgun. However, these limitations do not automatically follow through and restrict the operational scope of innocent agency. There is no inherent conceptual restriction of innocent agency to cases where the defendant has intentionally or purposefully caused or brought about the innocent agent's actions.[11] If the agent is truly to be regarded as no more than a mere conduit through which causal responsibility can flow, then in principle the doctrine should permit any form of liability if the defendant is culpable in the way required by the substantive offence. As noted in an early Model Penal Code commentary:

When crimes call for no more than recklessness or negligence for their commission, it should suffice, it is submitted, that one with such recklessness or negligence causes the required overt conduct by innocent or irresponsible persons; there is no reason for demanding that such conduct be caused purposely.[12]

Therefore, if P negligently fits a tyre to A's car causing it to run out of control and kill a pedestrian, it could be said that P is guilty of manslaughter through A's innocent agency.[13] Or, in the shotgun example, the father might be convicted of the postman's manslaughter even though he did not even deliberately supply the gun, let alone provide it with any homicidal purpose in mind.

However, whether innocent agency is the most appropriate mechanism for incriminating the morally guilty party in such circumstances is at least

---

[11] Fletcher, *Rethinking Criminal Law*, 666, implies that innocent agency is limited to situations where the defendant has purpose because (as in German criminal law) principal liability entails the concept of domination over or control of the agent's actions (hegemony over the act). Kadish also sees innocent agency as restricted to intended actions, but on the different basis that 'it rests on the notion of agency' ('Complicity, Cause and Blame', 391). This is, though, to place more weight than is really justified by the terminology, for of course the doctrine covers not merely human agents, but animals and inanimate means of perpetration — 'perpetration by means'. The nature of attribution of the agent's actions (and consequences) is arguably the key factor; see further below.

[12] Wechsler, TD 1 (1953), 17.

[13] At least two English decisions offer possible support for use of the doctrine beyond situations where the defendant wishes to bring about the agent's actions. In *Tyler and Price* A, a lunatic, led a gang of desperadoes 'having a common purpose of resisting the lawfully constituted authorities'. A in the presence of P shot an assistant constable who tried to apprehend A. P was held liable for the constable's murder. Despite the reasoning in Denman LCJ's judgment being complicated by the language of felony-murder, one construction of the evidence suggests P was convicted as a principal even though he had not wished A to shoot but had only foreseen A might do it. See also the *obiter* comments in *Quick* [1973] 1 QB 910 at 923. The manslaughter case of *Pagett* (1983) 76 Cr. App. Rep. 279 is implicitly against using innocent agency in non-intentional circumstances; instead general causal principles were applied to convict. See also the comments of Mason and Aickin JJ in *Matusevich* v. R. (1977) 51 ALJR 657.

questionable. A strong case, based partly on simplicity and fair labelling, can be advanced that in situations where the defendant does not intend the agent's actions, rather than innocent agency, the general language and principles of criminal causation are best resorted to.[14] Adopting this approach in determining *P*'s liability the broad question becomes whether his negligent fitting of the tyre was a proximate cause of the death. Again, the most conceptually coherent and consistent method of handling such (and more difficult) cases turns primarily on how closely causal attribution under innocent agency doctrine resembles direct non-agency cause. Asking whether *P* needs to act in a purposeful and manipulatory fashion is to pose this question more obliquely.

A form of agency action where this question of the proper scope of innocent agency implicitly surfaces is when the agent is responding to a situation largely created by *P*'s behaviour. The problem arises most vividly in police 'shoot back' cases where, for example, the police, in attempting to capture a suspect criminal (*P*), reasonably use force and in doing so accidentally shoot a third party, possibly *P*'s accomplice. Clearly *P* does not intend the police to shoot, whether at him or anyone else; and he may or may not foresee such a response. Can *P* be made liable for the injury or death of the third party? Although often clouded by the law and language of felony-murder, a sizeable cluster of mainly American decisions reveals two views of the proper solution to such cases.

Commonwealth v. *Moyer*[15] is an example of where *P* was held convictable as a principal offender for having performed acts deemed the proximate cause of the third party's harm. Against the *Moyer* proximate cause approach are decisions, such as *Commonwealth* v. *Redline*,[16] which treat the issue as determinable through complicity reasoning. However, in *Redline* and subsequent authorities, a further refinement expressly excluded 'shield cases'[17] from complicity, recognizing them as properly subject to

---

[14] See e.g. Williams, *CLGP* 352. Working Paper 43, proposition 3, specified that the defendant must 'intentionally' cause the innocent agent to act, whereas Law Commission Report 177, cl. 26 (1) stipulates 'the fault required for the [substantive] offence'. This is the approach adopted in the Model Penal Code s. 2.06 (2) (*a*). According to the commentary on TD 1 (1953) of the code 'This, it is submitted, probably is now the law; even more clearly, it should be the law' (18). Contrasting the American federal provision, s.18 (2) (*b*) requires the defendant 'wilfully' to cause the agent's conduct. 'Wilfully' appears to extend to possibly objective recklessness. But cf. the Final Report of the American National Commission on Reform of Federal Criminal Law (1971) following the Model Penal Code approach by proposing 'A person may be convicted of an offense based upon the conduct of another person when: (*a*) acting with the kind of culpability required for the offense he causes the other to engage in such conduct' (para. 401 (1)).

[15] 53 A. 2d 736 (1947). Followed in *Comm.* v. *Almeida* 68 2d 595 (1949) and *Comm.* v. *Thomas* 117 A. 2d 204 (1955).

[16] 137 A. 2d 472 (1958); also *Comm. ex rel. Smith* v. *Myers* 261 A. 2d 550 (1970) overruling *Almeida*, and *State* v. *Canola* 374 A. 2d 20 (1977).

[17] As the name suggests, where a third party is used by escaping suspects or those under siege as a shield against police gun-fire.

general causal principles. No clear reference to the relevance of innocent agency occurs in either the *Moyer* or *Redline* group of cases, although two California Supreme Court decisions, People v. *Washington*[18] and People v. *Gilbert*,[19] are a little more revealing. In *Washington* it was observed that

> where the defendant intends to kill or intentionally commits acts which are likely to kill with a conscious disregard for life, he is guilty of murder even though he uses another person to accomplish his objective (*Johnson* v. *State* 142 Ala 70 see also *Wilson* v. *State* 188 Ark 846 and *Taylor* v. *State* 41 Tex Ct. R. 504) . . . Defendants who initiate gun battles may be found guilty if their victims resist and kill . . . to invoke the felony-murder doctrine to imply malice is unnecessary and overlooks the principles of criminal liability that should govern the responsibility on one person for a killing committed by another.[20]

The language of *Washington* and the supporting authorities cited suggests innocent agency explanations are relevant to such cases where there is less than purposeful use of an agent. Distinctions drawn in judgments, such as *Redline*, between 'human shield' and other 'shoot-back' cases appear to rest on some notion of causal proximity, with only very proximate causes being accepted as sufficiently strong to warrant causal attribution. Proximity, of course, is a proper concern whether liability is being considered under general principles or the doctrine of innocent agency; although intended consequences are usually regarded as proximate and not too remote.[21]

However, the modern English 'shield-case' of *Pagett*[22] is implicitly against the use of innocent agency beyond intentionally caused actions. If such an example of strong causal attribution is not to be considered an innocent agency case, weaker ones are hardly likely to. 'At risk of scholarly criticism', the Court of Appeal in *Pagett* characterized the problem as one of cause in homicide and particularly as involving the effect of a *novus actus*

---

[18] 44 Cal. Rept. 442 (1965).

[19] 47 Cal. Rept. 909 (1965). 'When the defendant or his accomplice, with a common disregard for life, intentionally commits an act that is likely to cause death, and his victim or a police officer kills in reasonable response to such act the defendant is guilty of murder. In such a case the killing is attributable, not merely to the commission of a felony but to the intentional act of the defendant or his accomplice committed with conscious disregard for life. Thus the victim's self-defence killing or the police officer's killing in the performance of his duty cannot be considered an independent intervening cause for which the defendant is not liable, for it is a reasonable response to the dilemma thrust upon the victim or policeman by the intentional act of the defendant or accomplice' (at 917). Kadish, 'Complicity, Cause and Blame', 394, quite reasonably takes the court's reference to the police officer's actions not being considered as an 'independent intervening cause' as indicating use of general causal attribution principles rather than innocent agency.

[20] 44 Cal. Rept. 442 (1965), 445–6. *Johnson* is an early instance of innocent agency where innocence took the form of insanity. In both *Taylor* and *Wilson* robbers used a victim as a human shield for protection from police gun-fire which resulted in the victim's death from shots fired by the police. Citation of these cases alongside *Johnson* suggests the court considered them to be settled under the same principle.

[21] Hart and Honoré, *Causation* (1985 edn.), 42–3, 79.

[22] (1983) 76 Cr. App. Rep. 279. Cf. *Dalby* [1982] 1 All ER 916 and *Ahmed* [1990] Crim. LR 648.

interveniens. The capacity of the police's *novus actus* to relieve the defendant of liability depended on whether their intervention was voluntary; this, expressly borrowing Hart and Honoré's test, rested on whether the intervention was 'free, deliberate and informed'.[23] Two examples of non-voluntary conduct 'germane to the present case' were 'a reasonable act performed for the purpose of self-preservation, and an act done in performance of a legal duty'.[24] Moreover, it was open to a jury to conclude that the defendant had caused the victim's death not only in 'shield cases', but when 'an innocent bystander' is killed in circumstances where the police are making reasonable use of firearms.[25]

Whether 'shoot-back' and similar cases, where the defendant does not intend the police agent's acts, are best treated as examples of innocent agency (awkwardly making the policeman the defendant's agent to shoot *at* the defendant) or resolved under general causal principles may be of little or no practical consequence. The distinction, if any, turns on the nature of the attribution which occurs under innocent agency, a matter of some uncertainty considered in the next section. If innocent agency were viewed as no more than a particular application of general causal notions, then whether the language of cause or agency is employed would be no more than a matter of linguistic appropriateness in each case, rather than one of principle leading to different outcomes. However, some, such as Hart and Honoré, maintain that 'an element of intention (intending others to act in a specified way) is essential if one person is to be said to "cause" another to act but not when he is said to cause some event to happen'.[26] Distinctions between actions and events or results may have implications for the type of *actus reus* which innocent agency may be capable of reaching. If innocent agency attributes not just results but actions too, then it is arguable (following Hart and Honoré's claim) that it is restricted to intended or purposeful agency acts; the converse also being true. But the solidity of Hart and Honoré's principle is questionable. It rests on a blend of the 'natural'[27] use and meaning of cause and a body of case law dealing with

---

[23] *Causation* (1959 edn.), 296; (1985 edn.), 326. The Court of Appeal added cautiously: 'We must resist the temptation of expressing the judicial opinion whether we find ourselves in complete agreement with the definition; though we consider it to be broadly correct and supported by authority' — (1983) 76 Cr. App. Rep. 279 at 289.
[24] Ibid. at 289. Cf. *Bailey* v. *Comm.* 329 SE 2d 37 (1985), where the police were regarded as 'innocent agents' of the defendant.
[25] 76 Cr. App. Rep. 279 at 291. Cf. *Mkhwanazi* 1988 (4) SA 30, where the deceased was a member of a gang charged with his murder through having unintentionally provoked a third party to shoot him.
[26] *Causation* (1959 edn.), 327–8; (1985 edn.), 368. And Kadish 'Complicity, Cause and Blame', 396–7. Cf. the example of the father unintentionally making a shotgun accessible to his young son.
[27] *Causation* (1985 edn.), particularly 42 and 52. The distinction is not acknowledged in the Model Penal Code formulation of innocent agency, s. 2.06 (2) (*a*) and commentary TD 1 (1953), 17–18; nor in Law Commission Draft Report 177, cl. 26 (*c*) and commentary paras. 9.10–15.

particular instances of statutory and non-statutory use of the term.[28] Rather than an *absolute* principle of interpretation, Hart and Honoré demonstrate by the examples cited that either the essence of the offence necessitates intentionality or the particular offences involved are almost inevitably going to entail circumstances where there will be intentionality; which is essentially their initial premise.[29]

Borderline cases are imaginable where it is unclear whether they would be most appropriately considered as innocent agency cases under an intentionality requirement. For example, where although in one sense the agent's act is intended, its nature is in some vital respect different from that imagined by P. This would be so if P, a chemist, negligently gave M poison, instead of the intended medicine, to administer to M's son V. Certainly M's *action* of administering the substance given was intended by P, and therefore it could be said P had *caused* the poisoning. But would it be appropriate to describe P as having poisoned V — is M's act of administering poison attributable to P? This would appear to turn on whether the nature of the act is affected by the extent of P's knowledge of its essential qualities.

Such an example may be compared with one where, although there is an intentionally performed act, it is carried out by a different person, as occurred in *Michael*.[30] Michael intended her child V to be poisoned with laudanum through the innocent dosages of a nurse, but a single fatal dose was unexpectedly administered by another child aged 5 years. It was held that 'while the prisoner's original intention continued the laudanum was administered by an unconscious agent and the death of the child under such circumstances would sustain the charge of murder against the prisoner'. Although Michael intended the death of V at the hand of another and might have been willing to permit what occurred, it is likely that she never contemplated another administering the poison. However, despite the lack of continuity of intent between Michael and the child's actions, the court used the language of innocent agency to attribute the child's act to Michael.[31]

In sum, whether the principal in innocent agency must intend either his

---

[28] *Causation* (1985 edn.), 363–74.

[29] A variation of the theme of whether innocent agency doctrinally demands intention relates to whether manipulation or control is of the essence. One feature of manipulation or control is the 'innocent' state of the agent, but that is distinct from P's state of mind or attitude. In German criminal theory, innocent agency is restricted to cases where P dominates or manipulates the agent. There must be 'hegemony' over the act of the agent. See Fletcher, *Rethinking Criminal Law,* 666, and Schreiber, 'Problems of Justification', 627, and references to the leading German text on the subject, C. Roxin, *Täterschaft und Tatherrschaft,* 4th edn. (1984), cited therein.

[30] (1840) 9 Car. & P. 356; 173 ER 867. Cf. *Low* (1850) 3 C. & K. 123, 173 ER 489.

[31] Although it would have been sufficient for homicide to have attributed the *consequence* of death rather than the *act* of administering poison. Cf. Hart and Honoré's criticism of *Michael* (1985 edn.) 336–7. Applying the relevant provisions of Law Commission Report 177 would probably not convict Michael of the full offence, although a charge of attempted murder would be available. Under cl. 17 (2) she could not be held causally responsible for the death as the intervening agency of the child was (arguably) not foreseeable. Moreover, innocent agency

own initial actions or those of his agent is unresolved by case law, with authorities supporting several views. Although the outcome may be the same, the appropriateness of employing general causal principles rather than the concept of innocent agency sometimes turns on the particular circumstances involved. Agency has greater intuitive appeal in those cases where the principal has consciously pursued an objective through the manipulative use of an agent. Conversely (as in the shotgun example) where *P*'s act in relation to the agent has been unintentional, which in turn facilitates or acts as a necessary precondition of another party's 'innocent' behaviour, then general causal principles enjoy more obvious relevance. Between these two extremes many situations are susceptible to equally convincing theoretical analysis whichever approach is adopted. Beyond such questions of linguistic felicity is the related, though distinct, issue of how far agency doctrine is equivalent to general causal principles: is the agent really to be regarded as a causal conduit? Does the doctrine ascribe not only final consequences but also the agent's *acts* responsible for bringing them about? If the answer is 'yes', then, as already suggested, any claimed intentionality requirement is undermined for general causal principles operate throughout all levels of fault or mental culpability. The nature of causal attributability is considered in the following section.

(2) *In What Sense Does a Principal 'Cause' an Innocent Agent's Actions?*

Whilst judicial accounts rarely go behind simply designating one party the innocent agent of another, most[32] commentators' formulations of the doctrine expressly incorporate the requirement that *P* has *caused* the innocent agent to act. Such a claim prompts two types of question: first, what is the theoretical route or justification for causally ascribing the actions of one person (or their consequences) to another? Secondly, what exactly is being attributed to the principal?

---

under the code requires that the principal 'procures, assists or encourages' the agent, which might not extend to Michael's connection with the intervening child. See Williams, '*Finis* for *Novus Actus?*', 391, 399, and 405.

[32] e.g. Smith and Hogan, *Criminal Law*, 131. Williams, *Textbook*, 369 and the Model Penal Code, s. 2.06 (2) (*a*); also the New Zealand Crimes Bill 1989, cl. 56 (1) discussed by K. E. Dawkins 'Parties, conspiracies and attempts' (1990) 20 VUWLR monograph 3, 117, 119. Law Commission Report 177, rather than 'cause', uses 'procures, assists or encourages' cl. 26 (1) (*c*). In relation to complicity, according to explanatory note 9.13, 'Procuring connotes the idea of deliberately causing. A person assists another to commit an offence when, for example, he supplies tools or labour or information . . . or . . . any other act which facilitates the offence. A person *encourages* . . . an offence when, for example, he incites the principal'. Presumably the words carry the same meaning for principal liability through innocent agency. Because only 'procure' has a *clear* causal meaning (as well as the connotation of purposeful action) the implication is that the nexus between actions of *P* and of the agent may be less demanding and attribution more constructive than traditionally understood. The logic appears to be that requiring a stricter standard suggested by 'cause' might only have inhibited the intended scope of the provision to cover cases of 'semi-innocent' agents. (Commentary, paras. 9.13 and 9.14.) See below, section 2 (5).

104   *The* Actus Reus

The first question (the basis for causally attributing to *P* the agent's acts or their consequences) involves two complementary and opposite notions: how much control did a principal exercise over an agent's actions, and how voluntary or independent were the agent's actions? As already noted when discussing causation and complicity generally, actions (or their consequences) factually caused by one party (*A*) will be legally attributed to another (*P*) as principal where *P* has in some way set in motion or facilitated *A*'s behaviour and *A* is either an involuntary or not completely voluntary actor[33] — or, in the present context, an innocent or irresponsible agent.[34] Recognized examples[35] of 'innocence' include infancy,[36] insanity,[37] absence of *mens rea*,[38] and duress.[39] In all such cases the direct perpetrator is eliminated from the causal equation, so placing *P* in the front line of causal proximity to the substantive *actus reus*; *P* is legally its most immediate or direct cause.

One likely limitation on the use of the doctrine, seen as necessary on the grounds of fairness, is illustrated by the similar cases of *Bannen*[40] and *Valler*.[41] In *Bannen P* approached a die-sinker and, under the pretence of intended legitimate use, requested the production of a particular die. Being suspicious of *P*'s real motives, the die-sinker consulted the Mint which, for entrapment purposes, instructed him to carry out *P*'s orders. Despite this collaboration, *P* was convicted of forgery through the innocent agency of the die-sinker because he had 'innocent' rather than 'guilty knowledge'.[42] Besides being contrary to other indirect authorities implying the 'act of an innocent cannot be imputed to the defendant when the innocent agent was acting to incriminate him', it also arguably 'offends the sense of justice' to permit conviction of *P* of the complete offence rather than incitement.[43]

---

[33] Cf. the concept of the 'free, deliberate and informed' agent. Hart and Honoré, e.g. *Causation*, 326; refined by Kadish for innocent agency purposes, 'Complicity, Cause and Blame', 369–70. See Ch. 3 for critique relevant to complicity.

[34] Cf. Hart and Honoré, *Causation*, 336–7.

[35] Cf. Law Commission Report 177, cl. 26 (1) (*c*), and see below. The Model Penal Code refers to an 'innocent or irresponsible person' (s. 2.06 (2) (*a*)). No elaboration of the expression's meaning is provided; but see commentary 15–18 TD 1 (1953) and 300–3 (1985).

[36] *Mazeau* (1840) 9 C. & P. 676 and *Butt* (1884) 15 Cox 564.

[37] Cf. *Tyler and Price* and *People* v. *Monks* 24 P. 2d 508 (1933) and *Fritz* v. *State* 130 NW 2d 279 (1964).

[38] e.g., *Palmer and Hudson* (1804) 1 B. & PNR 96, 127 ER 395; *Butt* (1884) 15 Cox 564; *Boushea* v. *US* 173 F. 2d 131 (1949).

[39] Cf. *Bourne* (1952) 36 Cr. App. Rep. 125 and *Cogan* [1976] 1 QB 217.

[40] (1844) 1 Car. & K. 295, 169 ER 123.

[41] (1844) 1 Cox 84.

[42] In *Valler*, under similar circumstances, the court thought the agent had 'acted bona fide'.

[43] Williams, *CLGP* 777. Williams rightly cites *Eggington* (1801) 2 Leach 913, 168 ER 555, and *Johnson* (1841) Car. & M. 218, 174 ER 479. Note also *Lawrence* (1850) 4 Cox 438 and cf. *Chandler* (1913) 8 Cr. App. Rep. 82. By any reasonable standard, the reality of *Chandler* is difficult to distinguish from *Eggington* and *Johnson* where opposite conclusions were reached. See proposition 3 of Working Paper 43: 'A person is not guilty of committing an offence through an innocent agent when — the innocent agent acts with the purpose of preventing the commission of the offence or nullifying its effect'. Law Commission Report 177 provides no

Beyond such claims, the decisions in *Bannen* and *Valler* might be further faulted on causal grounds in that in neither case could it be said the agents were the defendants', rather they were agents of the authorities. In reality, the effects of the defendants' actions on the agents were terminated by the intervention of the Mint and the Dutch consul respectively. The illegal products were manufactured not in consequence of the defendants' instructions, but at the behest of the authorities.

As for the second more difficult question — *what* is attributed to the principal — the brief answer is that it depends on the strength of the causal nexus or degree of *P*'s control, which turns largely on the nature of the agency and the nature of the agent's *actions* which are to be attributed to the principal. Clearly if the defendant has killed *V* by using a remotely detonated bomb there is no question of suggesting that he has not caused *V*'s death; similarly where the defendant's highly trained mastiff kills at his command. Again, if the killing is accomplished by using a homicidal lunatic or by poison administered by an innocent acting at the defendant's direction, then it would be natural to say that the defendant had caused the death. But attribution of responsibility for *causing the death* in each case is distinct from claiming that the fatal *acts* were those of the defendant. Only in the first example could it be comfortably said that the defendant killed *V* by blowing him up. Here he could be sufficiently closely identified with the immediate cause of death for it to be reasonable to claim that it was his action. Once beyond inanimate means, and moving from animal to human agencies, the attribution to *P* of the *actions* most closely associated with the death becomes progressively more difficult and inapposite. If *P* encourages his mastiff dog to bite *V*, clearly few would claim *P* had 'bitten' *V*. Even suggesting *P* had 'attacked' *V* would still be somewhat artificial. The most natural course would be to employ a verb indicating that *P* had caused the dog's actions.

This holds even truer where a human agency is involved. Here it will usually be inappropriate to speak of the agent's actions as though they were the principal's. For example, if *A* (a lunatic) at *P*'s directions, stabbed *V* to death or shot him it would be unreasonable to say that *P* had stabbed or shot *V*; rather *P* would more naturally be described as having brought about or caused the stabbing, shooting, or *V*'s death.[44] Yet even where a human

---

similar defence. Would a charge of incitement be possible against *D* where he incites another to do an act which because of *A*'s innocence cannot be committed by him? See *Curr* (1968) 2 QB 944 where, as the appellant's counsel suggested, there probably could have been successful charges against the appellant for actual commission of the offences alleged to have been incited by him, through the innocent agency of the women. However, the Court of Appeal failed to respond to this speculation.

[44] Cf. s. 8 of the Accessories and Abettors Act 1861 which permits accessories to be 'indicted' as principals. This sanctioned the misleading practice of directly attributing actions of the principal to the accessory in the indictment particulars. The practice was soundly criticized by the House of Lords in *DPP for Northern Ireland* v. *Maxwell* [1978] 3 All ER 1140, where it was suggested that the true nature of the accessory's physical role be indicated by the indictment.

agency is employed there are occasions where it is perfectly reasonable to attribute the act of killing as well as the outcome to P. For instance, if P used an innocent to administer poison it would be quite natural to claim that P had poisoned V and not simply that P had caused V's death by poisoning. The difference may lie in the fact that in such cases the process of achieving a result and the final outcome are so closely associated, and the preliminary action of delivering the poison to V is itself neutral, that in normal usage no notice is taken of the linguistic distinction. Such conceptual uncertainty is an inevitable by-product of innocent agency's doctrinal dualism: an amalgam of liability through the use of an actual agent and also perpetration by means external to the principal.[45]

Questions of this nature have the greatest bearing on the use of innocent agency for conduct offences. When using the doctrine in consequence offences, such as homicide, there is no need to identify personally the *actus reus* element with P; it is enough that he has caused the death. However, where definitional elements stipulate either particular qualities as necessary for the defendant or specific forms actions, then innocent agency's capability may falter.

(a) Perpetrators Needing Prescribed Qualities or Status For offences where specific qualities or a prescribed status are needed to commit the offence (such as being 'any clerk, officer or servant',[46] or licensed to sell alcohol, or under a specified age) the fact that the agent satisfies such requirements should not permit use of the doctrine if the principal does not also have these attributes.[47] Therefore, if P a precocious 13-year-old boy incites A, a mental defective, to rape V, one reason preventing P's conviction as a principal would be his irrebuttably presumed incapacity.[48] Similarly if P, a bachelor, untruthfully but on reasonable grounds convinces A, who is already married, that A's estranged wife died three years ago, and in consequence A 'marries', then one reason why P could not be principally liable for bigamy would be his lack of the necessary status of one 'already married'. *Cogan*[49] is a counter-example where one objection to convicting the instigator was overcome by the court delimiting to direct personally

---

[45] Cf. the examples where the offence description embodies a technical notion, as in 'defrauding' or 'stealing'. In such cases, the principal could reasonably be said to have 'stolen' property or 'defrauded' another where an agent was used.

[46] Falsification of Accounts Act 1875, s. 1 (1). See e.g. *Oliphant* [1905] 2 KB 67.

[47] See e.g. Burchell and Hunt, *SA Criminal Law*, 412–13. Both Law Commission Working Paper 43, proposition 3 (2) *(a)*, and Report 143, cl. 30 (3) *(a)*, excluded from innocent agency coverage cases where either the offence required the principal to have certain characteristics or a particular status which the defendant did not have. This approach was abandoned in Report 177, cl. 26 (3) *(b)*. The Model Penal Code, s. 2.06 (2) *(a)*, in a modified variant of innocent agency resorts to no such limitation. But unlike the English provisions, the American ones make P not the principal offender but 'legally accountable'.

[48] *Groombridge* (1836) 7 C. & P. 582. For whether or not P could be an accessory, see below.

[49] [1976] QB 217.

performed acts the rule preventing cohabiting husbands from possible liability for raping their wives. Paradoxically, using an agent to perform the *actus reus* in such cases extended rather than restricted the potential criminal liability of husbands.

(b) *Offences Implicitly Requiring Personally Performed Actions* The second commonly suggested limitation on the availability of innocent agency is the imprecise notion permitting an agent's conduct to be imputed to a principal only where it is neither an affront to common sensibilities nor an abuse of language.[50] This view is premised on the implicit assumption that innocent agency is an inculpatory mechanism, extending beyond simply holding a party liable for *causing* another's actions, for also ascribing the *substance* of the actions. Thus, rather than saying *P* has caused *A* to act in a certain declared criminal fashion, the doctrine implies that *P* has committed the act: the *act* is *P*'s. Therefore, driving[51] a vehicle would be a 'non-proxyable' action,[52] as would sexual intercourse.[53] For without a 'violent wrench of the English language'[54] it could not be said that *P* has 'driven' when in fact *A* had, or that *P* had 'raped' *V* when *A* had been the perpetrator.

The essential question here is quite what marks out cases of this type from other generally accepted forms of innocent agency involving conduct offences such as stealing, falsification of accounts, burglary.[55] However, even these examples can generate difficulties: to say that *P* burgled premises in London, through the agency of a 9-year-old, whilst flying over the Atlantic, sounds distinctly unrealistic. Burglary's requirement of 'entering' premises as a trespasser, although creating a weaker expectation of personal action than other cases, still carries connotations of personal action. Certainly 'entering or being' on land under the Game Act 1831 has many times been held to require the principal defendant's 'bodily presence', the agency of a

---

[50] Smith and Hogan, *Criminal Law*, 132. Williams, *Textbook*, 369–71. Similarly in Law Commission Working Paper 43, proposition 3 (2) (*a*), and Law Commission Report 177, cl. 30 (3) (*b*); but abandoned in Report 177, cl. 26 (3) (*a*). The change was to avoid the complexity of the previously proposed 'mixed solution' whereby 'artificial' cases of innocent agency were dealt with as complicity liability. The 'oddity' of designating the 'artificial' cases as principal, see Report 143, cl. 30 (3) (*a*) and (*b*), was seen as 'one of nomenclature and not substance'; commentary paras. 9.11–12. Are not formal definitional requirements substantive?
[51] Williams, *Textbook*, 370 and *CLGP* 388; and as suggested by Working Paper 43, illustration (*c*), 13.
[52] This useful term is borrowed from Kadish, 'Complicity, Cause and Blame', 373.
[53] Smith and Hogan, *Criminal Law*, 132, and Williams, *Textbook*, 371, and Criminal Law Revision Committee, *Working Paper on Sexual Offences* (1980), para. 24. To the contrary, see Law Commission Report 177, cl. 26 (3) (*a*), illustration 26 (iv).
[54] Williams, *Textbook*, 371.
[55] See Hale, *PC* i. 555 and Smith and Hogan, *Criminal Law*, 597. But cf. *Pratt* (1855) ER & Bl. 380, 119 ER 319, *Pratt v. Martin* (1911) 2 KB 90, and *Plunkett v. Matchell* (1958) Crim. LR 252.

gun dog being insufficient.[56] Much the same could be claimed of assault and battery where, say, P incites a 9-year-old to punch another child. Claiming P 'entered' the building, or 'struck' a child implies personal conduct and in the given examples would at least be an unpleasing distortion if not a 'violent wrench' of language. The matter is one of degree rather than of clear and absolute categories of behaviour. The more specific and detailed the nature of the *actus reus* the greater the inclination to resist the use of innocent agency.

There is room for disagreement even in the strongest examples of personal conduct involving sexual intercourse and driving. In the case of driving, it could be argued 'drive' has 'such a strong bodily connotation that only the actual driver can be the perpetrator of a driving offence'.[57] However, with equal plausibility it could be maintained that driving is an activity 'characteristically done through instrumentalities, mechanical or animal, and it is therefore not unnatural to speak of driving through the instrumentality of another person'.[58] And, therefore, in what way does 'drive' have a stronger 'bodily connotation' than, for example, assault or battery?

It is, though, in the area of sexual offences, and particularly rape, that the strongest claim for non-proxyability can be put forward and where the greatest number of reported cases have arisen. In *Cogan*,[59] Leak forced his wife, V, to have sexual intercourse with Cogan, after convincing Cogan that V was a consenting party. Leak's conviction for rape was upheld via two different routes: the first, and most favoured, being principal liability through the doctrine of innocent agency; the second, conviction as an accessory.[60] According to the Court of Appeal, Leak had raped his wife by 'persuading Cogan to use his body as the instrument for the necessary physical act'. Endorsement for such uninhibited use of the doctrine is to be found in a fair scattering of authorities throughout a number of widely different jurisdictions including South Africa,[61] Australia,[62] and America.[63]

[56] In *Pratt* v. *Martin* [1911] 2 KB 90, Lord Alverstone CJ thought use of a dog could reasonably be regarded as 'entering or being' on land. However, he felt bound to follow unchallenged earlier contrary authorities. Cf. *Woley* v. *B. and O* [1986] Crim. LR 183.

[57] Williams, *Textbook*, 370. In *Thornton* v. *Mitchell* [1940] 1 All ER 339 a bus conductor was probably negligent (or reckless) in signalling to the bus driver to reverse, in consequence of which a pedestrian was knocked down and killed. The driver's acquittal for careless driving was taken to necessitate acquittal of the conductor for abetting the driver. The possibility of convicting the conductor of careless driving through the driver's innocent agency was not raised.

[58] Kadish, 'Complicity, Cause and Blame', 374. *Ball* v. *Loughlin* (1966) Cr. App. Rep. 266 involved a 'scout' car physically driven by one party partly on the information provided by another. Would it be unreasonable to describe the second party in such circumstances as a joint driver? Cf. *Tyler* v. *Whatmore* [1976] RTR 83.

[59] [1976] QB 217. Support for the *Cogan* principle(s) appears in *Howe* [1987] 1 All ER 771 at 775; and see below.

[60] It is just arguable that the Court of Appeal intended to suggest no more than that an indictment for complicity did not preclude the finding of principal liability where such existed.

[61] R. v. *D.* 1969 (2) SA 591 (RAD). But cf. *M.* 1950 (4) SA 101 (T) 102A. See Snyman, *Criminal Law*, 206.

[62] *Cogan* received *obiter* endorsement in *Matusevich* [1976] VR 470; and see Gillies, *Criminal Complicity*, 141.

[63] *State* v. *Dowell* 11 SE 525 (1890); cf. *State* v. *Blackwell* 407 P. 2d 617 (1965).

But the contentiousness of the issue is well illustrated by two contrasting modern American decisions. In *People v. Hernandez*,[64] P compelled her husband to have sexual intercourse with a non-consenting woman. On appeal it was held that P was properly convicted as a principal to rape, thereby demonstrating an 'even greater degree of hawkishness than displayed by the court in *Cogan* to call her a constructive man'.[65] Running against this extreme extrapolation of innocent agency doctrine, and the more moderate development in *Cogan*, is *Dusenbury v. Commonwealth*[66] where P forced both A and V to have intercourse against their will. On appeal P's conviction for V's rape was overturned on the basis that innocent agency did not extend to the type of personal actions involved in the definition of rape which only A could perform.

The judicial dilemma in such cases is clear; the defendant has indisputably behaved in a way deserving some criminal sanction, but, with orthodox complicity theory requiring a principal offence, a court must either acquit a morally culpable defendant or avoid this undesirable outcome[67] by convicting him through an uncomfortably distorting application of innocent agency. However, the extent of this distortion and departure from normal language usage may not always be as great as is often suggested. This, as noted before, depends on quite how innocent agency is seen as attributing the responsibility for the agent's actions to the usually manipulatory principal. If it is a complete identification and imputation of the agent's *behaviour* to the principal then there will always be a variable degree of unreality with the doctrine's use in conduct offences, especially where the verb is non-technical. Thus, returning to previous examples, to say P 'struck' V or 'entered' a building is a misleading but tolerated fiction;[68] to

---

[64] 96 Cal. Rept. 71 (1971).

[65] Part of Williams's commentary on *Cogan*, arguing that it is 'highly illogical that a man can commit rape through an innocent agent when a woman cannot, because if the notion of innocent agency is held to be applicable, so that the bodily acts of the innocent agent are attributed to the instigator, the sex of the instigator (the fact that the instigator lacks the sex organ of the innocent agent) becomes irrelevant: *Textbook*, 371. But matters of necessary qualities or status of a principal as specified in an offence's definition are distinct from the conceptual problems of attribution of personal acts. In rape the first conceptual hurdle is to accept attribution of the male agent's act to P the female instigator. There is then the additional formal statutory requirement of being 'a man': s. 1 (1) Sexual Offences Act 1956 and s. 1 (1) Sexual Offences (Amendment) Act 1976. Attribution of actions is distinct from attribution of characteristics.

[66] 263 SE 2d 392 (1980).

[67] Though the offence of incitement may sometimes be available.

[68] Cf. Hobbes, *Leviathan*, pt. 1, ch. 16, 'Of Persons, Authors and Things Personated'. Kadish ('Complicity, Cause and Blame', 372–83) gives greater credence to the notion of attributing actions under innocent agency. Although the force of judicial rhetoric in such matters should not be underestimated, as the Bromley CJ's comments in *Griffith* (1553), cited in Ch. 2, well demonstrate: 'Notwithstanding there is but one wound given by one only, yet it shall be adjudged in law the Wound of everyone, that is, it shall be looked upon as given by him who gave it, by himself and given by the rest by him as their Minister and instrument. And it is as much the Deed of the others as if they had all jointly holden with their hands the Club . . .'. Bromley's comments were made with reference to abettors and not innocent agency.

say P had forcible intercourse with V is normally too great a departure from linguistic reality to satisfactorily form the basis of charges against P. Yet there is nothing inherent in the notion of agency nor any firm and consistent line of authority requiring innocent agency to be conceived of and expressed in such a fashion. Rather, as its usual formulation suggests, the nature of the doctrine centres around its causal core: that P has *caused* A to perform in a certain way. Therefore in using the doctrine it should be alleged that P assaulted (battered) by 'causing' V to strike him, or that P burgled premises by 'causing' V to enter and remove property therefrom. Procedurally the bold *legal* claim that P assaulted V or burgled certain premises is unobjectionable when complemented by the *factual* account of how P caused the *actus reus* of the offence. In cases such as rape it would not be the inapplicability of this procedural formula that would prevent conviction of a woman as principal, but, instead, the fact that rape's definition limits principal liability to men;[69] definitional status demands are not properly susceptible to circumvention if innocent agency is grounded on causal attribution.

Alternative and complementary approaches to the possible limitations of innocent agency being able to cope with the morally culpable party are considered below. However, before doing so, and in order to clarify the extent of the 'lacunae cases', preliminary evidential and procedural groundwork needs to be undertaken.

2. Complicity and the Non-Conviction of a Principal Ofender or Convictions of Parties for Different Offences

(1) *Evidential and Procedural Matters*

A fundamental feature of complicity's derivative nature has been the need for a principal offence. As already seen, the entrenched rigidity and disabling effects of this requirement took its toll on the administration of criminal law over many centuries, with the common law showing a tenacious and blinkered unwillingness to compromise the rule. Many of complicity law's present characteristics were already discernible when Bracton was published (*c.* 1250). Prominent amongst these was the absolute necessity of conviction of the principal offender before any question of accessory liability could arise.[70] To a considerable degree, the requirement's

---

[69] If both status and linguistic objections are ignored and expressly overridden (Law Commission Report 177, cl. 26 (3)) would the style of indictment particulars in such principal liability be subject to the strong comments in *Maxwell* relating to the desirability of clearly indicating the factual nature of an accessory's role? If so, then e.g. would a woman be charged with raping another woman by 'causing' or 'procuring' another to have intercourse with the victim without the victim's consent? Cf. *People* v. *Hernandez* 96 Cal. Rept. 71 (1971).

[70] *Bracton*, trans. S. E. Thorne, ii. (1968). For details, see Ch. 2 n. 17.

The Derivative Nature of Complicity 111

existence could be attributed to the compound effects of primitive methods of proof (for example, by ordeal) and crude rules of evidence. Pollock and Maitland[71] rationalized the principle as being:

the outcome of strict medieval logic. If you convict the accessory while the principal is neither convicted nor outlawed, you beg a question that should not be begged. The law will be strained if the principal is acquitted after the accessory has been hanged. The modes by which guilt and innocence were proved were, or had lately been, sacred and supernatural processes which could not be allowed a chance of producing self-contradictory results. What should we think of the God who suffered the principal to come clean from the ordeal after the accessory had blistered his hand. Hence a complex set of rules which permit the escape of many accessories.

Coke[72] maintained that the Statute of Westminster I (1275) reflected the already existing common law condition that an accessory could not be forced to go to trial until the principal had been convicted or outlawed.[73]

Clearly some technique had to be devised for reducing the severely disabling impact of this rule[74] on the administration of the criminal law. Foster described both the difficulty and eventual (partial) solution:[75]

the great inconvenience of the rule I have mentioned touching the course and order of proceeding against accomplices in felony, tending, as it plainly did, to the total obstruction of justice in many cases and to great delays in others, induced the judges from a principal of true political justice, to come into the rule now settled, *That all persons present aiding and abetting are principals.*

This absurd state of affairs, whereby an accessory '*at* the fact' (abettor) could,[76] but an accessory '*before* the fact' could not be convicted and

---

[71] *History*, ii. 509. Note also *Proceedings before the Justices of the Peace in the XIVth and XVth century*, ed. B. H. Putnam (1938), cliii–cliv. But there could still be embarrassment where the principal was outlawed and the accessory tried, convicted, and attained, after which the principal returned, was acquitted (by judges resolution), which would reverse the conviction of the dead 'accessory': 9 *Co. Inst.* ix. 119.

[72] *Co. Inst.* ii. 183–4, and Hale, *PC* i. 623 and 625. Note also the view of Hawkins, *PC* i. 451.

[73] *Co. Inst.* ii. 183. 'If the principal be attained and has his clergy, or be pardoned after attainder, the accessory shall be put to answer': Hale *PC* i. 625. And see above, Ch. 2. The position was made a little less absurd by Anne 2, CS (1702) by which the accessory was subject to conviction provided a principal offender could have been convicted 'notwithstanding that such principal felon shall be admitted to the benefit of clergy, pardoned or otherwise delivered before attainder'. Stephen acidly comments: 'The result was, that if the principal died, stood mute, challenged peremptorily more than the proper number of jurors, was pardoned, or had his clergy, the accessory altogether escaped. This was found apparently upon a notion, half scholastic, half derived from the Roman law (a fertile mother of arbitrary rules put forward as self-evident truths) that *accessorius sequitur naturam principalis sui* . . . It is strange to observe how, even in our times a commonplace which is not even true may be made to look plausible by putting it in Latin'. *HCL* ii. 232.

[74] For others see Ch. 2.

[75] *Crown Law*, 348.

[76] *Griffith* (1553) 1 Plowd. 97, 75 ER 152, is an important early example of recognition of the modified position of abettors. See Ch. 2 for a discussion of the rationale for courts distinguishing accessories who were present at the commission of the offence and those who were absent.

sentenced prior to this happening to the principal,[77] subsisted from the sixteenth century, without reported resolution in *MacDaniel's Case*,[78] until the enactment in 1848 of 'An Act for the Removal of Defects in the Administration of Criminal Justice',[79] which provided:

after the passing of this Act, if any Person shall become an Accessory before the Fact to any Felony whether the same be a Felony made or to be made such Person may be indicted, tried, convicted and punished in all respects as if he were a principal Felon.

Only at this late stage in complicity's evolution were abettors/principals in the second degree and accessories before the fact treated similarly in respect of eligibility for trial and conviction.

Moving to evidential matters, as a broad principle, whilst conviction or acquittal of a person is conclusive *in rem* as to *that* fact (as a matter of record), it is conclusive only *in personam* so far as the accuracy or correctness of the verdict is concerned. Proof of the conviction of a principal offence for the purposes of establishing secondary liability admits no exception to this principle.[80] Therefore, under 'orthodox' complicity the existence of the principal offence must be established by evidence admissible in the proceedings against the accessory. However, under modern English law the principal's conviction is admissible evidence to prove the commission of an offence, although his acquittal remains inadmissible.[81]

Because of the possible effects of different evidence being admissible against the 'principal' and 'accessory', an accessory may be convicted without the conviction of a principal offender. This is permissible whether an accessory is tried before or after the principal, or jointly indicted with the principal.[82] Moreover an 'accessory' may be tried even though identification

---

[77] Eventually this procedural and evidential autonomy extended to conviction of an abettor even after the principal in the first degree had been tried and acquitted. *Taylor* (1785) 1 Leach 360, 168 ER 283.

[78] (1755) 19 St. Tr. 745; Foster, *Crown Law*, 121 and 364. Examples of the application of the rule before *MacDaniel's Case* being Benson v. *Offley* (1686) 2 Show KB 510, 89 ER 1071; *Walliss* (1703) 1 Salk 334, 91 ER 294; and after: *Taylor* (1787) 1 Leach 360, 168 ER 283; *Ashmall* (1840) 9 Car. & P. 236, 173 ER 817; *Wallace* (1841) C. & M. 200, 174 ER 471; *Phelps* (1841) C. & M. 180, 174 ER 463; *Hansill* (1849) 3 Cox 577. Cf. 1 Anne, St. 2, c. 9 (1702) which permitted trial of the accessory notwithstanding the principal's pardon or benefit of clergy etc.

[79] 11 & 12 Vic. c. 46. In 1826 the statute 7 Geo. IV, c. 64, s. 9, was enacted with the intention of bringing about a similar reform, but the courts were otherwise minded: *Russell* (1832) 1 Mood 356, 168 ER 1302.

[80] *Hollington v. Hewthorn* [1942] KB 587. And see R. Cross, *Evidence*, 6th edn. (1985), 97–100.

[81] Police and Criminal Evidence Act 1984, s. 74; a position proposed by the Criminal Law Revision Committee in its 11th Report, *Evidence*, Cmnd. 4991 (1972), paras. 217–20.

[82] Under s. 2 of the Accessories and Abettors Act 1861 an accessory may be tried before, with, or after the principal offender, whether or not the principal 'shall not be amenable to justice'. The provision was repealed by s. 10 (2) of the Criminal Law Act 1967. Although repealed, the effect of this section remains by virtue of s. 8 (as amended) of the 1861 Act, which abolished the procedural distinction between accessories before the fact and principals in the second degree so that the rule concerning trial applicable to (factual) principals in the second degree became of general effect in respect of accessories also. The 1861 Act was, of course,

The Derivative Nature of Complicity 113

of the perpetrator is impossible.[83] If acquittal of an alleged principal occurs after the conviction of the accessory, the accessory's conviction may not be challenged on the grounds of inconsistency, even if the evidence adduced at both trials was the same, as different juries are entitled to form different assessments of the probative weight of evidence.[84] Although not authoritatively settled, where both principal and secondary party are jointly indicted, it appears that an accessory may be convicted despite the principal's acquittal, provided the admissible evidence was different and, as against the accessory, it could be established that a principal offence occurred.[85]

---

declaratory of the existing common law in relation to misdemeanours: *Du Cros* v. *Lambourne* [1907] 1 KB 40. In *Gould & Co. Ltd.* v. *Houghton* [1921] 1 KB 509 at 522, it was observed that the 1861 Act 'recognise[s] the distinction in fact and in law between principals and accessories as existing even in cases of misdemeanour, and . . . enacts not that accessories are truly principals, but that they "shall be liable" to be treated as though they were.' See also *Wauby* [1895] 2 QB 482.

[83] *Anthony* [1965] 2 QB 189. In *Davis* [1977] Crim. LR 542, although it was clear that a burglary had occurred, the fact that the alleged accessory may not have been associated with the *actual* perpetrator (as distinct from the acquitted alleged perpetrator) seems to have been fatal to the charge against the alleged accessory.

[84] Cf. *Hughes* (1860) Bell, CC 242, 169 ER 1245. In *Surujpaul* v. *R.* [1958] 3 All ER 300 at 302 the Privy Council regarded *Hughes* as a case where the principal had been acquitted on the same indictment by the same jury. But cf. *DPP* v. *Shannon* [1975] AC 717, *semble* Viscount Dilhorne at 762. In some jurisdictions the rule preventing conviction of an accessory before the fact if the principal is acquitted has survived into modern times. See Crabtree, 'Accessory Liability: Acquittal of Principal' (Tennessee), [1984] 15 Memphis SULR 87. Cf. Model Penal Code s. 2.06 (7): 'An accomplice may be convicted on proof of the commission of the offense and of his complicity therein, though the person claimed to have committed the offense has not been prosecuted or convicted or has been convicted of a different offense or degree of offense or has immunity to prosecution or conviction or has been acquitted'.

[85] *Surujpaul* v. *R.* at 303; and *Humphreys and Turner* [1965] 3 All ER 689. Cf. Foster, *Crown Law*, 365, and the earlier decisions in *Walliss* (1703) 1 Salk 334, 91 ER 294; *Towle* (1816) R. & R. 314, 168 ER 820; *Taylor* (1785) 1 Leach 360, 168 ER 283. In *Humphreys and Turner* both defendants were in fact convicted. The case concerned abetting the commission of a misdemeanour, but since the enactment of s. 1 of the Criminal Law Act 1967 the distinction between felonies and misdemeanours has been removed. Therefore although expressly limited to misdemeanours the reasoning is applicable to all offences. As seen, earlier cases demonstrate that as all parties to misdemeanours were procedurally regarded as principals, there was no procedural difficulty in convicting the accomplice at the same trial at which the principal was acquitted. See e.g. *Burton* (1875) 13 Cox 71; *Gould & Co. Ltd.* v. *Houghton* [1921] 1 KB 509; *Daily Mirror Newspapers and Glover* [1922] 2 KB 530; *Morris* v. *Tolman* [1923] 1 KB 166. *Humphreys and Turner* was followed in *Sweetman* v. *Industries and Commerce Department* [1970] NZLR 139; and cf. *Harrington* [1976] 2 NZLR 763. See also *Runyowa* v. *R.* [1967] 1 AC 26 at 41; *Burrows* [1970] Crim. LR 419 and *Andrews-Weatherfoil Ltd.* [1972] 1 WLR 118 at 128. Two modern decisions which appear to be contrary to the general trend are *Rowley* [1948] 1 All ER 570 and *Anthony* [1965] 2 QB 189. In the former case it is far from clear whether Humphreys J. was purporting simply to lay down rules of procedure concerning the appropriate practice for trial of accessories after the fact, or whether he was addressing himself to substantive matters. In *Anthony* (distinguished in *Humphreys and Turner* on the grounds of it being related only to felonies) Lord Parker CJ observed, *obiter* (at 192), 'The jury cannot acquit the felon and at the same time find somebody guilty of counselling him to commit the felony.' Similarly in some American states, see e.g. *People* v. *Allsip* 74 Cal. Rept. 550 (1969) and *People* v. *Wyherk* 178 NE 890 (1931) and *State* v. *Austin* 228 SE 2d 507 (1976).

(2) *Substantive Considerations: Limitations of Derivative Liability*

As seen, although for procedural or evidential reasons it may not have been possible to convict anyone as the principal offender, it has been accepted that the accessory has been convictable provided that the evidence in the establishing of *his* liability supports the existence of a principal offence. But what is the 'accessory's' position if, as part of the evidence against him, it is clear that the perpetrator is not criminally liable for proscribed conduct or consequences because, for example, he lacked the necessary *mens rea*, or was insane, suffering from diminished responsibility, or had been subject to legally effective duress? As has been seen, where the perpetrator is fully exculpated the doctrine of innocent agency may be pressed into service to incriminate the 'accessory' as the principal offender. However, where the perpetrator has less than a complete 'defence', or if the doctrine of innocent agency is inappropriate, then the question arises whether the 'accessory' may still be convicted of complicity, and, if so, in what offence?

Providing solutions to such problems places the derivative nature of complicity under the severest strain. The moral and social case for convicting parties in situations of this type is plain; but the ability of orthodox complicity notions to accommodate them is questionable. When determining the conceptual capabilities of complicity in relation to these cases two broad categories can be identified which generate analytically distinguishable problems. They are, first, situations where the perpetrator is completely free of liability, and, secondly, circumstances where the perpetrator is liable for an offence but the level of his mental culpability is greater or less than the accessory's, thereby raising the question of the appropriate extent of criminality recordable against the accessory.

(3) *Where the Perpetrator is Free of Liability*

(a) *The Necessity of a Principal Offence or Only Harm?* Stating the problem through the medium of a classic example

which has tormented generations of students of criminal law. A, a bachelor, induces a married woman to believe, on reasonable grounds, but contrary to the facts known to him, that her husband is dead, whereupon she goes through a ceremony of marriage with X.[86]

In English law the woman will have a complete defence by virtue of her reasonable belief in her husband's death.[87] Alleging principal liability against *A* through innocent agency would, arguably, require an unconvincing attribution of behaviour to *A*; and, more important, *A* (not being

---

[86] R. Cross, 'Duress and Aiding and Abetting' (1952) 69 *LQR* 354 at 358. Cf. Smith and Hogan, *Criminal Law*, 132.
[87] *King* [1964] 1 QB 285.

married) did not have the necessary definitional attributes of a principal in bigamy. Assuming *A*'s behaviour deserves punishment, can an acceptable method or formula be devised for convicting him as a secondary party? Although, for example, Macaulay's Indian Penal Code provided for such occasions,[88] at common law, until relatively recently, the absence of a principal offence would have defeated any charge of secondary liability.[89] This seemingly self-evident consequence appears to have been affirmed by the Privy Council in *Surujpaul*[90] when adopting Turner's view

> That when the law relating to principals and accessories [and abettors] as such is under consideration there is only one crime, although there may be more than one person criminally liable in respect of it . . . There is one crime, and that it has been committed must be established before there can be any question of criminal guilt of participation in it.

In other words, the established attitude was that complicity is founded not simply on conduct or consequences 'caused' by another but only where it is recognized as criminal for the perpetrator.

However, two modern English authorities run counter to this clear-cut notion of dependency. Orthodoxy received its first jolt in *Bourne*,[91] although its severity was somewhat muffled by the ambiguity of reasoning in Lord Goddard's judgment. Having forced his wife to submit to buggery with a dog, Bourne was charged, *inter alia*, with aiding and abetting the offence; the wife was not charged. The Court of Criminal Appeal rested its

---

[88] Enacted 1860. S. 108 provides 'A person abets an offence who abets either the commission of an offence, or the commission of an act which would be an offence, if committed by a person capable by law of committing an offence with the same intention or knowledge as that of the abettor'. Cf. the more traditional (common law) formulation of the issue in the language of innocent agency by the Second Criminal Law Commissioners, 2nd Report, s. 3, arts. 2 and 3.

[89] *Vaux's Case* (1591) 4 Co. Rep. 44a; 76 ER 992 at 993 and cf. Foster, *Crown Law*, 365; *Tyler and Price* (1838) 8 C. & P. 616, 172 ER 643; *Gregory* (1867) 10 Cox 459. *Semble, De Marney* [1907] 1 KB 388, where it appeared to be accepted by the Crown and Alverstone LCJ that if a party acting from outside the jurisdiction was not potentially liable as a principal then the accomplice within the jurisdiction could not be either. In *Daily Mirror Newspapers Ltd. and Glover* [1922] 2 KB 530 at 542, although the guilt of the company originally charged as principal may have been proved, *procedurally* the company was not open to be tried and convicted. This form of immunity does not necessarily deny the existence of a principal offence. See below (cf. diplomatic immunity). Note also *Morris* v. *Tolman* [1923] 1 KB 166; *Semble, Griffiths* v. *Studebakers Ltd.* [1924] 1 KB 102 and *Thornton* v. *Mitchell* [1940] 1 All ER 339.

[90] Cit. n. 84, at 301, adopting Turner's view in *Russell*, 11th edn., i. 134, and 12th edn. 128; similarly in *US* v. *Ruffin* 613 F. 2d 408 (1979). See also the discussion of *Surujpaul* and related matters by Smith and Hogan, *Criminal Law*, 152–6.

[91] (1952) 36 Cr. App. Rep. 125. Cf. Williams, *CLGP* 389. See earlier American cases at Annot 84 ALR 2d 1017, 1022 (1962); and more recently, *Cody* v. *State* 361 P. 2d 307 (1961) and *Rozell* v. *State* 502 SW 2d 16 (1973). Cf. *State* v. *Kennedy* 1616 P. 2d 594 (1980). See also *Cain* v. *Doyle* (1946) 72 CLR 409 where the traditional view of the need for a principal offence was taken. In *Lewis* [1975] 1 NZLR 222 the New Zealand Court of Appeal expressly declined to rule on whether complicity required a principal offence. *Hartley* (1978) 1 NZLR 199 holds that an 'accessory' may not be liable for a greater offence than the principal. See below.

judgment on the assumption that if the wife had been charged as principal she would have been entitled to an acquittal on the grounds of duress. Nevertheless, the wife being 'excused'[92] from punishment was not, in the court's view, to say that no offence had occurred. Therefore Bourne's conviction for complicity in buggery could stand.

More recent is the Court of Appeal's consideration of the issue in *Cogan*.[93] As already noted, the upholding of Leak's conviction was achieved via two different routes: the first, and most favoured by the Court of Appeal, was principal liability under the doctrine of innocent agency; the second was conviction as an accessory. Expressed in a fashion similar to Lord Goddard's in *Bourne*, Lawton LJ had no doubt that 'The fact that Cogan was innocent of rape because he believed she was consenting does not affect the position that she was raped'.[94] The novelty and importance of the decision lies not only in the additional scope given to the doctrine of innocent agency, but in the suggestion that absence of *mens rea* in the perpetrator did not exclude the existence of an offence[95] for complicity purposes.

In the language of the law the act of intercourse without the wife's consent was the *actus reus*: it had been procured by Leak who had the appropriate *mens rea*, namely, his intention that Cogan should have sexual intercourse with her without her consent.[96]

---

[92] Lord Goddard characterized the defence of duress as a 'prayer by her to be excused from punishment'. *Lynch* [1975] AC 653 recognized duress as a substantive defence leading to an acquittal. Since *Howe* [1987] 1 All ER 771 it has become unclear whether its nature is justificatory or excusatory, or both. Law Commission Report 83 (1977) recommended 'that there should be a provision to ensure that, where the person compelled has the defence of duress, this should not affect the liability of any other person who participates': para. 34. In *Walters v. Lunt* [1951] 1 All ER 645 the Court of Criminal Appeal (again with Lord Goddard) held that a child under the age of criminal responsibility was not simply exempt from punishment but did not perpetrate a criminal offence, even for collateral purposes. Cf. *McGregor v. Benyon* [1957] Crim. LR 608 and *Kemp and Else* [1964] 2 QB 341 where quashing of the principal's conviction on the grounds of absence of *mens rea* was seen as necessitating questioning the abettor's conviction even though he did have *mens rea*.

[93] [1976] 1 QB 217.

[94] Ibid. at 222.

[95] The court cited *Humphreys and Turner* (cit. n. 85) as support for the general proposition that acquittal of the party charged as principal does not necessarily prevent conviction of another as abettor. As this was a case where the existence of a principal offender was proved (as against the abettor) its claimed relevance to the issue in *Cogan* is illusory. The Rhodesian case of *R. v. D.* 1969 (2) SA 591, cited by counsel for Leak, accepted that if a party *A* forced another by threats to submit to sexual intercourse with a third party *B*, then it would be rape on the part of *A*, as a principal under the doctrine of innocent agency if *B* were unaware of the absence of consent, and as an abettor if otherwise. The Supreme Court of Victoria in *Matusevich* [1976] VR 470 appeared to see no objection to convicting a party as an 'abettor' of an insane 'principal'.

[96] Even though it has long been possible to indict an abettor as a principal in the first degree this has not relieved the prosecution of the need to prove a principal offence. *Grey and Wise* (1835) 7 Car. & P. 164, 173 ER 72; *Crisham* (1841) C. & M. 187, 174 ER 466. This was also the case where the accomplice was indicted as accessory before the fact: *Brown* (1878) 14 Cox 144. Some support for *Cogan* may be extracted from the speeches of Lords Morris and Diplock in *DPP v. Merriman* [1973] AC 584. In *Quick and Paddison* the Court of Appeal noted

Although the practical outcome of cases such as *Cogan* is hardly criticizable, the theoretical justification is far from obvious. It has been seen that the operational scope of the doctrine of innocent agency is generally not restricted by the nature of the agent's innocence: it may be absence of *mens rea*, lunacy, duress, infancy. By implication, therefore, it could be claimed that the doctrine's very existence is hostile to the notion that complicity extends to situations where, for example, the 'principal' lacks the necessary *mens rea*. However, such historically based reasoning could be met by interpreting innocent agency as imputing the acts themselves to the 'accessory' rather than just the legal responsibility for causing them. On this basis there is no coupling of the *mens rea* of one party with the actions of another: both mental culpability and actions are regarded as combined in the principal. Treated in this way the implicit doctrinal conflict with innocent agency may, up to a point, be circumvented.

In settling the conceptual propriety of *Cogan*—whether it is a legitimate development of complicity liability—the central question remains: from what is an accessory's liability derived? As seen, *conviction* of a principal offender has long been unnecessary, but is establishment of more than the conduct or consequences proscribed by the substantive offence required? Are the reasons why the perpetrator of the conduct or consequences is not convictable relevant to the question of their capacity to sustain secondary liability? It has already been noted that rigidly taking the principal's liability[97] as the basis of the accessory's would produce several inconvenient consequences; particularly that neither (in old terms) the abettor nor the accessory before the fact could be liable for greater liability than the principal, as greater liability cannot be derived from a lesser level of liability. This has not been the case for abettors since at least the sixteenth century. An abettor's liability could be more[98] or less[99] than the principal's for the same actions because the principal's actions were regarded in law as those of the abettor also.[100] However, for accessories before the fact, as Foster explained,

> The accessory is indeed a felon, but guilty of a felony of a different kind from that of the principal. It is, if I may use the expression, a derivative felony connected with and arising out of that of the principal and cannot exist without it.[101]

Merriman as being authority on only the procedural issue of whether the conviction of a party jointly indicted could stand where no verdict against the other had been taken on the joint charge. Perhaps significantly, later in *Quick*, when dealing with the question of whether a person can abet another who has been 'adjudged not guilty', the court thought the answer was 'a qualified yes' depending on the individual circumstances.

[97] Fletcher characterizes this as the 'narrow theory' of secondary liability: *Rethinking Criminal Law*, 642.
[98] *Salisbury's Case* (1553) 1 Plowd. 97, 75 ER 152; *Tooley* (1709) 2 Ld. Raym. 1296, 92 ER 349 at 352. Hale, *PC* i. 438; Hawkins, *PC* i, ch. 31, ss. 31 and 50; East, *PC* i. 350.
[99] *Stanley's Case* (1663) Kel. J. 86, 84 ER 1904; *Lord Mohun* (1692) Holt KB 479, 90 ER 1164; Hale, *PC* i. 437–8.
[100] *Griffith* (1553) 1 Plowd. 97, 75 ER 152; Hawkins, *PC* i, ch. 29, s. 7.
[101] *Crown Law*, 343. Cf. *Donnelly and Vaughan* (1816) Russ. & Ry. 310, 168 ER 818.

Yet the logic supporting the procedural distinction between abettors and accessories which permitted the trial and conviction of an abettor before that of the principal was not followed through to the next stage by recognizing that abettors could be convicted even though no principal *offence* was established. Whether abettor or accessory, at least the commission of a principal offence needed to be proved. In other words, only independently criminal acts were attributed to abettors; those which were not for some reason criminal could, where appropriate, only form the basis of innocent agency liability. The further conceptual step along the path laid to convict abettors, whereby the socially or individually objectively harmful component of the perpetrator's actions is accepted as the basis upon which a secondary party's liability rests,[102] was not taken[103] until modern times.

The fact that some situations are open to both complicity and innocent agency approaches is not in itself an overwhelming doctrinal objection, for whether conviction is as a secondary party or as a principal the potential punishment is the same. Furthermore, overlapping forms of liability already occur with incitement and conspiracy. Clearly in certain circumstances innocent agency would have more natural or intuitive appeal, especially where there has been a manipulative effect by the 'accessory' to achieve a particular result. The stronger the 'accessory's' causal role and the weaker the perpetrator's, the greater should be the inclination to label the actions as 'principal' through innocent agency.[104] But borderline examples are unavoidable for, as seen, [105] 'procuring' may be a recognized case of complicity where strong causation exists—occupying a causal no-man's-land between complicity and principal liability. On the other hand, offences requiring perpetrators with a special quality or status, or implying personal behaviour, may be more comfortably accommodated within complicity.

(b) Objective Harm or Wrongfulness Where the Perpetrator Lacks the Necessary Criminal Fault Taking the broad function of complicity to be punishment of those culpably associated with bringing about proscribed harmful conduct or consequences set out in the definitions of substantive offences, should this core of harm, regardless of the perpetrator's convictability, function as the foundation of accessorial liability? Whether such recognizable harm may exist in isolation from and independently of a convictable perpetrator probably turns on the combined effect of the definitional structure of the offence and the reason(s) for the perpetrator's

---

[102] Cf. Fletcher's imported Franco-German 'broad theory' of secondary liability based on the perpetrator's wrongful act. *Rethinking Criminal Law*, 643–4.
[103] Cf. Hawkins, *PC* ii, ch. 29, s. 7.
[104] Cf. Kadish, 'Complicity, Cause and Blame', 379, who appears to advance an account of a causally sharper distinction.
[105] Ch. 3 (1) (1).

non-convictability. Where the perpetrator lacks the necessary fault (subjective or objective) it is arguable that he is not liable because although he may have caused *harm* he has done no *wrong*.[106] Only when coupled with the required fault element (and in the absence of justification)[107] does causing the proscribed harm constitute behaviour worthy of punishment. However, the analytical cleavage between what is just harmful and what is criminally wrong, whilst acceptable as an account of a single actor's principal liability, is less immediately convincing when operating in complicity.

As a general proposition, what is designated criminally wrong will be based on a foundation of recognized individual and social harm. Depending on the context and circumstances, when the level of social or individual harm reaches a certain threshold it will achieve the status of criminal harm—it will be criminally wrong. Actions or consequences which are either individually or socially objectively harmful may be legally inert for principal liability unless carried out or caused by an actor with a prescribed degree of mental culpability.[108] Thus in homicide if the actor factually causing the death of another is not at least grossly negligent (reckless?) he will not be criminally responsible. The harm is obvious (if there is no positive justification) but, in the circumstances, not of a nature or wrong in a way which attracts a criminal sanction. However, the same objective harm would be recognized as manslaughter if the actor were grossly negligent and murder for the secondary party if he had the necessary *mens rea*.

Where does the, so to speak, 'extra wrongfulness' come from to support the secondary party's conviction for greater harm? One explanation lies in recognizing that for complicity the degree of wrongfulness of the killing is not determined at one level and for all purposes by the culpability (or otherwise) of the perpetrator. Therefore, if the degree of harm and wrongfulness is partly affected by the individual culpability levels of each party then why should the accessory's culpability not be linked with the *otherwise* (in respect of the perpetrator) *sub-criminal* or inert harm of the death to make him liable for murder? As noted, the degree of wrongfulness of the killing can move up from that determined by the perpetrator's culpability, from manslaughter where he is grossly negligent, to the higher level required for murder where the accessory has the necessary mental culpability. Why can a similar process of increasing or elevating wrongfulness not occur, but starting from sub-criminal wrong or harm, where the perpetrator is not criminally liable? Thus, returning to *Cogan*, the harm done to Mrs Leak by the forced submission to intercourse was not

---

[106] Kadish, 'Complicity, Cause and Blame', 381, termed 'innocent wrongdoing' (382).
[107] Fletcher, *Rethinking Criminal Law*, 511.
[108] On the risks of analytically separating *mens rea* and *actus reus*, Hall warns, if 'a sharp bifurcation is drawn between the external situation and *mens rea*, unfortunate conclusions are reached': *General Principles*, 231.

recognized as criminally harmful and wrong as against Cogan because of his lack of *mens rea*. But when linked with Mr Leak's mental culpability the harm changes character, being activated or raised to a recognized criminal level which constitutes the foundational wrongful harm from which secondary liability is derivable. Perhaps 'law newly minted',[109] yet it is, arguably, a conceptually legitimate development of complicity consistent with its derivative nature.[110]

(c) *Objective Harm or Criminal Wrongfulness Where the Perpetrator Has a Complete Defence* So far, harm and wrongfulness have been considered in situations where the perpetrator incurred no liability because he lacked the necessary fault. Beyond absence of fault, a perpetrator may have a positive and complete defence. It has been maintained by some commentators that whether a particular defence has implications for the liability of any 'secondary parties' to the perpetrator's act turns on whether the defence is justificatory or excusatory in nature.[111] The revival[112] and refinement of these terms, along with the consequential analytical apparatus in Anglo-American criminal jurisprudence,[113] besides assisting general evaluative[114]

---

[109] Williams, *Textbook*, 372.

[110] Rather than seeing such a conclusion as a possible development of common law, Fletcher appears to arrive at a similar conclusion via the Franco-German 'broad' theory of accessorial liability. In his view, Cogan's act was 'wrongful but excused' and therefore Leak could 'properly' to be held an accessory: *Rethinking Criminal Law,* 667. Here Fletcher seems implicitly to follow the approach that objective wrongfulness can exist without the necessary fault element of the offence. However, fixing Fletcher's view on whether this is always the case, or only for some offences, is problematic: compare 475–8, where the thesis of objective wrongdoing without fault is advanced, with 691–8 where fault seems to be seen as a necessary element of wrong.

[111] Here, for expositional purposes, the necessary fault element in an offence is treated separately from defences. However, it is accepted that it is at least debatable whether an offence's definitional fault element should be treated distinctly or as a variety of excuse. Some commentators (Fletcher and Robinson) favour separate classification; on the other hand, Williams cogently argues that both approaches are supportable: 'The Theory of Excuses' [1982] Crim. LR 732–5. Although pertinent to disputes over the existence, or otherwise, of a clear theoretical distinction between definitional elements and defences, its relevance to the present issue is insubstantial. For example, whether rape is defined as sexual intercourse subject to the *defence* of consent or remains in its present formulation, has no *significant* implications for the judgment when forcible intercourse is personally and socially harmful and morally wrong. On the question of definitional elements and defences, see e.g. G. L. Williams, 'Offences and Defences' (1982) *LS* 233 and K. Campbell, 'Offence and Defence', in I. H. Dennis, ed., *Criminal Law and Justice* (1987), 73.

[112] See Stephen, HCL iii. 11, and Hart, *Punishment and Responsibility,* 13, for the view that the medieval distinction between justification and excuse involves no legal consequences. Cf. Williams, *CLGP* 20 and J. L. Austin, 'A Plea for Excuses' (1956), reproduced in A. J. White, ed., *The Philosophy of Action* (1968), 19.

[113] Most prominently, through the efforts of Eser (e.g. 'Justification and Excuse' (1976) 24 *Am. J. Comp. L.* 621); Fletcher (e.g. 'The Individualization of Excusing Conditions' (1974) 47 *S. Cal. LR* 1269 and *Rethinking Criminal Law*); and Robinson (e.g. 'Criminal Law Defenses: A Systematic Analysis' (1982) 82 *Col. LR* 199 and *Criminal Law Defenses* (1984)).

[114] e.g. Horowitz, 'Justification and Excuse' (1986) 49 *Law and Contemp. Probs.* 109 and Kadish, 'Excusing Crime' (1987) 75 *Cal L.Rev.* 257.

processes in substantive law also carries potentially important implications for complicity.[115]

Separation of justified from excused actions represents and underscores moral and policy judgments or assumptions; and although a fair crop of problematic examples of moral and policy ambiguity can be adduced, demonstrating the futility of attempting to 'delineate bright line'[116] distinctions between justification and excuse, *broad* contrasting generalizations are still possible. Justificatory defences focus on the defendant's conduct, which is not simply regarded as non-culpable but as something socially approved of. Justified behaviour is not objectively wrong; it is morally appropriate. Justified action represents an element in a programme of criminal justice aimed at encouraging laudable behaviour—it 'modifies the legal norm'. Consequently, it is claimed that third parties may lawfully assist or encourage an actor performing a justified action without incurring accessorial liability. Most commonly, harm inflicted in the course of a lawful arrest, self-defence, or preventing the commission of an offence is classified as justifiable.[117]

On the other hand, an excused act entails the admission of unacceptable harm but a claim of no personal culpability. Excuses include infancy, insanity, and possibly duress and mistake.[118] Absence of culpability rests on

---

[115] Under s. 29 of the German Criminal Code 1975, as a general proposition, each participant's liability to punishment is determined without regard to the liability of others. However, there can be no accessorial liability for instigation or facilitation which is not unlawful (ss. 26, 27) because of the absence of the required fault element in the perpetrator's act or because his act is justified (s. 34). Although there may be accessorial liability where the perpetrator is excused by 'excusing necessity' (s. 35). See Eser, 'Justification and Excuse', 622, and Schreiber, 'Problems of Justification', 622–3; and more generally, Roxin, *Täterschaft und Tatherrschaft*.

[116] K. Greenawalt, 'Distinguishing Justifications from Excuses', (1986) 49 *Law and Contemp. Probs.* 89, 99. Similarly, J. Hall, 'American Penal Law viz a viz German Penal Theory', in *Law, Social Science and Criminal Theory* (1982), 165; J. Dressler, 'New Thoughts about the Concept of Justification in the Criminal Law: A Critique of Fletcher's Thinking and Rethinking' (1984) 32 *UCLA LR* 61; D. N. Husak "Justifications and the Criminal Liability of Accessories" (1989) 80 J. Crim. L. and Crim. 491 and Smith, *Justification and Excuse in the Criminal Law* (1989). However, see the categorization in the Canadian Law Reform Commission Report 31 (1987) proposals on complicity, s. 4 (2) (*b*).

[117] Difficult borderline cases are possible; e.g. where P uses excessive force in self-defence, if reasonable in the circumstances as imagined to exist by P he will (unless intoxicated) be free of liability. (*Williams* (1984) 78 Cr. App. Rep. 276.) However, rather than justified (see *Devlin* v. *Armstrong* (1971) NI 13) P's actions in such circumstances are, arguably, excused because it can hardly be maintained they are desirable and deserve the law's encouragement. Therefore if A, knowing the true circumstances, assists P it could be said that A was either an accessory to P's *excused* wrongdoing or a principal through P's innocent agency. See Fletcher, *Rethinking Criminal Law*, 762; Robinson, '*Criminal Law Defenses*', 235–6, 240; and Williams, 'The Theory of Excuses', 739. More generally on such cases see K. Greenawalt, 'The Perplexing Borders of Justification and Excuse' (1984) 84 Col. LR 1897.

[118] The classification of some defences as excuses is contentious—e.g. the form of insanity under the McNaghten Rules relating to the actor's inability to understand the nature or quality of his act is a denial of *mens rea*. However, if it is claimed that the actor could not understand what he was doing was wrong then, unless it is regarded as an additional superimposed fault

some form of incapacity, whether mental or physical, inhibiting the 'meaningful exercise of free will',[119] thereby making it morally inappropriate to punish the actor. In consequence, excused acts may be lawfully resisted or prevented but, unlike justified ones, not lawfully assisted or encouraged by others. Those arguments already advanced in respect of imposing complicity liability where a perpetrator lacks the necessary fault apply *a fortiori* in the case of excuses.[120]

Therefore, for example, where A coerces P into taking money from P's employer, excusing P on the grounds of duress might be said to leave untouched the harm or wrongfulness of P's actions. It may then, as with the absence of criminal fault, be claimed that A's accessorial liability is derived from such remaining criminally wrongful harm. Conceptual implausibility[121] is undoubtedly a weakness in this technique of producing liability from a coupling of the accessory's culpability with the perpetrator's objective wrongdoing; although the plausibility of the process varies with the nature of the perpetrator's excuse. For instance, incriminating the instigator of a 13-year-old 'rapist' for complicity in rape or convicting an

---

element, it is an excuse as awareness of wrongfulness is not part of the fault requirement of most defences. As absence of the necessary fault element or excuse for an actor arguably have the same effect on complicity liability this problem of classification is without consequence. The same is also true in the case of an actor's mistake which, depending on the circumstances, may most appropriately be regarded as either negating the fault element or constituting an excuse. Duress, although clearly classified in *Lynch* as an excuse, took on a justificatory guise in *Howe* [1987] 1 All ER 771 (particularly the speeches of Lord Hailsham at 777, and Lord Mackay at 796). The appropriate classification of duress is also disputed amongst commentators; see, for instance, Robinson, *Criminal Law Defenses*, i. 347 (excusatory) and La Fave and Scott, *Criminal Law*, 432 (justificatory). See *US* v. *Bailey* 444 US 394 (1980) where the Supreme Court drew no distinction between necessity and duress defences, implicitly running together justification and excuse; cf. *US* v. *Lopez* 662 F. Supp. 1083 (1987) treating duress as an excuse and not preventing complicity liability, but regarding a necessity defence as justificatory and barring complicity liability.

[119] Robinson, 'Criminal Law Defenses', 221; similarly Kadish's formulation: 'the underlying principle is that of voluntariness, in two senses, literal and metaphorical', 'Excusing Crime', 265. Cf. Moore: 'excuses are all related to the exercise of the actor's practical reasoning capacities'; excused acts are performed by less than 'fully rational agents', 'Causation and the Excuses', 1148. However, an excuse of diplomatic or other form of immunity does not rest on such a basis. See *Austin* [1981] 1 All ER 374, recognizing a principal offence for complicity purposes but protection from prosecution of the perpetrator.

[120] Rather than explain cases such as *Cogan* through notions of objective wrongdoing, a sharper, more judicially accessible formula could be where the *actus reus* of an offence has been 'caused' by one party, the liability of an 'accessory' will turn on each person's *mens rea*. (Cf. Smith and Hogan, *Criminal Law*, 140.) However, although this approach would in most cases produce the same result as the more elaborate identification of what constitutes the objective wrongdoing in an offence, it is, in certain respects, incomplete. First, it does not reveal the substance of the theory by which the *mens rea* of the accessory can be coupled with the actions of another to produce complicity. Secondly, by not taking account of the justification/excuse distinction, justified actions have the potential to serve as the basis of complicity (cf. *Howe*). Thirdly, for some offences the *actus reus* and wrongful act are not 'coterminous', as e.g. in perjury. Cf. Taylor, 'Complicity and Excuses', 660–2.

[121] Cf. Kadish, 'Complicity, Cause and Blame', 380.

inciter of complicity in theft carried out by a 9-year-old child involve excusing the actor from liability because of deemed incapacity; yet the substance of criminally wrongful harm is still apparent. But even in less persuasive examples the implausibility or awkwardness is not of any greater order than that experienced in many traditionally accepted cases of innocent agency.

As already conceded, under such an expanded form of complicity the overlap or doctrinal duality with innocent agency would be considerable. In the example of theft executed through the use of a 9-year-old, the instigator (P) could be liable as a principal or accessory. Does saying P committed theft as principal really carry more obvious linguistic conviction than claiming P was an accessory to the child's excused liability for theft?[122] Moreover, realistically, the level of evidence needed to establish both the existence of a principal offence and the particular circumstances of its commission may be quite low. The common law has never been greatly concerned in this respect — nothing need be proved beyond the actions of a perpetrator whose characteristics may be quite unknown, and therefore, possibly an infant, insane, or entitled to the benefit of some defence. Although the prosecution must discharge its burden of establishing the definitional elements of the substantive offence, it is, of course, not obliged to rebut every conceivable defence that might be raised by the unknown perpetrator.[123]

For offences,[124] such as manslaughter, based on objective fault, the question of complicity in an act, whether the perpetrator has been excused or found to lack the necessary fault (as with subjective fault), turns on the existence of criminally wrongful harm. Whether such wrongfulness can exist despite a finding of no fault by the perpetrator rests on the substance and definition of the offence in issue. In cases such as careless driving it could be maintained that the offence's criminal wrongfulness is entirely limited to driving carried out in a careless fashion. Therefore acquittal of the driver of such charges necessarily constitutes a denial of *any* objective wrong element.[125] The harming or endangering of others by 'simple' driving is not a wrong within the scope of *that* offence. Unlike most offences, careless driving does not incorporate objective or wrongful harm beyond

---

[122] Objections of this nature would diminish if the verdicts in each case where excusatory defences were successfully pleaded were more forthcoming in articulating the nature of exculpation; e.g. that as a consequence of duress P was excused from liability for committing offence X. Although failure to establish the necessary fault element is not amenable to such an approach.

[123] *Mancini* v. *DPP* [1942] AC 1. In relation to proving some principal offender existed, see *Anthony* [1965] 2 QB 189, at 192 and *US* v. *Harper* 579 F. 2d 1235 (1978). Cf. e.g. *Agresti* v. *State* 234, A. 2d 284 (1967) and *People* v. *Turner* 229 NW 2d 861 (1975).

[124] See ch. 6 (5) 'Complicity in Offences of Negligence'.

[125] Cf. the similar outcome of neither complicity nor principal liability through innocent agency under Law Commission Report 177, cl. 26 (1) (c); and commentary para. 9.15.

the fault required. However, such wrongdoing could, if death occurred, be accommodated by manslaughter where the actor's non-culpability is immaterial to the question of the existence of criminally wrongful harm.[126] For under general causal principles (or innocent agency) the perpetrator is simply the medium through which ascribable cause flows back to the culpable 'secondary' party.

(4) *Statutory Development of 'Causing' Offences*

Development of complicity theory in the arguably defensible direction manifested in *Cogan* had in some respects been statutorily anticipated and rendered unnecessary in some American jurisdictions.[127] The leading provision roughly duplicating the effects of *Cogan* is section 18 (2) (*b*) of the US Federal Code whereby

> whoever wilfully causes an act to be done which if directly performed by him or another would be an offence ... is punishable as a principal.[128]

Introduced in 1948 to complement standard complicity provisions,[129] section 18 (2) (*b*) inculpates one who causes the external elements of an offence through an innocent agent or other means.[130] In particular, enactment of section 18 (2) (*b*) was prompted by the perceived need to convict manipulatory parties, lacking prescribed principal status or qualities, for offences carried out by qualified but innocent agents. Whether the nature of liability produced by section 18 (2) (*b*) and similar provisions[131] is

---

[126] Taylor, 'Complicity and Excuses', 656 in discussing *Thornton* v. *Mitchell* [1940] 1 All ER 339. Cf. Smith and Hogan, *Criminal Law*, 154–5. The arguable importance of settling the nature and boundaries of the element of objective wrongfulness in an offence is well demonstrated by determining liability for procuring or suborning perjury under s. 7 of the Perjury Act 1911 which appears to restate s. 8 of the Accessories and Abettors Act in the context of perjury.

[127] Some pre-s. 18 (2) (*b*) American cases suggest the possibility of such liability before the enactment of s. 18 (2) (*b*). See D. Lanham, 'Accomplices, Principals and Causation' (1980) 12 *Mel. ULR* 490, 500.

[128] 1982 version.

[129] S. 18 (2) (*a*): 'Whoever commits an offence ... or aids, abets, counsels, commands, induces or procures its commission, is punishable as a principal' (1982 version).

[130] The provision was intended to remove 'all doubt that one who puts in motion or assists in the illegal enterprise [or] causes the commission of an indispensable element of the offence by an innocent agent or instrumentally, is guilty as a principal'. See A. White, 'The Scope of Accomplice Liability under Section 18 USC section 2 (b)' (1981) 31 *Case West RL Rev.* 386, n. 63 and generally on this provision.

[131] Cf. the Model Penal Code, s. 2.06 (2) (*a*) which makes a person 'legally accountable for the conduct of another person when: acting with the kind of culpability that is sufficient for the commission of the offence, he causes an innocent or irresponsible person to engage in such conduct'. This is a form of liability *distinct* from the MPC complicity provision under s. 2.06 (3). A number of state code reformulations follow this approach, including Georgia (1983 Code Ann. s. 26-801 (*b*) (2)), Colorado (1978 Rev. Stat. s. 18-1601) and Missouri (1983 Rev. Stat. Ann. title 17-A s. 57 (2) (*a*)). Other states such as California (1970 Penal Code, s. 31), achieve a similar result through expanded complicity provisions. See Robinson, 'Imputed

complicitous in complexion or a modified and expanded variety of innocent agency is debatable.

Regarding such 'causing' offences as a development of complicity is difficult because the causer's liability is neither derived from nor does it rest on the perpetrator's wrongful harm. Rather, liability depends on causing the external elements of an offence—a specification which in one respect is narrower and in another wider than complicity. Limiting liability to *positively* proved 'caused' actions is probably narrower than the necessary relationship between an accessory and principal (see Chapter 3 above, section 2 (3) (c)). In the opposite direction, by making no attempt to fix the basis on which the perpetrator's act is deemed not criminal [132] the conduct which may generate 'causing' liability includes justified and therefore objectively non-wrongful behaviour. This takes the potential scope of a 'causing' liability beyond that possible under a developed, but still derivatively based, *Cogan* form of complicity.

The extent of the resemblance between 'causing' liability and innocent agency turns largely on which theoretical account of the doctrine is adopted. As seen, it is arguable whether innocent agency rests on imputing the agent's *actions* to the principal or on the less constructive basis of causal responsibility. If the former explanation of innocent agency is accepted then positively proved 'causal' liability along the lines of section 18 (2) (b) could rightly be regarded as an entirely novel form of liability.[133] However, accounting for innocent agency as a long-established mechanism for the attribution of causal responsibility for the agent's actions would mean the degree of innovation entailed in 'causing' type offences was far more limited. It would then be most appropriate to view such liability as constituting an expansion of traditional innocent agency doctrine in order to accommodate more comfortably *less* proxyable forms of behaviour and to criminalize unqualified defendants for status offences committed by their qualified agents.[134]

Criminal Liability' (1984) 93 *YLJ* 609, 631 n. 72; and cf. old state codes which treated innocent agency as a form of complicity noted in the Model Penal Code commentary TD 1 (1953), 16 n. 9.

[132] Model Penal Code s. 2.06 (2) (a) refers to an 'innocent or irresponsible person'. These terms are not defined although the commentary (TD 1 (1953), 17–18) implies they are intended to relate to an actor who is either excused or lacks the necessary fault. For constructional difficulties see Robinson, 'Criminal Law Defenses', 282. Cf. Williams who proposes a version of s. 2.06 (2) (a) in which necessity and provocation are included as grounds for exempting the actor but a basis for 'causing' liability. It appears that necessity and provocation here may be limited to a hybrid of justification and excuse. 'The Theory of Excuses', 737 and 740. But cf. *Howe*'s hybrid reasoning for duress.

[133] Cf. Kadish, 'Complicity, Cause and Blame', 382.

[134] Despite this being a declared legislative objective for enacting s. 18 (2) (b), for sometime federal courts often displayed a marked reluctance to recognize that the 'causer' did not need to have the specified attributes required of a direct perpetrator. Most particularly in *US* v. *Chiarella* 184 F. 2d 903 at 910 (1950). Judge Learned Hand characterized such an interpretation of the provision as 'revolutionary'. Ineptly obscure drafting long delayed the acceptance of this legislative purpose. See Model Penal Code s. 2.04 (2) (a) TD 1 (1953),

As already suggested, it is maintainable[135] that innocent agency, if posited on an openly causal basis, has the capacity to reach those cases targeted by section 18 (2) (*b*). However, such a move would require a degree of judicial creativity even bolder than that apparent in *Cogan* where, although it was accepted that the defendant had caused his wife to submit to non-consensual intercourse, the court was not required also to circumvent the definitional requirement of the principal being a man. To use innocent agency in such a case where the defendant (*P*) is a woman, would require the charge that '*P* raped *V* by causing *A* to have intercourse with *V* without *V*'s consent'. Such a formulation might quite reasonably be seen as failing to satisfy the definitional necessity of the principal offender being a man.[136]

The question of quite how extensive liability *should* be under a 'causing' provision has already been indirectly touched upon in relation to the existing scope of innocent agency under English law. As noted, the uncertain limits of the doctrine turn largely on the necessary mental culpability of the defendant and what degree of influence or manipulation constitutes a sufficient (causal) connection. In relation to mental culpability, nothing inherent in innocent agency doctrine requires its limitation to intended or purposive use or manipulation of an agent, although the strong tendency in offences of recklessness and negligence has been to invoke general causal notions rather than innocent agency.[137] The federal provisions under section 18 (2) (*b*) require 'wilfully' caused actions or consequences, although the scant case law suggests that recklessness (probably objective) supplies the necessary culpability.[138] In contrast, section 2.06 (2) of the Model Penal Code specifies no more than 'the kind of culpability that is sufficient for the commission of the offence'.[139] Those points already raised in respect of innocent agency have similar relevance here, as does the earlier discussion of 'innocence' and cause.

Overall, the practical demand in English law for a provision along the lines of section 18 (2) (*b*) is hardly pressing. Most, though not all, unusual examples of inter-party collaboration can be reached by either innocent

---

commentary 15–17. The intended effect of s. 18 (2) (*b*) was finally established in *US* v. *Wiseman* 445 F. 2d 792 (1971). See also *US* v. *Ruffin* 613 F. 2d 408 (1979) discussed by White, 'Scope of Accomplice Liability'; and *US* v. *Tobon-Builes* 706 F. 2d 1092 (1983).

[135] Cf. Williams, 'The Theory of Excuses', 737.

[136] S. 1 (1) Sexual Offences Act 1956 and s. 1 (1) of the Sexual Offences (Amendment) Act 1976. But cf. the American decision of *People* v. *Hernandez* 96 Cal. Rept. 71 (1971) and Law Commission Report 177, cl. 26 (3) (*b*).

[137] See self-defence 'shield' cases, discussed above, and see also Lanham's review of the meaning given to 'cause' in 'Accomplices, Principals and Causation'.

[138] See *Pereira* v. *US* 347 US 1, 1–9 (1954) and Robinson, 'Element Analysis', 735 n. 242; but cf. the comments in *US* v. *Lester* 363 F. 2d 68 (1966) at 73.

[139] Most states that have followed the Model Penal Code approach of separate 'causing' and complicity provisions have taken the same view on culpability for causing. A few have not: e.g. the Georgia State Code specifies intention (s. 26-80 (*b*) (2), 1983). For a discussion of interpretational problems with the culpability element of s. 2.06 (2) see Robinson (1983) 'Element Analysis' at 734–6.

agency or complicity. *Bourne* and *Cogan* show that courts nowadays are not so easily thwarted by doctrinal niceties as in the past when presented with activities seen as deserving punishment. However, achieving the ultimately right result can, of course, never be an end to the matter. Although, theoretically legitimate routes can be mapped out leading to the desired results, the necessary reasoning may be a little too rarefied for comfort, bearing in mind the desirability of making the basis and nature of criminal liability reasonably apparent. It is in this respect that the relative clarity and directness of 'causing' offences have greatest appeal and advantage over common law developments.

(5) Where Accessory and Principal are Liable for Different Levels of Criminality: Complicity and 'Semi-Innocent Agency'

It has been observed that where a perpetrator of objectively wrongful harm is completely free of criminal responsibility, because of absence of required fault or availability of an excusatory defence, other participants in such behaviour may nevertheless be found criminally liable. Depending on the particular circumstances, their liability may be either principal or secondary in nature. Where a perpetrator is to some extent criminally responsible for his actions the question arises whether a 'secondary' party, because of his greater mental culpability, is open to conviction of a more serious offence.

For a considerable period of time the common law has accepted that there can be different degrees of liability amongst parties for the same unlawful killing. Thus an *abettor* could be convicted of manslaughter while the principal was liable for murder in the same killing. Conversely, an abettor could be convicted of murder when his principal was liable for manslaughter.[140] However, this flexibility did not extend to accessories before the fact because, as Blackstone notes,

> It is a maxim that *accessorius sequitur naturam principalis sui*, and therefore an accessory cannot be guilty of a higher crime than his principal . . . being only punished, as a partaker of his guilt.[141]

---

[140] e.g. Hale, *PC* i. 437–8; Hawkins, *PC* i, ch. 31, ss. 31 and 50; East, *PC* i. 350 and ii. 666.

[141] *Comm.* v. 36, citing *Co. Inst.* iii. 139. Notable variations exist in various 19th-cent. codes as to how this issue is handled. Macaulay's Indian Penal Code, ss. 38 and 110, appears to permit any secondary party, circumstances allowing, to be punished at a level appropriate to his personal mental culpability regardless of the perpetrator's. Wright's 1877 draft Jamaican Criminal Code broadly follows the same course: ss. 12 (ii) and 32. On the home front, the First Criminal Law Commissioners' 7th Report code (1843) does not refer to the question in its complicity provisions. However, the Second Criminal Law Commissioners' 2nd Report code (1846) provides that where the perpetrator 'would himself be justified or excused in the doing of any act, such justification or excuse shall be deemed to extend to any person acting in his aid or assistance' (art. 15). The remit of the Second Commissioners was for 'Revising and Consolidating' the criminal law, but art. 15 constituted a very distinct departure from the then current law without any explanation.

The basis of the distinction between abettors and accessories before the fact was that *procedurally* an abettor's liability could be established without reference to *conviction* of the principal. But although procedurally autonomous, an abettor's liability was *substantively* derivative in the same way as that of an accessory before the fact: in both cases proof of a principal offence needed to be established. It would, therefore, be a misunderstanding to regard the basis of an abettor's liability as non-derivative because of the rhetorical fiction induced by procedural convenience and 'true political justice [that] all persons present aiding and abetting are principals'.[142]

The existence and operation of this rule of permissible variation in levels of liability between principals and abettors is demonstrated by common purpose cases where the less culpable abettor is convictable of manslaughter although the principal is liable for murder.[143] Further, in the non-common purpose case of *Kwaku Mensah*,[144] the Privy Council found no difficulty in accepting that, in respect of a killing, the perpetrator could be convicted of murder and his accomplice of complicity in manslaughter because the latter only intended to assault the victim. Conversely, when the accomplice's mental culpability is *greater* than the principal's it has been recognized in a number of situations that his liability may be higher than the principal's. The perpetrator's lower culpability may either follow from a lesser degree of *mens rea* or fault than the accessory's, or because he qualifies for a partial defence. Modern illustrative authorities of where the *mens rea* of an accomplice is greater than the perpetrator are scant[145] and contradictory.

---

[142] Foster, *Crown Law*, 348. Although Bracton, without elaboration, notes a distinction between accessories *before* and *at* the fact (abettors) in respect of the availability of a defence: 'When both are present and the principal has been convicted, the accessory though present is not to be convicted on that accord since he may have his independent defence' — F. 142 and 144.

[143] e.g. *Lord Mohun* (1692): 'In case a man shall murder another, whether all those in his company at the time of the murder, are so necessarily involved in the same crime, that they may not be separated from the crime of the said person, so as in some cases to be found guilty only of manslaughter? Ans. The crime of those who are in the company at the time of the murder committed, may be so separated from the crime of the person that committeth the murder, as in some cases they are only to be found guilty of manslaughter — Holt KB 479, 90 ER 1164. Also *Betty* and *Reid*; but cf. *Lovesey and Peterson* and *Dunbar* and see Ch. 8.

[144] [1946] AC 83 at 91. See also *Murtagh and Kennedy* [1955] Crim. LR 315 and cf. *Garforth* [1954] Crim. LR 936. The conceptual basis for achieving such a result under Scottish complicity law is still unclear. See *Melvin* v. *HM Advocate* 1984 SCCR 113 and comment in Scottish Law Commission Report 93, 'Art and Part Guilt of Statutory Offences' (1985), para. 8.

[145] Cf. *Millard* (1921) 59 DLR 34, *Remillard* (1921) 59 DLR 340 (based on the Canadian Criminal Code 1906 which embodied common law principles) Hebert (1986) 51 CR (3d) 264; *State* v. *Gray* 39 P. 1050 (1895); *State* v. *McAllister* 366 So. 2d 1340 (1978); *State* v. *Dault* 608 P. 2d 270 (1980); *Jones* v. *State* 486 A. 2d 184 (1985); *Tonkin* [1975] Qd. R. 1, for which see Gillies, *Criminal Complicity*, 146. For American case law adhering to a rule preventing greater accessorial liability see Annot. 9 ALR 4th 972, 995, 1981 and Supp. The New Zealand decisions in *Lewis* [1975] 1 NZLR 222 and *Hartley* [1978] 2 NZLR 199 suggest that an accessory may not be convicted of a more serious offence than the perpetrator, although he could be convicted of a lesser.

The most recent, but inconclusive, considerations of the position in English law are found in *Richards*[146] and *Howe*.[147]

At issue in *Richards* was whether the defendant, who had hired two others to injure her husband seriously, could be convicted as an accomplice to the offence of wounding with intent although the perpetrators of the attack were liable only for the lesser crime of unlawful wounding.[148] Implicitly adopting Hawkins's account of the law, the Court of Appeal accepted that although an *abettor* might be liable for a more serious offence than the principal, it was an 'uncontroverted rule' that the liability of an accessory before the fact could not be greater, 'it seeming incongruous and absurd that he who is punished only as a partaker of the guilt of another, should be adjudged guilty of a higher crime than the other'.[149] And as the defendant 'was not truly in a position' formerly describable as an 'abettor', she could not be convicted of an offence more serious than the perpetrator's.

[T]here is proved . . . in this case one offence and one offence only, namely the offence of unlawful wounding [s. 20] without the element of specific intent. We do not think it right that one could say that that which was done can be said to be done with the intention of the defendant who was not present at the time and whose intention did not go to the offence which was in fact convicted . . . If there is only one offence committed, [s. 20] then the person who has requested that offence to be committed, or advised that that offence be committed, cannot be guilty of a graver offence than that in fact which was committed.[150]

While not directly[151] necessary for their decisions, both the Court of Appeal[152] and House of Lords in *Howe* expressed disapproval of *Richards*. In the Court of Appeal, Lord Lane CJ took the view that *Richards* was 'incorrectly decided'; that where, for instance,

---

[146] [1974] 3 All ER 1088, surprisingly, not *Curia adviseri vult*.
[147] [1987] 1 All ER 771.
[148] Under ss. 18 and 20 of the Offence Against the Person Act 1861. The defendant wanted to put her husband 'in hospital for a month'. Because of the defendant's proximity to the attack she was almost certainly an abettor rather than an accessory before the fact. See Ch. 2 (2). The defendant was also probably liable for incitement to wound with intent.
[149] *PC* ii ch. 29, s. 15. The real import of Hawkins's remarks are disputable on technical grounds: 'It may well be that by "higher offence", Hawkins meant higher *category* of offence—petit treason as opposed to felony or felony as opposed to misdemeanour'. Smith and Hogan, *Criminal Law*, 5th edn. 140, with acknowledgements to P. R. Glazebrook.
[150] (1974) 3 All ER 1088, 1092.
[151] And, therefore, technically not overruled. The second certified question in *Howe* was: 'Can one who incites or procures by duress another to kill or to be a party to a killing be convicted of murder if that other is acquitted by reason of duress'. As in *Cogan*, the 'innocence' of the perpetrator did not prevent the court considering both innocent agency and accessorial liability. Lord Hailsham may have intended to endorse the principle(s) in *Cogan*, when observing that '*Cogan* if it had been followed in *Richards* seems to me to dispose of the matter' (775); followed by Lords Bridge and Griffiths. The suggestion may be that the *Cogan* principle (relating to complicity and innocent agency) supersedes the old rule espoused in *Richards*.
[152] Lord Lane CJ [1986] QB 626 at 641–2.

A hands a gun to D informing him that it is loaded with blank ammunition only and telling him to go and scare X by discharging it. The ammunition is in fact live (as A knows) and X is killed. D is convicted only of manslaughter . . . It would seem absurd that A should thereby escape conviction for murder.

In the court above, Lord Mackay[153] found this 'reasoning . . . entirely correct', affirming the view that

where a person has been killed and that result is the result intended by another participant, the mere fact that the actual killer may be convicted only of the reduced charge of manslaughter for some reason special to himself does not, in my opinion in any way result in a compulsory reduction for the other participant.

However, in neither *Richards* nor *Howe* is any serious attempt made to offer a *theoretical* account of the substance of the dispute or of its resolution. Concern in *Richards* to emphasize the commission of 'one offence and one offence only' is strongly reminiscent of *Russell*'s proposition expressly endorsed by the Privy Council in *Surujpaul*. But whereas the comments in *Richards* were apparently limited to an accessory before the fact, *Russell*'s proposition relates to abettors as well. The implicit contrary reasoning in *Richards* seems to be that an abettor commits a distinct offence; a view with resonances of the ancient claim that the perpetrator's act is regarded as that of the *abettor* also. By disapproving of this distinction between types of secondary party, *Howe* may perhaps be taken to endorse the *Richard*'s view of abettors as being relevant to all parties.

As previously suggested in respect of perpetrators who lack any liability, attribution of the perpetrator's actions and incrimination of an 'accessory' may be possible through either an innocent agency causal explanation or through a developed form of orthodox (derivative) complicity resting on the notion of objectively harmful wrongdoing. Clearly, where the perpetrator, as in *Richards*, is criminally responsible for his actions he is not 'innocent' in the usual sense; but he may be innocent in that he lacks the necessary fault for a more serious offence sharing a common *actus reus*. Like cases of complete innocence, the actions of the 'semi-innocent' perpetrator[154] may be characterized as caused in so far as the perpetrator does not enjoy a full knowledge of the nature or circumstances of his actions. Thus, taking Lord Lane's example in *Howe*: D's unawareness of the type of ammunition could be said to make his actions of discharging the gun less than fully voluntary and, to the extent of harm caused beyond what was intended or foreseen, his actions could be described as innocent. However, contrary to the view expressed in *Howe* (by both the Court of Appeal and the House of Lords), Lord Lane's illustration is not, on *this* analysis, at odds with the verdict in

[153] [1987] 1 All ER 771, 799, endorsed by Lords Bridge, Brandon, and Griffiths; and commentary [1987] Crim. LR 480 at 484–5.
[154] Williams, *CLGP* 391, and *Textbook*, 373–4. Macaulay's Indian Penal Code treats innocent agency circumstances as one form of complicity ('abetment'). See s. 108, 'Explanation 3' and 'Illustrations'.

Richards. For although Mrs Richards was the moving force behind the attack, it is difficult to accept that she 'caused' the attack in the strong ('direct') sense used in relation to innocent agency and neighbouring notions. The two perpetrators were fully acquainted with the nature of their actions and the material circumstances and were in no sense volitionally incapacitated. It would have been otherwise, and comparable with Lord Lane's example, if, say, secretly knowing of her husband's perilously high blood pressure, she had induced others to threaten and chase him, achieving the desired aim of causing a heart attack, and so making her *principally* liable for the more serious offence.

However, applying the alternative objectively harmful wrongdoing analysis to the facts of *Richards* arguably produces a different conclusion and outcome. Taking the wounding as the common source of objective harm from which an accessory's liability may be derived for either wounding with intent or unlawful wounding, it could be maintained that with the necessary mental culpability Mrs Richards's actions constituted *complicity* in the more serious offence of wounding with intent. Just as the objective wrongfulness in *Cogan* existed whether or not the immediate perpetrator had *mens rea*, so here *a fortiori* where the perpetrator has less rather than no fault at all. Although an intended act of non-consensual intercourse is a greater social and personal wrong than a mistaken one (as demonstrated by the fact that the first is rape and the second is not) that is not to deny the undesirable core of objective harm in both cases. Similarly for wounding with intent and unlawful wounding: the extent of the objective wrongdoing could be claimed to increase according to the perpetrator's or secondary party's mental culpability.

Beyond such cases of different *mens rea* levels are established examples where the culpability disparity is the consequence of one party's personal entitlement to a partial defence. Although open to both a 'semi-innocent' agency and complicity analysis, usually the latter approach is adopted to incriminate the accomplice. For instance, an accessory or principal may successfully plead diminished responsibility without 'affect[ing] the question whether the killing amounted to murder in the case of any other party to it'.[155] Similarly, infanticide provisions[156] allow a special defence to murder for a woman suffering from the effects of childbirth which, as in the case of diminished responsibility, reduces the offence of killing her child from murder to manslaughter; yet, unlike diminished responsibility, there is no express provision relating to the selective autonomous effect of reducing either party's liability. However, limited case law[157] recognizes the same

[155] Homicide Act 1957, ss. 2 (3) and (4).

[156] S. 1 of the Infanticide Act 1938 provides that the defendant shall be 'dealt with and punished as if she had been guilty of the offence of manslaughter of the child'; it does not convert the offence into one of manslaughter.

[157] *Conroy* [1954] Crim. LR 141. Both husband and wife were charged with murdering a child which the latter had given birth to. At trial, Glyn Jones J. directed that the jury, *if* it

ability for courts in infanticide cases to convict the accessory of a higher offence than the principal's. This may also be possible where the partial defence of provocation[158] is raised:

[T]he instigator may act in hot blood, in which case he will be guilty only of manslaughter, while the perpetrator may act coolly, and thus be guilty of murder. The converse also, may be true; the instigation may be cool and deliberate the execution in hot blood by a person whom the instigator finds in a condition of unreasoning frenzy.[159]

But provocation, as with diminished responsibility and infanticide,[160] defies confident classification as being either justificatory of excusatory. As J. L. Austin neatly observed:

[W]hen we plead ... provocation there is a genuine uncertainty or ambiguity as to what we mean — is *he* partly responsible, because he roused a violent impulse or passion in me, so that it wasn't truly or merely me acting 'of my own accord' (excuse)? Or is it rather that, he having done me such injury, I was entitled to retaliate (justification)?[161]

If provocation were regarded as justificatory, the theory of objectively harmful wrongdoing would delimit the accessory's liability to that unjustified portion of the principal's actions — responsibility for manslaughter. However, if provocation is taken to be excusatory then, where appropriate, an accessory could be convicted of murder as the quality of the wrongful harm is unchanged by such a defence personal to the perpetrator. The same would be true if the theory of 'semi-innocent' agency were applied; but here the basis of liability would be the 'principal' having caused

---

believed the balance of the wife's mind had been upset at the time of the killing, could convict her of infanticide and the husband of murder. It was not clear which party had actually killed the child, but the direction was given on the alternative that the wife was the perpetrator.

[158] According to the Privy Council in *Lee Chun-Chuen* v. *R.* [1964] AC 220 at 228, the defence does not constitute a denial of *mens rea*; also *Parker* v. *R.* [1964] AC 1369.

[159] *Moore* v. *Lowe* 180 SE 1 (1935); quoted by Williams, *CLGP* 391. Cf. *Remillard* (1921) 59 DLR 340 and Macaulay's Indian Penal Code, s. 38 illustration. The wording of s. 3 of the Homicide Act 1957 does not obviously preclude application of the defence to a secondary party.

[160] In both diminished responsibility and infanticide the basis of the plea is one of diminished *volitional* control as opposed to cognitive power or ability, and, therefore, arguably, not amounting to a plea of no *mens rea*; although possibly a denial of a voluntary action. The basis of these partial defences, as in the case of complete defences, is of some importance. If justificatory, then by allowing the accessory's liability to rise higher they would constitute statutory modifications to the theory of objective wrongdoing. See Robinson's schematic tables, 'Criminal Law Defenses', 242–3. For present purposes, though, whether they are best classified as 'failure of proof' defences or, most likely, 'excuses', they cannot reasonably be regarded as justifications. The effects of intoxication, although similarly concerned with incapacity, more clearly relate to defects of perception or understanding and therefore, like insanity, are excusatory. Cf. *McCarron* [1977] Crim. LR 559.

[161] 'A Plea for Excuses', in White, ed., *The Philosophy of Action*, 20. For a consideraton of the position in English law note Alldridge, 'The Coherence of Defences' [1983] Crim. LR 665, at 669–72. See also F. McAuley, 'Anticipating the Past' (1987) 50 *MLR* 133 and J. Dressler 'Provocation: Partial Justification or Partial Excuse?' (1988) 51 *MLR* 467.

the perpetrator's not fully volitional actions.[162] Moreover, 'semi-innocent' agency reasoning is attractively free of the classificatory disputes over the substance of different defences.

3. CONCLUSIONS

Looking back at the pattern of historical development of complicity's derivative nature, the common law has over many hundreds of years progressed from a highly restrictive and debilitating inflexibility to a position capable of accommodating most forms of culpability operating (one way or another) at a secondary level. The various stages of this evolution represent responses to demonstrated and acknowledged need – or more grandly, 'from a principle of true political justice'.[163] Early absolute notions of derivativeness, whereby *punishment* of the principal offender had to precede any question of secondary liability, gradually retreated giving way to recognition of the procedural and evidential autonomy of secondary parties, albeit (irrationally) to a lesser extent for accessories before the fact. While the common law's capacity to imprison itself for centuries in doctrinal *cul de sacs* is not unknown, with limited exceptions this has not happened to any marked degree in complicity or the complementary theory of innocent agency.

As previously suggested, innovation apparent in cases such as *Cogan* can be accounted for as a legitimate development within the concept of parasitic or derivative complicity. Such developments may be regarded as the final phase of a gradual, if hesitant, progression towards a less derivatively based and more atomistically reconstructed liability. It constitutes conceptual growth which corresponds with, and is a proper response to, the steady subjectivizing of criminal responsibility; and one which facilitates a more adequate and accurate recognition of both the reality and (im)morality of the secondary party's role. This is not to claim that the doctrinal limits of derivative complicity have an infinite elasticity, but rather that modern developments should not be viewed as constituting a doctrinal break. The point is worth emphasizing, for providing a practical solution to a local embarrassment or lacuna in the criminal law's coverage is in itself no complete justification for the wholesale distortion or breaking away from a long established and proven system of criminalization. Piecemeal subversion of a generally satisfactory theoretical structure may unsettle

---

[162] Cf. Kadish, 'Complicity, Cause and Blame', 387, for suggested objections to the notion of 'semi-innocent agency'. If Othello is guilty of manslaughter on the grounds of Iago's provocation, then could not Iago be liable for murdering Desdemona as a *principal* through Othello's (not fully voluntary) 'semi-innocent agency'? This outcome appears to be recognized under Law Commission Report 177, cl. 26 (1) (*c*) (iii).

[163] Foster, *Crown Law*, 348.

legitimate assumptions and aims elsewhere within the system. A *true* departure from a derivative basis for complicity would carry strong implications of it taking on a distinctly inchoate complexion coupled with an increased role for principal liability through an expanded doctrine of innocent agency. For such reasons, disputing whether changes in complicity's derivative nature are doctrinally evolutionary or revolutionary is a far from sterile exercise.

However, providing theoretically convincing explanations to justify accessorial liability without a principal offence, or how an accessory may be convicted of a more serious offence than the perpetrator, is not to demonstrate conclusively that such developments are the best or most appropriate methods of criminalizing the forms of behaviour involved. To many operating within the Anglo-American or other common law influenced systems, the concept of objective or innocent wrongdoing may easily be perceived as some form of theoretical dandyism or overrefinement: alien, often obscure, and, with its civil or continental law gloss, quite untranslatable. Criminal law ought to enjoy a reasonable degree of comprehensibility. Apparent, as well as real, incoherence to non-lawyers is generally subversive of any system's credibility and proper functioning. Conceptually defensible results or distinctions may appear bafflingly capricious to those not tolerably well schooled in the metaphysical fringes of criminal jurisprudence. Moreover, academic and judicial dispute over the proper classification of many defences as either excuses or justifications — well illustrated by duress — badly undermines the tenability of 'objective wrongdoing' as a reliable and acceptable basis for settling secondary liability. This is one weakness not suffered by the relatively simple notion of semi-innocent agency. For reasons of this nature, fresh and historically untrammelled legislative provisions have distinct appeal. On grounds already given,[164] they would be an expanded form of innocent agency[165] (or, preferably, 'causing' liability)[166] capable of most

---

[164] Assuming no radical changes to complicity's parasitic structure. The great appeal of a non-parasitic or non-derivative system is its relative simplicity. An inchoate (or endangerment) based form of complicity, by focusing mainly on the defendant's mental culpability, would avoid the problems associated with causal contribution. However, unless an unwavering attachment to subjectivistic notions of criminality is held to and the *causing* of harm denied relevance, where a secondary party *has* been demonstrably instrumental in bringing about a certain proscribed consequence it could be claimed that inchoate liability understates or incompletely represents the full degree of criminal culpability (see Ch. 3). Cf. the proposed hybrid system of the Canadian Law Commission Codification Report 31 (1987); and see R. J. Buxton, 'Complicity in the Criminal Code' (1969) 85 *LQR* 252.

[165] Cf. the Model Penal Code provisions, s. 2.06 (2) (*a*) and the 'semi-innocent' agency approach in Working Paper 43 (proposition 3 (1) explained at 17) and Law Commission Report 177, cl. 26 (1) (*c*) (ii); commentary para. 9.13 and illustration 26 (iii). For a general critique of innocent agency see P. Alldridge, 'The Doctrine of Innocent Agency' (1990/1) Crim.L. Forum (forthcoming).

[166] Cf. s. 18 (2) (*b*) of the American Federal Code.

appropriately and clearly characterizing the real substance of the criminality involved[167] in problematic cases of 'secondary' participation.

[167] Neither Working Paper 43 nor Report 177 (cf. commentary para. 9.4) considered the ability of inchoate liability (and particularly incitement) to deal with the problem cases of innocent agency and semi-innocent agency. Without modification, incitement would be inapplicable in *Cogan* type cases unless the instigator believes the agent is lacking *mens rea* or the necessary capacity. Cf. *Curr* [1968] 2 QB 944. Attempt would be open to a similar claim of linguistic inappropriateness as much as the full offence.

II

The Mental Requirement

The scope for extreme complexity in settling an appropriate level of mental culpability in complicity is immediately obvious. With two sets of actions (possibly followed by intended or unintended consequences) and two accompanying mental states, the range of permutations for cross linkage of these separate elements is considerable.

In the first place, there is the (potential) accessory's mental state in respect of his own actions, their possible consequences or effect on the (potential) principal's actions, and any further consequences thereof. Along with these matters of knowledge or foresight is the accessory's attitude; whether he wishes or has the purpose of bringing about any principal (re)action.

Moving to the accessory's perceptions of the principal: where there is no instigation by the accessory, how specific must his knowledge or belief be as to the principal's possible behaviour and the circumstances in which it may occur? How likely must the accessory believe the principal's actions to be? Is it sufficient for an accessory simply to 'know' the principal's *mens rea*, or must he also share it?

Most, or all, of these factors have a bearing on the extent of the accessory's identification with or commitment to the occurrence of the principal offence. The degree of accessorial mental culpability may be calibrated or marked off against these distinct but interconnecting units of fault, whether of knowledge, foresight, or attitude. Quite how complicity doctrine manifests itself through these possible mental linkages between accessory and principal is considered under four related heads.

First, the accessory's purpose or knowledge that his actions will assist or encourage the principal. Chapter 5 examines the extent to which an accessory must consciously associate his own actions with those of the principal. What accessorial attitude is required towards the occurrence of the principal offence? Must an accessory act with the purpose of assisting or encouraging and bringing about the principal offence, or will less be sufficient?

Second, in Chapter 6, is specificity: the necessary extent of the accessory's knowledge of the principal offence. Here consideration is given to the broad question of what matters relating to the principal's actions a non-instigatory accessory must be aware of. In particular: how specific must his knowledge or foresight be of the planned actions, the likelihood of their taking place, the perpetrator's mental state, and the presence, or otherwise, of any necessary incriminating circumstances? To what degree will the answer be determined by whether the principal offence is one of intention, recklessness, negligence, or strict liability?

In Chapter 7 variations in performance by the principal from that contemplated by the accessory are considered. Following on from the previous chapter's treatment of 'specificity' is the issue of how flexibly the law treats such demands. How far may the principal's behaviour (and any consequences) deviate from that anticipated by the accessory before the necessary degree of foresight is regarded as no longer present? What is the relevance of the voluntariness, or otherwise, of the principal's variations?

Chapter 8 reviews the nature and status of the 'doctrine' of common purpose, asking whether it is simply a linguistic or a substantive variant of complicity's general *mens rea* requirements. In considering this question its relationship with 'variation' issues and the role, if any, of consensuality in complicity are also both examined.

5

The Accessory's Purpose or Knowledge that His Actions Will Assist or Encourage the Principal

1. Nature of the Problem

A well-established scattering of judicial comments confirms that an accessory must both intend[1] his acts of assistance or encouragement and be aware of their ability to assist or encourage the principal offender.[2] Therefore, a voyeuristic onlooker's mere presence at the scene of a rape could not make him a party to the offence, even if his presence actually encourages the perpetrator, unless the onlooker is at least aware of this effect. But, beyond this initial requirement of an accessory's awareness of the possible effects of his behaviour, must he also intend the principal offence to occur? Does complicity require anything approaching a 'coincidence of purpose'[3] between principal and accessory?

---

[1] *NCB* v. *Gamble* 1 QB 11, 20. Cf. Law Commission Report 177, cl. 27 (1) (*a*): complicity requires that the accessory 'intentionally procures, assists or encourages the act which constitutes or results in the commission of the offence by the principal'. Report para. 9.25 makes it reasonably clear that 'intentionally' here relates to the accessory's actions and not to the principal's. Giving assistance under protest or purely for payment does not prevent the accessory's action being carried out 'intentionally', for 'he knows that its effect in the ordinary course of events will be to assist him . . . A motive to assist or encourage the principal is not necessary'. The code team's original draft did not require the accessory to have such a strong belief that his actions would assist or encourage the principal; it was enough that he 'intends that what he does shall, or is aware that it will or may cause or assist or encourage' (Report 143, cl. 31 (4) (*a*)). Therefore, if, for instance, A sold P a rope ladder which he believed might be used to enter premises from the roof and commit burglary, would A be an accessory if he was uncertain as to whether it was long enough to do the trick? Apparently A would not be liable under cl. 27 (1) (*a*) because he did not at least believe it would 'in the ordinary course of events assist him' — he believed that it might. This uncertainty would not have prevented liability under cl. 31 (4) (*a*). Case law provides no clear authority on the point.

[2] e.g. *Coney* (1882) 8 QBD 534, 557: 'Encouragement [or assistance] does not of necessity amount to aiding and abetting, it may be intentional or unintentional, a man may unwittingly encourage intentionally by expressions, gestures, or actions intended to signify approval. In the latter case he aids and abets, in the former he does not'. See also *Allan* [1965] 1 QB 130; *Clarkson* [1971] 1 WLR 1402; *Jones* (1977) 65 Cr. App. Rep. 250; *DPP for N. Ireland* v. *Maxwell* [1978] 1 WLR 1350, 1371.

[3] *NCB* v. *Gamble* [1959] 1 QB 11, 15.

The range of attitudes which an accessory may have towards whether the principal offence occurs is extensive. At one extreme the accessory may instigate the principal's actions; at the other, he may furnish assistance with the fervent hope that the principal does not go through with the criminal venture. Between these opposites many imaginable attitudes are possible: the accessory whilst not openly encouraging may assist with the undisclosed purpose or objective of the offence being carried out; a less interested party might not have a 'stake' in the outcome but still consent to or approve of the enterprise; even less involved is the provider of assistance who is totally indifferent to whether the principal offence takes place. What attitude must an accessory entertain towards the carrying out of the principal offence? Or, to pose the question differently, is the accessory's purpose or reason for acting relevant to his liability?[4]

Whether or not immediately participating in the commission of an offence alongside the perpetrator, probably most examples of complicity involve accessories with some positive interest in the criminal enterprise's successful outcome. However, the question of whether a lesser degree of involvement may incriminate still carries considerable implications for complicity's scope, raising awkward questions of both a theoretical and practical nature. Open consideration of whether purpose or just some variety of knowledge was a necessary ingredient in complicity has been hampered until relatively modern times by the criminal law's general disinclination clearly to acknowledge and apply a substantive distinction between the two mental states. This is transparently evident from any perusal of various nineteenth-century codes and commentaries.[5] In the context of complicity the issue received its first substantial airing in the conflicting American federal appeal cases of *US* v. *Peoni* (1938) and *Backun* v. *US*[6] (1940) which have come to represent bench-mark decisions of the

---

[4] The general issue is the accessory's attitude towards whether the principal offence is committed. The main aspect considered here is the accessory's attitude to the effect or use which is made of his own actions (usually) via the principal i.e. what the principal's consequential behaviour will be. Additional questions concerning the accessory's mental state as to the *circumstances* and/or *consequences* in cases where the principal offence involves such definitional elements are considered in Ch. 6.

[5] Bentham's notion of intention included 'oblique' intention which was wide enough to include consequences contemplated as 'likely'. *Introduction to the Principles of Morals and Legislation*, ch. 8, s. 6. See also J. Austin, *Lectures on Jurisprudence*, 4th edn. (1879), ii, 'Notes on Criminal Law', 1092–4. 19th-cent. Criminal Law Commissioners' Reports, such as the 4th Report (1839), treat purposeful and indifferent action similarly, as e.g. in the prefatory remarks on homicide. Likewise in the 1879 Draft Criminal Code and Wright's 1877 draft Jamaican Criminal Code, particularly s. 10 and illustrations. Stephen on various occasions in different contexts notes the law's practice of generally not distinguishing between 'intention and reckless indifference': *HCL* iii. 56 and 80–5; *Digest*, 158–61 and 362–70. Cf. a modern manifestation of this attitude in *Hyam* v. *DPP* [1975] AC 55.

[6] For American developments see Westerfield, 'The Mens Rea Requirement'; and La Fave and Scott, *Criminal Law*, 582–4. The Model Penal Code's requirement of purposive action (s. 2.06) produces the following non-complicitous examples: 'A lessor rents with knowledge that the premises will be used to establish a bordello. A vendor sells with knowledge that the subject of the sale will be used in commission of a crime. A doctor counsels against an

The Accessory's Purpose or Knowledge 143

two main approaches to the question. English courts did not seriously encounter the problem until *NCB* v. *Gamble* (1959), on which occasion it appeared to be settled that the accessory's indifference as to the offence's commission would not prevent his liability.[7] However, attendant interpretational difficulties of *NCB* v. *Gamble* eventually surfaced indirectly for review by the House of Lords in *Gillick* v. *West Norfolk and Wisbech AHA*[8] where elements in certain speeches suggested the necessity of a more positive accessorial attitude than hitherto generally believed. At the very least, the ambiguities of *Gillick* open up the possibility of English courts reconsidering the meaning and standing of *NCB* v. *Gamble*, and whether theoretical and practical considerations prompt an open change of position.

2. ENGLISH CASE LAW

Construction of the relevant authorities, although few in number, has shown itself capable of producing intense dispute and rarefied case analysis amongst commentators.[9] For some time the decision in *NCB* v. *Gamble*[10] has generally been taken[11] to decide that complicity requires nothing

abortion during the third trimester but, at the patient's insistence, refers her to a competent abortionist. A utility provides telephone or telegraph service, knowing it is used for bookmaking. An employee puts through a shipment in the course of his employment though he knows the shipment is illegal. A farm boy clears the ground for setting up a still, knowing that the venture is illicit.' (s. 2.06, comment at 316, 1985). Under existing English law — in so far as it can be confidently stated — each example has the potential to form the basis of complicity.

[7] Williams, *Textbook*, 342, rightly comments that 'The decision was a turning point in the law of complicity'.

[8] [1986] AC 112.

[9] Particularly the vigorous debate between G. R. Sullivan, 'Intent, Purpose and Complicity' [1988] Crim. LR 641, [1989] Crim. LR 166; and I. H. Dennis, 'Intention and Complicity: A Reply' [1988] Crim. LR 649, [1989] Crim. LR 168, and 'The Mental Element for Accessories', in P. F. Smith, ed., *Criminal Law* (1987), 40. And cf. Williams's commentary in 'Complicity, Purpose and the Draft Code' [1990] Crim. LR 4, and R.A. Duff, 'Can I help you?' (1990) 10 LS 165.

[10] As the report's headnote accurately states: 'M The servant of the firm of hauliers took his lorry to a colliery of the National Coal Board where it was filled with coal from a hopper and was then taken to a weighbridge, where the weighbridge operator H, who was employed by the board, weighed the lorry and its load and told M that the load was nearly 4 tons overweight. M, saying that he would risk taking the overload, took the weighbridge ticket from H and left the colliery premises. He was subsequently stopped by the police.' The NCB was convicted of aiding and abetting the offence of driving an overloaded lorry. All three judgments in the case assumed the weighbridge operator was aware that he was entitled to refuse to allow the lorry to leave the board's premises overloaded. Without this knowledge the Divisional Court thought no conviction was possible. Further, the NCB accepted liability for the acts of its employee although, strictly (*Ferguson* v. *Weaving* [1951] 1 KB 814), knowledge of the necessary facts could not be imputed to it.

[11] e.g. Smith and Hogan, *Criminal Law*, 1st edn., 73, and 6th edn., 126–7, and Lanham, 'Limitations on Accomplice Liability' (1982) 6 *Crim. LJ* 306, 317. Williams finds the case 'theoretically inconclusive': *Textbook*, 342. See also particularly Dennis, 'The Mental Element', 52. Since *Attorney-General's Reference (No. 1 of 1975)* [1975] QB 773 the argument seems necessarily to relate to complicity except where procuring is alleged. In

beyond intentional or voluntary and informed help or encouragement; mere indifference on the part of the accessory to the commission of an offence does not prevent incrimination. Two of the three Divisional Court's judgments in NCB v. Gamble present no interpretational difficulties. Lord Goddard CJ (by then author of a string of decisions relating to problems of specificity of knowledge in complicity cases) found no problem in supporting the conviction; the defendant had the requisite knowledge and 'that amounted to an aiding and abetting of the offence'.[12] Equally clear was Slade J.'s dissenting opinion requiring proof that the accessory's act or omission was 'done or made with a view to assisting or encouraging the principal offender . . . in other words, with a motive of endorsing the commission of the offence'.[13]

The judgment of the court's third member was uncharacteristically[14] ambivalent. According to Devlin J., aiding and abetting required 'proof of *mens rea*, that is to say, of intention to aid as well as knowledge of the circumstances, and proof of the intent involves proof of a positive act of assistance voluntary done'.[15] By 'intention' Devlin J. may simply have meant an act 'voluntarily done'. However, this interpretation is undermined by the subsequent comment that

> proof that the article was knowingly supplied is not conclusive evidence of intent to aid[16] . . . But prima facie . . . a man is presumed to intend the natural and probable consequences of his act [although] it is always open to the defendant as in *Steane*, to give evidence of his real intention. But in this case the defence called no evidence.

The imprecise implication here seems to be that evidence produced of unwillingness or a lack of desire for the principal offence's occurrence negates *mens rea*. Yet in the succeeding paragraph Devlin J. appears to face the opposite direction when suggesting

> *Attorney-General's Reference* the Court of Appeal ruled that 'procurement' meant 'to produce by endeavour. You procure a thing by setting out to see that it happens and taking the appropriate steps to produce that happening' (779). However, later elements of the judgment foster the impression that it might be sufficient if a person is merely aware that his conduct would probably bring about an offence. See Ch. 2. The common law once drew distinctions between requirements for proceedings against accessories before the fact and principals in the second degree. Whether or not the actual substantive demands differed is debatable, but at least differences existed in relation to levels of proof or evidence required as to the defendant's association with the principal offence. See Westerfield, 'The Mens Rea Requirement'. In the case of accessories before the fact 'affirmative' proof of *mens rea* was necessary. For abettors this could be 'inferred' from presence and knowledgeable actions.

[12] *NCB* v. *Gamble*, 19.
[13] Ibid. 26.
[14] Castigated by Williams as a 'judgment of unwanton indecision', *Textbook*, 342; and 'a specimen of extraordinarily poor judicial thinking', 'Complicity, Purpose and the Draft Code', 15. Cf. Devlin, 'Criminal Responsibility and Punishment' [1954] Crim. LR 661, 666–7.
[15] *NCB* v. *Gamble*, 20.
[16] Ibid. 22–3, citing *Fretwell* and *Steane*. Four years before in *Bullock* [1955] 1 WLR 1, 4, Devlin J. mysteriously alluded to some constituent of *mens rea* beyond knowledge: 'mere knowledge is not of itself enough, there must be something further'. No clarification of its nature was provided.

The Accessory's Purpose or Knowledge

Evidence of an intent in the crime or of an express purpose to assist it will greatly strengthen the case for the prosecution. But an indifference to the result of the crime does not of itself negative abetting. If one man deliberately sells to another a gun to be used for murdering a third he may be indifferent about whether the third man lives or dies and interested only in the cash profit to be made out of the sale, but he can still be an aider and abettor. To hold otherwise would be to negative the rule that mens rea is a matter of intent only and does not depend on desire or motive.[17]

Constructional difficulties aside, *NCB* v. *Gamble* was subsequently taken as authority for the proposition that motive is immaterial to complicity, with House of Lords endorsement of this principle appearing in *DPP for Northern Ireland* v. *Lynch* and *DPP for Northern Ireland* v. *Maxwell*. In *Lynch*, Lord Morris maintained that a defendant acting with knowledge 'in pursuance of a murderous plan' would be an accessory 'even though he regretted the plan or indeed was horrified by it. However great his reluctance, he would have intended to aid and abet'.[18] Similarly, Lord Simon interpreting *NCB* v. *Gamble*:

Slade J thought the very concept of aiding and abetting imported the concept of motive. But Lord Goddard CJ and Devlin J disagreed with this. So do I . . . one may lend assistance without any motive, or even with the motive of bringing about a result directly contrary to that in fact assisted by one's effort.[19]

Three years later, in *Maxwell*, their Lordships[20] endorsed the view that the *mens rea* of complicity 'goes to intent only and does not depend on desire or motive'.[21]

---

[17] Ibid. 23.
[18] *Lynch*, 678. In the Court of Criminal Appeal of Northern Ireland, Lowry CJ deemed 'intent to assist' was proved by 'participation together with knowledge' [1975] NI 35, 37. Contrastingly in his dissenting judgment, O'Donnell J. argued 'assistance plus knowledge is not in itself sufficient . . . while I accept that care must be taken not to confuse "motive" or "purpose" with "intention", nevertheless it seems clear that some subjective element is required . . . there must be a mens rea' (60–1). Though never clearly identified, the gist of the judgment suggests that willingness or consent might have been this extra element. Cf. Lord Porter in *Lang* v. *Lang* [1954] 3 WLR 762.
[19] Ibid. 699.
[20] Edmund-Davies [1978] WLR 1350, 1369, 1371; citing *NCB* v. *Gamble* and *Lynch*. *Howe*, though directly on duress and murder, implicitly takes the same view on the complicity issue. And cf. *Ahmed* [1990] Crim. LR 648.
[21] Lowry CJ. The speeches of the rest of their lordships do not directly advert to the issue. No dissenting comments were raised on Lowry CJ's statement. See also e.g. *De Marney* (1907) 1 KB 388; *Ladbrokes* (1971) 1 WLR 110; *Cook* v. *Stockwell* 15 Cox 49; and *Cafferata* v. *Wilson* [1936] 3 All ER 149. In *Clarke* (1984) 80 Cr. App. Rep. 344 the Court of Appeal observed 'motive is indeed irrelevant' to liability, citing *Lynch* and *NCB* v. *Gamble* (347). But the court did concede that where the defendant claimed 'he acted with or within the law' (347) the position could be different, as where 'conduct . . . is overall calculated and intended not to further but to frustrate the result' (348). Such a 'defence' would be 'exceptional and rare'. The theoretical status of this 'defence' is problematic in that it would appear excusatory and not deny the existence of *mens rea*, but it is permitted for overriding policy reasons of crime detection (justificatory?). The judgment is unclear on this point, though it twice uses the expression 'defence'. The existence of such a defence, though, is not obviously consistent with Lord Simon's observations in *Lynch* that 'One may lend assistance without any motive, or even with a motive of bringing about a result directly contrary to that in fact assisted by one's effort'

Set against such received orthodoxy is a small body of contrary *dicta*, once believed extinct but revitalized, principally by *Gillick*.[22] Prominent amongst these authorities is the nineteenth-century case of *Fretwell*.[23] Here the defendant unwillingly supplied Bradley, his pregnant friend, with an abortifacient after she had threatened suicide if he did not. Bradley's consumption of the substance killed her. On a reserved case Fretwell was acquitted as an accessory to Bradley's 'self murder'. Erle CJ and Chanell B. saw Fretwell's unwillingness for Bradley to take the substance as crucial: 'the facts of the case are quite consistent with the supposition that he hoped and expected that she would change her mind and not resort to it'.[24] However, the court's other three members found against conviction on different grounds not directly involving motive or intention.[25] Arguably *Fretwell* is, therefore, best viewed as a decision entailing constructional issues of participation in particular statutory offences, carrying no clear general relevance to the *mens rea* requirement in complicity.[26]

(699). Cf. Law Commission Working Paper 43, 47 illustration (*f*) and 51, where the approach is similar to that in *Clarke* and seen as 'restating existing law'. Report 177, cl. 27 (6) (*a*) provides that 'A person is not guilty of an offence as an accessory by reason of anything he does — (a) with the purpose of preventing the commission of the offence'; and see Report commentary para. 9.33.

[22] See n. 8 and also *Salford Health Authority ex p. Janaway* [1988] 2 WLR 442. Here a medical secretary who typed a letter to a consultant to arrange a patient's possible abortion was held not to be a party to procuring the abortion. In the Court of Appeal's view, by simply typing the letter the secretary 'would have been intending merely to carry out the obligations of her employment, and not endeavouring to produce a result consisting of an abortion' (452). The special connotation of 'procure' recognized in *Attorney-General's Reference* (No.1 1975) — 'to produce by endeavour' — seems to have been in the Court of Appeal's mind in the present case. In that sense its *general* relevance to complicity is suspect. However, although affirming the overall decision in *Janaway*, the House of Lords [1988] 3 WLR 1350 did so on a different basis, preferring to reserve its position on the question of complicity and employment duties. Carrying out employment obligations as a reason for finding no *mens rea* wears the appearance of the broader question of when compliance with any civil obligation may prevent incurring liability. See *Lomas et al.* (1913) 9 Cr. App. Rep. 220.

[23] (1862) Le & Ca 161; 169 ER 1346.

[24] Ibid. 1346.

[25] Martin B. believed Fretwell's acts were 'too remote from the death'; Blackburn and Keating JJ rested their opinions on the fact that Fretwell had 'neither administered the poison nor caused it to be taken' (1347) — more a denial of the *actus reus* of the particular offence involved. These references relate to the felony of abortion which required both intent to procure a miscarriage and either administering the poison or causing it to be taken (s. 58, Offences Against the Person Act). Fretwell had neither the *mens rea* nor the *actus reus* of the offence, rather he committed the misdemeanour of supplying the poison (s. 59). Therefore even if Bradley had taken the substance to kill herself Fretwell could not, on an equivalent to the felony—murder rule, have been party to her self-murder; *a fortiori*, he could not be a party to her death where she intended only to abort herself. Erle CJ based at least part of his judgment on the difference between the felony of abortion under s. 58 and the misdemeanour of supplying an abortifacient under s. 59 of the 1861 Act.

[26] Cf. Williams, *CLGP*, 367–8. The difficulty of deducing a clear generally acceptable ratio from *Fretwell* is illustrated by its citation for the prosecution in *Lomas* (1913) 9 Cr. App. Rep. 220, 221, as supporting the proposition that 'knowledge, coupled with assistance, is enough to constitute a person an accessory'. Against this, Devlin J. in *NCB* v. *Gamble* took *Fretwell* to support the view that intent to aid was not conclusively established simply if an 'article was

Although presenting acute interpretational difficulties, *Gillick* contains sufficient ammunition to embolden lower courts to reconsider the standing of *NCB* v. *Gamble*. This declaratory action included the issue whether a doctor's provision of contraceptive advice and treatment for girls under 16 necessarily constituted aiding and abetting unlawful sexual intercourse under section 6 of the Sexual Offences Act 1956.[27] Without attempting an extensive analysis of the law, Lords Fraser, Scarman, and Bridge saw the answer turning on the particular nature of the doctor's intention. Lord Fraser thought liability 'unlikely' where the doctor acted 'honestly . . . in the best interests of the girl'.[28] Lords Scarman and Bridge expressly adopted the relevant portion of the case's first instance judgment of Woolf J.[29]

As a starting-point, Woolf J. accepted that contraceptive advice or assistance given with the 'intention thereby of encouraging [unlawful] sexual intercourse' would incriminate. However, if whilst 'firmly against unlawful sexual intercourse' a doctor provided advice or assistance 'in the

knowingly supplied' [1959] 1 QB 22–3. A different interpretation is offered by Turner in *Russell*, 152. Employing the authority of *Co. Inst.* i. 182, Hale, *PC* i. 615–16, Foster, *Crown Law*, 126 and 348, and Hawkins, *PC* ii, ch. 29, s. 16, Turner concludes that in addition to knowledge an accessory must have 'approved of or assented to' the principal's conduct. Support for *Russell's* interpretation is found in *Bernard* (1858) 1 F. & F. 240, 175 ER 709, where Lord Campbell CJ gave a similar account of what was 'laid down in our books'. The First Criminal Law Commissioners' 7th Report (1843), s. 4, art. 10 and 11, and the Second Commissioners' 2nd Report (1846), s. 3, art. 8, required an accessory to 'procure or promote' the principal offence. According to art. 11, 'a party shall be deemed to procure or promote [the principal offence] who shall by commandment, counsel, advice, consent, aid, or otherwise, either directly or indirectly cause, incite or encourage [the principal offence]'. Use of the expression 'or otherwise' seems to suggest that any form of association between accessory and principal could incriminate, so long as it 'cause[d], counsell[ed] or encourage[d]'. *Taylor* (1875) LR 2 CCR 147 required not just assent but also some element of direct encouragement. This clearly is a matter of *actus reus* rather than part of the mental element, and, as *Russell* notes, appears to exceed 'ancient principle' (152).

[27] S. 6 of the Act creates the principal offence of unlawful intercourse. As a particular form of complicity, this offence is catered for by a specific provision under s. 28 (1) whereby it is 'an offence for a person to cause or encourage . . . the commission of unlawful sexual intercourse with . . . a girl under the age of 16 for whom he is responsible'. S. 28 (3) provides 'persons who are to be treated for the purposes of this section as responsible for a girl are . . . any other person who has the custody, charge or care of her'. At first instance Woolf J. ruled, [1984] QB 581 at 588, that an offence under s. 28 (1) could not be committed as the girl would not be in the 'care' of the clinic or doctor under s. 28 (3). His subsequent comments on complicity all relate to the general law. This identification of two forms of complicity—the specific and the general—did not occur in the Court of Appeal where Parker LJ conflated the two (134). The Court of Appeal, in the event, chose not to express a view on the relevant criminal law. In the House of Lords, Lord Fraser adopted Parker LJ's approach and referred to 'aiding and abetting' under s. 28. Lord Scarman expressly followed both Woolf J., and Lord Fraser (190). Lord Bridge simply followed Woolf J.; with Lords Brandon and Templeman dealing exclusively with the general law of complicity; all in all, a true hotchpotch of a decision.

[28] Ibid. 175. The girl's 'best interests' entailed considering whether 'unless she receives contraceptive advice or treatment her physical or mental health or both are likely to suffer' (174).

[29] Lord Scarman (190), Lord Bridge (194). Lord Templeman limited his reference to the issue by suggesting that the 'purpose' (along with other factors) of providing contraceptive advice was relevant to liability (199).

best interests of the girl in protecting her from unwanted pregnancy and the risk of sexually transmitted disease' would there then be criminal complicity? It was a situation where Woolf J. 'found the greatest difficulty in applying the law'. On the authority of *NCB* v. *Gamble* and *Lynch*,[30] Woolf J. agreed that it was 'necessary to distinguish between motive and intent', and that an 'unimpeachable' motive would not itself negate intention and liability.[31] Therefore what, if anything, would prevent undesirable incrimination of a doctor who acted with socially and medically sound motives? Rather than lack of the necessary 'intention', Woolf J. (unconvincingly)[32] saw absence of liability turning on either the contraceptive advice not directly assisting in unlawful intercourse, or the prescribing doctor's insufficiently specific knowledge of the circumstances of the unlawful intercourse.

Lord Scarman's position is further complicated by not only his adoption of the judgment of Woolf J. but also by his comment that the 'bona fide exercise by a doctor of his clinical judgment would be a complete negation of the guilty mind which is an essential ingredient of the criminal offence of

---

[30] [1959] 1 QB 11, 20: 'proof of . . . intent involves proof of a positive act of assistance voluntarily done' per Devlin J. [1975] AC 655, 699: 'One may lend assistance without any motive, or even with the motive of bringing about a result directly contrary to that in fact assisted by one's effort' per Lord Simon.

[31] This path had been trodden before by Woolf J. in *Attorney-General* v. *Able* [1984] QB 795. Taking a passage in *Russell* (12th edn., 150–1, rather than the more natural course of using a modern authoritative text) as representing the requirements of accessorial liability, Woolf J. accepted the need for assent to the principal offence (809). But 'intention to assist need not, however, involve a desire' that the principal offence be committed (811). (Cf. *Nedrick* (1986) 83 Cr. App. Rep. 267.) Interestingly, Woolf J. saw the reasoning of Erle CJ in *Fretwell* (taken to decide 'that the mere provision of the means of committing a crime is insufficient) as not in 'accord' with his own view. Furthermore, *Fretwell* was seen as inconsistent with *NCB* v. *Gamble*. These comments again leave the reader in the dark as to what 'intention to assist' means if it is not desire and not mere indifference to use of the assistance. Presumably, adopting a general meaning of 'intention', awareness of the virtual certainty that an act will assist the principal, although not *necessarily* 'intention', is evidence from which intention may be 'inferred': *Moloney* [1985] AC 905, and *Hancock and Shankland* [1986] AC 455. Cf. *Walker and Hayles* [1990] Crim. LR 44 where the Court of Appeal accepted that reference to a 'very high degree of probability' was not a misdirection for murder, offering a sufficient basis on which a jury might infer 'intention' to kill.

[32] As for the lack of direct assistance, it is probably sufficient if the likelihood of the offence being committed is increased by the accessory's act. Generally there is no necessity that assistance must be essential to commission of the principal offence, so long as it made some difference to the perpetrator's performance. See Ch. 3. It would be reasonable to say that the principal offender had been assisted by the doctor's action because it would encourage the girl and thus assist the man's commission of the offence. Furthermore, if he knows of it, the man may be encouraged by the contraception. On the question of specificity, *Bainbridge* and *Maxwell* (see Ch. 6) permit conviction without knowledge of the date and place of the offence. Not knowing the identity of the principal offender is unusual, but by knowingly making intercourse more likely the doctor is facilitating the offence even if the identity of the principal offender is unknown to him, for it is the commission of the principal *offence* which complicity seeks to prevent. (*Cooper and Wicks* (1833) 5 Car. & P. 536, 172 ER 1087.) Furthermore, if *A* provides *P* with materials to rob a bank then *A* will not only be the accessory of *P* but also all of *P*'s accomplices, provided he foresaw the possibility of others carrying out the offence in a fashion similar to *P*. But cf. *Davis* [1977] Crim. LR 542.

aiding and abetting the commission of unlawful sexual intercourse'.[33] Having apparently accepted Woolf J.'s opinion that motive or desire is immaterial to the *mens rea* of complicity, it is difficult to see quite what Lord Scarman was alluding to when purporting to agree with Woolf J. Furthermore, of those grounds on which Woolf J. thought a doctor might be excluded from liability, only the issue of specificity of knowledge relates to *mens rea*, which is hardly a matter of 'intention'—the subject of Lord Scarman's discussion.[34]

Can any confident statement of the current law be offered in the light of these conflicting and confusing *dicta*?[35] As already noted, the possible range of attitudes which an 'accessory' could have towards the commission of the principal offence extends from the desire or wish for it to come about, through to a neutral or indifferent state, or even open hostility to the enterprise. Whilst the weight of authority still suggests that the accessory's reason or purpose for acting is irrelevant to liability,[36] an arguably plausible *via media* can be offered which is capable of accommodating cases such as *Fretwell* and *Gillick* without demanding that the accessory acts with the purpose of bringing about the principal offence. Accordingly, while an accessory need not endorse the offence's commission, evidence of 'disapproval of or non-consent to the principal's act may negative the mental element required for an accessory'.[37] And although the feasibility of using approval as a condition of liability may be questionable, it nevertheless approximates to what *Russell* refers to as the 'assent' always required by

---

[33] *Gillick* [1986] AC 112, at 190.

[34] Lord Brandon unblinkingly saw the giving of contraceptive advice or assistance as 'necessarily involving promoting, encouraging or facilitating the having of sexual intercourse' because it removed 'the inhibition arising from the risk of unwanted pregnancy' and 'making contraception available to girls under 16 is unlawful, whether the parties know of and consent to it or not' (ibid. 197 and 199).

[35] An alternative ingenious explanation for the majority view in *Gillick* on complicity liability is that of a 'concealed defence of necessity', put forward by J. C. Smith [1986] Crim. LR 117–18, and in *Justification and Excuse in the Criminal Law* (1989). Undeniably *dicta* of Lords Scarman, Fraser, and Templeman can be pressed into supporting such an interpretation. Endorsed by Spencer, 'Trying to Help Another Person Commit a Crime', 164. And cf. Williams's suggestion that the decision in *Fretwell* 'can be explained on the grounds that the deceased's threat of suicide raised the case of duress or necessity': *CLGP* 368. However, standing in the way of a necessity account of *Gillick* are the solid objections that the defence is never openly alluded to nor is any supporting authority cited (cf. Dennis, 'The Mental Element', 65 n. 104). Furthermore, Lord Scarman bases his conclusion on 'a complete negation of the guilty mind' (190). The defences of duress and necessity rest on an excusatory or justificatory rationale, not the negation of *mens rea*. See *Lynch* and the confirmation of this point in *Howe* [1987] 1 All ER 777, per Lord Bridge 783. But cf. *Steane* and commentary on *Howe* [1987] Crim. LR 483. Law Commission Report 177, cl. 27 (6) (*b*), provides that there will be no complicity liability if a party acts 'with the purpose of avoiding or limiting any harmful consequences of the offence and without the purpose of furthering its commission'; *quaere* the function of the last conditional clause of the defence? See commentary para. 9.34.

[36] Unless there is legally effective duress or, possibly, necessity.

[37] Dennis, 'The Mental Element', 52.

ancient authorities on complicity.[38] However, despite lingering strands of support for this view in some 'common purpose' decisions, the predominant attitude[39] manifested in modern case law is against 'assent'[40] based liability, favouring instead responsibility resting on foresight alone.

3. Practical Consequences of Not Requiring Purpose or 'Assent'

By not requiring that an accessory has a stake in or even assents to the criminal venture many examples of everyday conduct appear to satisfy the conditions of criminal complicity. For instance, the ordinary commercial sale of any commodity or substance which the seller is aware will facilitate

---

[38] *Russell*, 12th edn., 151–2 and authorities cited. *Russell's* reference to 'assent' is noted approvingly by Stephen J. in *Johns* v. *R.* [1980] 143 CLR 108, 118; and see references to 'assent' by Mason, Murphy, and Wilson JJ, 131. This explicit statement of the need for 'assent' does not appear before the 11th edn. of *Russell* (1958). Earlier edns. cite *Fretwell* as illustrative of the general need for 'some degree of direct incitement': e.g. 5th edn. (1877), 165. Dennis, 'The Mental Element', 52, translates (and apparently shifts the emphasis of) assent or consent into an 'in order to' test: did the accessory act in order to assist the principal actions? The accessory acts purposefully, not in the sense of 'endorsing' the offence but rather 'in the sense of the defendant's reason for acting; the outcome or state of affairs that he had decided to achieve by his act'. This apparent distinction between the necessity of A acting *in order to assist* the principal carry out the offence and (the unnecessary) acting *in order to bring about the offence* is exceedingly subtle. It is a distinction which would appear to convict in cases where: 'I'm supplying this gun in order to assist you (P) to kill V, although I'm completely indifferent as to whether you actually shoot V.' But the distinction would lead to acquittal in cases where: 'I'm supplying the gun purely for the high profit involved whilst well aware you will probably shoot V with it, which is too bad as business comes first.' Moreover, if Devlin J.'s judgment in NCB v. *Gamble* is taken to support this analysis, how did Slade J.'s dissenting judgment in NCB v. *Gamble* differ from the 'in order to' test? He spoke of 'motive' and 'endorsement' but also asked if the act was 'done . . . with a view to assisting'. For an early use of the expression 'in order to' in complicity, see Macaulay's Indian Penal Code (1837), s. 107, explanation 2: 'Whoever . . . does anything in order to facilitate the commission of [an] act, and thereby facilitates [its] commission . . . , is said to aid . . . the . . . act'. Stokes, *Anglo-Indian Codes*, i. 127–8.

[39] It has been argued (most cogently by Dennis, 'The Mental Element') that reference to the necessity of 'intention' for complicity must be interpreted in the light of general trends towards, effectively, giving 'intention' a (probably) narrow scope, close to purposive action. (See *Moloney* [1985] AC 905 and *Hancock* [1986] AC 455; discussed by G. L. Williams, 'Oblique Intent' [1987] CLJ 417 and Smith and Hogan, *Criminal Law*, 55–61.) The Court of Appeal gave support to such a view in *Barr* (1989) 88 Cr. App. Rep. 362, and in *Smith* [1988] Crim. LR 616. However Lord Lane CJ on two other occasions specifically rejected the relevance of *Moloney* and *Hancock* to complicity: *Ward* (1986) 85 Cr. App. Rep. 71, 76 and *Slack* [1989] 3 All ER 90.

[40] In *Lynch* Lord Morris refers to complicity liability despite regrets and being horrified by the principal's actions; and Lord Simon suggests liability would exist even if the accessory acted with the motive of thwarting the principal's plans. It is difficult to say that there had been 'assent' in such cases. Obvious theoretical conflict arises in connection with the defence of duress if assent or purpose is an element of the *mens rea* of complicity. An accessory's claim of acting under coercion is necessarily a denial of purpose because the defendant is claiming he acted to avoid the harm threatened and not with the purpose of bringing about the principal offence. If an 'accessory' submits to pressure less demanding than that sufficient to satisfy

another's offence may constitute complicity: supplying petrol to the driver of an unroadworthy or uninsured vehicle, or selling alcohol to intending drivers.[41]

A related issue, touched upon in *NCB* v. *Gamble,* is how far assisting in the course of satisfying civil obligations will expose a party to criminal liability. If at least assent or willingness for assistance to be used towards criminal ends were required, then simply meeting a civil obligation would not potentially incriminate. However, if indifference as to outcome suffices then fulfilment of civil duties may incidentally incriminate the performer. In *Lomas*[42] the defendant returned a jemmy in his possession to King, its owner, knowing that King intended to use it for burglary. The Court of Criminal Appeal's grounds for quashing Lomas's conviction as an accomplice are far from obvious. Counsel for the Crown submitted that liability required 'knowledge coupled with assistance'. In *arguendo* Lush J. appeared to suggest Lomas had insufficient knowledge of the principal offence to incriminate him.[43] Isaacs LCJ ruled that, even if the Crown was correct in its account of the law ('we do not say that we agree with it'),[44] the facts did not incriminate Lomas on such a basis.

In the same way as Devlin J.'s judgment in *NCB* v. *Gamble* defies a reasonably clear interpretation on the relevance of motive, so does that aspect of the judgment concerning the effect of civil obligations on criminal liability.[45] *Lomas* was interpreted as authority for the view that giving assistance in any form because the principal 'has a right to demand it' could not be the basis of liability as it was only a 'negative' act; Lomas was 'only refraining from detinue'.[46] But 'forcible detention' of materials would be

---

duress, and was exculpated on the grounds of not assenting, then the policy embodied in the defence of duress conditions would, indeed, be in danger of being 'outflanked' (Dennis, 'Intention and Complicity', 659). In overruling *Lynch*, the House of Lords in *Howe* [1987] 1 All ER 771 confirmed that a party may still be an accessory to murder even though he assisted under threats of death. Cf. Williams [1990] Crim. LR 4 for the suggestion of circumventing the problem by making the accessory's 'purpose' relate to the perpetrator's *act*, not any *result*. But use of a 'purpose' standard would still acquit an 'accessory' who supplies deadly information or weapons for money with the firm expectation of their murderous use, a case morally not greatly distinct from the purposeful supplier.

[41] Williams, *Textbook*, 341. In *Attorney-General's Reference* (No. 1, 1975) it was suggested that leaving the consumer of alcohol to take his own decision whether to drink and drive would circumvent the possible argument that the supplier was an accessory. But the intervening and autonomous decision of the principal always exists in complicity, therefore it is difficult to see how this fact alone prevents the supplier's liability. Cf. HMSO, *Road Traffic Law Review Report* (1988), ch. 7, rejecting a 'specific offence of sale of alcohol to drivers'; and see above Ch. 2 'Modes'.
[42] (1913) 9 Cr. App. Rep. 220.
[43] Ibid. 22.
[44] Ibid. 222.
[45] See J. C. Smith [1972] B *CLJ* 197, at 208–11, and Williams, *CLGP* 370–7.
[46] [1959] 1 QB 11, 20. *Bullock* [1955] 1 WLR 1, was also cited in support where Devlin J. held that in *Lomas* the defendant was 'not in a position to withhold the jemmy' (4).

'justified' in the case of a felony.[47] Ownership and the question of exactly when title passed also figured in Lord Goddard's reasoning; the implication for both judges being that if title had passed the lorry driver would have had the irresistible right to remove coal and commit the offence; an apparent principle of the 'proprietary interest of the owner of a chattel [prevailing] over the public interest' of individuals not voluntarily assisting the commission of offences.[48] Adding to this confusion is *Garrett* v. *Arthur Churchill (Glass) Ltd.*[49] where, effectively, it was ruled that an agent's withholding of delivery of property to his principal would not entail any civil liability where the property was intended for illegal exportation. Therefore the agent's compliance with the principal's request to surrender, though he was aware of the intended unlawful exportation, constituted 'being knowingly concerned' in the offence.

On the question of the entitlement of a party to thwart the commission of an offence by withholding possession of property from another, provisions authorizing the prevention of crime by the use of reasonable force would seem to have potential relevance. Detention or retention of property, whether with or without force, would presumably be included within the scope of such provisions.[50] Certainly the American federal case of *Backun*[51] drew an explicit connection in arguing that 'every citizen is under a moral obligation to prevent the commission of a felony, and has the legal right to use preventative force, so it is difficult to see why selling with knowledge is not an offence'. However, use of a general interventionary power carries with it the problem of proportionality of force. Consequently, for anything less than the most serious offences, the lawfulness of the use of force to retain possession of property would be open to doubt. Yet the problem of proportionality would, arguably, be present even if the civil entitlement were suspended or overridden (as suggested in *Garrett*) by some independent rule. This is so because the possessor for the time being of another's property could not lawfully resist under the rules of self-defence (of person or property) attempts by the owner to regain possession with *any* level of force, regardless of the known illegal purpose for which the owner wished to use his property. Here again the possessor could only employ reasonable

---

[47] Burglary was a felony at the time under the pre-1967 law. How could a forcible detention at the same time be lawful yet constitute detinue?

[48] Smith [1972] B *CLJ*, 210. And cf. n. 22, *Salford Health Authority ex p. Janaway*, on the question of complicity liability through complying with employment obligations which may incidentally assist the commission of an offence.

[49] [1969] 2 All ER 1141. Although not involving complicity, the issue of when proprietorial interest can be overridden by the need to avoid facilitating an offence is similar. The court referred to whether the defendant had 'lent himself to the idea' of illegal exportation; a possible reference to the need for willingness to allow the unlawful activity. Law Commission Report 177, cl. 27 (6) (*c*), provides that supplying assistance will not incur liability if done in the belief that the party is 'under an obligation to do it and without the purpose of furthering the commission of the offence'; and see commentary para. 9.36.

[50] Criminal Law Act 1967, s. 3. Cf. Williams, *Textbook*, 344, n. 3.

[51] 112 F. 2d 635 (1940).

force. (*Quaere*, whether the owner is entitled to use any force to retrieve his property for criminal use.)

In sum, ownership or the passing of title, as raised in *NCB* v. *Gamble*, provides an unsatisfactory determinant of the accessory/supplier's liability on two grounds: first, on account of the difficulties in settling these technical civil matters; secondly, because such rights of the principal offender and owner are either overridden or superseded by a special rule (*Garrett*) or by general interventionary provisions permitting retention by the possessor.

4. Theory and Solutions

Apart from the practical implications of an accessory's attitude on complicity's reach, are there prescriptive forces within complicity's general theoretical structure favouring (though not requiring) assent if not purpose? The common law does not follow any rule of equivalence of *mens rea* between accessory and principal. However, while there are no direct theoretical requirements, other features of complicity and general principles of criminal justice have certain implications, although pulling in opposing directions.

The most tangible reason for requiring purposive action (or, at the very least, 'assent') is that sellers should not be their buyers' keepers; legitimate trading should not be hampered or exposed to the risk of criminal proceedings;[52] liability based on anything less than purpose or assent is unacceptably intrusive and restrictive of reasonable social and commercial activity. Beyond such considerations the nature of the causal element in complicity also carries indirect *mens rea* implications and particularly for the appropriateness of requiring purposeful action. It has already been suggested that the more limited the causal requirement the stronger the claim for a closer connection between the accessory's mental state and the principal's action. As an accessory lacks final control over the principal's conduct, the distinction between an accessory desiring (or at least assenting to) the principal action and his mere foresight of it assumes greater significance than in respect of a principal who always retains the power not to act. Furthermore, if, in addition to a causal requirement, the accessory need only foresee the 'type' of the principal's actions as a possibility, then without accessorial purpose (or perhaps assent) the whole basis of his derivative liability appears decidedly thin and remote from the principal source of criminality. Without some joining in or identification with the criminal venture, at an intuitive level, it becomes more difficult convincingly

---

[52] See the Model Penal Code (1962). The original view of the American Law Institute was that such considerations should be subordinated to those of more extensive law enforcement. TD 1 (1953), 27–32; and see revised commentary (1985), 314–19.

to attribute some responsibility for the principal's actions to the accessory.[53]

Against this view a number of counter-arguments may be deployed. First, as claimed in *Backun*, freedom to trade is subject to overriding moral duties to prevent crime; a seller or supplier cannot 'wash his hands of the aid he has given the perpetrator'; the 'larger interest'[54] of suppressing crime must be paramount. The force of this claim is affected by the level of knowledge or foresight required by the accessory as to what the buyer intends to do with the materials and the perceived likelihood of such action. A low level knowledge requirement argues for a purposive attitude from the seller if trading is not to be made unfairly hazardous and the association between the accessory's and principal's standard of culpability too tenuous. Secondly, because an accessory, particularly one not present at the commission of the offence, is one stage removed or detached from active criminality, the opportunity and ability to reflect on the consequences of actions is liable to be greater. Consequently, in one sense, there may be more of an element of 'calculation' in indifference to the effects of the conduct. Finally, where a supplier is virtually certain that the other party will carry out a criminal act the indifferent supplier's moral culpability is hardly distinguishable from a party whose object in supplying is to bring about the principal offence.

Such competing and inconclusive arguments on the appropriate attitudinal requirement for an accessory suggest that the most acceptable approach or 'solution . . . is found not in logical abstraction, but in the effort to make a proper adjustment between conflicting social interests'.[55]

The solution to these problems obviously turns on their nature. There is no natural or automatically ascertainable proper level of mental involvement or culpability; it is a normative issue of what mental states, bearing in mind the social circumstances and consequences and possibilities for control, ought to be taken as appropriate subjects for criminal sanctions. A number of initial questions arise in relation to accessorial attitude: should there be a universal standard applicable to all circumstances of complicity? Should differences in levels of mental commitment to or association with the principal offence be reflected in scales of punishment—whether formally prescribed or informally enforced? Should differences in the *mens rea* requirement be dependent on the mode of complicity?

In favour of a generally applicable standard is simplicity and certainty. This approach rests on the assumption that discernible variations in culpability occurring between accessories can be fully accommodated in the

[53] Agency, as one possible theoretical basis of complicity (see Ch. 3), entails the notion of consent to or willing identification with another's actions. As Kadish notes ('Complicity, Cause and Blame', 5) under the civil law of agency what counts is the appearance or objective manifestation of consent rather than true consent. However, the business rationale of such an approach clearly has no direct relevance to criminal liability.
[54] Model Penal Code, TD 1 (1953), 32.
[55] Perkins, *Criminal Law*, 746.

sentencing process. Such a stance implicitly denies that the circumstances of the accessory's acts may themselves be crucial in determining whether they should be deemed criminal or not. These variations may be as to the mode of complicity (particularly whether the accessory is present at the commission of the principal offence) or the background nature of the transaction or association between accessory and principal, or the gravity of the principal offence. Each of these factors may, arguably, be the basis for a differential in the requirement of the accessory's attitude towards the principal offence. And although the practicalities of formulation and usage would be likely to rule out anything beyond crude or broad differentials, nevertheless it is worth briefly reviewing the possibility.

In respect of the mode of complicity, 'procure' seems almost inevitably to entail a purposive state of mind. Realistically *almost all* cases of encouragement will be purposeful; but the present question is whether encouragement generally is intrinsically different from assisting in a way which warrants a distinct attitudinal requirement. It is very doubtful whether this is so, for the liability of the non-purposeful encourager, as with an assister, depends on an indirect contribution being made towards the commission of the principal offence. And even though assistance may be a more tangible form of involvement, the encourager's and assister's moral positions are not obviously distinguishable.[56]

An alternative modal distinction is whether the presence of the accessory should affect *mens rea* requirements. Being present at the commission of the principal offence often provides the accessory with the potential for greater influence over the principal, thereby making the accessory's indifferent attitude less remote from the principal criminal source.[57] However, in addition to the problem of settling when a party is present, there are many imaginable examples where the nature of the assistance provided would tend to cancel out any worthwhile distinction based on presence: compare the selling of a gun to a notoriously violent criminal, later murderously used, with refreshments being sold to individuals in the act of illegal gambling.

The context of the transaction is another possible criterion for distinguishing appropriate levels of accessorial *mens rea*. In particular, there is the position of the commercial trader who supplies goods or materials purely for profit. It has been suggested that, subject to specifically identified exceptions, there should be no liability where such a party is 'acting in the ordinary course of lawful business'.[58] Indirect support for this approach is

---

[56] See Ch. 2. *Contra* Williams [1990] Crim. LR 4 who argues in favour of a 'purpose' requirement for encouragement and a selectively modified foresight standard for assisters or helpers.

[57] See the discussion of different levels of proof of *mens rea* formerly required in English law according to whether the secondary party was an accessory before the fact or principal in the second degree. Westerfield, 'The Mens Rea Requirement', 155–8.

[58] Williams, *Textbook*, 343.

supplied by a solid body of mainly eighteenth- and nineteenth-century English authorities whereby the supplier of goods or services who facilitated the purchaser's subsequent criminal behaviour was entitled to enforce the contract, provided nothing out of the ordinary run of legitimate business practice had been followed. Therefore, for example, selling a dress to a prostitute with the awareness of its intended use in the buyer plying her trade,[59] or the sale of spirits with the knowledge of the buyer's intention of illegal resale,[60] did not prevent recovery of the contract price and, by implication,[61] did not make the supplier a party to the buyer's offence.

Conversely, where the seller's conduct deviates from standard commercial behaviour the contract will be unenforceable and he may also be *particeps criminis*, as where goods were specially packed to facilitate smuggling.[62] Useful as this technique may be for filtering out assistance in minor criminality, its applicability to more serious offences is doubtful. Would it, for instance, be acceptable in cases for the supply of weapons believed to be destined for use in violent crimes? Furthermore, even for less serious offences, is a test of ordinary trade practice workable? What *degree* of departure from the seller's usual trading pattern would be enough to incriminate him? Would it need to be demonstrable that it was of value to the purchaser? For example, would staying open half an hour later than usual for the purchaser's convenience, or extending unusually favourable credit arrangements, be a sufficient deviation? In truth, the substance of this method of distinguishing 'ordinary' commercial transactions from those which are thought appropriate to punish is a variant of determining whether the supplier has done sufficient to involve himself in the buyer's criminal venture for it to be said that he has identified himself with or has a stake in it. The distinction may possibly be looked at as evidential: supplying help or assistance raises a presumption of associated purpose rebutted by evidence that the basis of the transaction was nothing beyond standard commercial practice.[63]

---

[59] *Bowry v. Bennett* (1808) 1 Camp 348, 170 ER 981, followed in *Smith v. White* (1866) LR 1 Eq. 626. Similarly washing a prostitute's clothes, *Lloyd v. Johnson* (1798) 1 Bos. and Pul. 340, 126 ER 939.

[60] *Hodgson v. Temple* (1813) 5 Taunt 181, 128 ER 656; followed in *Pellecart v. Angell* (1835) 2 CM & R. 311, 150 ER 135, and *Foster v. Driscoll* [1929] 1 KB 496, 518.

[61] *Cafferata v. Wilson* and *Cook v. Stockwell* are clearly against this approach.

[62] *Biggs v. Lawrence* (1789) 3 TR 454, 100 ER 673; and similarly in *Weymell v. Reed* (1794) 5 TR 599, 101 ER 335. Discussed by Williams, CLGP 374–5, and Perkins, *Criminal Law*, 746–7, for additional American case law.

[63] In similar vein, there is the possible distinguishing test of liability turning on whether what was supplied was a generally available 'marketable commodity'. But even assuming that identification of such is usually feasible (cf. Smith and Hogan, *Criminal Law*, 129) one possible reason for excluding liability in such cases might be causal — that what was supplied could have been obtained elsewhere and consequently that the supplier's role was not an essential precondition of the principal offence. But this is to misunderstand the causal element in complicity; see Ch. 3.

Finally, using the gravity of the principal offence as a method of discriminating between where criminal purpose should or should not be required has been widely canvassed.[64] Clearly, the more serious the likely resulting social harm the greater the individual's moral responsibility to ensure that assistance is not rendered; and, further, a certain level of personal and commercial convenience is overborne by the larger social interest of preventing serious criminal behaviour. Therefore, in such serious cases, assistance provided by a party indifferent to its use is justifiably incriminated. However, it might be countered that particularly in the case of serious offences where punishment is potentially most severe, the need to establish high personal culpability through a 'purpose' requirement is strongest. True as this is, the claim gives insufficient weight to the role that actual or threatened consequential harm performs in gauging an actor's culpability. Beyond this at least two further objections may be raised which cast doubt on the efficacy of using the seriousness of offence approach. First is the problematic determination of *what* should be regarded as a 'serious' offence;[65] how far would the circumstances of a case be allowed to vary its classification as 'serious' or not? For example, would all thefts regardless of the value of the property involved be treated similarly? Secondly, the cumulative effect of complicity in the commission of a large number of similar but fairly trivial offences might be thought to be sufficiently culpable to warrant punishment,[66] even where the complicitous actions were non-purposeful.

5. Facilitation Offences

The difficulties for existing complicity law in providing an appropriate attitudinal requirement across the complete range of criminal association suggest the need for a more radical and structured change than the potentially discriminating factors so far considered might permit. In particular a solution is needed which incorporates sufficient flexibility to cope with actors who, although less than purposefully involved in the principal's criminality, have played a substantial role in bringing about the

---

[64] See Perkins, *Criminal Law*, 746; La Fave and Scott, *Criminal Law*, 509. More sceptically, see Smith and Hogan, *Criminal Law*, 129. One indicator of seriousness will be the level of mental culpability—the most serious offences requiring 'intention'. Following a scheme of using the principal culpability standard as that also demanded of the accessory indirectly achieves a similar discriminatory standard; see below, Ch. 6, s. 7, 'Conclusions'.

[65] e.g. Smith and Hogan, *Criminal Law,* 129. It has been proposed that purposive aid should be required unless either the principal offence involves 'treason or serious violence to person or property' or the accessory is 'present' at the principal offence. Lanham, 'Limitations on Accomplice Liability', (1982) 6 *Crim. LJ* 306, 325.

[66] Cf. Spencer, 'Trying to Help Another Person', 162. And see Law Commission Working Paper 104, *Conspiracy to Defraud* (1987), app. C, for a brief review of the possibility of using a facilitation offence as an alternative to conspiracy to defraud.

actus reus. Such cases, it could be argued, deserve punishment because the totality of the accessory's criminality is the combined product of his mental culpability and the degree to which he has actually contributed to the bringing about of the principal offence; limited mental culpability is compensated for by a strong *actus reus* contribution. An approach of this nature seeks to achieve some sort of rough equalization between the necessary aggregate criminality of each accessory by balancing complicity's *mens rea* and *actus reus* components. Whether, so to speak, trading off *mens rea* and *actus reus* levels in this fashion is theoretically coherent is debatable;[67] certainly its practicability must be doubtful. A *reductio ad absurdum* example could be an accessory's perception of the remote chance of the principal offence occurring being compensated for or set off against his provision of overwhelmingly strong assistance.

Rather than pursuing such an approach within the confines of complicity, some modern reforms — particularly in American jurisdictions — have looked towards the enactment of separate and distinct forms of liability to complement standard (purposeful) complicity liability.[68] A pioneering provision in this area was article 115 of the 1967 New York Penal Code [69] which created a new offence of criminal facilitation:

A person is guilty of criminal facilitation ... when believing it probable that he is rendering aid to a person who intends to commit a crime, he engages in conduct which provides such a person with means or opportunity for the commission thereof.[70]

---

[67] Cf. Model Penal Code, TD 1 (1953), s. 2.04 (3) (*b*), and TD 4 (1955), s. 2.06 (3) (*b*). Under the code's original proposal complicity liability would be imposed where a person either purposefully facilitated an offence or 'knowingly substantially facilitated its commission'. The commentary of TD 1 (1953), 27–30 seems to imply something approaching a rationale of balancing *mens rea* and *actus reus*.

[68] Not the Model Penal Code (1962). It has been criticized for this omission. The majority of state penal code reforms have followed the code provisions and required purpose; see P. H. Robinson and J. A. Grall, 'Element Analysis in Defining Criminal Liability: The Model Penal Code and Beyond' (1983) 35 *Stan. LR* 681, 739 n. 260. Of those states that do not through a code provision expressly require purposive assistance, most do so by case authority. La Fave and Scott, *Criminal Law*, 508, n. 15. A small number of states have enacted new codes incorporating a knowledge only requirement; see Robinson, 'Imputed Criminal Liability', 637 n. 100.

[69] See Ch. 3 (3), 'Conclusions' for *actus reus* references. Note N. R. Sobel, 'The Anticipatory Offences in the New Penal Law: Solicitation, Conspiracy, Attempt and Facilitation' (1966) 32 *Brooklyn LR* 257, 269–71; and 'The Proposed Penal Code of New York' (1964) 64 *Col. LR* 1469, 1523. Cf. Californian Penal Code Rev. Project TD 1 (1967), art. 452, and Michigan Rev. Criminal Code, art. 415 (*b*), 1967.

[70] Amended in 1978 to create four degrees of facilitation. It was an approach taken up in the proposed federal code, although, instead of a 'means and opportunity' basis, use is made of a 'substantial assistance' formula. Art. 1002 (1) of the proposed federal code states: 'A person is guilty of criminal facilitation if he knowingly provides substantial assistance to a person intending to commit a felony and that person in fact commits the crime contemplated or a like or related felony employing the assistance as provided. The ready lawful availability from others of the goods or services provided by a defendant is a factor to be considered in determining whether or not the assistance was substantial.' See P. Doherty, 'A New Crime: Criminal Facilitation' (1971) 18 *Loyola LR* 103; also 'The Proposed Federal Penal Code'

The explicit twin bases of facilitation offences have been acceptance of the need to punish conduct falling outside complicity requiring purposive assistance and recognition that assistance which is provided 'knowingly' merits not only a lower range of sanctions than that purposefully given but also warrants a separate and distinctive criminal designation. Jurisdictions (as is probably the case in England) where knowledge or foresight alone is the *mens rea* of complicity, obviously do not suffer from any lacunae preventing prosecution of indifferent suppliers or aiders. Rather, the question is whether the philosophy and benefits of this two-tier system[71] of punishing involvement in the offences of others are sufficiently attractive to prompt abandonment of the existing single liability structure.

Common law[72] (or common law influenced)[73] jurisdictions divide on whether an accessory's liability requires purpose to further or promote the principal offence.[74] Although tending to favour a purposive standard

(1972) 47 *NYULR* 320, 341; and S. C. Charen and J. P. Colangelo, 'The Proposed New Federal Criminal Code' (1976) *An. Survey of Am. Law* 313, 337. The level of the facilitator's foresight of the likely commission of the principal offence must be high in the case of the New York provision; the offence must be foreseen as 'probable'. *People* v. *Gordon* 295 NE 2nd 777 (1973). The proposed federal code simply requires the defendant to 'knowingly' assist; what strength or foresight would satisfy this expression is unclear.

[71] And whether the drawbacks of the present single standard liability are sufficiently uncomfortable.

[72] Australian common law states would appear to require no more than knowledge; see Gillies, *Criminal Complicity*, 60–1, and *Harding* (1976) VR 129. Cf. C. Howard, *Criminal Law* (1983), 262; and s. 7 (*b*) of the Queensland and Western Australian Codes both of which, in addition to express provisions concerning aiding, counselling, and procuring, separately refer to a party acting with 'the purpose of enabling or aiding another person'. See a similar provision in s. 66 (1) (*b*) of the New Zealand Crimes Act 1961 concerning 'aiding'. However 'purpose' is not included in s. 66 (1) (*c*) in relation to labelling'. Cf. *Lewis* [1975] 1 NZLR 222, *Paterson* [1976] 2 NZLR 394 and *Curtis* [1988] 1 NZLR 734. The Canadian Criminal Code, s. 2 (1), specifies 'purpose' which has been given a meaning that 'closely approaches' motive'; V. G. Rose, *Parties to an Offence* (1982), 14. See *F. W. Woolworth Co. Ltd.* (1974) 18 CCC (2d) 23; *Curran* (1978) 38 CCC (2d) 151; *Glushek* (1978) 41 CCC (2d) 380; *Popen* (1981) 60 CCC (2d) 232; *Roan* (1985) 17 CCC (3d) 534 at 537. California is a relatively recent example of a jurisdiction expressly moving through case development from a standard of indifference or knowledge to one of purpose. See the 1984 California Supreme Court decision in *People* v. *Beeman* 674 P. (2d) 1318, discussed by C. Carpenter, 'Should the Court Aid and Abet the Unintending Accomplice' (1984) 24 Santa Clara LR 343.

[73] South Africa takes a knowledge-only approach; Burchell and Hunt, *SA Criminal Law*, 425; and see *Tshwape* 1964 (4) SA 327 and *S.* v. *O'Brien* 1970 (3) SA 405 at 409; and cf. the equivocal judgment in *S.* v. *Quinta* 1974 (1) SA 544 at 547. In Scotland the provision of assistance 'in the normal course' of business is 'probably' not a sufficient basis for complicity. But quite how much deviation from normal business practice is necessary is not firmly indicated by authority; see *HM Advocate* v. *Johnstone* (1926) JC 89 and cf. *HM Advocate* v. *Semple* (1937) JC 41. Gordon suggests that to incriminate the assisting party must be in some way 'in it' with the principal: *Criminal Law*, 142–4.

[74] As variations between American states reveal, even those sharing a standard of purposeful assistance part company on means and modes of proof to such an extent as to produce considerable differences in the practical scope of complicity liability. Some states enforce a high standard of proof requiring *direct* and positive evidence of a community of purpose; others seek evidence demonstrating either a pecuniary interest or conspiracy; while some jurisdictions readily permit an inference of purpose simply from knowledge of a possible principal offence. See the American case law reviewed by Westerfield, 'The Mens Rea Requirement', 161–7.

coupled with a separate facilitation offence, reform proposals have displayed widely differing attitudes to precise resolution of the question.[75] Judgments on the *right* standard — whether in a theoretical or practical sense — are impossible without due allowance being given to the nature of the other elements of any *particular* system of complicity — most especially to the demands of the remaining components of *mens rea* and the substance of causal requirements. Aggregate culpability requirements must be weighed along with assessment of the particular contributing elements.

As already maintained in relation to causal demands, adhering to a single broad concept of participation in another's criminality is unwieldy, necessitating compromises in definitional clarity and anything approaching finesse in designating certain forms of behaviour to be of the same species of criminality. The issue of accessorial attitude further illustrates orthodox complicity's problem in satisfactorily spanning distinct and diverse forms of criminal activity. It will be seen in Chapter 6 on 'specificity' that many acute difficulties relating to accessorial 'knowledge' or foresight of the principal's possible actions follow on from, or are aggravated by, the absence of a purpose requirement.[76] Consequently, incorporation of such a condition in complicity coupled with the enactment of a facilitation provision is desirable in that it would relieve other areas of tension within secondary liability beside that immediately concerned with accessorial attitude.[77]

[75] Proposition 7 (1) (*a*) and (*b*) of Law Commission Working Paper 43 specifies intention or knowledge. Law Commission Report 143, cl. 31 (4) (*a*), effectively settled for the lower standard of recklessness by imposing liability where assistance is provided which a party believes 'may, cause, assist or encourage the principal' etc. Thus e.g. in trading cases the seller would be liable under proposition 7 if he acted with knowledge (a belief or expectation) of a planned offence, whereas under s. 31 acting with awareness of the risk of assisting or encouraging a principal offence would suffice. However, Law Commission Report 177, cl. 27 (1) (*a*) restates the law in apparently narrower terms (see n. 1) similar to those in Working Paper 43. As with the Model Penal Code, s. 2.06 (3) (*a*), the Canadian Law Reform Commission's Draft Criminal Code 1986, ss. 4 (2) and 2 (4) (*d*), requires purposeful activity for the proposed new offence of 'furthering'.

[76] Requiring only an accessory's assent or consent to the principal offence would cut back the scope of complicity from where it probably now stands in English law. *Gillick* e.g. would be more clearly outside complicity. However, conduct presently unlawful, such as in *Bainbridge*, would still warrant some degree of punishment, thereby making some form of facilitation liability a necessary substitute. Setting complicity at the lower culpability level of assent rather than requiring purposeful behaviour has the drawback of it being a state of mind less easily demonstrated or disproved. How easily, for instance, could it be determined whether a seller of firearms assented to their use for criminal purposes? Would the dealer who knew of such likely use exonerate himself by displaying a notice in his shop proclaiming his disapproval of the criminal use of firearms?

[77] For the distorting effects on inchoate and other areas of criminality caused by the law's *indirect* efforts to incriminate facilitation and attempts at such, see Spencer, 'Trying to Help Another Person', 148.

6

Specificity: The Necessary Extent of the Accessory's 'Knowledge' of the Principal Offence

1. The Accessory's Need for 'Knowledge' of 'Essential Matters' of the Principal Offence

(1) *Case Law*

Not until comparatively recently has the nature of an accessory's *mens rea* requirement received much in the way of concentrated judicial consideration. And even now, as will become apparent, many complexities in this area of complicity law lie waiting to be prodded into action by the occurrence of less than fanciful situations. The broad modern *mens rea* formula finally emerged from a cluster of decisions in the late 1940s and early 1950s, and most particularly in the Divisional Court case of *Johnson* v. *Youden*[1] where Lord Goddard CJ explained that :

[1] [1950] 1 KB 544 at 546. In this case and in a considerable number of the authorities discussed, Lord Goddard uses the expression 'aiding and abetting' in a general sense connoting all forms of complicity. Only in cases where the terminology adopted by the court is clearly of significance will notice be taken. House of Lords approval of *Johnson* v. *Youden* was given in *Churchill* v. *Walton* [1967] 2 AC 224 at 236, and *DPP for Northern Ireland* v. *Maxwell* [1978] 1 WLR 1350 at 1355. In similar vein see e.g. *Ackroyds Air Travel Ltd.* v. *DPP* [1950] 1 KB 933 at 936 citing the court's (pre-*Johnson* v. *Youden*) decision in *Wessel* v. *Carter Paterson and Pickfords Carriers Ltd.* [1947] 2 All ER 280. *Thomas* v. *Lindop* [1950] 1 All ER 966 at 968; *Ferguson* v. *Weaving* [1951] 1 KB 814 at 820; *Sayce* v. *Coupe* [1952] 2 All ER 715; *John Henshall (Quarries) Ltd.* v. *Harvey* [1965] 1 All ER 725 at 728. Earlier examples of the express or tacit acceptance of the rule are *Callow* v. *Tillstone* (1900) 19 Cox 576 at 579; *Chivers* v. *Hand* (1914) 24 Cox 520 at 522; *Bowker* v. *Premier Drug Co.* [1928] 1 KB 217 at 229 and 230. *Provincial Motor Car Co. Ltd.* v. *Dunning* [1909] 2 KB 599 and *Carter* v. *Mace* [1949] 2 All ER 714 are decisions where secondary liability was imposed despite the absence of knowledge or even negligence on the part of the controlling secondary party. In the former case the court held that breach of traffic regulations committed by the accessory's employee was 'not to be regarded as a criminal offence in the full sense of the word; that is to say there may be a breach of regulation without criminal intent or *mens rea*' (at 602). In *Carter* v. *Mace* where the principal offender was an independent haulage contractor, in relation to the accessory Lord Goddard held (as accurately stated in the headnote) 'it was the appellant's duty to see that the person whose vehicle he hired could lawfully carry out the contracts which he had made, and in hiring a lorry from an owner whose licence did not enable him to carry the goods in question the appellant was guilty of aiding and abetting that lorry owner'. The ruling in *Carter* v. *Mace* was effectively neutralized by its author in *Davies Turner & Co.* v. *Brodie* [1954] 1 WLR 1364 when characterized as being one 'decided entirely on the particular facts which were striking'.

Before a person can be convicted of aiding and abetting the commission of an offence he must at least know the essential matters which constitute that offence. He need not actually know that an offence has been committed . . . If a person knows all the facts and is assisting another person to do certain things, and it turns out that doing of those things constitute an offence, the person who is assisting is guilty of aiding and abetting the offence.

This fundamental rule holds true whether or not the offence requires knowledge of 'essential matters' by the principal offender;[2] although if the absence of such knowledge can be attributed to 'wilful blindness'[3] then ignorance of essential matters will not bar secondary liability.

Having settled that an accessory must have knowledge of essential matters, the further question requiring judicial attention was exactly what constituted 'essential matters'. With what degree of specificity was an accessory required to 'know' the facts of the principal offence? References in briefly reported early twentieth-century cases[4] suggest the need for an accessory's awareness of the possible commission of a particular offence. A contrary approach was taken in *Bullock*.[5] However, although expressly unwilling to accept the earlier view, the court in *Bullock* felt a ruling on the issue[6] was unnecessary, being content

> that once the Jury were satisfied . . . that he did know that it was being used for an unlawful purpose, there was no need to give an elaborate direction whether the unlawful purpose was merely a general purpose or the intent to commit one or other of the crimes.[7]

---

[2] As e.g. in *Callow* v. *Tillstone*, where it was suggested even negligence would not suffice. Cf. the continuing doctrinal uncertainty over the appropriate 'culpability structure' — whether subjective or objective — for American federal provisions relating to *civil* damages actions for complicity under the Securities Exchange Act 1934, as amended. See J. T. Vangel, 'A Complicity-Doctrine Approach to Section 10 (*b*) Aiding and Abetting Civil Damages Actions' (1989) 89 Col. LR 180.

[3] *Antonelli and Barberi* (1905) 70 JP 4; *Davies Turner & Co. Ltd.* v. *Brodie*, and *Thomas* v. *Lindop*, discussed below. And cf. the notion of a 'blank cheque', below.

[4] Especially *Lomas* (1913) 9 Cr. App. Rep. 220. Particularly Lush J. in *arguendo*: 'If the verdict merely means that the appellant handed King's jemmy to him with the knowledge that he would commit *some* burglary with it, it is not enough' (emphasis added). Similarly, Shearman J. in *Bowker* v. *Premier Drug Co.* offered the view that 'A crime must be a specific intentional act, and I know of no case saying that a man can be an aider and abettor if he knows nothing of the act or the date or the person against whom the criminal offence is committed' (230). Shearman J. appeared to use 'or' between 'act', 'date', and 'person' conjunctively: an accessory needed to know both when the act would occur and also the victim's identity.

[5] (1955) 38 Cr. App. Rep. 151.

[6] 'It is no doubt true that if an accused merely suspects that if he lends something it may be used for a general criminal purpose it may not be enough to make him an accessory before the fact; it is not necessary for the purposes of this case that we should express a view one way or another on that point. If an accused lends a man a revolver believing that it may be used to commit a crime of violence but with nothing specific in mind, it may not be enough, but this is not a case of that sort': per Devlin J. at 153.

[7] Ibid. at 154.

Specificity of Knowledge

Soon after *Bullock* the problem was unavoidably confronted by the Court of Criminal Appeal in *Bainbridge*[8] where Lord Goddard's successor, Lord Parker CJ, whilst recognizing that it was 'not altogether easy to lay down a precise form of words', held 'that there must be not merely suspicion but knowledge that a crime of the type in question was intended'. It was insufficient if 'a man knows that some illegal venture is intended'.[9]

The combined policy and practical issue faced in *Bainbridge* was typical of those which the criminal law constantly throws up: what is the appropriate level of culpability and how can it be captured in a usable formulation? Although always latent in the rules of variation, introduction of the 'type' test of specificity was a watershed decision in complicity's developmental history — in one sense representing an open decoupling of an accessory's mental culpability from a *particular* anticipated offence and substituting an attachment to a *class* of offences, the specific details (venue/time/victim) of which need not be known to the accessory. Remarkably, in so far as (lack of) reported decisions are a reliable indicator, *Bainbridge*'s 'type' test produced few difficulties of practical application; but a fair harvest of latent problems exists to reward reasonably imaginative commentators. Most particularly, how far does technical classification or description determine the 'type' of offence? For example:

If D lends a jemmy to P, contemplating that P intends to enter a house in order to steal, is D guilty of any offence if P enters a house intending to rape?[10]

---

[8] [1960] 1 QB 129 at 134 and 133. In producing his 'type' test Lord Parker drew on Foster's formula proposed for cases of variation by the principal from the conduct anticipated by the accessory: 'if the principal totally and substantially varieth and knowingly committeth a felony of another, he will stand single in that offence', *Crown Law*, 369. See Chs. 7 and 8 for a discussion of variation issues.

[9] On the problem of clearly distinguishing 'suspicion' from 'knowledge', see below, Ch. 6 (4). The essential facts of the case were that Bainbridge purchased oxygen-cutting equipment subsequently used by another a few weeks later to break into a bank. Bainbridge admitted that he had purchased the equipment for another whom he believed was intending to use the same 'for something illegal' possibly 'for breaking up stolen goods'. The courts ruled that to convict the defendant his knowledge must have been such that he knew an offence involving breaking and entering and stealing was planned. In *Payne* [1965] Crim. LR 543 it was held to be sufficient that the defendant knew an offence involving fraud was contemplated, for even though he did not know the precise nature of the fraudulent statements employed he knew the type of offence involved. Lord Pearce, in the Privy Council case of *Thambiah* v. *R.* [1966] AC 37 at 46, when reflecting on how much particularity of *mens rea* must be shown in proving complicity, observed: 'this is a matter which must clearly be affected by the extent and degree of the abettors' activities and their proximity to the actual crime'. These words seem directed rather more at the issue of evidence of knowledge rather than degree of knowledge necessary for an accessory. According to *Bettles* [1966] Crim LR 503, knowing the principal was going to engage in some 'dishonest and unlawful purpose' was insufficiently specific to satisfy the 'type' test. In *Calderwood and Moore* [1983] 10 NIJB at 30, Hutton J. contrasted knowledge or contemplation of a prospective offence with mere suspicion of its possible commission which would not support a conviction. Cf. Law Commission Working Party 43, 53, illustration *a* discussed below.

[10] Example of Smith and Hogan, *Criminal Law*, 145.

Will the fact that both forms of behaviour constitute burglary mean they would be regarded as of the same type of offence? If formal classification is not the sole determinant of 'type', then what particular features reveal 'type'? A further potential difficulty is whether the method employed to achieve the principal objective is relevant to 'type'. The means used to bring about an agreed goal may determine the offence committed:

If, for instance, D tells P to take V's gold watch by snatching it from V's wrist, but P obtains the watch by threatening to expose V's criminal record to his golf club, will D be liable as an accessory to blackmail?

There has been no variation of ends, but will the unforeseen means be considered sufficiently similar to make the whole enterprise of the same type?[11]

The limitations and standing of *Bainbridge* were eventually reviewed by the House of Lords in the leading case of *DPP for Northern Ireland* v. *Maxwell*.[12] Using his own car, Maxwell, a member of the illegal Ulster Volunteer Force (UVF), guided other members of the organization occupying a second car to a public house which had been 'targeted' for some form of terrorist attack. While aware the second car carried the necessary

---

[11] Proposition 7 (2) (a) of Law Commission Working Paper 43, 57, was intended to preserve the test in *Bainbridge*, but an illustration of the perceived scope of the test provided by the Working Party suggests an expansion (possibly inadvertent) of the ambit of the test as well as possible incompatibility with proposition 7 (1). Illustration *a* (53): 'The defendant lent A oxy-acetylene apparatus, knowing that A intended to use it for breaking into premises or for breaking into stolen safes or some other dishonest purpose. The defendant is an accessory to any such offence of dishonesty for which A uses the apparatus.' If in *Bainbridge* the defendant had suspected 'that some illegal venture is intended' or 'the equipment was to be used to dispose of stolen property' that would not have been sufficient to incriminate him ([1960] 1 QB 129 at 133). Yet in the Working Party's example it appears the degree of specificity of knowledge (foresight) required of the defendant is hardly greater than a suspicion of some 'illegal venture'; and if inaccurate suspicion of one form of dishonesty is not sufficient (i.e. breaking up stolen property, *Bainbridge*) why should a *general* suspicion of dishonesty embracing many inappropriate offences incriminate in the actual offence committed? Cf. *Bullock* in which it was remarked that awareness that another person intended a crime of violence with a revolver may not be sufficiently specific to convict. And cf. also *Bettles* (cit. n. 9). Further, it is difficult to follow how the requirement of knowledge of external elements stipulated in proposition 7 (1) can be satisfied in circumstances such as those in the example provided. Has the offence of burglary the same external elements as, say, receiving? Law Commission Report 177 makes no reference to 'type' nor to the accessory's 'contemplation'. Instead it seeks to achieve the result of liability without detailed knowledge of the principal offence by providing that 'a person may be guilty of an offence as an accessory although he does not foresee, or is not aware of, a circumstance of the offence which is not an element of it (e.g. the identity of the victim or the time or place of its commission, where this is not an element of the offence), cl. 27 (4). Report 143, as well as incorporating a similar provision, cl. 31 (5), refers to the accessory's awareness of 'an act of the kind' the principal did. The change may be of substance as well as style, for 'kind' seems to envisage a class or type of act, not necessarily the particular act foreseen. Would two different *acts* be regarded as the same 'kind' as each other if both were punishable as the same offence, as e.g. in burglary?

[12] [1978] 1 WLR 1350. In one sense the specific and unspecific elements known to the accessory in *Maxwell* were the converse of those in *Bainbridge*: the latter case involving a specific (known) type of offence and non-specific (unknown) details of occasion and location; the former case involving unspecific offences but a specifically known occasion.

Specificity of Knowledge 165

means for such an attack, Maxwell claimed not to have known exactly what was planned; although he knew the 'attack would be one of violence in which persons would be endangered or premises seriously damaged'.[13] On arriving at the public house a bomb was planted by an occupant of the second car. Maxwell was convicted as an accessory to two offences under the Explosive Substances Act 1883.[14] Dismissing an appeal[15] against conviction, the House of Lords held the basis of liability to be the accessory's 'contemplation' of the principal offence committed, but that the accessory's contemplation need not be specifically focused on the actual offence carried out, it being sufficient if that offence was within a range of possible offences foreseen by the accessory. This important decision warrants a number of comments.

First, does the 'type' test devised in *Bainbridge* survive *Maxwell*,[16] or has it been either partly or completely superseded by it? Although none of their lordships doubted the correctness of *Bainbridge*, both Lords Dilhorne and Scarman appeared to see the contemplation principle as a superior approach, rendering the 'type' test redundant. According to Lord Dilhorne, *Bainbridge* established the broad proposition that a person could be an accessory, 'without his having knowledge of the actual crime intended'. In the present case no 'useful purpose' was to be served by employing the 'type' test. And, more generally, an accessory's liability 'should not depend on categorisation'.[17] Lord Scarman was even more explicitly critical of *Bainbridge*'s shortcomings:

I think *Bainbridge* was correctly decided. But I agree . . . that in the instant case the Court of Criminal Appeal in Northern Ireland has gone further than the Court of Criminal Appeal for England and Wales found it necessary to go in *Bainbridge* . . . The guilt of an accessory springs according to the [Court of Criminal Appeal in Northern Ireland]:

'from the fact that he contemplates the commission of one (or more) of a number of crimes by the principal and he intentionally lends his assistance in order that such a crime will be committed . . . The relevant crime must be within the

---

[13] Ibid. 1358, Lord Hailsham quoting trial judge MacDermot J.
[14] S. 3 (*a*): doing an act with intent to cause by explosive substances an explosion of a nature likely to endanger life or cause serious injury to property; s. 3 (*b*): possessing an explosive with similar intent. S. 5 of the Act expressly provides for complicity in any offence under the Act.
[15] The question certified for the House by the Court of Criminal Appeal in Northern Ireland was: 'If the crime committed by the principal, and actually assisted by the accused, was one of a number of offences, one of which the accused knew the principal would probably commit, is the guilty mind which must be proved against an accomplice thereby proved against the accused?'
[16] *Bainbridge* was applied in *McClafferty* [1980] 11 NIJB. The Ontario Court of Appeal in *Yanover and Gerol* (1985) 20 CCC (3rd) 300 at 329, took *Maxwell* as authority for the 'type' test.
[17] [1978] 1 WLR 1356. Lord Dilhorne nowhere directly adopts the test of the accessory's contemplation. However, he approvingly cites a passage from Lowry LCJ's judgment which incorporated the elements of the test: 1355–6.

contemplation of the accomplice, and only exceptionally would evidence be found to support the allegation that the accomplice had given the principal a completely blank cheque'.

The principle thus formulated has great merit. It directs attention to the state of mind of the accused . . . it avoids definition and classification . . . Although the court's formulation of the principle goes further than the earlier cases, it is a sound development of the law and in no way inconsistent with them.[18]

Unlike Lord Scarman, Lord Edmund Davies adopted Lowry LCJ's judgment without further elaboration, believing it to be a 'sleeveless errand' to do otherwise.[19] The Lowry judgment itself makes no direct or explicit attempt to change or circumscribe the 'type' test, although its guiding principle was that 'guilt springs from the fact that [the accessory] contemplates the commission of one (or more) of a number of crimes . . . and he intentionally lends his assistance in order that such a crime will be committed'.[20]

The remaining two members of the House felt able to uphold Maxwell's conviction without recourse to any culpability formulation beyond *Bainbridge*. Lord Hailsham was quite 'content for this purpose to adopt the words of Lord Parker CJ in . . . *Bainbridge*' and apply the 'type' test.[21] Similarly, Lord Fraser spoke the language of and employed the formula from *Bainbridge*.[22]

It would appear, then, that a majority of the House of Lords[23] adopted as a requirement of complicity liability the contemplation (or foresight) of the principal offence occurring. However, it remains impossible to state with confidence whether the 'type' test still performs a recognized and legitimate role alongside, or complementary to, the *Maxwell* approach.[24] Clearly the issue is only of significance if the two formulae are capable of producing different or conflicting results. Conceptually, Lord Scarman took *Maxwell* to be no more than a 'sound development' of *Bainbridge*. Therefore cases with facts like those in *Bainbridge* should still be decided in the same way under the contemplation test.

For example, if a defendant supplies breaking equipment expecting it to be used to steal from the vaults of Lloyd's Bank, Fleet Street on the last day

---

[18] [1978] 1 WLR 1362–3.

[19] Ibid. 1359.

[20] Ibid. 1374. Sir Robert Lowry noted 'Once the "particular crime" theory of guilty knowledge is rejected in favour of the *Bainbridge* principle, the question arises how far that principle goes. In a practical sense the question is whether the principle applies to the facts proved in this case.' Cf. *Hamilton* [1987] 6 NIJB 1.

[21] Ibid. 1357.

[22] Ibid. 1360–1.

[23] Lords Dilhorne, Scarman, and Edmund Davies.

[24] Most commentators, by implication, have taken the view that *Bainbridge* has survived *Maxwell*, at least in part. See, particularly, Smith and Hogan, *Criminal Law*, 143, 145, where *Maxwell* is accepted as a consistent development of *Bainbridge*; and Williams, *Textbook*, 336; Ashworth, 'The Elasticity of Mens Rea', 66–7. Cf. R. J. Buxton, 'The Extent of Criminal Complicity' (1979) 42 MLR 315. The WLR headnote is misleadingly simplistic in its unqualified restatement of the 'type' test.

of January, and instead it is employed in a burglary of Silversmiths in Chancery Lane on the 1st February, will a court be entitled to find that the defendant has contemplated the offence which took place?

In a strict literal sense *that* offence was not contemplated. And, if the conceptual basis of the *Maxwell* approach entails insisting upon a real subjective nexus between what is known or foreseen and the actual principal offence, then no accessorial liability should follow. Underlying *Bainbridge* is a notion of free-floating culpability, operating within the confines of 'type'. It is objective in the sense that the accessory may be incriminated for complicity in a particular offence completely unforeseen by him. His culpability rests on willingness to risk facilitating a range[25] of a particular type of criminality fixed by his foresight — not a range of particular *offences* as is seemingly prescribed under *Maxwell*.[26]

However, set against this interpretation of *Maxwell* are certain difficulties. First, and most obviously, *Bainbridge* was expressly accepted by all of their lordships as correctly decided. Yet the accessory in *Bainbridge* was only aware that a burglarious type of offence was planned somewhere, sometime in the future. In no realistic sense did he contemplate *the* offence eventually committed. Secondly, Lowry LCJ expressly accepted that 'the "particular crime" theory' was disposed of in *Bainbridge*, thus making liability in cases of future repeated use of equipment turn on 'whether the crime actually committed is *fairly described* as the crime or one of a number of crimes within the contemplation of the accomplice' (emphasis added).[27] By 'fairly described' Lowry LCJ seemed to be alluding to the sort of latitude that would permit conviction in cases such as *Bainbridge*, for it would be difficult to see how a succession of future offences could be contemplated in the degree of detail which would mark out a particular offence. The third difficulty is Lowry LCJ's acceptance of the 'blank cheque' (or carte blanche) principle of complicity.

Assuming that *Bainbridge* has survived *Maxwell*, then used in combination they are capable of producing liability in circumstances where neither, if applied singularly, could. The test of specificity of accessorial knowledge incorporating the two approaches would be whether the offence committed was within the contemplated range of offences, if not, then was it of the

---

[25] See Ch. 9, 'Limitation', and Ch. 10, 'Withdrawal', for the issue of repeat offences.
[26] At what point does, say, an uncrystallized intention to use equipment to burgle a bank in the London area become specific enough to constitute a particular offence? If its venue and time need not then be fixed what factor converts it from an intent to burgle at large to something particular enough to attach complicitous liability? It is unclear in Lowry CJ's comment, where the 'accomplice has only offence A in contemplation and the principal commits offence B [the accomplice] is not guilty of aiding and abetting offence B' (1375), whether offences 'A' and 'B' are different in 'type' or just different in being carried out in unforeseen circumstances, as where a robbery is carried out at a Bristol rather than a Birmingham branch of Barclays. Buxton e.g. seems to adopt the latter construction, 'Extent', 317–18.
[27] Ibid. 1375.

same type as any of those offences contemplated?[28] Therefore, if *D* lent *P* a gun believing it might be used either to murder some unknown party or to rob an unidentified security vehicle, it is not certain that when applied alone the *Maxwell* or *Bainbridge* tests would convict *D*. For if *P* subsequently committed a murder with the gun it would be difficult to say *D* had contemplated the particular offence in the sense[29] arguably required in *Maxwell*[30] and, furthermore, it could not be said that *D* knew a particular 'type' of offence would be committed as demanded by *Bainbridge*. However, a blend of the two tests would secure *D*'s conviction, for the murder was within the range of the type of offences contemplated.[31] In combination the two decisions produce a hydra-like notion of 'knowledge' through which each particular crime contemplated as a possibility by the accessory in turn sprouts its own range of same 'type' offences.

A final area of considerable interpretational uncertainty relates to whether an accessory's liability may rest on his having given a 'blank cheque' to the principal. The point was left open by Devlin J. in *Bullock* who accepted that it 'is no doubt true that if an accused . . . merely suspects . . . a general criminal purpose, that may not be enough to make him an accessory [but] it is not necessary . . . that we should express a view one way or another on that point'.[32] Lord Parker CJ in *Bainbridge* rejected liability based on assistance coupled with belief that 'some illegal venture is intended'.[33] The issue also surfaced indirectly in the drugs possession case of *Patel*[34] where the Court of Appeal balked at accepting a direction that it was sufficient to incriminate the defendant as an accessory if 'he knew that the bag contained something and was content to aid in its possession whatever it might be'.

---

[28] Cl. 27 (4) of Law Commission Report 177 is capable of this construction, but the wording is such that it could be more restrictively construed. Commentary, at para. 9.26, appears to indicate that a wider interpretation is intended. This is more clearly the case in Report 143, commentary para. 10.15.

[29] The precise point is dealt with by Judge Aarvold in *Bainbridge* who directed that 'it is not enough to show that he either suspected or knew that some crime was going to be committed, some crime which might have been a breaking and entering or might have been disposing of stolen property or anything of that kind'. Lord Parker held that this whole direction 'cannot be criticised' [1960] 1 QB 129, 132–3.

[30] By Lowry LCJ and Lords Scarman and Edmund Davies.

[31] A further illustration of the problems of 'type' is provided by the contrasting views of Lords Hailsham and Fraser. Lord Hailsham considered that 'bullet, bomb, or incendiary device, indeed most if not all types of terrorist violence, would all constitute offences of the same "type"' (1358). For Lord Fraser throwing 'poison gas into the Inn' would have been an offence of a different type (1361) and he may have been correct in that 'poison gas' might not have been an 'explosive substance' under the 1883 Act. But a common design of terroristic attack in whatever form would, as Lord Hailsham suggests, reasonably be considered of the same type of offence.

[32] [1955] 1 WLR 1, 5.

[33] [1960] 1 QB 129, 133. Similarly Lord Parker in *Bettles* [1966] Crim. LR 503.

[34] [1970] Crim. LR 274. The Court of Appeal required Patel to know that the bag contained some kind of dangerous drug; it was unnecessary that he should know it was cannabis. See Williams, *Textbook*, 352 for comments on *Scott* (1978) 68 Cr. App. Rep. 164 where a similar approach was taken in respect of conspiracy.

However, according to Lowry LCJ, 'exceptionally ... evidence [could] be found to support the allegation that the accomplice had given the principal a completely blank cheque'. Exactly what, then, would an accessory need to do to issue effectively an incriminating blank cheque? Presumably, if, for example, D has a standing arrangement with P under which P may use D's car at any time to carry out 'general criminal purpose[s]', then D may be an accessory to *any* offence — from abduction to gun running — carried out by P with the use of the car, even though P's professional versatility was beyond D's wildest dreams. As a question of social policy, is there a significant moral distinction between an accessory who furnishes aid believing the principal could use it for 'just about anything criminal', and one who anticipates that offence W, X, Y, or Z may be carried out — and offence X is committed? A further point is whether D's willingness to facilitate any offence needs to be communicated to P? It is difficult to see what relevance it has (other than evidential) once the 'blank cheque' principle is conceded. If it exists, the blank cheque principle represents an explicit admission that 'knowledge' or detailed foresight is not necessarily the basis of complicity in all cases. Rather, for the accessory who has, at least in his own mind, given the principal carte blanche, liability can be founded on subjective recklessness in its widest and loosest variety.

(2) *Theoretical Implications*

Following *Johnson* v. *Youden*, Lord Parker stoutly affirmed in *Bainbridge* that there must be 'not merely suspicion but knowledge' of the type of offence in prospect. 'Knowledge', as used here, must extend to belief[36] as to what the principal intends. To limit 'knowledge' to its strict sense would be self-defeating for an 'accessory' cannot *know* the essential matters of an offence until it has been committed. Therefore the real question here is *how strong* the accessory's belief or foresight must be. Both the facts of *Maxwell* and the contemplation test make the point abundantly clear. *Bainbridge* introduced an erosion of the subjective link that was possible if 'knowledge' was confined to belief in the existence of the 'essential matters' of the

[35] [1978] 1 WLR 1350, 1375. None of their lordships took issue with this observation, although Lord Hailsham accepted that there must be a 'minimum significance attached to the expression "essential ingredients"' (1359). See the Canadian decision of *Hartford and Frigon* (1979) 51 CCC (2d) 462 at 468 where the British Columbia Court of Appeal used *Maxwell* as the basis for incriminating an accessory supplying assistance for 'no matter which of a number of crimes [the principal] chose to commit'. Followed in *Howard and Trudel* (1983) 3 CCC (3rd) 399 at 409. Is 'blank cheque' culpability a close relation of conspiracy as an auxiliary mode of complicity? See Ch. 2 (4).

[36] Cf. Buxton's discussion of this point, 'Complicity in the Criminal Code' (1969) 85 *LQR* 252, 258–61. For the peculiar complicity difficulties generated by offences where the burden is cast on the principal offender to establish his innocence by proving a negative state of affairs, e.g. the absence of corruption, see the Privy Council's majority and minority judgments in *Mok Wei Tak and Mok Chiu Yee Man* v. *R.* [1990] 2 WLR 897. And also see below for consideration of the meaning of 'knowledge' and 'belief' in relation to circumstances.

principal offence. It could then be reasonably asserted that the accessory's culpability was consciously connected with *that* principal offence from which accessorial liability was derived. *Bainbridge*, whilst retaining subjectivity at the core of liability, decoupled it (or made the direct link unnecessary) from a particular principal offence by substituting a substantially autonomous form of mental culpability together with an objective referential test of 'type'. Although the language of the House of Lords (and Lowry LCJ) is heavily laced with 'knowledge', *Maxwell* consolidates this approach which in all essentials is one of recklessness: did the defendant foresee the occurrence or existence of the 'essential matters' constituting the principal offence?

In the case of 'blank cheque' liability (if it exists) all pretence of linking the accessory's mental culpability with the principal offence is abandoned. Liability is founded on an unfocused subjective recklessness at large. Perhaps with a slight degree of disingenuousness, the broad theoretical line of complicity liability could be held by claiming that it was just the extreme end of the range of contemplation—that in such cases the defendant contemplates that all and everything is possible with the enviably versatile principal. Yet while accessorial liability of someone who is criminally worldly wise might convincingly be accounted for by this argument, the devoted but dull-witted criminal associate could not be. A variant of the 'blank cheque' problem is membership of a large criminal organization ('Crime Incorporated') where an individual will be aware that he is in some way contributing towards the carrying out of a virtually limitless range of offences—involving, say, prostitution and unlawful drugs through to murder by unknown principals.[37] Although the question in such cases is more often seen as one of conspiracy, complicity may also be at issue. But rather than complicity liability being escaped because of the absence of *mens rea*, it is more likely that there would be failure to establish the necessary *actus reus* elements.

However, whether the case is one of issuing blank cheques or of actual foresight or contemplation of an extremely large range of possible principal offences, the conceptual difficulty is the tenuousness of the association between what the accessory foresees and the occurrence of a particular principal offence. Underlying complicity notions of parasitic or derivative liability look painfully strained if, for example (combining *Bainbridge* and *Maxwell*), D is convicted as an accessory to an offence of P's which is of a similar type to one within an extensive range of crimes contemplated as open to commission by P. Incrimination in such circumstances arguably raises objections that a principle of 'fair' or 'representative labelling' of culpability is being infringed: that the real nature of the defendant's

---

[37] As is suggested in Working Paper 43, 53, illustration *a*, there is no general principle that an accessory must know the identity of the principal offender; supported by Foster, 125. Cf. Woolf J. in *Gillick* at 590. See also Ch. 2 (4).

criminality is not being fairly represented by its form of legal designation.[38] Rather than seeing the accessory's culpability as linked to and being dependent on the offence actually carried out by the principal, the true substance of the accessory's criminality is just as appropriately viewed as inchoate — although even inchoate liability tends to be more orientated to specific offences.

Much of the difficulty encountered with specificity is the product of not requiring anything resembling a purposeful attitude from the accessory towards the commission of the principal offence. Where an accessory instigates or wishes an offence to take place, it will usually be one particular offence that is in the accessory's mind, the details of which are clear. This is one important reason why American jurisdictions, where purposeful accessorial attitudes are generally necessary, have experienced fewer[39] problems with the specificity issue. However, although far less likely, problems of specificity can arise where, although there is a purposeful attitude, the principal offence is not firmly settled upon at the time of rendering assistance. This would be so when in cases similar to *Bainbridge* the accessory supplying essential equipment (unlike *Bainbridge*) had a stake in the outcome of the principal's criminal venture. This expectation (if not an inflexible requirement) of involvement in or commitment to the offence goes some way in explaining the virtual absence of reference to the specificity question in early reported decisions and also its neglect in various nineteenth-century code proposals or digests of complicity. Both the 1843[40] and 1846[41] Criminal Commissioners' Report proposals, for instance, obliquely specify the mental requirement for accessories through the *actus reus* elements where the language focuses on acts which have 'procured or

---

[38] For concise accounts of this theory see particularly Ashworth, 'The Elasticity of *Mens Rea*', 53–6, and Williams, 'Convictions and Fair Labelling' 85. Paradoxically the House of Lords firmly favoured that as a matter of good practice the indictment particulars should make clear the nature of the accessory's role and not directly attribute to him the performance of the acts of others. In count 1, Maxwell was alleged to have 'placed' the bomb; and in count 2, to have had the bomb 'in his possession or control'.

[39] Although see e.g. *State* v. *Davis* 682 P. 2d 883 (1984). The Model Penal Code formulation under s. 2.06 leaves limited potential for such problems and incorporates no express 'variation' provisions.

[40] Seventh Report of the 1st Criminal Law Commissioners appointed in 1833 to consolidate the criminal law, 'disencumbering it from the superfluities and inconsistencies under which it labours' and to 'relieve it from many useless accumulated burthens, by which its bulk is increased and its energy diminished'. Unlike Macaulay's earlier Indian Penal Code (drafted in 1837, enacted 1860) the reform proposals for home consumption were not a freehanded Benthamite attempt to create law from first principles; rather the Commissioners sought to provide a 'more accessible and intelligible' restatement of the existing law, 'deviating as little as may be from either the ancient or more modern law' (Report, 1–2).

[41] Second Report of the 2nd Criminal Law Commissioners appointed 1845. The approach in the 1846 report was essentially that of the 1843 report. A few revisions were introduced, notably in relation to eliminating the procedural and punishment distinctions between complicity in treason, felonies, and misdemeanours.

promoted' the principal offence.[42] The 1879 Criminal Code Bill Commission's Draft Code[43] is even less forthcoming, forcing readers to resort to current expositions of case law, such as Stephen's *Digest of Criminal Law*, where aiding and abetting is indicated as requiring knowledge only of the principal's necessary *mens rea*.[44]

Turning away from matters of specificity of foresight, two further distinct but overlapping features have a bearing on the question of the extent of the accessory's mental culpability, both relating to the accessory's understanding of the state of the principal's mind at the time of complicity. These are, first, the perceived likelihood or chance of the principal actually carrying out the contemplated actions; and secondly, whether the principal is anticipated as having a culpable state of mind at the time of such actions.

The first of these two factors is obviously of greatest relevance to situations where the accessory, rather than instigating, provides the principal with some form of assistance to carry out a pre-existing or planned criminal venture. Clearly, there is greater moral culpability in furnishing aid to a party seen as desperately anxious to commit an offence, than in assisting one who it is believed might *in extremis* do so. Again, as in other areas of complicity, the problem is an amalgam of two elements: what is the appropriate level of culpability, and how is this to be expressed in a usable formula? This issue is considered in the next section as 'The perceived likelihood of the principal offence occurring'. The further separate question of whether the perpetrator is believed to have the *mens rea* necessary for principal liability also affects the *nature* of the 'accessory's' criminality in that it determines whether it is either principal (through the doctrine of innocent agency) or secondary. This question is examined in section 3 as 'The accessory's knowledge of the principal's mens rea'.

---

[42] As do the introductory observations: Report, 29–30. Both the 1843 and 1846 codes distinguish between abettors present at the commission of the offence and accessories. Abettors must have by 'consent'/'assent' or by 'other means' have helped or encouraged the offence (arts. 8 and 6 respectively). Accessories are required to have an even stronger or more positive attitude towards commission of the offence: 'by commandment, advice, consent, aid, encouragement or otherwise . . . procured or promoted' the principal offence (arts. 10 and 11, and 8 respectively). The separate treatment of abettors and accessories is probably explicable in terms of evidential presumptions about the intention to further an offence when an accomplice was present and providing some form of assistance or aid. Surprisingly, more space is devoted in both codes to the conditions of withdrawal than to matters of *mens rea*: arts. 9, 12, and 18 in the 1843 code, and arts. 7, 9, and 14 in the 1846 code.

[43] Although containing a number of substantive innovations, the code was professedly no more than a digest of existing law. This appears to be true of complicity (Report, 19).

[44] Art. 37, *Digest*. For accessories before the fact an element of instigation is suggested as necessary. Art. 39, *Digest*: an accessory must do 'something to encourage [the principal offence's] commission actively'. Stephen notes that 'instigate' is used as 'equivalent to "counsel, procure or command"' referring to the Draft Code provisions s. 71. *Quaere*, and *vice versa*? Under Macaulay's Indian Penal Code (as amended) complicity required either active instigation or the provision of assistance 'in order to facilitate' the principal offence. See s. 107, 'Explanation 2', 126–7 in Stokes, *Anglo-Indian Codes*, i.

2. The Perceived Likelihood of the Principal Offence Occurring

Where assistance is provided with the desire or objective of bringing about the principal offence there will be liability without any foresight or expectation that an offence will occur. If *D* is the initiator or instigator of a crime to be carried out by *P* he cannot have any knowledge or foresight of *P*'s yet to be formed criminal state of mind. In such cases the accessory's mental culpability could be said to reside in his purposeful identification with the principal offence. Alternatively, it might be maintained that the broad requirement of 'knowledge' for accessoryship is subsumed within and satisfied by the higher mental culpability of purposeful action. This harmonizes with the view that instigation is necessarily a more culpable form of complicity than assistance; an attitude incorporated, for example, in the structure of German criminal law.[45] Furthermore, as in principal liability where, broadly, desired consequences of actions will never be considered too remote,[46] so also in complicity a parallel argument supports liability where the accessory initiates or instigates. Logically the same does not hold where, rather than openly seeking to encourage criminal actions, the defendant provides assistance while clandestinely hoping for the principal's success.

The question of the accessory's perception of the likelihood of the principal offence arises where the accessory lacks purposeful intention and foresees that his assistance may facilitate an offence. In one sense, as already noted, the more the principal offence is perceived as likely to occur by the accessory the greater is his culpability. Providing another with a revolver, believing that it will almost certainly be used to kill a rival mobster, is far more reprehensible than if the killing were foreseen as only a very remote possibility: in the latter situation the supplier is being less reckless. The central question is how likely must an accessory perceive the principal offence as being? How reckless must the accessory be in this respect?

At one time English law offered no authoritative statement on this issue beyond a few unfocused judicial comments. For instance, Lord Simon in *Lynch* noted that 'it must be foreseen [by the accessory] that the instrument or other object or service supplied will probably (or possibly and desiredly) be used for commission of a crime'.[47] Similarly, Lord Parker in *Bainbridge* appeared to assume the necessity of the accessory's belief in the principal's commitment to carry out an offence by requiring 'not merely suspicion but knowledge that a crime of the type in question was intended'. However, the

---

[45] Schreiber, 'Problems', 624–5.
[46] Cf. Hart and Honoré, *Causation* (1985), 43–4, 170–1; and Smith and Hogan, *Criminal Law*, 324–5.
[47] [1975] AC 653, 698–9. For earlier references see e.g. *Cruse* (1838) 8 C. & P. 541, 173 ER 610.

high level of likelihood implied by such *dicta* did not find favour in a number of subsequent decisions.[48]

The underlying principle of *Maxwell* itself implicitly subverts anything resembling a requirement that an accessory must foresee commission of *the* principal offence as being (say) highly likely. As already suggested, by allowing liability to be imposed where the accessory contemplates the commission of one of a virtually unlimited range of offences, the resulting subjective nexus between accessory and principal offence may be exceedingly tenuous. Furthermore, in relation to the question of perceived likelihood of the offence occurring, if for example *D* believes *P* will almost certainly commit one of a dozen offences it cannot be maintained that *D* contemplated *the* offence as almost a certainty — rather it would be no more than a one in twelve chance, or whatever: a mere possibility. Yet even *Maxwell* contains a sprinkling of open-ended observations indicating concern over the question of how likely the accessory foresaw the principal offence to occur. In particular, Lowry LCJ felt it worth emphasizing that a 'bombing attack on the Inn must have been one of the likeliest jobs to occur to [Maxwell] when he was briefed for the mission. This is, in our view, a crucial point so far as the requirement of guilty knowledge and intent is concerned'.[49] Was this an oblique suggestion that the offence finally committed must have been foreseen as more than just a possibility?[50]

However, direct authority on the question was subsequently provided by the Court of Appeal and the Privy Council. In *Chan Wing-Siu* v. *R.*,[51] when reviewing an accessory's *mens rea* relevant to murder in the course of a robbery, the Privy Council considered how far the murderous acts needed to have been foreseen as being as a possible incident of carrying out the primary criminal objective of robbery. Taking its lead from Australian[52] and New Zealand[53] decisions, the Privy Council declared it to be a matter

---

[48] Both Lord Simon's and Lord Parker's observations are open to narrow interpretations; see Dennis, 'The Mental Element', 47–8.

[49] Although elsewhere he refers to violence that 'may be resorted to'.

[50] [1978] 1 WLR 1350 at 1370. In Lord Dilhorne's opinion, accessoryship required knowledge that the principal's acts 'may be or are intended' (1355). Without suggesting it to be necessary, Lord Scarman twice referred to *Maxwell*'s contemplation of a bomb attack as 'very likely' (1363).

[51] [1985] 1 AC 168.

[52] *Johns* v. *R.* (1980) 143 CLR 108 and *Miller* v. *R.* (1980) 55 ALJR 23 where the expression 'substantial risk' was employed. See also *Harding* [1976] VR 129 and Annakin (1989) 13 Crim. LJ 405.

[53] *Gush* [1980] 2 NZLR 92 following *Johns* even though s. 66 (2) of the Crimes Act 1961, when specifying the test for liability in common purpose cases, uses the word 'probable'. The New Zealand Court of Appeal felt that the objectives of the Act would have been frustrated if 'probable' was held to mean 'more probable than not'. *Hamilton* [1985] 2 NZLR 245: in murder the accessory 'must at least have seriously contemplated' the principal's intent to kill or cause serious harm (at 250). *Tomkins* [1985] 2 NZLR 253: 'knew that there was a substantial or real risk' (at 256). *Piri* [1987] 1 NZLR 66: knew that it 'could well happen' (at 84). Cf. the South African standard of foresight of a possibility: *S.* v. *Kazi* 1963 (4) SA 742 (W) 750; and *S.* v. *Khoza* 1982 (3) SA 1019 (A) 1041; or 'reasonable possiblity', *S.* v. *Beukes* 1988 (1) SA 511 (A).

for the 'jury (or other tribunal of fact) to decide whether the risk as recognised by the accused was sufficient to make him a party to the crime'. And the accused should be convicted (of complicity in murder)[54] unless the contemplated risk was negligibly remote. Risks will be more than negligible and not too remote if they can be designated a 'substantial risk, a real risk, a risk that something might well happen'.[55] But in directing a jury 'no one formula is exclusively preferable; indeed it may be advantageous in summing up to use more than one'.

Soon after *Chan*, the Court of Appeal (although professing to adopt *Chan*) followed a distinctly different path in *Jubb and Rigby*.[56] Here, in another joint enterprise case where robbery was the primary objective and murder the incidental outcome, rather than adopting the *Chan* standard of what amounts to a non-negligible possibility, the Court of Appeal held that to 'avoid uncertainty in the future it would be preferable if judges were to use a constant phrase, and "probably" would be the proper one to use'.[57] Although the clear signification of degrees of risk or likelihood is a notoriously slippery subject, 'probably' in both common and judicial parlance tends to suggest a higher degree of risk than 'possibly'. This was certainly thought so in *Chan* and the Commonwealth cases considered by the Privy Council. A differently composed Court of Appeal returned to the question in *Ward*,[58] where, without reference to *Jubb and Rigby*, *Chan* was applied, being taken to require foresight of a possible result. Several issues are raised by these cases.

First, *Chan*, *Jubb*, and *Ward* are all 'common purpose' cases where the *mens rea* problem centres not on the primary criminal objective but on one which is incidental to or contingent on that offence—most typically, as in *Chan*, a robbery with the express or tacit agreement to use all necessary force to overcome any opposition encountered. As will be seen, this form of complicity has a long history of courts applying an indistinct form of *mens rea* differential whereby the culpability requirement for the incidental offence has been at a lower level than for the primary objective. Yet, logic and limited authority suggest the standard(s) applied here in this trio of decisions to be of general application beyond common purpose cases. In *Maxwell*, Lowry LCJ when laying down the test of contemplation drew an analogy with common purpose rules where

two persons who agree to rob a bank on the understanding, either express or implied from conduct (such as the carrying of a loaded gun by one person with the

---

[54] The case does not deal with the question of possible liability for manslaughter where the accessory has insufficient *mens rea* for murder. See Ch. 8, for consideration of the conflicting case law.
[55] [1985] 1 AC 168, 179.
[56] [1984] Crim. LR 616.
[57] Ibid. 617.
[58] [1987] Crim. LR 338; (1986) 85 Cr. App. Rep. 71.

knowledge of the other), that violence *may* be resorted to. The accomplice knows, not that the principal *will* shoot the cashier, but that he *may* do so: and if the principal does shoot him the accomplice will be guilty of murder.[59]

However, although not without interpretative difficulties,[60] the judgment in the non-common purpose case of *Attorney-General* v. *Able* seems to require the principal to be 'contemplating' an offence as a 'real likelihood',[61] which could just as easily be taken to mean 'probability' as much as 'possibility'. If the standard were to be different — a higher level of foresight being required for the primary criminal objective — anomalous results might arise. For example, D makes his car available to P for use as a getaway vehicle in one of a long series of robberies should P's own very reliable car break down and P wish to carry on. In addition to contemplating this possible use of his car, D also contemplated the possibility of serious violence being employed by P during one of the robberies. A few months later P's own car breaks down and P decides to take advantage of D's offer. If when using D's car for his twentieth robbery, P murders someone, then application of distinct tests requiring different levels of foresight could point to D's conviction as an accessory to murder (the incidental or contingent offence) but non-convictability for complicity in robbery (the primary criminal objective) because D only foresaw his assistance through use of his car as a slight possibility and not (say) a probability as the differential might prescribe.

A second issue raised by *Chan*, *Jubb*, and *Ward* concerns the role of a jury in settling the question of the accessory's foresight of the chances of the principal offence occurring. According to *Chan*, not only is it the jury's function to determine the defendant's estimation of the chances of an offence happening, but, more controversially, to decide whether it was 'negligible' and therefore insufficient to convict. In some respects, it is a form of *de minimis* restriction, although, unlike that rule, here the limitation concerns *mens rea* rather than *actus reus*. If, by the defendant's standards, one chance in ten is too insignificant to worry about, it does not follow that that will be the jury's conclusion. What is negligible to one jury may be criminally significant to another; the standard is flexible and undesirably variable in likely result. Whilst far from a complete parallel, this subjective assessment by the jury invites some of the objections legitimately aimed at the notion of dishonesty.[62] In reaching their conclusion the Privy Council offered two guides to juries: that awareness of 'lethal weapons' being carried by others meant the defence [of negligible risk] should succeed only very rarely'; and generally, the judge 'is entitled to warn the jury to be

---

[59] [1978] 1 WLR 1350 at 1374–5.
[60] See Dennis, 'The Mental Element', 46–8.
[61] Woolf J. [1984] QB 794, 812 and 811.
[62] e.g. E. Griew, 'Dishonesty: The Objections to Feely and Ghosh' [1985] Crim. LR 341.

Specificity of Knowledge

cautious' before acquitting on the grounds of negligible risk.[63] Rather than risk the vagaries of jury views on what is or is not more than negligible, the simpler (if not simple) approach in *Jubb* of a 'constant phrase' should be adopted—whether probability or possibility—with the greater hope of a uniform standard being applied.[64]

Finally, as a matter of broad policy, a low level of foresight (of a possibility) has strong appeal: why should a party

> who lends himself to a criminal enterprise knowing it involves the possession of potentially murderous weapons which in fact are used by his partners with murderous intent . . . escape the consequences . . . of their conduct by reliance upon nuances of prior assessment of the likelihood that such conduct will take place.[65]

Probably few would complain at convicting D as an accessory to murder where previous experience has shown that only in the rarest of instances would he and his gun-carrying principal risk disturbance in their burglarious ventures. However, such rhetoric loses some of its attractiveness where patently deadly weapons are not involved or where the offence is of a less serious nature. It then becomes questionable whether complicity should extend to these cases, bearing in mind the overall remoteness possible between what the accessory knows or foresees and the final outcome. For, at present, taking the likely core *mens rea* requirement to be the combined effect of *Maxwell* and *Bainbridge*, it would appear that D may be convicted where he contemplates that by furnishing assistance one of a range of offences (or one of a similar type to each case within that range) may possibly be committed at an unknown time and place. It is the absence in English complicity law of a purposeful attitude requirement on the accessory's part which is the prime source of these difficulties and dilemmas relating to perceived risk levels. This is discussed further in the Conclusion to this chapter.

3. The Accessory's Knowledge of the Principal's *Mens Rea* or Culpable State of Mind

Even though an 'accessory' may foresee the chance of certain future conduct by the perpetrator as more than 'negligible', he may still be insufficiently certain or aware of the perpetrator's mental state to know if that conduct will constitute an offence by the perpetrator. How will the 'accessory's' awareness, or otherwise, of this aspect of the perpetrator's mental state

---

[63] [1985] 1 AC 168, 179.

[64] The 'no one formula' view in *Chan* was affirmed by the Court of Appeal in *Slack* [1989] 3 All ER 90. Cf. Law Commission Report 177, cl. 27 (1) (c), which makes no attempt to set the level of the accessory's recklessness in respect of the likelihood of the principal acting; see ex. 27 (v).

[65] Counsel for the Crown in *Chan*, ibid. 172; adopted by the Privy Council, 177.

affect the accessory's liability? Put another way, is the mental element necessary for the principal's liability part of the 'essential matters' of which an accessory must have 'knowledge'? In answering this question an initial distinction needs to be drawn between cases where a potential accessory has instigated the enterprise and others where this has not been so and the accessory has later joined in or facilitated existing activity.

In the case of instigation, where, for example, A successfully encourages P to steal from V, the accessory necessarily can have no knowledge of P's then non-existent mental state or attitude towards the theft. A's liability springs from his instigatory actions rather than from a 'knowledge' based form of culpability. However, even here there are imaginable circumstances where the legal outcome is less than certain. Suppose, without any right to do so, A wishes to destroy a wooden hut belonging to V and persuades P to burn it down. If, contrary to A's belief, P lacks the necessary *mens rea* for criminal damage, what is A's position? It would appear that A may be liable as the principal through P's innocent agency despite his being unaware of the agent's 'innocence'.[66] Alternatively, it seems, according to *Cogan*[67] that A could also be an accessory. If in the same example, the mistake were the other way (A erroneously believed P to have been unaware of the unlawfulness of the action) then A will be free of liability if knowledge of the principal's *mens rea* is an element of complicity.[68]

Where the accessory is not a moving force in the criminal enterprise different considerations arise. Although it is true that in most situations where assistance is provided knowledge of the principal's actions will include awareness of the accompanying mental state, this will not invariably be so. For instance, A may lend equipment to P to enable P to remove a car from certain premises. If P's actions are theft will A be an accessory if he was unaware of P's culpable state of mind? Conviction of A would be plainly unacceptable unless he at least contemplated that P might not be entitled to do what he did — that A believed P had the mental state necessary for theft. If A did not even consider the possibility, then to make him P's accomplice would be to exclude subjectivity from a central component of complicity in the offence. Particularly in conduct offences, such as theft, where the activity's criminality turns substantially on the actor's mental state, an accessory's 'knowledge of essential matters' clearly must include the principal's *mens rea*. Furthermore, for offences of different degrees of seriousness which share a common *actus reus* but differ in respect of the prescribed level of mental culpability (such as murder and manslaughter) the only way[69] of fixing the extent of the accessory's liability is by reference to what he understood the likely state of the principal's mind to be. This is

---

[66] Cf. *Tyler and Price*, cit. in Ch. 4 n. 13.
[67] [1976] QB 217.
[68] It is arguable that in such cases A might be liable for attempt: see Ch. 4, 'Innocent Agency'.
[69] Assuming an underlying subjective basis to complicity.

implicitly[70] borne out in the bulk of common purpose cases discussed below, and by more direct authority. According to Stephen:

> When the existence of a particular intent forms part of the definition of an offence, a person charged with aiding or abetting the commission of the offence must be shown to have known the existence of the intent on the part of the person so aided.[71]

Against the general run of authority and demands of internal coherence which suggest that an accessory must know the mental element necessary for the principal's liability there is the problem presented by the *Cogan* type of case: the need to convict the accomplice where the actor has no *mens rea* and the doctrine of innocent agency is inappropriate.[72] Here the actor's lack of *mens rea* for rape — and consequential inability of the accessory to have knowledge of it — did not prevent the Court of Appeal from declaring (probably *obiter*) that in addition to innocent agency responsibility there could be accessorial liability. Cases of this nature are best regarded as exceptional *ad hoc* concessions to the obvious practical need to punish the accomplice in such situations.[73] As already suggested,[74] they are perhaps most satisfactorily accommodated by statutory creation of a special form of 'causing' offence.

4. The Accessory's Knowledge of the Circumstances and Consequences of the Principal Offence

So far, consideration of the broad issue of the accessory's foresight of the principal's possible behaviour has been largely limited to foreseen principal

---

[70] The support is not direct as the doctrine of common purpose has, in the past at least, often carried the implication that the *mens rea* requirement may not be the same for complicity in the *primary* and *incidental* (or contingent) principal offence — see Ch. 8.

[71] Art. 37, *Digest*. And see *Cruse* (1838) 8 C. & P. 541, 173 ER 610. More recently see *Wilcox* v. *Jeffery* [1951] 1 All ER 464 at 466, and *Quick* [1973] QB 910 at 923. And cf. *Adams* (1989) 49 CCC (3d) 100. Stephen offers no explanation as to why the requirement is limited to abettors. Possibly he saw the chances of an absent instigator not being aware of the perpetrator's mental state as being too remote to justify discussion. Law Commission Working Paper 43, proposition 7 (1) (*b*) requires help with 'knowledge . . . of any necessary mental state of the principal'. Law Commission Report 177, cl. 27 (1) (*c*), provides that an accessory must intend that the principal 'shall act, or is aware that he is or may be acting, or that he may act, with the fault (if any) required for the offence'. This precludes cases such as *Cogan* being determined as examples of complicity liability. Instead, it would be treated as a case of principal liability through innocent agency principles; see cls. 26 (1) (*c*) and (3) (*a*), and commentary at paras. 9.11–12. Such an approach has the theoretical appeal of harmonizing with the requirement that in the inchoate offence of incitement the inciter 'intends or believes that the other' will have the necessary fault; cl. 47 (1) (*b*). Permitting complicity where there is no 'principal' fault involves a degree of theoretical asymmetry between these distinct though related forms of liability.

[72] See Ch. 4 generally. *Bourne* (1952) 36 Cr. App. Rep. 125 is best viewed as a case where the actor possessed the necessary *mens rea* but was excused under the defence of duress.

[73] Cf. Law Commission Report 177, cl. 26 (1) and (3) which treat such cases as principal liability. Report 143 favoured regarding them as examples of complicity. See the commentary on this change, paras. 9.11–12.

[74] See Ch. 4 (3).

actions or conduct. However, the criminality of a perpetrator's behaviour frequently takes its colouring from the circumstances in which it occurs; or the criminality flows from a specific harm consequent on the perpetrator's conduct. How far does complicity law require an accessory to be aware of or foresee such matters? Although made with specific reference to strict liability offenders, the statement in *Johnson* v. *Youden* that complicity requires knowledge (actual or constructive)[75] of 'essential matters' has been taken, subject to limited exceptions, to have universal application. But does the requirement apply not simply to the principal's conduct but to the circumstances[76] and consequences of the conduct?

The answer to both these questions is uncertain. For offences requiring *mens rea* of some description (intention or subjective recklessness) and stipulated consequences case law establishes the need for foresight of such consequences. Anything less would have the quirky effect of lowering the culpability level for complicity in consequence offences in comparison with complicity in offences based on conduct alone. However, the position for offences of negligence (offences of unforeseen consequences) is contentious, as is even the extent to which 'knowledge' of *circumstances* may be cleanly separated from 'knowledge' of *consequences*. Both these matters are discussed in the next section after the question of 'knowledge' of circumstances has been examined.

In the case of circumstances, although most authorities[77] appear to accept the need for knowledge of or belief in[78] the circumstances specified in the principal offence, a few examples of contrary *dicta* can be found. The most notable is *Carter* v. *Richardson*[79] where, according to Lord Widgery CJ, the

---

[75] Constructive knowledge in the sense of wilful blindness; see e.g. *Antonelli and Barberi* (1905) 70 JP 4; *Davies, Turner and Co. Ltd.* v. *Brodie* [1954] 3 All ER 283; *Thomas* v. *Lindop* [1950] 1 All ER 966, 968; *Bateman* v. *Evans* [1964] Crim. LR 601; *D. Stanton & Sons Ltd* v. *Webber* [1973] RTR 86. And, similarly e.g. the Canadian decision of *McDaid* (1974) 19 CCC (2d) 572 and the Australian High Court decisions of *Crabbe* [1985] 156 CLR 464, and *Giorgianni* v. *R.* [1985] 156 CLR 473, 482.

[76] Occasionally difficulties can arise in settling whether something is conduct or consequence, see generally Williams, *Textbook*, ch. 6.

[77] Including *Maxwell* which emphasized the need for knowledge of the particular constituents of each of the range of offences contemplated by the accessory, although the case itself focused on knowledge or foresight of the principal's conduct rather than the circumstances in which they occurred.

[78] See e.g. Ashworth, 'Belief, Intent and Criminal Liability', 9.

[79] [1974] RTR 314. Cf. *Crampton* v. *Fish* (1969) 113 Sol. Jo. 1003, [1970] Crim. LR 235. The supervisor of a learner driver was convicted of complicity in the latter's driving with an excessive blood/alcohol level. The defence's contention that until a recognized test had been carried out it was impossible to know the 'essential matters' of the offence, convinced the justices at first instance but not the Divisional Court, where Lord Parker saw the totality of evidence sufficient for a reasonable inference being drawn that the supervisor knew of the driver's unlawful state. At least two post-*Johnson* v. *Youden* decisions include *dicta* which come perilously close to suggesting negligence as being sufficient as to circumstances. In *Davies, Turner & Co. Ltd.* v. *Brodie*, Lord Goddard himself noted that 'If a person shuts his eyes to the obvious or, perhaps refrains from making enquiry where a reasonably sensible man would make enquiry I think the Court can find that he was aiding and abetting': [1954] 3 All ER 286.

supervisor of a learner driver with an excessive blood/alcohol concentration was convicted of aiding and abetting the driver's offence on the basis that the supervisor was either 'aware that the principal consumed an excessive amount of alcohol or was *reckless* as to whether he had done so'.[80] Quite what was meant by 'reckless' needs clarification. As previously noted, 'knowledge' used in relation to complicity must include foresight[81] as to possible conduct by the principal, for obviously the accessory cannot 'know' something yet to occur.[82] In the case of circumstances, although 'knowledge' could be restricted to actual direct perception of an existing fact (such as a driver having been seen to consume a half-dozen double whiskys) or firm belief, courts have generally not taken this approach. Rather 'knowledge' has been employed in the sense of a belief of the existence or likely existence of a fact or state of affairs.[83] The crucial point is how far from construing 'knowledge' in the strictest sense will (and should) courts go before deciding the accessory did not 'know'? Essentially, what difference in this context is there between 'knowledge' and 'recklessness'?

The Model Penal Code defines 'knowledge' as being at least belief or awareness of the 'high probability' that something exists;[84] the English Draft Criminal Code (1989) tightly confines knowledge of circumstances to

---

The introduction of reasonableness into this account of wilful blindness is rather baffling. Similarly, in *Bateman* v. *Evans* [1964] Crim. LR 601, the Divisional Court invoked a test of the 'reasonably sensible man'. However, in *D. Stanton & Sons Ltd.* v. *Webber*, the Divisional Court firmly dismissed this form of liability apparently employed by the trial justices to convict.

[80] Emphasis added. Although the offence was one of strict liability, there is no suggestion that the standard of recklessness employed was intended to be restricted to strict liability offences only. While it is certainly arguable (see commentary on *Smith* v. *Mellors and Soar* [1987] Crim. LR 421, 422) that Lord Widgery's reference to recklessness was *dictum* only, most commentators see the decision in more solid terms; see e.g. Smith and Hogan, *Criminal Law*, 129–30, and Williams, *Textbook*, 359, and [1975] *CLJ* 182. In *Giorgianni* v. *R*. [1985] 156 CLR 473 the Australian High Court rejected recklessness as to circumstances as an adequate basis for complicity: 'Suspicion of the existence of facts, although relevant when the accused has deliberately shut his eyes does not by itself amount to or take the place of knowledge . . . Recklessness, in the sense of not caring whether the facts exist or not [is insufficient unless] it amounted to wilful blindness' (487; and at 488 and 508). The court viewed the ratio of *Carter* v. *Richardson* narrowly as not including acceptance of recklessness.

[81] As is clear from a succession of authorities including *Bainbridge*, *Lynch*, and *Maxwell*.

[82] Other than inevitable physical phenomena, such as night following day and round objects rolling down hill.

[83] Lord Widgery in *Carter* v. *Richardson* referred to the supervisor knowing that it was 'probable' that the driver was over the limit. The Model Penal Code stipulates (s. 2.02 (7) 1962): 'When knowledge of the existence of a particular fact is an element of an offence, such knowledge is established if a person is aware of a high probability of its existence, unless he actually believes that it does not exist.' Law Commission Report 177, cl. 27 (1) (*b*), requires that an accessory 'knows of, or (where recklessness suffices in the case of the principal) is reckless with respect to, any circumstance that is an element of the offence'. According to cl. 18 (*a*) 'knowingly' covers awareness that a circumstance 'exists or will exist'. Unlike Report 143, cl. 22 (*a*), and the Model Penal Code, it does not extend to belief that something almost certainly exists.

[84] Ibid.

belief that a state of affairs 'exists or will exist'. English case law offers no firm guidance.[85] When it comes to offering accounts of 'recklessness' both the American and English codes require an actor's actual perception of socially unjustifiable risk, although whereas the English Draft Code is unspecific as to the level of risk perceived the American Code demands a 'substantial' risk.[86] English judicial authority on the general concept of criminal recklessness gives it both a subjective and objective connotation,[87] but does not in its subjective version carefully seek to specify the necessary levels of likelihood of the perceived risk materializing.[88] Case law in complicity, despite a small quantity of fragmentary *dicta* to the contrary, does not accept objective culpability in respect of the circumstances of the principal offence.[89] In English law the distinguishing feature between 'knowledge' and 'recklessness' as to circumstances is arguably not generic but one of degree: 'knowledge' of circumstances is reserved for the perception or belief that something is very likely to exist; subjective 'recklessness' as to circumstances covers the perception that something may exist where the degree of likelihood is insufficiently high to warrant the description 'knowledge'. In other words, there is no sharp-edged boundary between the two; the one runs indistinctly into the other.[90] They both deal with the perceived likelihood of a state of affairs existing;[91] that is, with the perceived *risk* of a state of affairs existing.

Therefore, for example, suppose A successfully encouraged P to seduce a 15-year-old girl. A believed W to be at least 15 and probably 16 years old,

[85] See the 'no substantial doubt' formula in Law Commission Report 89. The meaning of 'knowledge' or 'knowing' has caused much judicial activity in relation to handling. See J. C. Smith, *The Law of Theft* (1989); E. Griew, *The Theft Acts 1968 and 1978* (1986); and G. L. Williams, 'Handling, Theft and the Purchaser who takes a Chance' [1985] Crim. LR 432. Law Commission Working Paper 43 thought the position of complicity and handling 'analogous' on the problem of knowledge (49).

[86] Law Commission Report 177, cl. 18 (c); Model Penal Code, s. 2.02 (2) (c). The codes' verbal formulations also differ in that the former requires disregard of the risk to be 'unreasonable', the latter specifies a 'gross deviation' from the normal 'standard of conduct'.

[87] *Cunningham* [1957] 2 QB 396 and *Caldwell* [1982] AC 341.

[88] Occasionally in specific offences the law has imposed a particular standard, as was the case for murder under *DPP* v. *Hyam* [1975] AC 55.

[89] In the case of consequences, see below.

[90] Except that for recklessness the standard involves reference to whether the risk was justified in the particular circumstances. Cf. E. Griew, 'Consistency, Communication and Codification: Reflections on Two Mens Rea Words', in P. R. Glazebrook, ed., *Reshaping the Criminal Law* (1978), 72–3.

[91] An additional layer of difficulty is added by the potential application of the uncertain notion of wilful blindness. *Davies, Turner & Co. Ltd.* v. *Brodie*, supra 1; and generally in respect of *principal* liability, *Roper* v. *Taylor's Central Garages Ltd.* [1951] 2 TLR 284, and *Westminster City Council* v. *Croyalgrange Ltd.* [1986] 1 WLR 674. Views differ as to the scope of 'wilful blindness'. For instance, Smith and Hogan, *Criminal Law*, 110, see it as 'closely akin to recklessness', whereas Williams, *Textbook*, 125, suggests the 'best view is that it applies only when a person is virtually certain that the facts exist'. This very restrictive interpretation has little support outside the law of handling. Of course, a high level of recklessness (e.g. where something is seen as being highly probable) is approaching a 'virtual certainty'. Cf. *Giorgianni* (cit. n. 80) 487.

but was not really sure. Will *A* be an accessory to *P*'s offence under section 6 of the Sexual Offences Act 1956? How strong would *A*'s belief need to be that *W* was probably 16 before a court could find that he has 'knowledge' of the 'essential matters', or even have been sufficiently 'reckless' as to them?[92] Again, what if *A*, not being sure whether a car had been abandoned, helped *P*, who was similarly unsure, to remove certain parts from it. If the car had not been abandoned could *A* be a party to *P*'s theft because *A* had no 'knowledge' of this 'essential' matter?

What is, or would be, the appropriate level of the accessory's foresight of the probable existence of circumstances specified in the principal offence? At what point is this on a continuum running from certainty to foresight of some possibility?

Various reform proposals reveal a considerable fluidity in attitudes and ideas. In 1972 the Law Commission's Working Party suggested that an accessory should have 'knowledge of the external elements' of the principal offence; mere recklessness would be insufficient.[93] No attempt was made to define 'knowledge' in this context[94] but, by implication, the meaning offered in Law Commission Working Paper 31 was adopted: 'A person knows of circumstances not only when he knows they exist but also when [either] he has no substantial doubt that they exist [or] he knows they probably exist.'[95] Final Report 89 settled for the 'no substantial doubt' formulation of knowledge.[96] In contrast with the 1972 report, Law Commission Report 143 set down a standard of accessorial recklessness (of an unspecified level) as to both the conduct and circumstances of the principal offence: potentially a considerable difference between the proposals with virtual certainty set against foresight of a possibility. Subsequently, in Law Commission Report 177, recklessness as to circumstances was deemed sufficient for complicity only where it also satisfied the fault element for the relevant principal offence.

In so far as there can be a single 'right' solution, the answer turns first on whether theory and/or practicality demands the same standard of accessorial culpability in respect of circumstances as of conduct; and secondly, if this is not so, then what would be the most appropriate standard?

As to both these questions, it has been seen that, in relation to the principal offender's conduct, the accessory needs to foresee with a certain

---

[92] Cf. the similar knowledge/recklessness issue as to material circumstances in attempt. See e.g. discussion by Smith and Hogan, *Criminal Law*, 288–9 and Buxton, 'Circumstances, Consequences and Attempted Rape' [1984] Crim. LR 25.

[93] Working Paper 43, proposition 7, 47. In the Working Party's view, 'one reason for this restriction is that otherwise there would be a risk of bringing within the penal law persons who have no specifically wrongful intention and who are acting in the ordinary course of business dealings'.

[94] Knowledge 'means that he must know the facts required for the commission of the offence', 49.

[95] Working Paper 31, s. 7, A (3).

[96] See n. 6.

level of specificity the details of the principal offence. Distinct from this is the matter of the accessory's perception of the likelihood of the principal's conduct. It has been noted that the main, but not only, element of this is the degree of resolution or commitment demonstrated by the principal and it was concluded that the principal's conduct need be foreseen as no more than a (non-negligible) possibility; recklessness of a low order suffices. Does it then follow that the accessory's mental culpability in respect of any definitional *circumstances* of the principal offence is of the same level? Is any degree of subjective recklessness adequate?[97]

Principal liability may be made up of more than one degree of culpability in respect of different definitional elements of the offence, whether they be conduct or circumstances or consequences, and there is no absolute imperative preventing adoption of a similar pattern in complicity. Policies embodied in principal liability and manifested in individual mental requirements will have broadly similar relevance to every element of accessorial liability.[98] As already suggested in respect of conduct, departing from the paralleling or mirroring of principal culpability in that specified for complicity may be justified on the basis of the accessory's more remote position *vis-à-vis* the proscribed principal harm — a fact which may even argue for a higher standard of culpability on the accessory's part. For circumstances the case for requiring the same culpability level as that of the principal is equally strong. However, current law seems to require a uniform standard of recklessness regardless of the culpability appropriate to principal liability, which may be higher or lower. Therefore, returning to the example of inciting the seduction of a 15-year-old girl, the principal could be liable even if he reasonably believed the girl to be of age, whereas the accessory must at least *actually* recognize that she might be under 16.[99]

In sum, under English law there appears to be a common standard of subjective recklessness, of an unspecified level, for the following mental

---

[97] In relation to the perceived chances of the principal's *conduct* occurring, the accessory's culpability level turns on his answer to the question 'How likely is it?' In relation to *circumstances*, the accessory's culpability turns on the question 'How likely is it that certain material circumstances will exist if the principal acts?' Although the two issues of perception relate to different aspects of the principal offence, both concern taking risks over the (culminating) occurrence of the proscribed criminal harm.

[98] Cf. MPC, TD 1 (1953), 34. The Model Penal code specifies accessorial purpose as to the 'commission of an offense' and the same level of culpability as stipulated for the principal offence in respect of any specified result: s. 2.06 (3) (*a*) and (4). But, surprisingly, no express attempt is made to deal with the question of culpability as to *circumstances*. Arguably, the code's internal logic and consistency suggest that circumstances be treated in the same way as results. Note particularly the discussion of P. H. Robinson and J. A. Grall, 'Element Analysis in Defining Criminal Liability' (1983) 35 *Stan. LR* 681, 740–3. Law Commission Report 177, cl. 27 (1), requires an accessory's acts to be 'intentionally' performed with the expectation that such actions will assist or encourage the principal's actions. At the same time, the accessory must have knowledge or (if sufficient for the principal) be reckless as to any circumstance element of the offence. The accessory need be no more than reckless in respect of the presence of the principal's fault: cl. 27 (i) (*c*), see report commentary, para. 9.28.

[99] Subject to the special defence for defendants under 24; Sexual Offences Act 1956, s. 6 (3).

components of accessorial liability: the nature and external particulars of the principal offence, the perceived likelihood of the commission of the offence's external elements, the presence of any necessary *mens rea* for the principal and any necessary surrounding circumstances by the offence.

Still to be considered is an accomplice's liability for unforeseen consequences of foreseen conduct (effectively, complicity in offences of negligence) and for complicity in strict liability offences.

5. Unforseen Consequences of Foreseen Conduct: Complicity in Offences of Negligence[100]

An initial distinction needs to be drawn between conduct and consequence offences. For offences of negligent *conduct*, such as careless driving, under complicity's general *mens rea* requirement an accessory must know or foresee the existence of circumstances making the conduct negligent.[101] For example, if A lends his unsafe car to P, then P could be liable for careless driving if he *ought* reasonably to have known of its defective state, but A would not be an accessory to the offence without at least foresight of these 'essential matters'. In the case of negligent *consequence* offences the question is the extent to which a party will be liable for the unintended [102] and unforeseen criminal consequences of another's conduct encouraged or assisted by him. Is liability coextensive with that of the principal offender?

The only significant manifestation of the problem arises where the unintended consequence of the principal's act is unlawful homicide.[103] In

---

[100] And offences of objective recklessness. References to 'negligence' should, circumstances permitting, be taken to include offences of objective recklessness.

[101] Hilbery J. in *Rubie* v. *Faulkner* [1940] 1 KB 571 at 574–5; *Du Cros* v. *Lambourne* [1907] 1 KB 40. This distinction appears to be embodied in Working Paper 43, proposition 7 (4).

[102] The point at issue here is *unintended* consequential harm following on from encouraged or assisted action. This is distinct from accessorial liability for conduct deliberately performed by the principal *beyond* that contemplated by the accomplice. This problem is dealt with in Chs. 7 and 8. The present question involves *consequences* of non-deviant principal conduct. However, the two issues may be found operating in combination or individually: e.g. if A counselled P to assault V with a wooden stick and P uses an iron bar then the first problem of deviation of *action* arises. If, under the appropriate rules, A is still liable for P's actions it does not also follow that A must be liable for *consequences* of the action. Therefore if V dies the further question of secondary liability for the unintended consequences arises.

[103] Until the 19th cent., case law and commentators denied the possibility of there being an accessory before the fact to manslaughter: *Bibithe's Case* (1597) 4 Co. Rep. 43b, 76 ER 991; *Goose's Case* (1597) Moore KB 461, 72 ER 695; Hale, *PC* i. 437 and 614–16; East, *PC* i. 218; Hawkins, i, ch. 30, ss. 1–2. This attitude rested on the logic that as manslaughter was a consequence of an unpremeditated act (it 'ensue[d] upon a sudden debate or affray', *Bibithe's Case* at 44a) there could be no prior complicity — whether before or at the fact. Whether a rigid rule of law or not, practically speaking the possibility of the appropriate circumstances are remote but not impossible for 'accessories at the fact' (abettors): e.g. if P in a greatly provoked state asks for and gets a knife from his companion and kills V. Cf. *Moore* v. *Lowe* 180 SE 1

such cases is the risk of the unintended death an 'essential matter' of which the accessory needs to be aware? As already seen, complicity in murder requires at least contemplation by the accessory that the principal might inflict serious harm; there is no requirement that death be intended or even foreseen. Clearly no more can be required of an accessory to manslaughter; nor can the same be sufficient otherwise there would be no culpability distinction between complicity in murder and manslaughter. Rather, for negligence based offences, fidelity to the general complicity principle of 'knowledge of essential matters' must be limited to awareness of the dangerous potential of the principal's conduct through 'knowledge' of the surrounding circumstances.[104] However, limited authority suggests following an alternative 'principle of parallelism'[105] under which an accessory is only required to be at fault in the way required for liability as a principal, in respect of both consequences and circumstances—thus, for example, making the supplier of a defective vehicle liable for complicity in the offence committed by its driver, even though the supplier had no actual knowledge of the defects.

The difference in outcome between these two approaches may be marked. For example, if *M* manufactured and delivered inadequately tested cheap 'cold cures' to a retail chemist who sold them to customers with fatal results in some cases, the chemist could be liable for manslaughter if found to have been grossly negligent.[106] This would be so even if the chemist at no time actually perceived any risk of poisoning, provided the risk was objectively apparent. However, the liability of *M* for complicity in such manslaughter would turn on whether the same test is applicable. The cold cure's dangerousness is part of the circumstances of the chemist's conduct, circumstances of which accessories must be aware, or at least subjectively

(1935). Or *A* encouraged *P* to an act of excessive self-defence which kills *V* and *P* were liable for manslaughter (see *Palmer* v. *R*. [1971] AC 814) would not *A* be an accessory to the offence? The general prohibition against accessoryship in manslaughter was refined to cover voluntary manslaughter only, involuntary manslaughter clearly not being subject to the spontaneity argument: *Hargrave* (1831) 5 Car. & P. 70, 172 ER 925; *Mastin* (1834) 6 Car. & P. 396, 172 ER 1292; *Smith and Taylor* (1847) 2 Cox 233; *Swindall* (1846) 2 Car. & K. 230, 175 ER 95.

[104] Effectively, the standard expressed in Law Commission Report 143, cl. 31 (4) (*a*) and (*b*), citing *Baldessare* as an example of the principle. And the view adopted by Smith and Hogan, *Criminal Law*, 137–8 and 148, and by Williams, *Textbook*, 360. Law Commission Report 177, cl. 27 (1) (*a*), requires an accessory to 'intentionally' procure, assist, or encourage the act which results in the offence. As to risky circumstances, cl. 27 (1) (*b*) refers to knowledge or recklessness (in a subjective sense) 'where recklessness suffices' in respect of 'any circumstance that is an element of the offence'. This has no relevance to manslaughter as the offence does not include a *circumstance* element. Cf. commentary at para. 9.27. Moreover, the effect and applicability of cl. 27 (1) (*c*) is not obvious. This provision requires recklessness as to principal 'fault (if any)'. Either an accessory must actually foresee those risks which are at least objectively foreseeable and the basis of the principal's liability, or an accessory need have no greater fault than the principal.

[105] See Ch. 1.

[106] See Smith and Hogan, *Criminal Law*, 352–4. The same objective standard applies to unlawful act manslaughter, ibid. 345–52.

reckless. But the case law is equivocal on this question of whether, unlike the principal, an accessory must have 'knowledge' of these factual circumstances which make the principal's actions dangerous.

The authority approaching closest to confirming this differential in knowledge between principal and accessory in the case of offences of negligence is *Robert Millar (Contractors) Ltd*.[107] Here the defendants knowingly permitted an employee to drive a lorry with a dangerously worn tyre which burst causing a fatal accident. In affirming the employer's conviction as an accessory of the driver's offence of causing death by dangerous driving, the Court of Appeal appeared to operate on the assumption that knowledge of the defective state of the tyre was an essential element of the employer's liability.[108] Although aware of the dangerous state of the vehicle, the driver would still have been liable if, objectively, he *should* have known, whether or not he knew.

Two earlier abortion – manslaughter cases of *Buck*[109] and *Creamer*[110] are silent on the question, although, because of the inherently risky nature of abortion,[111] the issue of the accessory's knowledge of its dangerousness would be unlikely to receive explicit attention. Much the same point may be made in relation to the dangerous driving cases – whether or not the parties occupied the same vehicle. In these cases, because of the nature of the behaviour, each party would be equally aware of the patently dangerous circumstances.[112] However, the facts of the late

---

[107] [1970] 2 QB 54. Followed in the factually similar case of *Giorgianni* v. *R*. [1985] 156 CLR 473. See also *Reid* (1976) 62 Cr. App. Rep. 109 at 112.

[108] Ibid. at 71*d–e*, 72*c–f*, 73*g–h*; and see Smith and Hogan, *Criminal Law*, 148 n. 19 who take the same construction of the judgment. Cf. *State* v. *McVay* 132 A. 436 (1926) where a shipowner was held to be an accessory to manslaughter caused by an exploding ship's boiler because he had 'with full knowledge of the possible danger to human life, recklessly and wilfully advised . . . the captain an engineer to take a chance by negligent action or failure to act'. Cited by La Fave and Scott, *Criminal Law*, 511.

[109] (1960) 44 Cr. App. Rep. 213.

[110] (1966) 1 QB 72. Following *Buck*, Lord Parker ruled in relation to an illegal abortion 'it is quite consistent that a man who has counselled and procured such an illegal and dangerous act from which death, unintended, results should be guilty of being accessory before the fact to manslaughter' (82). Cited with approval in *Giorgianni* v. *R*. [1985] 156 CLR 473, 503.

[111] Noted by Edmund Davies J. (1960) 44 Cr. App. Rep. 213, 219, and 224.

[112] e.g. *Swindall* (1846) 2 Car. & K. 230, 175 ER 95; *Longbottom* (1849) 3 Cox 439; *Du Cros* v. *Lambourne* (1907) 1 KB 40; *Baldessare* (1930) 22 Cr. App. Rep. 70. Of *Swindall* Williams suggests, 'the point seems to have been that as regards each driver, looked upon as an accessory, what mattered was not his own negligence but the fact that he knew that his friend (regarded as the perpetrator) was driving as he was and knew all the circumstances that made driving negligent': *Textbook*, 360. Cf. the modern American road-racing examples of *Stallard* v. *State* 348 SW 2d 489 (1961) and *Comm.* v. *Root* 170 A. 2d 310 (1961). In *Stallard* the starter and first racer in a road race were held to be accessories of a second racer who recklessly ran into and killed V. However, in *Root* where one of two road racers was killed when colliding with a lorry, the surviving racer was, on appeal, acquitted of manslaughter. Rather than complicity, the issue was regarded as one of whether the actions of the surviving racer could be accepted as a sufficiently proximate cause of the deceased's death. The distinction between the two cases is an exceedingly fine one; there is no clear reason why *Root* should not also have been treated as a complicity situation. (Cf. the similar case of *Jacobs* v. *State* 184 So.

nineteenth-century decision in *Salmon*[113] are less easily open to such construction:

> Here, Salmon and two others practised target shooting within a quarter of a mile of houses with a rifle 'deadly at a mile'. Each member of the group fired a round, one of which killed a boy in the garden of a neighbouring house. Although the identity of the party who fired the fatal shot could not be ascertained, the five judges of the Court for Crown Cases Reserved unanimously held all participants to be rightly convicted of manslaughter, either as principals or accessories.

None of the court's short judgments contains any suggestion that to be an accessory, rather than a principal, it was necessary to have knowledge or at least foresight of the particular circumstantial dangers that materialized in the boy's death. Certainly they were not so overwhelming as to be *necessarily* obvious to the shooting party.[114] Lord Coleridge CJ was content with observing that acting dangerously without 'taking proper precautions' constituted manslaughter by all parties if death resulted. Similarly, Stephen J. was concerned with the duty to take proper care, rather than any question of actually perceived danger:

> There is a duty tending to the preservation of life to take proper precautions in the use of dangerous weapons or things. It is the legal duty of everyone who does any act, which without ordinary precautions is or may be dangerous to human life, to employ these precautions in doing it. Firing a rifle under circumstances such as in the present case was a highly dangerous act, and all are responsible, for they unite to fire at the spot in question, and they all omit to take any precautions whatever to prevent danger.[115]

Of course, whether or not an accessory must be aware of all the surrounding circumstances which make the conduct or consequences of the principal actor criminally negligent, there is the basic separate requirement that the accessory must have intended to assist or encourage the acts which produced principal liability. Therefore, for example, A would not be an *accessory* to manslaughter by negligently leaving a shotgun lying around his house which is later fatally used by his 12-year-old son. For complicity in constructive or unlawful act manslaughter the qualifying conduct will be

---

2d 711 (1966) where the defendant was convicted as a principal.) It is arguable (see especially Kadish, 'Complicity, Cause and Blame', 399–400) that *Stallard* and *Root* are distinguishable on the basis that in the former the particular act which caused the death was excessive speed, something which the defendant had encouraged; whereas in *Root* the cause of death was a particular act of reckless overtaking, something which the defendant did not intend. However, precise atomizing of what is intended or foreseen by road racers is not wholly convincing. Characterizing the attitude and contemplation of participants as one of 'anything goes' seems at least as plausible, and therefore, a basis for complicity liability. Cf. the 'blank cheque' attitude considered above.

[113] (1880) 6 QBD 79; used as an illustration in Working Paper 43, 59.
[114] But cf. Williams, *Textbook*, 360, and [1990] Crim. LR 98, 104.
[115] (1880) 6 QBD 79, 83.

intentionally assisting or encouraging a distinct offence, usually an assault; for other varieties of manslaughter, where the basis of liability is less firmly focused, problems are possible in settling whether the accessory's behaviour has a sufficient link with that of the principal's. The most common situation where the difficulty arises is where a vehicle is lent to a driver known by the lender to be intoxicated. Clearly the permutations for fatally dangerous driving are limitless, with a range of American decisions demonstrating uncertainty by courts as to quite how much (if any), knowledge or foresight of the principal's criminal actions the accessory must have.[116]

English case law, such as *Robert Millar (Contractors) Ltd.*, suggests that there must be at least an intent to assist or encourage the principal to drive in dangerous circumstances, but does not reveal with what degree of particularity the dangerousness must be foreseen. At issue here is the problem[117] of specificity of the accessory's foresight in another guise; the accessory has intentionally facilitated conduct leading up to the principal offence, but may have little or no idea of the likely outcome of his actions. And as in offences of *mens rea*, so also for negligence based liability, the policy question concerns the limits within which the accessory's liability be kept. However, as will be seen below, a facilitator's negligence, although insufficiently informed to incriminate him as an accessory, paradoxically may form the basis of direct principal liability.

This general case law equivocality, as to whether an accessory must be aware of the factual circumstances making the principal's behaviour negligent, has ramifications for consequence offences such as manslaughter and death by negligent ('reckless') driving. This follows because if for complicity the *circumstances* of the conduct which produces the proscribed consequences must be known, then that itself will inevitably go some way to subjectivize culpability in relation to the *consequences*. In other words, knowledge or foresight of circumstances necessarily entail some level of foresight of consequences. The facts of *Robert Millar (Contractors) Ltd.* illustrate this: the employer/accessory needed to be aware not simply that the lorry tyre was defective, but that it was dangerous; nothing is dangerous *in vacuo* but only in relation to some possible result or consequence – in this case having the potential to burst and cause the vehicle to become uncontrollable. As the Court of Appeal explained:

if a driver is sent out by his employer to drive a heavy vehicle on a trip ... with a dangerously defective ... tyre ... who knows that the tyre is dangerous, and there is

---

[116] e.g. see *Freeman v. State* 362 SW 2d 251 (1962) and *People v. Pitts* 270 NW 2d 482 (1978); and generally the cases referred to by La Fave and Scott, *Criminal Law*, 511–12 and Kadish, 'Complicity, Cause and Blame', 347–9. Obviously there could always be complicity in the simple act of driving over the prescribed alcohol limit; its seriousness depending on how intoxicated the driver was. And see also Ch. 2 (3) (3) (b).

[117] There may also be questions of causation to be determined; see above.

a serious risk of harm resulting to other road users, then if that tyre does burst and thereby causes an accident killing somebody the employer is guilty of counselling and procuring death by dangerous driving.[118]

Obviously in most cases the consequential risks attendant upon the circumstances needed to be known by the accessory will be readily apparent, and therefore the claimed circumstance/consequences demarcation will not be visible; but this will not always be so. For example, returning to the hypothetical case of the faulty cold cure, the supplier's awareness of the cure's defectiveness could be limited to its ineffectiveness. Not until the enquiry is pursued beyond the bland contextual circumstantial facts and reference is made to potential consequences can 'knowledge of circumstances' have the meaning attributed to it by some later case law and commentators.[119] Again, taking the classical example of high level demolition workers blithely and blindly throwing rubble down into a street: those who actually throw the materials will be liable for manslaughter if any passer-by is killed, provided they were objectively 'reckless'[120] as to the risk of harm. Their complete obliviousness to danger is irrelevant; but the workmate who hands across the materials for dumping presumably would need to be aware of the possibility of people down below (part of the surrounding circumstances), thereby also giving him foresight of the risk of consequential harm.[121]

However, as indicated, in some situations although the defendant's negligent behaviour is insufficiently informed to incriminate him as an accessory, he may be liable as a principal. This is possible where the relevant offence is unspecific as to how the proscribed criminal result is brought about — as in manslaughter by gross negligence or recklessness. To convict the 'accessory' as a principal offender clear causal responsibility for the death would need to be ascribed to his initial negligence. This would probably require the direct perpetrator to be free of liability and, effectively, to be an innocent agent for the negligence of another. But, as was noted when considering notions of cause and directness, this designation of causal roles to participants may be problematic.[122]

[118] Fenton Atkinson LJ [1970] 2 QB 54, 72.
[119] According to *DPP* v. *Newbury* [1977] AC 500, principal liability for unlawful act manslaughter requires the actor to perform an unlawful and dangerous act; there being no need for the principal to understand its dangerous potential so long as 'all sober and reasonable people recognise its danger'. If an accessory needs to have knowledge of the facts which make the principal's act negligent would this not coincide with the foresight of 'all sober and reasonable people'?
[120] *Seymour* [1983] 2 AC 493. As to how much harm must be objectively foreseeable, see e.g. Smith and Hogan, *Criminal Law*, 352-5.
[121] In *Newbury* the House of Lords may implicitly have applied the same objective standard of fault to all of the parties, principal and secondary.
[122] See, Ch. 4, 'Innocent Agency', and Ch. 3, 'Causation'. D would probably be principally liable for manslaughter if he employed X, an unskilled worker, to supervise a chemical process carried out by Y and Z who are killed in an explosion due to X's diligent but inadequately informed supervision.

6. COMPLICITY IN OFFENCES OF STRICT LIABILITY

It has been seen for offences of negligence (and objective recklessness) that, where the accessory 'intentionally' assists or encourages another party, there may be complicity in the criminal consequences of the assistance or encouragement, provided the accessory displayed a similar level of culpability to that required of the principal: he intended or foresaw the occurrence of the principal's actions but not their consequences, nor *possibly* even relevant surrounding circumstances. However, a more rigid adherence in strict liability offences to the principle that complicity requires the accessory to have 'knowledge' of the 'essential' circumstances of the principal offence was affirmed in *Johnson* v. *Youden*, itself a case involving strict liability. With such a policy for strict liability offences the criminal law presents the apparent paradox of requiring subjective accessorial fault when no fault is necessary for the principal, whereas complicity in negligence offences *may* not demand culpability beyond that necessary for the principal. Although not unwavering[123] in their application of this principle, English courts were enforcing it long before *Johnson* v. *Youden*; with the clearest and best known early decision being *Callow* v. *Tillstone*.[124]

In part, the approach is a particular consequence of the entrenched common law assumption that some form of *mens rea* is a necessary element of criminal responsibility[125] and that complicity (despite its procedural restatement in the 1861 Act), as a creature of the common law, is subject to this underlying requirement. But, this alone obviously fails to provide a complete explanation for strict liability's position for, as seen, courts have not felt much inhibited by the common law principles of *mens rea* when wishing to convict parties of complicity in negligence offences. Rather, a good part of the attitude towards complicity in strict liability offences is attributable to the general suspicion with which strict liability is regarded. As one commentator has suggested:[126]

---

[123] *Provincial Motor Cab Co. Ltd.* v. *Dunning* [1909] 2 KB 599 and *Wheat* v. *Stocks* [1921] 2 KB 119 are contrary decisions. *Gough* v. *Rees* (1929) 29 Cox 74 is suggested by Williams to be wrongly decided (*CLGP* 394 n. 2). However, Hewart LCJ clearly affirms that 'a man cannot counsel or procure unless he knows and intends what is done'. The previous convictions of the accessory in similar situations suggest the basis of the decision was possibly wilful blindness as to the circumstances (at 80). And cf. *Carter* v. *Richardson* [1974] RTR 314.

[124] (1900) 83 LT 411. Here, relying on a veterinary surgeon's certificate of fitness for human consumption, unsound meat was offered for sale by a butcher. The butcher was found liable for the offence of exposing unsound meat for sale, but the veterinary surgeon's negligence was held insufficient to incriminate him as an abettor. Although unnecessary for the butcher's principal liability, knowledge that the meat was contaminated was held to be essential for the veterinary surgeon's. See also e.g. *Chivers* v. *Hand* (1914) 24 Cox 520; *Bowker* v. *Premier Drug Co. Ltd.* [1928] 1 KB 217; *Tinsley* [1963] Crim. LR 520.

[125] e.g. Lord Diplock in *Sweet* v. *Parsley* [1970] AC 132 at 162; and Wright J. in *Sherras* v. *deRutzen* [1895] 1 QB 918 at 921.

[126] Williams, *CLGP* 395. Cf. *Textbook*, 361.

the doctrine of absolute prohibition is of dubious policy and whatever may be said for it where the defendant is directly within the words of the statute it would be going too far to extend responsibility to secondary parties who have no knowledge of facts . . .

Certainly a reasonable case can be made out supporting the status quo. The accessory's usually more removed, less informed, involvement with the actions or consequences constituting the offence suggests a different (higher) standard of culpability is appropriate to compensate for this — although a similar claim could be made for complicity in negligence offences. Moreover, particular reasons justifying absence of fault liability for direct perpetrators often will not apply to secondary parties. Yet despite such arguments this inflexible approach is, for several reasons, far from being invulnerable. Several counter-arguments can be mustered.

First, as *Callow* v. *Tillstone* well demonstrates, patently unjust and anomalous results can follow where a negligently culpable secondary party, who is, in one sense, primarily responsible for the actions of the convicted but blameless principal, may go unpunished.[127] Secondly (accepting for present purposes the broad logic of strict liability), the specific social objectives behind much legislation construed as imposing liability without fault are more likely to be achieved if all parties associated with the proscribed behaviour are subject to a similarly severe basis of liability. For example, if in *Alphacell* v. *Woodward*[128] inspection and maintenance of the automatic pumps had been the responsibility of an independent contractor, then, arguably, the possibility of unlawful river pollution would have been further diminished by the greater vigilance of both the factory owners and the contractors, prompted by a regime of strict liability.[129] Again, for instance, should not a firearms dealer, who honestly but erroneously encourages a customer to purchase what is believed to be an antique revolver, be convictable as an accessory in a firearms certificate offence committed by the customer when the expressed judicial rationale of his strict liability was that 'the danger to the community resulting from the possession of lethal firearms is so obviously great that an absolute prohibition against their possession without proper authority must have been the intention of Parliament'.[130] Thirdly, the broad front of opposition to strict liability in complicity is already breached in a limited form by vicarious liability. Here, provided there is an employer/employee relationship, the essential matters constituting the criminal offence performed by the employee need not be known to the employer for the latter to be criminally responsible. As acknowledged by the House of Lords in *Tesco*

---

[127] The veterinary surgeon's behaviour in *Callow* v. *Tillstone* would now be convictable under the Food and Drugs Act 1953.
[128] [1972] AC 814.
[129] Cf. Lord Salmon, ibid. at 848. Similarly in *Callow* v. *Tillstone*.
[130] *Howells* [1977] 3 All ER 417 at 425.

Specificity of Knowledge

Supermarkets Ltd. v. *Nattrass*,[131] the function of vicarious liability is akin to that of strict liability: to bring about the most efficacious enforcement of the great bulk of regulations governing the many facets of trade and commercial activities. Vicarious liability loosely represents a selective form of complicity operating within the confines of an employer/employee relationship where the special circumstances or social benefits are seen as warranting abandonment of the requirement of 'knowledge', if not of any form of fault.

Viewed as a matter of general policy extending beyond immediate issues of complicity theory, the arguments for extending strict responsibility to complicity are weighty. In response several possible courses are open as alternatives to existing law. The least controversial is the approach already followed in relation to a few specific statutes that, effectively, impose strict complicity liability.[132] It would mark a true departure from present English[133] practice if courts allowed themselves the freedom to construe individual statutory provisions as ousting the presumption of *mens rea* for both principal liability and complicity; or, more radically, that dispensing with the requirement of *mens rea* for the principal offender carried with it the implicit corollary of a similar dispensation for complicity in the offence. Given sufficient verbal latitude, on general principles of statutory construction it is difficult to see what there is to prevent even a court of first instance from interpreting a particular statutory offence as imposing strict liability on any participant. Where liability is not expressly spelt out, as is often the case, it is simply a question of degree as to how clear the language of the statute has to be, in the eyes of the interpreting court, in order to exclude fault. A third approach, and in some respects the most appealing one, is the compromise of requiring an accessory to be at least negligent. This enjoys the attraction of avoiding the more perverse effects of the present disparity between the fault requirements of accessories and principals, and at the same time goes some way to meeting reasonable concern over the possible excessive breadth of complicity in many trivial cases. However, even this modest development would clearly require either legislation or the House of Lords reversing itself,[134] both of which possibilities are remote.

---

[131] Particularly Lord Diplock [1972] AC 153 at 194.

[132] See Williams, *Textbook*, 980–5, and cf. 'Complicity, Purpose and the Draft Code', 107–8.

[133] Most common law (influenced) jurisdictions take the current English approach; for Canada see *F. W. Woolworth Co. Ltd.* (1974) 18 CCC (2d) 23 and *Hamel* (1968) 64 WWR 173; in South Africa *S.* v. *Obrien* 1970 (3) SA 405 at 409; in American jurisdictions, see La Fave and Scott, *Criminal Law*, 512. The Model Penal Code, s. 2.06, leaves the question open. Australian jurisdictions are divided: two exceptions to the requirement of *mens rea* are South Australia and Queensland; see Gillies *Criminal Complicity*, 79–86 for a discussion of the case law development.

[134] See approval of the current position in e.g. *Churchill* v. *Walton* [1967] AC 224, Lord Dilhorne at 236. Working Party Paper 43, proposition 7 (4) follows existing law; and cf. the restatement in Law Commission Report 177, cl. 27 (1) and commentary at para. 9.27.

7. Conclusions: The Accessory's Mental Culpability and Complicity Theory

As in any other area of criminal liability, settling the question of the offender's appropriate level of mental culpability or fault requires that regard be had both to theoretical or doctrinal constraints and to matters of policy. Desirable policies often may not coincide with entrenched doctrine; what is theoretically appropriate may become undesirable or outmoded as a matter of social policy. In one sense established doctrine is a distillation of past practice and received wisdom, serving the current legislator (judicial or otherwise) as an aide-memoire. The speculative nature of so many of complicity's theoretical demands frequently offers the policy-maker a fairly free hand — a latitude especially apparent in relation to specificity of accessorial 'knowledge'. Yet, conceding this is not to deny the existence of any theoretical expectations. Indeed, at least two indirect implications arise from other features of complicity law which, while not clearly legitimizing (or otherwise) particular levels of mental culpability, do offer some guidance on what might be more or less appropriate.

First, as already suggested, the accessory's attitude towards the criminal venture may be seen as a form of counterweight to his knowledge of it when assessing his overall degree of mental culpability: to achieve a rough balance, the uncommitted or even hostile helper arguably ought to know more than one who acts purposefully or has a 'stake in the outcome'. However, this is the opposite of the natural position in most situations, for the purposeful accessory will tend to know more of the venture precisely because of his concerned involvement; and, by the same token, the indifferent accessory will tend to be less aware of the details of the planned offence. English law's likely modern dispensation with any need for accessorial approval of, or stake in, the principal's actions throws the emphasis on the extent of an accessory's foresight; beyond the initial intention to act, it has become the only necessary source of mental culpability. This reliance or focus on foresight in turn raises expectations as to the appropriate specificity of such foresight. Rather than meeting this expectation of a high level of specificity the contrary position has evolved, with the *Maxwell/Bainbridge* formula relying on free-floating culpability, allowing conviction of parties where the level of foresight is low, or possibly non-existent in 'blank cheque' cases. Moreover, decoupling the accessory's mental culpability from a particular principal offence in this way is not altogether consistent with complicity's derivative nature; in some respects it implies a move towards relocating the substance of liability in inchoate territory. It is a claim also underscored by the desirable objective that the real nature of any particular form of criminality should be properly and accurately represented, descriptively as well as conceptually. Arguably, this decoupling process, endorsing transferable or mobile culpability, raises a

Specificity of Knowledge 195

variety of 'fair labelling' dispute: that the culpability tie or nexus between accessory and principal offender and offence may be too tenuous to support, in a realistic and convincing fashion, the designating of one party the 'accessory' to the commission of any particular offence.

A second area of indirect theoretical relevance to the specificity issue is that relating to the causal element in complicity. As previously maintained, accepting the need for some form of causal requirement has few, if any, direct or necessary theoretical implications for the question of mental culpability. But, indirect connections exist in that the more demanding causal requirements are the less demanding the mental element may need to be when an acceptable overall level of criminality is sought. Further, it could be claimed that complicity's derivative quality must convincingly reside at least in either *mens rea* or *actus reus* components. Therefore, diminution in demands on the *mens rea* side has repercussions for the causal element as part of the *actus reus*; and *vice-versa*. Again, though admittedly unrefined, such reflections on the interrelation (or interdependence) of complicity elements do illustrate implications which developments in one portion of complicity law may have for others.

In the absence of anything approaching a doctrinal commitment to arguably desirable[135] parallel levels of *mens rea* or fault between accessory and principal, the scope for increasing or limiting complicity's reach is extensive. However, set against this are two long-standing features which make the policy-maker's task exceedingly problematic: these are complicity's universal coverage of offences of whatever seriousness, and the eligibility of all parties to similar punishment. Accommodating participation in the most and the least serious of offences with a largely fixed culpability standard forces a compromise formulation incapable of properly reflecting the culpability or fault nuances built into individual substantive offences. Three examples illustrate the point. First, under English law P would be convictable of V's murder only if he acts with the 'intention' of causing serious harm, or worse. But A is convictable of complicity in murder if he has supplied the means of causing injury with no more than indifferent foresight that P might possibly act in that way if particular contingent events materialize: a considerable disparity in culpability between principal and secondary parties.[136] Such disparity all but disappears when dealing with moderately serious offences requiring a subjectively reckless perpetrator. Thus, P is convictable of stealing V's disintegrating car if he sells it believing that V may or may not have abandoned it. A, who supplies P with a duplicate set of ignition keys would incur complicity liability if he was

---

[135] Generally followed in the Model Penal Code provisions, but subject to interpretational difficulties; for which see G. Mueller 'The Mens Rea of Accomplice Liability' (1988) 61 S. Cal. LR 2169.

[136] *Chan Wing-Siu* [1985] AC 168, confirmed by the Court of Appeal in *Slack* [1989] 3 All ER 90; disapproving of contrary views in *Barr* (1989) 88 Cr. App. Rep. 362, and, by implication, *Smith* [1988] Crim. LR 616.

similarly subjectively reckless as to circumstances. Finally, the culpability disparity reappears when moving to strict liability offences. Here, in contrast with complicity in serious offences stipulating intentionality for the principal, the disparity runs in the opposite direction with accessory needing full 'knowledge' of the circumstances of the offence and the principal offender none. Complete sentencing flexibility is complicity's complementary feature through which such disparities may be met and individually appropriate punishment meted out. Yet this does not approach being a completely convincing answer to the extent that culpability and punishment are viewed as reflected in the social stigma attaching to particular offences as well as magnitude of sentence. And designating an indifferently acting accessory a party to an offence requiring intention may (as in the example of murder) be inappropriately severe.

Introducing (or reintroducing) purposefulness into complicity would reduce objections of this nature. Requiring an accessory to act both with the purpose of encouraging or assisting the principal, *and* also with a similar[137] level of culpability in respect of circumstances and results to that necessary for principal liability, offers an even more measured and appealing correlation between accessory and principal fault demands.[138] Indifferent, non-purposeful assistance, presently punished as complicity, could then more appropriately be treated as less serious facilitatory liability. As previously argued in relation to the issue of an accessory's attitude towards the occurrence of the principal's actions,[139] dividing secondary participation in such a two-tier fashion would properly reflect conceptually distinguishable types of criminality. A change of this nature would constitute a desirable refinement of possible roles which non-perpetrators may perform, and more harmoniously complement modern attempts to grade principal culpability with greater subtlety.

---

[137] Except for strict liability, see above, section 6.
[138] A few American states seek to achieve this effect through a simple formula of requiring that the accessory was 'acting with the mental culpability' demanded by the principal offence; see e.g. the New York Penal Code, s. 20.00, which is unspecific in relation to circumstances and consequences.
[139] See above, Ch. 5 (5).

7

Variations in Performance by the Principal from that Contemplated by the Accessory

1. The Relationship of Variation and Common Purpose

The general problem considered here and in the following chapter is what degree of deviation is possible by a principal from the behaviour foreseen by the 'accessory' before the 'accessory' ceases to be a party to such behaviour. Although clearly from the same genus of *mens rea* and *actus reus* issues, problems relating to the doctrine of common purpose and those raised as 'variation' are distinguishable, in respect of the factual circumstances where each tends to operate and of certain specific matters which may arise outside a common purpose context and are exclusive to 'variation'.

As will be seen, the paradigm common purpose problem centres on a principal acting beyond an agreed course of conduct and committing a different offence from that anticipated by the accessory. Typically, this entails the commission of an offence in addition to, or a more serious version of, that agreed. Common purpose questions are tied up with deviation in abetting situations—where the accessory is present at the commission of the principal offence. Problems traditionally labelled or viewed as ones of 'variation' almost invariably concern counselling—where the accessory is not present. Beyond this initial difference of categorization is that of the scope of 'variation' questions: like common purpose they may involve liability for an offence beyond or different from that foreseen; but, unlike most imaginable common purpose situations, 'variation' also extends to a principal's mistaken or accidental deviation, and to changes of victim or subject-matter.

Therefore, for expositional convenience and clarity and frequent analytical and judicial practice of separating the two overlapping areas of common purpose and 'variation' problems will be followed. However, expositional separation neither denies the need for nor prevents the search for conceptual and judicial consistency in the solution of common issues.

Principal liability has its own techniques for meeting problems loosely characterizable as involving 'variation'—where what an actor wants or expects to occur does not do so because of a mistake by him or because of some accidental event. When, owing to some failure of perception by the actor, a mistake is made as to subject-matter or identity of the victim, then, unless the definition of the offence involved specifies otherwise, the actor's responsibility will be unaffected. In the case of accidents, the doctrine of transferred malice, when applicable, is used to fix the actor with liability. Similar problems of mistake and accident are possible where accomplices are involved. Here the question is whether rules relevant to principals, where variation is not deliberate, are equally applicable to accomplices. Additionally, there is a range of variation possibilities exclusive to the accessory/principal relationship where there is no ready-made mechanism to determine the 'accessory's responsibility because the principal's deviation is voluntary and therefore no special means are required to settle *his* liability. Here the existence of complicitous activity necessitates particular rules without any obvious equivalent in principal liability to serve as a model.

Overall, the complexity of deviation within complicity is the product of the several permutations derivable from three soft-edged variables: whether the principal's departure was deliberate, accidental, or mistaken; the degree of the principal's deviation from the originally conceived behaviour; and the particular nature or substance of the deviation. To this, an extra layer of complexity is added by the need to consider not only *mens rea* but also causal dimensions of the problems.

Although not without risks of misclassification, the least imperfect approach is to take the deliberateness, or otherwise, of the deviation as analytically the most significant distinguishing feature.[1]

2. Mistaken or Accidental Deviation

Where there has been an accidental or mistaken change of victim or outcome,[2] the predominant[3] view in English law is that the accessory's liability remains unaffected.

---

[1] e.g. adopted by Smith and Hogan, *Criminal Law*, 145–8; and Gillies, *Criminal Complicity*, 151–4. Cf. the contrary approach by Lanham, 'Accomplices and Transferred Malice'.

[2] The Model Penal Code's general provision relating to causal attribution states: 'When purposely or knowingly causing a particular result is an element of an offence, the element is not established if the actual result is not within the purpose or the contemplation of the actor unless: (*a*) the actual result differs from that designed or contemplated . . . only in the respect that a different person or different property is injured or affected or that the injury or harm designed or contemplated would have been more serious or more extensive than that caused; or (*b*) the actual result involves the same kind of injury or harm as that designed or contemplated and is not too remote or accidental in its occurrence to have a just bearing on the actor's liability or on the gravity of his offence' (s. 2.03 (2)).

[3] Foster, *Crown Law*, 370, s. 4; Hawkins, *PC* ii, ch. 29, s. 22; Stephen, *Digest*, art. 41. The approach is adopted in Law Commission Working Paper 43, proposition 7 (2) (*b*) and (*c*), and in Law Commission Report 177, cl. 24 (1). Both *Co. Inst.* iii. 51, and Hale, *PC* i. 617, deny liability, at least in the case of murder.

Deviation will be the consequence of a *mistake* where, for example, A instigates P to kill or rob V, but vain and acutely myopic P, who refuses to wear glasses, mistakenly attacks W. Clearly, the mistake in no way affects P's liability, as the victim's identity is irrelevant to the definitions of the offences involved. And, as Foster suggests,[4] an acquittal of A where there has been a mistake over the identity of the 'Man marked out for Destruction' would be a 'Merciful Opinion'. Similarly, if P shot at V but instead *accidentally* killed W, then the doctrine of transferred malice would hold P responsible for W's death. Rather than transferred malice, Foster's[5] and Stephen's ground for conviction of an accessory in both mistake and accident cases is the potentially narrower one of the offence being 'in the ordinary Course of Things the probable Consequence'.[6] The general question of the theoretical coherence and acceptability of this and other objective standards of complicity liability for different or additional offences is considered below as part of 'Common Purpose'.

The core rationale of transferred malice for principal liability is the definitional immateriality of the changed victim or subject-matter. Whatever criticism may be levelled at its operation for principal liability is equally applicable to complicity;[7] although, incriminating the accessory through extension of the doctrine is treating him no less fairly than the principal. However, the theoretical explanation of the accessory's liability in such circumstances presents similar problems to those relating to deliberate deviation. Essentially, the suggested incapacity of exclusively *mens rea* accounts to provide a complete analysis of the problems of deliberate deviation also holds true for accident and mistake. As will be seen, in all cases the accessory's *mens rea* is a constant, the difference lies in the effect the principal's varied actions may have on their causal attributability to the accessory. In accidental or mistaken deviation, where change is unintended or involuntary, there is no completely unassisted or uninfluenced action

---

[4] *Crown Law*, 370.
[5] 'The Events, though possibly falling out beyond his original Intention, were *in the ordinary Course of Things the probable Consequences of what B did under the Influence, and at the Instigation of A. And therefore in the Justice of the Law He is answerable for them.*' (Foster's emphasis.)
[6] Foster, *Crown Law*, 369–70, similarly Stephen, *Digest*, art. 41; Hawkins, PC ii, ch. 29, s. 22. Some jurisdictions still apply this test; see Gillies, *Criminal Complicity*, 154–5 for Australian states and New Zealand, and Rose, *Parties*, 139 for Canada. Scotland appears to favour a 'reasonably probable outcome' test: Gordon, *Criminal Law*, 152, paras. 5–44. Note also the examples cited in Ch. 8, 'Common Purpose'. Whilst accident and mistake are analytically separable, the issues raised in complicity do not require any distinction to be made. Both old and most modern commentators treat the cases together: see e.g. Foster, Hawkins, Smith and Hogan, *Criminal Law*, 146–7, and Kadish, 'Complicity, Cause and Blame', 351; the doctorine of transferred malice is seen as generally relevant. Cf. Ashworth, 'Transferred Malice', 77.
[7] Cf. the critical views of Williams (*CLGP* 135, *Textbook*, 181) and Ashworth ('Transferred Malice', 88–9, and 'The Elasticity of Mens Rea', 56–7) with Smith and Hogan, *Criminal Law*, 74–5.

and, consequently, no difficulty in identifying the necessary causal nexus between the accessory's actions and those of the principal.[8]

3. Deliberate Variation

Judicial opinion is scarce but the general consensus of institutional authorities suggests that a principal's deliberate substantial variation from the originally anticipated action will prevent accessorial liability. The scope for principal deviation is considerable, possibly relating to any one of a number of matters: the victim or subject-matter, the nature of the offence, or the manner of execution. Broadly, in so far as there is a collective view amongst institutional authorities, whether or not the 'accessory' will be liable despite variation is summed up by Foster:

> If the Principal totally and substantially varieth, if being solicited to commit a Felony of One kind He wilfully and knowingly committeth a Felony of Another, He will stand single in that Offence, and the Person soliciting will not be involved in his Guilt. For on his part it was no more than a fruitless ineffectual Temptation ... But if [he] in Substance complieth with the Temptation varying only in Circumstance of Time or Place or in Manner of Execution ... the Person soliciting to the Offence will ... be an [accessory].[9]

This principle of accessorial exculpation if there is substantial variation (or liability through substantial compliance) initially appears to be consistent with the likely standard *mens rea* requirement set out in *Bainbridge* and

---

[8] It is in cases of complicity by encouragement, rather than through assistance, that the distinction between deliberate and unintentional deviation is clearest. If the means are provided for committing an offence of, say, theft of a particular thing and they are used to steal something else, then, as already argued, there should be complicity in both cases — sufficient *mens rea* and causal connection being present. However, where A encourages P to steal a particular object and P steals something else, and deviation is deliberate, the causal effect of A's actions on P's behaviour is unlikely to be demonstrable or assumed (See Ch. 3). Where deviation is accidental or mistaken this will not be the case as the principal will be attempting to carry out the original purpose. This is an occasion where agency or authorization theory appears to offer a plausible alternative account to causation. It could be said that in cases of mistake and accident the accessory remains liable for the principal's deviant actions because he was attempting to carry out authorized actions. If his variation is deliberate the principal has stepped outside his authority. However, as already argued (Ch. 3), agency or authorization accounts are, unlike causation, incapable of providing an *overall* coherent explanation of complicity's *actus reus* requirements and derivative structure. And see below, 'Expressed Limited Authority'.

[9] *Crown Law*, 369. Similarly, Hawkins, *PC* ii, ch. 29, s. 20; Hale, *PC* i. 436, 616–7; Co. *Inst.* iii. 51; and Plowden's commentary on *Saunders and Archer* (1576) 2 Plowd. 473, 475. Cf. the modern US decisions in *Benchwick* v. *US* 297 F. 2d 330 (1961), *Simmons* v. *State* 594 SW 2d 760 (1980), and *McGhee* v. *Comm.* 270 SE 2d 729 (1980). Arguably matters of time, place, or manner of execution may be of substantial importance to the accessory. Williams suggests that, if A insures his wife against traffic accidents and hires P to kill her by pushing her under a lorry, A will not be a party to her murder if a knife is used. *Textbook*, 346. However, A has instigated murder and if P's actions are in some way causally attributable to A then he should and may be an accessory to it despite the changed mode of execution.

Maxwell: it is irrelevant that an accessory has no knowledge of the time, place, or mode of execution of the 'type' of offence contemplated. Therefore, if it is clearly agreed with A that P burgles Lloyds Bank at Bristol on 1 December by tunnelling into the premises, but, without consulting A, P uses A's sponsoring funds to burgle Barclays Bank at Leeds on 2 December, gaining access by bribery, then presumably A would be an accessory to the burglary. This would be so unless satisfaction of the standard *mens rea* requirement is insufficient, with liability being overridden by either some separate negating effect of the highly specific agreement, or by the absence of an essential causal element.

In attempting to identify any conflict (or qualification) between the general *mens rea* requirement and particular rules of deviation, Foster's[10] account of the basic rule of variation requires amplification in two major respects. First, just what amounts to substantial variation—how is it determined? Secondly, *why* should this free the 'accessory' from responsibility—does it signify that some underlying requirement is missing?

According to Hawkins[11] and Foster,[12] there will be a variation of 'substance' if the principal ignores a specified or understood requirement as to a particular person or thing[13] whereby an offence 'of quite a different nature' is committed. Direct supporting judicial authority is severely limited, but the South African decision of *Robinson*[14] is an example of where the issue of substantiality of variation arose. Here, as part of a scheme to obtain life assurance monies, V arranged with P, X, and Z that P should kill V. However, V changed his mind, communicating this to P, X, and Z, but P still killed him. Because the agreement had been killing with consent P alone was liable for murder, with X and Y accessories to attempted murder only, their support being contingent on consent.[15] Despite the fact that killing with or without consent was murder,[16] the court held that P had acted beyond the common purpose—killing without consent was, by implication, a substantial variation.[17]

In determining what is 'substantial' reference needs to be made to the

---

[10] And those authorities cited.

[11] PC ii, ch. 29, s. 21: 'if a Man command another to commit a Felony on a particular Person or Thing, and he do it on another; as to kill A and he kills B or to burn the House of A and he burns the House of B or steal an Ox, and he steals a Horse; or to steal such a Horse, and he steal another; or to commit a Felony of one kind and he commit another of a quite different Nature in the Night, and there steal the Plate; it is said, That the Commander is not an Accessory, because the Act done varies in Substance from that which was Commanded'.

[12] Foster, *Crown Law*, 369–72. And cf. *Leahy* [1985] Crim. LR 99.

[13] On one interpretation *Saunders and Archer* confirm this.

[14] 1968 (1) SA 666. In *Davis* [1977] Crim. LR 542 the change in mode of performance was the change of principal actor. By implication, *Davis* seems to suggest such a variation could prevent accessorial liability.

[15] There was no evidence that X and Z contemplated P would kill without consent.

[16] In South Africa consent has the effect of providing greater sentencing flexibility. S. v. *Hartman* 1975 (3) SA 532.

[17] Cf. *Dunning* v. *Graham* (1985) unreported, Smith and Hogan, *Criminal Law*, 146.

particular circumstances of each case, but does this enquiry extend beyond a purely objective assessment of the nature of the enterprise to embrace any special requirements or stipulations of the parties? Most centrally, can an accessory limit the extent of his participation and liability by narrowly specifying the criminal objective (person or thing) even though he contemplates other possibilities? For example, will A be an accessory to V's murder if he sells P a gun on the express understanding that it will be used to shoot X? Here murder was foreseen and committed with the means supplied. The answer turns on the theoretical basis used for determining cases of deliberate variation. Divergent views emerge from both limited judicial authority and commentators. Two main conceptual approaches are identifiable and merit consideration: (1) express authority or agreed limitation as to the mode, object, or victim of the offence;[18] and (2) the causal notion of the principal's informed voluntary interposed act, independent of the earlier association with the 'accessory'.[19] Although applying one test in preference to another will not normally change the outcome, this is not invariably so, with the choice of test being crucial in a few cases.

(1) *Expressed Limited Authority*

Returning to the hypothetical bank robbery and murder examples above, applying the express authority test suggests that A would not be an accessory to the robbery of Barclays because he had clearly stipulated Lloyds and had not authorized anything else; nor would A be an accessory to V's murder because the gun was supplied for shooting X. Such conclusions present two awkward problems: first, just how finicky can an accessory be? Can he delimit his liability by insisting upon a particular crime be committed on, say, 26 February because that is his birthday? If substantiality is introduced to avoid such absurd consequences then how much remains of the original authorization test? It also still leaves the question of what *is* 'substantial'? Both robbery and murder examples involve no change of offence but does the change of victim substantially alter the nature of the criminality entailed? The second difficulty is the apparent conflict between the authorization theory and the general *mens rea* requirement set out in *Bainbridge* and *Maxwell*. These authorities incorporate no qualifying references to the power of accessories to restrict the scope of their complicity by declaration or express agreement with the principal—

---

[18] Cf. Williams, *Textbook*, 346: 'the alleged accessory is entitled to delimit the scope of his participation in an intended crime'. Also Hale, *PC* i. 617, and Hawkins, *PC* ii, ch. 29, s. 21.

[19] See Ch. 3 generally and cf. Hart and Honoré, *Causation* (1985), 383–4; and Kadish, 'Complicity, Cause and Blame', 367–8.

Variations by the Principal

if deviation from a hoped for or agreed course of action is *contemplated* then it will not be exculpatory deviation.[20]

This is underscored by the weight of decisions demonstrating the immateriality of the accessory's approval or willingness to endorse the anticipated proposed action,[21] so long as the act of assistance or encouragement is 'intentional'. Similarly, as will be seen (despite persistent equivocality), the doctrine of common purpose now effectively bases liability on commonly agreed actions plus whatever is foreseen[22] as possible incidental, albeit unauthorized, conduct by the principal. To accept that an expressly stipulated purpose can restrict the range of an accessory's liability entails a distinction being made between an accessory who foresees the real possibility of the principal's deviation and says nothing to the principal, and the accessory who does. In both cases there is contemplation of undesired actions which eventually materialize, thereby, according to *Maxwell* and *Bainbridge*, satisfying all necessary *mens rea* requirements.[23] It is very difficult to believe that the House of Lords would have regarded Maxwell's position in an entirely different light if he had told the principal offenders that he would guide them to the Crosskeys Inn only to carry out a robbery and not engage in any bombing activity which he foresaw as likely. A distinction turning on express stipulations not only lacks any clear modern authority, but also runs contrary to the subjectively based risk rationale espoused in *Maxwell* and *Bainbridge* that now underlies English complicity.[24]

(2) *The Voluntary and Causally Independent Principal*

A second theoretical approach to cases of deliberate variation recognizes complicity's essential causal component (or link) between an accessory's actions and those of the principal. Where the principal's behaviour demonstrates a detached independence, free of the 'accessory's' causal influence, and the principal follows the 'Suggestions of his own wicked

---

[20] It is accepted that neither *Bainbridge* nor *Maxwell* are cases where the accessory had expressly stipulated particular use for his aid. However, the general tenor of the speeches in *Maxwell* strongly suggests that their lordships were intending to lay down universal principles of complicity liability which reject the 'particular crime' theory of liability. (And see also Lowry LCJ [1978] 1 WLR 1350 at 1374.) Williams appears to accept this point with the example of P, who having been 'instructed' by A to burgle a particular house, deliberately burgled another house. Williams assures his worried interlocutor that conviction of A as an accessory would probably follow from his 'contemplation' of the changed plan. *Textbook*, 357.

[21] Especially *Lynch*, see Ch. 5.

[22] In the past in English law and still in some jurisdictions, *objectively* foreseeable, see Ch. 8.

[23] Assuming there is an 'intention' to provide the assistance or encouragement; see Ch. 5.

[24] Also see *Chan Wing-Siu* [1985] AC 168. Implicitly accepted in Law Commission Report 177, for under cl. 27 (5) an accessory can only effectively limit liability by agreement with the planned perpetrator 'in respect of a specified person or thing'. The provision does not appear to cover any agreement to limit the level of force which is subject to the general fault test under cl. 27 (1) and (4). But see report ex. 27 (iv), and see below Ch. 8 (3), for the issue of variation in mode of performance and degree of violence or harm.

Heart',[25] there can be no complicity.[26] Therefore, even though it might be contended that the 'accessory' satisfied *mens rea* requirements by having the appropriate level of foresight, he would not be a party to principal liability because of the absence of the essential causal element. It is a line of reasoning indirectly confirmed by the attitude of courts towards mistaken or accidental variation, where an identical (to cases of deliberate variation) mental state on the accessory's part is seen as sufficient to incriminate, even though a particular victim or subject-matter was specified by him.[27] By implication, it could be said that in such cases because the variation was not 'voluntary' the principal has not detached himself from the causal effects of the accessory's actions.[28]

The relevance of this approach to deliberate deviation can be illustrated by the much discussed sixteenth-century case of *Saunders and Archer*,[29] where Saunders, wishing to dispose of his wife, consulted Archer, who suggested a poisoned apple. In Archer's absence, Saunders gave his wife such an apple, but she unexpectedly passed it on to their daughter who, in Saunders's presence, ate it and died; his failure to intervene and prevent his daughter's poisoning being motivated by fear of detection. Although Saunders was convicted of murder, Archer was acquitted as an accessory because the child's poisoning was a 'distinct thing' which Archer had 'neither advised ... assented [nor been] privy to'. Saunders's conviction as principal appeared to rest on equating his allowing the scheme to miscarry with a deliberate deviation.[30] Yet seeing Saunders's behaviour in

---

[25] Foster, *Crown Law*, 372.
[26] See Ch. 3 generally.
[27] Cf. Hart and Honoré, *Causation*, 384, and Kadish, 'Complicity, Cause and Blame', 367.
[28] In addition to citing specific instances of substantial and insubstantial deviation, Foster uses an objectively probable consequence explanation to distinguish between substantial and insubstantial deviation. Cases of insubstantial deviation are those which 'were in the ordinary Course of Things the probable Consequences of what [the principal] did under the [accessory's] Influence'. The test combines a causal rule with a negligence standard of culpability. Cf. *Cooper* v. *Wicks* (1833) 5 Car. & P. 535, 172 ER 1087; and *Bernard* (1858) 1 F. & F. 240, 175 ER 709. The test is employed (via the 1879 English Draft Code) in the Canadian Criminal Code, s. 22 (*b*). Cf. the apparently combined causal and objective culpability test of 'direct and proximate result' which incriminates an 'accessory' whenever it is possible to trace back to the accessory a 'substantial cause' of the principal's actions — to say that the criminal result 'flows directly from P's attempt to commit the crime suggested'. Lanham, 'Accomplices and Transferred Malice', 110–14 and 121. Under this test the verdicts in *Saunders and Archer*, *Robinson*, and *Longone* could have been different because in each case it is arguable that the outcome was the result of the accessory's involvement. Unlike Foster's approach, here a result is attributable to the accessory though it was not objectively *probable*.
[29] (1578) 2 Plowd. 473. The court in *Saunders and Archer* was lukewarm about the practical consequences of its decision; as Foster notes 'the Judges however did not think it advisable to deliver [Archer] in the ordinary Course of Justice by Judgment of Acquittal. But for Examples sake They kept Him in Prison by frequent Reprieves from Session to Session' till He had procured a Pardon from the Crown. A Measure Prudence will often suggest in Cases of a doubtful or delicate nature' (371).
[30] e.g. Smith and Hogan, *Criminal Law*, 147; Hart and Honoré, *Causation*, 383; and Williams, *Textbook*, 358, although at *CLGP* 403 he suggests 'Where the principal finds himself in the dilemma of having to let the wrong victim suffer unless he confesses to the serious

this light[31] does not reveal the nature of the grounds for acquitting Archer. Describing the child's poisoning as a 'distinct thing' is to say it was outside the permitted degree of variation from that 'advised' or 'assented' to: issues of *mens rea* and the (then) likely necessary positive attitude of accessories. Additionally, it might have been claimed that Saunders acted without being causally influenced or affected by Archer's behaviour for 'it was no more than a fruitless ineffectual Temptation'.[32]

In sum, current English law in relation to deliberate deviation admits to neither a completely clear account of result nor theoretical explanation. Although a line of institutional works[33] suggests a similar *broad* solution — that deliberate *and* substantial deviation exonerates the 'accessory' — there

---

crime of attempted murder which he is not willing to do, the case wears the appearance rather of an involuntary miscarriage of the plan than of a deliberate change of victim'. And cf. De Villiers JA in *Longone* 1938 AD 532, 542.

[31] Saunders clearly set in motion events which led to the child's death. His actions were *aimed* at his wife's death. Without his intervention or change of objective the ultimate harm miscarried, killing the wrong party. Saunders's actions differ from the undisputed example of transferred malice, where a blow is aimed at one party but accidentally strikes another, in two respects: the miscarrying medium is another person and the principal has the recognized power to halt the process before the objective miscarries. Does and should this make transferred malice inapplicable?

[32] Foster, *Crown Law*, 369. Continuing: 'The Fact cannot with any Propriety be said to have been Committed under the Influence of that Temptation'. Foster used *Saunders and Archer* as authority for his 'probable consequence' rule (370); the ultimate consequence in this case not being 'probable' ruled out Archer's liability as an accessory. On the facts of *Saunders and Archer*, Archer not only encouraged the wife's murder but also provided information on how to commit the killing. If the information actually assisted Saunders, Archer's causal involvement would not have been completely absent from the child's death. The modern equivalent of *Saunders and Archer* is the SA Supreme Court decision in *Longone* 1938 AD 532. (See also *Mapolisa* 1965 (3) SA 578 (PC)). In *Longone* L supplied poison to C to enable C to poison his wife. After poisoning the drinking water in the hut usually occupied by his wife, C discovered the hut would be occupied by V and another. For fear of self-incrimination, C did nothing, permitting V fatally to drink the poisoned water. One explanation for L's acquittal of complicity in V's murder by C is that he was liable only for acts authorized by him and such steps that 'he should have reasonably contemplated, or foreseen as likely to be taken by . . . the principal and what occurred . . . was not a reasonable probability which should have been foreseen by the accused'. However, the judgments of Tindall and de Wet JJA imply that the absence of accessorial liability was due to C's failure to intervene to prevent the plan miscarrying, so converting C's behaviour into the equivalent of voluntary deviation. Cf. Burchell and Hunt, *SA Criminal Law*, 426.

[33] Cf. Macaulay's Indian Penal Code, s. 111, which employs a probable consequence test for both voluntary and accidental or mistaken deviation. Wright's 1877 draft Jamaica Criminal Code (s. 33) was innovatory in a different manner. Whether variation concerned a person, thing, or manner of execution, where the actual offence was not a probable consequence nor substantially the same as that foreseen the accessory was still liable for complicity in the offence *anticipated*. Where the actual offence was a probable consequence or substantially the same there was complicity in that offence. Being for colonial consumption, neither Macaulay's nor Wright's criminal code was limited to reiterating common law complicity notions. Under the First English Criminal Law Commissioners' 7th Report (1843), art. 13, variation as to circumstances or means would not prevent liability, provided the 'object intended and the crime perpetrated be substantially the same' or the offence is 'a probable consequence' of the intended offence. Three years later the 2nd Report of the Second Criminal Law Commission (1846) offered a more elaborate provision, imposing liability where the crime 'intended and the

is no express high judicial endorsement of this. Moreover, modern case law setting down the standard *mens rea* requirement for accessories runs counter to the belief that accessories are able to delimit the range of their liability, expressly or impliedly. Consensuality in some degree may previously have played a greater role in complicity, however the *mens rea* of complicity is now substantially one of subjective foresight.[34] The question of how much latitude or flexibility *should* be permitted between what the accessory contemplated in the way of principal action and what he is made responsible for is, of course, a matter of penal policy, supported by coherent and consistent theory.

As a matter of policy, it might be suggested that variations from the behaviour contemplated by the accessory which do not change the essential nature of the criminal enterprise should not prevent complicity liability. The various forms of the substantiality test all represent attempts to incorporate this attitude.

While a degree of imprecision is inevitable, flexibility is already adequately built into the system with the *Maxwell/Bainbridge* formula. Although most immediately bearing on mental culpability, the wide *Maxwell/Bainbridge* test[35] also has implications for causal attribution; for what is actually contemplated or deemed to have been contemplated is unlikely to be considered causally too remote or a 'substantial' deviation.[36] Provided the necessary causal relationship and mental elements exist, it is difficult to find convincing justifications for making specific agreements or stipulations[37] (as to a victim's identity or particular subject-matter) fundamental to the nature of the offence and a basis for exempting the accessory from liability.[38] As in situations where the deviation is accidental

one perpetrated be substantially the same and the person or thing against whom or . . . which such crime is perpetrated' was intended by the accessory, unless the plan miscarries as a consequence of a mistake or accident. In the case of a mistake or accident there would be liability for any act that was a 'probable consequence' of the 'endeavour' (art. 10). The brief provisions of the 1879 code provide a stark contrast: s. 72 declares liability is unaffected by variations in mode of performance, and that an accessory's liability extends to all offences which he 'knew or ought to have known to be likely to be committed' in consequence of his actions. No reference is made to cases of change of victim or object. Foster is cited as the source of this view of the law. See also Stephen, *Digest*, arts. 40 and 41.

[34] But even if purposeful complicitous action were required (Ch. 5) the issue would remain how much variation from *that* desired outcome could occur without freeing the accessory from liability.

[35] Cf. the *Bainbridge* 'type' text with the Model Penal Code's 'same kind of injury or harm' test in its general causation provisions: s. 2.03 (2) (*b*).

[36] See Ch. 3 for complicity's causal demands.

[37] *Saunders and Archer* might mean that simple awareness of the intended victim's identity *alone* (without any restrictive agreement) will limit the accessory's range of possible liability. If so, then the more knowledge a potential accessory has of the planned crime the greater the effect of restricting his possible liability.

[38] Cf. Law Commission Report 177, cl. 27 (5) which restates such exceptions. The special 'Scrutiny Group' which reviewed the complicity provisions in Report 143 did not favour the exceptions relating to stipulated 'person or thing'. The code team notes (commentary para. 9.31) that the provision would not except the accessory in cases similar to *Robinson* where

or mistaken (when liability remains), the extent of the accessory's mental culpability is unchanged by a deliberately deviating principal. Therefore, if A provides P with a gun to kill V which is used to murder X, then why should A not be a party to X's murder *if* he has both *causally* facilitated it and has sufficient *mens rea* according to *Maxwell* and *Bainbridge*.[39] Stipulations as to victim should (contrary to institutional authorities) not prevent his liability any more than it would if P had mistakenly or accidentally shot X instead of V. The substance of A's criminality has not changed; he is as morally culpable as one who provides a gun suggesting that P shoots the first person he meets with green eyes. Change of victim should not be regarded as a 'distinct thing' or change of 'substance' any more than it is for the principal offender.[40] This remains true whether or not an accessory's purpose, or assent, is necessary to incriminate him; for even if it were necessary the issue should *not* be 'Did A desire or consent to *that* murder?' but 'Did A desire or consent to participation in *an* offence of murder?'

Furthermore, rather than looking (solely) to a *mens rea* account of deviation, a more complete and internally consistent explanation is found by also registering the presence or absence of the necessary causal relationship between the accessory's and principal's acts. It is 'consistent' in the sense of not running counter to the subjective risk philosophy implicit in *Maxwell* and *Bainbridge*, and not resorting to the dubious use of negligence as would any incriminating formula based solely on objectively probable consequences. A complementary causal analysis follows on from the necessary establishment of some causal relationship in all forms of complicity; or, put in a negative form, the absence of an unassisted or uninfluenced independently acting perpetrator. Therefore, in cases of deliberate deviation (assuming appropriate *mens rea*) the essential question will be whether or not the principal was acting uninfluenced by and independently of the accessory's assistance or encouragement.[41] If he was

---

there was no change of victim. Cf. *Calhaem* (1985) 2 All ER 266. Other than suggesting the principle was 'well-established', it is not revealed why identity or subject-matter is thought to demand special treatment, and neither does the code commentary discuss the role, if any, of causation here. Bearing in mind the absence of clear and strong authority, there was scope for a *de novo* solution with supporting argument. See also Working Paper 43, proposition 7 (2) (c), which also excludes liability where there is a deliberate change of victim or property.

[39] On the *Bainbridge/Maxwell* test A probably has sufficient *mens rea*: he has committed the same 'type' of offence as murder was 'contemplated' by A; limiting stipulations are contrary to the fault basis espoused in *Bainbridge* and *Maxwell*, rejecting the 'particular crime' theory (see Ch. 6).

[40] It is accepted that arguments against 'transferred malice' reasoning have similar relevance to the accessory's position. The Canadian Law Reform Commission Report 31 (1987) proposals on complicity, s. 4 (6) (*b*) do not recognize variation in the victim's identity as exculpating the accessory.

[41] Where A provides P with a means of killing V, but P deliberately kills W, although there is probably sufficient *mens rea* to satisfy the *Maxwell/Bainbridge* requirement, is there a causal link? If P had always intended to kill W and was just waiting for the appropriate means, then

acting in this way there can be no complicity. If there is a factual[42] causal relationship then it should be regarded as sufficient, on the basis that the *Maxwell/Bainbridge* culpability demands also indirectly act to discriminate between appropriate and inappropriate causal attribution.

his action would be independent of *A*'s influence although facilitated by *A*. Whether a sufficient causal link is made out in such cases depends on whether it is seen as comparable to a situation where *A*, *knowing P* intends to kill an unidentified person, simply provides a weapon. Here there would be liability even though there is no influence on *P* who in *this* sense was acting independently. Unless it is claimed the accessory can limit his liability to a particular victim, there is no significant distinction between the two examples. Therefore an 'independent' principal actor must extend to independence of accessorial influence *or assistance*. Cf. Hart and Honoré's narrower concept of independence in Ch. 3. Williams maintains 'the fact that you supply an accomplice with a gun with murderous intent does not involve you in every murder the accomplice chooses to commit with the weapon. The inciter does not become involved in a murder merely because he has incited murder in the abstract. He must have incited the particular murder...': *Textbook*, 347. But will not (and should not) *A* be an accessory to every murder *P* commits if *A* supplies a gun foreseeing that *P*, an escaped mass murderer, is likely to shoot anyone on sight?

[42] Of the nature described in Ch. 3.

8

The Doctrine of Common Purpose

A standard formulation of the broad theory of the doctrine of common purpose is provided by Alderson B. in the mid-nineteenth-century case of *Macklin*:[1]

> It is a principle of law, that if several persons act together in pursuance of a common intent, every act done in furtherance of such intent by each of them is, in law, done by all. The act, however, must be in pursuance of the common intent.

According to Pollock CB in the later case of *Skeet*,[2] the doctrine's function and nature, at least in earlier times, was plainly a form of collective felony — murder

> [arising] from the desire on the part of the old lawyers to render all parties who are jointly engaged in the commission of a felony responsible for deadly violence committed in the course of its execution. But that doctrine has been much limited in later times, and only applies in cases of felony, where there is no[3] evidence of a felonious design to carry out the unlawful purpose at all hazards, and whatever may be the consequences.

However, whatever perceived practical need may have motivated the doctrine's creation, its nature, status, and relationship to general complicity concepts and requirements have been and, to a fair degree, still remain hazy.

Resort to the terminology of common purpose ('common design' or 'common pursuit') occurs most frequently where the issue is the liability of an accessory for an offence additional or collateral to the primary principal offence. Most typically, during the course of a robbery an intervening third party is killed by one of the robbers. Here the primary offence or objective of the common purpose is robbery, the killing being a collateral or additional degree of criminality. When determining the liability for

---

[1] (1838) 2 Lew. CC 225, 168 ER 1136. One of the very earliest statements of a variety of common purpose theory is given in Fitzherbert's *Corone*, fo. 256*b*, pl. 314 (3 Edw. III) (1329): 'Note that all those who come in company to a certain place with a common consent where a wrong is done, whether homicide or robbery or other trespass, each one shall be held a principal actor, although he was standing by and did no wrongful act'.

[2] (1866) 4 F. & F. 931, 176 ER 854 at 857.

[3] The word 'no' is obviously a slip of the judicial tongue or reporting error. Cf. the policy of 'old lawyers' and the allegation made in respect of *S. v. Safatsa* 1988 (1) SA 868 (A) and refs. in Ch. 3 n. 33.

collateral offences, the central question has been whether, if at all, the basis of responsibility is different from that used in settling liability for the primary offence. More particularly, in relation to specificity of knowledge, does the *mens rea* necessary for complicity in the primary offence in any way act as a substitute for or dilute the full accessorial *mens rea* that would normally be required for the collateral offence? Further, on the question of the accessory's attitude towards the criminal venture, the doctrine carried, and still may harbour, notions of consent or authorization hostile to the 'contemplation' of risk basis for complicity as authoritatively laid down in *Bainbridge* and *Maxwell*. Put directly, the overall question is whether the doctrine is no more than a linguistic variant of a single general culpability standard or whether it embodies a substantive culpability distinction.

Before approaching an analysis of modern case law relating to these two areas of contention, a brief review of mainly Victorian developments will serve to illustrate the theoretical and policy uncertainties that still, in some measure, inhabit current judicial pronouncements.

1. Nineteenth-Century and Earlier Developments

As the comments of Pollock CB in *Skeet* suggest, common purpose decisions have mostly concerned collateral liability for homicide, although many reported examples exist involving other offences.[4] However, it is in relation to homicide that the doctrine has attracted—and continues to attract—the most frequent and careful judicial consideration.

Early reports, and particularly pre-nineteenth-century cases, too often offer interpretational problems, partly through their brevity and also because of the operation of, usually, unspoken rules of procedure and evidence. These difficulties are aggravated and magnified in complicity cases by problems relating to the substantive offence(s) being overlaid with those particular to complicity itself. Compounding such difficulties is the language and operation of the formerly extensive range of examples of constructive liability, most especially unlawful act manslaughter and felony-murder. However, despite such constructional obstacles, a general account of detectable trends during this period may be hazarded.

Over the three hundred years, or so, running from early in the sixteenth century to the Victorian period, in line with the gradual general subjectivizing of criminal responsibility, the common purpose doctrine

[4] e.g. theft: *Standley* (1816) Russ. & Ry. 305, 168 ER 816, *Bolster* (1909) 3 Cr. App. Rep. 81; possession of housebreaking implements: *Thompson* (1869) 11 Cox 362; possession of weapons: *Goodfellow* (1845) 1 Den 81, 169 ER 159; possession of counterfeit coins: *Rogers* (1839) 2 Mood. 85, 169 ER 34; burglary: *Cornwall's Case* (1730) St. 881, 93 ER 914; poaching: *Passey* (1836) 7 Car. & P. 282, 173 ER 124, *Lockett* (1836) 7 Car. & P. 300, 173 ER 133, Cf. *Sotton* (1844) 5 QB 493, 114 ER 1333; concealment of birth: *Skelton and Batting* (1853) Car. & K. 119, 175 ER 488.

developed with increasing particularity the enquiry into how much the accessory knew of (or should have known of) how the principal might act. Reported decisions suggest movement from constructive liability for collateral offences through the qualifying guilt of complicity in the primary offence to the application of an objective probable consequences test[5] and, later, some form of subjective requirement.[6] But no tolerably clear authoritative principle emerges from the case law. Typical of the division in judicial opinion was that relating to the responsibility of an accessory for violence of a confederate in carrying out a robbery. Some decisions held an accessory liable for any principal action performed in pursuance of the common purpose of robbery,[7] whilst others required positive evidence of a common design to execute the common purpose with all necessary force.[8]

Clearly influential was the individual judicial attitude taken towards constructive liability and its legitimate role in complicity. Pollock CB's observations in *Skeet* mark some attempt to limit the harshness of the felony-murder rule in complicity to circumstances where there had been agreement to use serious force. But such comments were exceptional, leaving unresolved the question of the extent of accessorial liability for acts unforeseen or beyond the confines of the common purpose. Most particularly, was there responsibility for overzealous principal actions which, although outside the common design, were carried out in its pursuance and were objectively foreseeable? The contentiousness and uncertainty surrounding the answer to this important question, and the effects on it of particular criminal jurisprudential predilections, are revealed by the treatment given to it in successive editions of *Russell*. During Charles Sprengel Greaves's editorship (the 1843 and 1865 editions)[9] no reference is made in *Russell* to such an objective principle in connection with common purpose.[10] However, Samuel Prentice, Greaves's successor, in the 1877 edition of the work, although retaining Greaves's text in a virtually unaltered form, inserted at the end of the common purpose section a purported summary[11] of the law:

---

[5] In the case of riot or affray: 'if several persons come to a house with intent to make an affray, and one be killed, while the rest are encouraged in riotous and illegal proceedings, though they are dispersed in different rooms, all will be principals in murder': J. Chitty, *Criminal Law* (1816), i. 256–7, citing Hale, PC i. 439; Hawkins, PC ii, ch. 29, s. 28; East, PC i. 258. See also e.g. *Griffith* (1553) 12 Plowd. 97, 75 ER 152; *Mansell* (1556) 2 Dyer 1286b, 73 ER 279; *Lord Mohun* (1692) Holt KB 479, 90 ER 1164; *Ashton* (1698) 12 Mod. 256, 88 ER 1304; *Wallis* (1703) 1 Salk. 334, 91 ER 294; *Edmeads* (1828) 3 Car. & P. 390, 172 ER 469; *Cooper* (1846) QB 533, 115 ER 976.

[6] The exact nature of the subjective element is often far from clear; see e.g.: *Hodgson* (1730) 1 Leach 6, 168 ER 105; *White v. Richardson* (1806) Russ. & Ry. 99, 168, ER 704; *Collison* (1837) 4 Car. & P. 565, 172 ER, 565, 172 ER 827, *Franz* (1861) 2 F. & F. 580, 175 ER 1195.

[7] e.g. *Bowen* (1841) Car. & M. 149, 174 ER 448; *Harvey and Caylor* (1843) 1 Cox 21.

[8] *Price* (1858) 8 Cox 96; *Luck* (1862) 3 F. & F. 483, 176 ER 217; *Caton* (1874) 12 Cox 624.

[9] 3rd and 4th edns.

[10] See bk. i, ch. 2, and bk. iii, ch. 1, in both edns.

[11] 5th edn., p. 164.

It is submitted that the true rule of law is, that where several persons engage in the pursuit of a common unlawful object, and one of them does an act which the others ought to have known was not improbable to happen in the course of pursuing such common unlawful object, all are guilty.

No supporting authority is cited for the proposition, and no relevant new case law appears to have been reported between Greaves's last edition of *Russell* and Prentice's. This suggested objective probable consequence rule wears all the appearance of editorial kite-flying. But, bearing in mind *Russell*'s role as the standard work of reference for Bench and Bar in English criminal law during the nineteenth century (and for much of the twentieth too) the significance of Prentice's modification was potentially considerable.

In the face of disputed and disparate case law and underlying uncertainty, it might be expected that someone like Greaves, with a background of relatively liberal reforming inclinations,[12] would during his editorship not wish to promote a form of culpability of which he probably disapproved. However, the most curious feature of this unspoken dispute over the function (if any) of a probable consequence rule for common purpose liability (with its relevance to abetting) is Greaves's acceptance of Foster's objective formulation for accessories before the fact.[13] For although Foster's well-known pronouncement occurs in that part of his treatise dealing with matters of 'variation' and accessories before the fact, he also included abettors as being subject to the same rule of objective probability.[14]

Yet this practice of limiting the probable consequences test to accessories before the fact is also to be found in a series of early and mid-nineteenth-century code reform proposals. Both the 1843 and 1846 codes contain 'probable consequence' provisions for accessories before the fact but not for parties to a common purpose.[15] However, the 1879 Criminal Code Bill

[12] Greaves was involved in much legislative consolidation and drafting reforming measures, mainly between the late 1840s and early 1860s. He was joint draftsman of the Criminal Law Amendment Bill (Nos. 1 and 2) (1852–3) aimed at amending and consolidating a large slice of the criminal law, basing his efforts on the 4th Report (1848) of the Second Criminal Law Commissioners. Greaves's most lasting legislative drafting monuments are the 1861 Criminal Law Consolidation and Amendment Acts. See R. Cross, 'The Reports of the Criminal Law Commissioners (1833–1849)', in Glazebrook, ed., *Reshaping the Criminal Law*. Greaves's own proposals on criminal appeals were distinctly radical for his time. For instance, in his evidence to the Committee on the Criminal Law Amendment Bill (1848) Greaves argued for 'an absolute and unconditional right to every prisoner who is convicted to appeal to one of the common law courts in Westminster Hall': Minutes of Evidence 62, 18 May 1848.

[13] *Crown Law*, 372: 'in the ordinary Course of Things a probable Consequence'. And see, Ch. 7; similarly Chitty, *Criminal Law*, i. 263.

[14] *Crown Law*, 369, s. 2: 'But if the Principal in Substance complieth with the Temptation, varying only in Circumstance of Time or Place, or in the Manner of Execution, in these Cases the Person Soliciting to the Offence will, *if Absent, be an Accessory Before the fact*, if *Present a Principal*' (emphasis added). Ss. 3 and 4 explain the relevance of the probable consequence test and are linked to the general statement of outcome contained in ss. 1 and 2.

[15] Criminal Law Commissioners' Report of 1843, art. 13; Report of 1846, art 10. Both codes limit the extent of abettors' liability to what is within the 'scope of such common design' 1843 code, arts. 16 and 17; 1846 code, arts. 12 and 13.

The Doctrine of Common Purpose

Commission's draft code (largely Stephen's work) breaks free of this practice by including such a provision in both portions of the code dealing with abettors and accessories.[16] It is reasonably clear from his *Digest of Criminal Law* (editions preceding and following the code) that the probable consequence rule was generally seen as limited to accessories before the fact. Therefore Stephen must have believed that the code proposals were novel.[17] Bearing in mind the lead offered by Prentice's 1877 edition of *Russell* and by the 1879 code, it seems probable that Stephen did not favour this possible extension of complicity liability, and that the code provision was incorporated to cater for the preferences of his fellow commissioners rather than his own:[18] an approach consistent with his long-standing dislike for most manifestations of the felony-murder rule.[19]

Prentice's submission was retained, completely unaltered, despite several changes of author(s)[20] until Turner's 1958 edition. Turner's 1950 version of *Russell* made no attempt to modify or explain the submission other than cite the unsupporting case of *Pridmore* (1913) (see next section) as every earlier author had done since 1923. Neither does Turner offer any reason for the paragraph's omission in 1958. The explanation for this may lie in one or both of two significant (for complicity) events occurring between 1950 and 1958. By far the most important and likeliest reason for Turner's modification was the unequivocal affirmation of the principle of 'knowledge' set out in *Johnson v. Youden, et al.*[21] Secondly, the elimination of felony-murder by the Homicide Act 1957 may have been taken as indicative of the formal discrediting of the most unacceptable manifestations

---

[16] Ss. 71 and 72. S. 71 makes anyone who 'aids or abets' 'counsels or procures' a 'party' to the offence. Its final paragraph extends 'common purpose' liability to any offence committed in pursuance of the common purpose or which 'ought to have known to be a probable consequence of the prosecution of such common purpose'. This provision, therefore, applies to any party whether present or not when the collateral principal offence is committed. Curiously, s. 72 deals specifically with the case of variation as to the 'way' a 'counselled or suggested' offence was committed. Here the party 'counselling or procuring' is liable for every offence committed in consequence which 'ought to have [been] known to be likely'. The reason for the separate treatment is not obvious as the generality of s. 71 would seem to extend to variation in the case of counselling and procuring. It may be that, to make the position absolutely clear, what was implicit in s. 71 was expressly spelt out in s. 72. Quirky drafting is an explanation for the use of 'probable' in s. 71 and 'likely' in s. 72. The 1879 code was meant to be a clear exposition of existing law, however, as the authors admit, many reforming innovations were incorporated; see the report of the Criminal Code Bill Commissioners, particularly 19. The marginal note against s. 71 states 'this section is so framed as to put an end to the nice distinctions between accessories before the fact and principals in the second degree, already practically superseded by 24 and 25 Vit c. 94'.

[17] See *Digest*, art. 41 which makes an instigator liable for all crimes actually committed that were 'likely to be caused by [his] instigation'. The word 'instigate' is the 'equivalent to "counsel, procure or command"' (n. 2 to art. 39). All the examples provided to illustrate the operation of the rule are cases of accessories before the fact.

[18] Cf. Stephen's own 1878 code bill.

[19] See e.g. Stephen J.'s direction in *Serne* (1887) 16 Cox 311 at 313, and *HCL* iii. 468.

[20] See those listed in the 12th edn. of *Russell*.

[21] This is set out in a new section in Turner's 11th edn. of *Russell*, 156.

of constructive liability, so making probable consequence liability in complicity visibly anomalous. Furthermore, in many old complicity decisions the basis of liability seems to have been an amalgam of this and the felony-murder rule—as in *Betts and Ridley*. However, when discussing accessories before the fact (as distinct from abettors and common purpose) Turner in each of his editions of *Russell* cites Foster's principle (as applied in *Betts and Ridley*) as authority for the objective test; although latterly he suggests 'Nowadays . . . the test should be subjective'.[22] This account of the law is difficult to follow for two reasons: by then *Bainbridge* had removed any possible doubts that the 'knowledge' principle applied to accessories and abettors; and, additionally, *Betts and Ridley* was clearly a common purpose case of abetting.[23] Therefore, if regarded as binding, the probable consequence rule was equally applicable to abettors.

2. Modern Case Law Issues

Against this background of confused and ambivalent commentaries on the doctrine of common purpose and the role of the probable consequence approach, the main features of the doctrine's erratic modern developments can be charted.

In *Rubens*[24] during the course of a robbery carried out by Mark and Morris Rubens, Sproull was fatally stabbed by Mark Rubens. The evidence supported the conclusion that there had been an agreement to use violence but did not suggest Morris Rubens knew of the knife. Contrary to earlier decisions[25] brought to the notice of the Court of Criminal Appeal by defence counsel, Morris Rubens's conviction for murder was sustained on the basis that in such circumstances 'it has been long laid down that Morris is also responsible for the blow'.[26] *Rubens* appears to be a case of the felony-murder rule being applied automatically to any accessory without further inquiry into the question of whether the nature and extent of the violence was different from or beyond that agreed to or contemplated. It was a retrograde approach at odds with a more progressive line of authorities[27] according to which 'constructive homicide' in felony cases

---

[22] See the 11th and 12th (final) edns. of *Russell*, 172 and 162 respectively. Kenny, in his *Outlines of Criminal Law* (1st edn., 1902) never adopts the 'probable consequences' formulation for abettors, although he follows Foster in relation to accessories (see ch. VI).
[23] Although Foster was expressly applied (1930) Cr. App. Rep. 148 at 154.
[24] (1909) 2 Cr. App. Rep. 163.
[25] *Price* (1858) 8 Cox 96, and *Caton* (1874) 12 Cox 624.
[26] (1909) 2 Cr. App. Rep. 163 at 167 per Darling J. Two months before these remarks in his direction to the grand jury at Liverpool on 9 Mar. 1909, Lord Alverstone CJ had made clear his disapproval of any watering down of the felony-murder rule: 'The experience of the judges shows that there are so many cases of death caused by attempts to commit felonies, that, for the protection of human life, it is not desirable to relax the rule which treats such crimes as murders'. Quoted in *Kenny*, 13th edn., 139.
[27] Such as *Price* and *Caton*.

would not in itself incriminate accessories unless they had agreed to the fatal level of violence or to carry out the common design 'at all hazards'.[28]

Until *Betts and Ridley*, with two exceptions,[29] there appear to be no other reported decisions relating to common purpose and murder. Of those cases concerning other offences where common purpose is discussed, only *Pridmore*[30] and *Pearce*[31] provide anything more than a brief reference to the doctrine.[32] Four years after *Rubens*, in *Pridmore*, the Court of Criminal Appeal was required to rule on the nature of common purpose where the charge was shooting with intent to murder, arising from a poaching incident in which a bailiff was shot. What is most significant is the response of Pickford J. (one of the court's three members) to the prosecution's suggestion, quoting Prentice's addition to *Russell*, that where a common unlawful design is pursued each party is responsible for every act of another confederate which he 'ought to have known was not improbable to happen'. As Pickford J. pointed out, 'If such an act is probable in the course of night poaching there would be a common purpose in every case'.[33] In general tenor, the court's judgment is towards requiring evidence of at least an implied understanding of the use of force to resist apprehension, but no clear indication is offered as to *how* much force must be contemplated.[34] No such ambiguity is found in the factually similar case of *Pearce*, with Avory J. for the Court of Criminal Appeal insisting on evidence of an arrangement to assault with a gun or other weapons *and* 'also to resist apprehension at all costs'.[35]

---

[28] e.g. *Skeet*, *Luck*, and *Franz*.

[29] The two murder cases of *Stewart and Lincoln* (*The Times* 21 Jan. 1926) and *Browne and Kennedy* (*The Times* 28 Apr. 1928) are of relevance but limited in their discussion of the issue considered here. In the former a submission of no case to answer was successfully made by counsel for the alleged abettor on the grounds that *more* than a design to rob with violence was necessary — knowledge that the other party was carrying and intended to use a pistol was also required to convict the abettor of murder. In the notorious police murder case of *Browne and Kennedy* the trial direction was to the effect that it was sufficient to incriminate Kennedy if he was aware of Browne's possession of the revolver used to shoot the policeman, at any moment before the shooting, if they were acting in concert in order to prevent arrest. See the report of Avory J.'s direction in *Notable British Trials*, ed. Shaw, 169–88, particularly 182–3. Both decisions, although after *DPP v. Beard*, demonstrate that the abettor was required to have foresight of the *degree* of violence likely to be used by the principal.

[30] (1913) 8 Cr. App. Rep. 198.

[31] (1929) 21 Cr. App. Rep. 79. Cf. *Kerr* (1921) 15 Cr. App. Rep. 165 at 168.

[32] *Bolster* (1909) 3 Cr. App. Rep. 81 involved larceny; the report contains no more than brief references to common purpose. See similarly *Joachim* (1912) 7 Cr. App. Rep. 222 and *Connor* (1913) 8 Cr. App. Rep. 152.

[33] (1913) 8 Cr. App. Rep. 198 at 201. The difficulty of interpreting earlier cases is well illustrated by the citation of *Edmeads* by counsel for both sides, each claiming it to be in 'my favour' (201).

[34] Ibid. 203. Neither *Pridmore* nor *Pearce* involved felony-murder.

[35] (1929) 21 Cr. App. Rep. 79 at 81. The charge was assault of a bailiff by clubbing him with the stock of a gun. In *Short* (1932) 23 Cr. App. Rep. 170, as in *Pridmore*, the conviction appealed was shooting with intent to murder. In the view of Lord Hewart CJ 'the question really is, whether there was any evidence fit to go to the jury that the appellant was a party to a common design to affect the felonious purpose, if necessary, by the use of firearms' — possibly a higher degree of culpability than may have been stipulated in *Pridmore*.

Betts and Ridley was the first reported case to contain a relatively lengthy examination of common purpose and murder after the House of Lords' restatement of the felony-murder rule in *DPP* v. *Beard*.[36] Other than whether or not Betts used a weapon, the facts of the case were simple and undisputed. In pursuance of an agreement between the defendants, a bag of money being carried by Andrews was snatched by Betts while Ridley waited close by in a car. During the course of the robbery, Betts struck Andrews a fatal blow to the top of his head. Ridley admitted to having agreed or anticipated that Andrews would be pushed to the ground during the robbery; although he might possibly have foreseen the risk of greater violence being employed. On the basis of *Beard*, Betts was properly convicted of felony-murder:[37] Ridley's conviction for complicity in the murder was sustained by the Court of Criminal Appeal on the grounds that he was a party to the 'felonious act of robbery with violence', and had anticipated at least some violence even though not of the degree employed by Betts.[38] Only if Ridley had not contemplated that any violence would be used against Andrews would he have been free of complicity in murder. In the Court of Criminal Appeal's view, by using greater violence than anticipated or agreed, Betts had not gone beyond the limits of the common purpose but had varied only in 'manner of execution'.

Extracting the *ratio* of *Betts and Ridley* is problematic. The most tenable view is that it represents a direct unmodified application of *Beard*'s felony-murder rule to complicity: in one sense making the liability strict since no foresight or even negligence is required in respect of the infliction of the fatal act.[39] Alternatively, it has been argued that the Court of Criminal Appeal decided the case on the basis of the objective probable consequence test.[40] The primary source of this interpretational difficulty is the Court of Criminal Appeal's express resort to Foster's discussion of variation rules. As has already been seen, Foster sought to account for his rules of variation by the unifying probable consequence principle.[41] What is not clear from the judgment in *Betts and Ridley* is whether when invoking the substantial variation rule the court intended or felt it had to accept the accompanying general probable consequence principle. In concluding that there had been no substantial variation by Betts, the court fixed on the expression 'manner

---

[36] (1920) AC 479. The judgment arguably expanded the definition of malice aforethought that was accepted in many earlier decisions at the end of the 19th cent. to include cases where death was caused by 'an act of violence done in the course, or in furtherance of . . . a felony involving violence' (493). See *Russell*, 12th edn., 481–93; and also the discussion of the doctrine's scope before *Beard* in D. A. Stroud, *Mens Rea* (1914), ch. IX.

[37] (1930) 33 Cr. App. Rep. 148 at 152.

[38] Ibid. 154–5.

[39] See Lanham, 'Accomplices and Constructive Liability', 79–81, and adopted in the Australian case of *Soloman* [1959] Qd. R. 123.

[40] A view taken by Turner in *Russell*, 12th edn., 161 n. 5 and in the Canadian decision of *Bannister* (No. 2) (1936) 66 CCC 357.

[41] *Crown Law*, 370–2.

of execution' as the key to its decision; no reference was made to what was a probable consequence of Ridley's actions. The court's only allusion to objective contemplation occurs at the very end of the judgment where it is observed that the jury must 'have found that [Ridley] was actually a party and privy to an act which was calculated in the judgment of ordinary people' to cause death. Rather than an oblique reference to the probable consequence test, this was no more than the court using the trial judge's direction in respect of Betts to demonstrate Betts's culpability was greater than that strictly demanded by the *Beard* felony-murder rule.

Overall, the decision in *Betts and Ridley*, like *Rubens*, was the product of applying the felony-murder rule and, unlike many earlier authorities,[42] effectively ignoring (or very narrowly construing) variation rules.[43] Once it had been established that the principal's actions were in pursuance of the common purpose offence (of violence) no variation would excuse the accessory. The effect of the *Betts and Ridley* application of felony-murder to complicity was followed through with the slight modification of the rule recognized by Lord Goddard in *Grant and Gilbert*.[44] No attempt is made in these modern felony-murder cases to mitigate the rule's severity in complicity by applying Foster's probable consequence test which could easily have affected the outcome (in the accessory's favour) in a number of decisions.

Use of the language and concept of common purpose facilitated the application of the felony-murder rule to complicity. Common purpose

---

[42] Such as *Stewart and Lincoln* (1926) and *Browne and Kennedy* (1928), and also in *Price and Caton*. Cf. the slightly later case of *Mastin* (1934) 26 Cr. App. Rep. 177 at 184. The court's discomfort with the severity of the result of felony-murder within complicity is perhaps indicated by its invitation at the end of its judgment (as in *Rubens*) for the possible exercise of executive clemency.

[43] Ten years after *Betts and Ridley* the Court of Criminal Appeal returned to a related problem in *Appleby* (1940) 28 Cr. App. Rep. 1. The case involved the special rule of constructive malice aforethought then existing in respect of murdering 'an officer of justice' in the course of violently resisting arrest, however, *obiter* observations carry more general relevance. After citing extracts from Stephen's *Digest* and from *Russell* the court concluded that 'a much less degree of violence may be sufficient to justify a verdict of guilty of murder in the case of a police officer who is killed in the execution of his duty, in arresting a person . . . than would suffice in the case of another person' (5). In the case of the arresting police officer 'real violence, . . . something more than a mere refusal to submit to arrest' needed to have been part of the common design; 'real violence' here meaning apparently no more than assault. How much more violence would 'suffice' in other cases is not specified. On the question of exceeding the anticipated level of violence, as in *Betts and Ridley*, the court resorted to the same interpretation of Foster's rule of (in)substantial variation, implying the difference between basic assault and deadly violence to be no more than a non-substantial change in the 'manner of execution'.

[44] (1954) 38 Cr. App. Rep. 107. The case confirmed that felony-murder applied not only to felonies intrinsically involving violence, but also to felonies (such as theft) carried out with a degree of violence responsible for death. See the critical comment of Turner in *Russell*, 12th edn., 497. The arbitrary effect of the rule is illustrated by contrasting the non-felony-murder homicide cases of *Garforth* [1954] Crim. LR 936 with *Grant and Gilbert*. Cf. also *Mutagh and Kennedy* (1955) 39 Cr. App. Rep. 72 and *Headley* (1945) 31 Cr. App. Rep. 35.

terminology tends to encourage the imputation of the principal's *mens rea* to the accessory by equating a joint primary objective with accessorial *mens rea* in respect of any collateral offence of the principal committed in 'pursuance of the common purpose'. Unmitigated in its effect even by the probable consequence test, felony-murder represented the most extreme form of departure from the general expectation of accessorial *mens rea*. As has been seen, even outside felony-murder examples, considerable uncertainty persisted as to quite what level of *mens rea* an accessory was required to have in respect of any collateral offence committed by the principal. Abolition of felony-murder left the law of complicity with several outstanding issues; more particularly:

(1) whether there was substantive significance in the notion of an agreement or common design between parties as opposed to mere foresight
(2) what was the relationship of the doctrine of common purpose and principles of variation?
(3) when was it appropriate to convict the principal of murder or manslaughter and the accessory of manslaughter?

As will be seen, modern post-felony-murder case law has yet to provide unequivocal responses to these questions.

3. Agreement or Foresight?[45]

Although in most instances of what was (and often still is) described as 'aiding and abetting' there will have been an agreement which also constitutes a conspiracy, it is not an essential ingredient of this form of complicity.[46] Where there is no common purpose, the culpability of each participant must be determined separately.[47] Where a common purpose does exist, it is said that, broadly, each party is responsible for the acts of others carried out in pursuance of the agreement, but not responsible for those actions going beyond the agreement. Agreements may be 'express or tacit' and any consequential force or violence need have been no more than contingent upon certain events occurring.[48] The doctrine's many formulations are pervaded by a strong impression that action which goes outside what has been expressly or tacitly agreed will not incriminate an accessory, even if the collateral liability was actually foreseen by the accessory. This notion of the limitation of accessorial liability by agreement is consonant both with agency accounts of complicity and claims that at least 'consent' or

---

[45] See Ch. 7 for consideration of the issue in relation to 'variation'.
[46] *Kupferberg* (1918) 13 Cr. App. Rep. 166.
[47] *Abbott* (1955) AC 497; *King* v. *R.* (1963) AC 199.
[48] e.g. *Chan Wing-Siu* [1985] AC 168; and *Slack* [1989] 3 All ER 90; [1989] Crim. LR 903.

The Doctrine of Common Purpose 219

willingness as to the principal offence's commission is an essential component of all complicity liability.[49] But 'consent', as already argued, is probably no longer necessary, even if it has been in the past. The language of most modern common purpose case law, even before *Maxwell*, accommodates this fact by frequent references to 'contemplation' rather than simply to agreement.[50]

However, this is not true of all modern judicial expositions. In *Anderson and Morris*[51] and in *Lovesey and Peterson*[52] the judgments appear to suggest that common purpose liability rests on consensuality and that unauthorized actions in breach of such agreement would not incriminate other parties.

Anderson and Morris involved the fatal use of a knife by Anderson which Morris, his 'co-adventurer', claimed to be outside their common criminal design to beat up Welch without use of weapons. No part of the Court of Criminal Appeal's judgment includes any reference to what Morris foresaw or contemplated Anderson would do, rather the language is a combination of notions of authorization and causation. Lord Parker CJ accepted for the five-member court that

if one of the adventurers goes beyond what has been tacitly agreed as part of the common enterprise, his co-adventurer is not liable for the consequences of that unauthorised act [and] it is for the jury in every case to decide whether what was done was part of a joint enterprise, or went beyond it and was in fact an act unauthorised by that joint enterprise.[53]

Again, in *Lovesey and Peterson*, the judgment at no point poses or reflects on the question whether the fatal attack if not agreed to was at least foreseen by the party who did not actually inflict grievous harm. Instead there is repeated employment of the terms 'common purpose' and 'common

---

[49] See Ch. 5. Williams notes (*Textbook*, 354) that the supplier of a weapon expected to be used in a robbery 'may be indifferent to the question whether robbery is committed or not, or devoutly hope that it may not be, but he knows of the plan and that makes him an accessory'. Therefore for this and other reasons 'it is desirable to avoid the expression common purpose, and to speak instead of the contemplation of the alleged accessory'. However, puzzlingly, Williams later suggests (355) that the accessory 'D2 is not liable, if he believed that D1 [the principal] would not use such force [as actually used] or if the use of such force was specifically excluded by agreement between them (even though in the later case, D2 realised that D1, being an unreliable person, might possibly use it)'. Is it being implied that the position turns on whether accessory is present at the offence?

[50] See e.g. *Davies* v. *DPP* [1954] AC 378 at 401; *Betty* (1963) 48 Cr. App. Rep. 6 at 10; *Penfold* (1979) 71 Cr. App. Rep. 4 at 8, 9, 12; *Chan* [1985] AC 168 at 175–8.

[51] [1966] 2 QB 110.

[52] [1970] 1 QB 352. See also *Smith* [1963] 1 WLR 1200: 'Several persons . . . at the death of a man may be guilty of different degrees of crime—one murder, others of . . . manslaughter. Only he who intended that unlawful and grievous bodily harm should be done is guilty of murder. He who intended that the victim should be unlawfully hit and hurt would be guilty of manslaughter if death results' (Slade J. at 1205–6).

[53] [1966] 2 QB 110 at 118–19. See 120 for consideration of Lord Parker's resort to lack of causation as a ground for acquittal from liability for manslaughter.

design' with a concluding reference to liability being limited to 'authorised' acts.[54]

Subsequently the Privy Council' decision in *Chan Wing-Siu* went some way to (finally) settling the point, although distinct traces of confusion are still discernible in the continued use of consensus terminology. According to Sir Robin Cooke for the Privy Council,

> It should first be recalled that a person acting in concert with the primary offender may become a party to the crime, whether or not present at the time of its commission, by activities variously described as aiding, abetting, counselling, inciting or procuring it. In the typical case in that class, the same or the same type of offence is actually intended by all the parties acting in concert. In view of the terms of the directions to the jury here, the Crown does not seek to support the present convictions on that ground. The case must depend rather on the wider principle whereby a secondary party is criminally liable for acts by the primary offender of a type which the former foresees but does not necessarily intend.
>
> That there is such a principle is not in doubt. It turns on contemplation or putting the same idea in other words, authorisation, which may be express but is more usually implied. It meets the case of a crime foreseen as a possible incident of the common unlawful enterprise. The criminal culpability lies in participating in the venture with that foresight.[55]

Mystifying as it is for 'contemplation' to have been equated with 'authorisation', the repeated emphasis and use of the foresight formula throughout the judgment neutralizes Sir Robin's confused slide into the language of consensus.[56] Much the same may be said of the High Court of Australia's influential decision in *Johns* v. *R.*,[57] approvingly cited in *Chan*. Although each judgment is overwhelmingly approving of the universality of the foresight test in complicity, at one point Stephen J. briefly lapses into positing liability on 'what is contemplated, and both approve[d] of . . . and in some way encourage[d]'.[58]

---

[54] [1970] 1 QB 352 at 356. Both *Lovesey* and *Morris* were expressly followed by the Court of Appeal in *Dunbar* [1988] Crim. LR 693; as well as authorization, the court referred to the accessory's 'contemplation'.

[55] [1985] AC 168 at 175. Similarly in the New Zealand Court of Appeal cases of *Gush* [1980] 2 NZLR 92; *Hamilton* [1985] 2 NZLR 245 at 250, 'liability turns on contemplated albeit unwanted consequences'; and *Tomkins* [1985] 2 NZLR 253, and *Piri* [1987] 1 NZLR 66. Under the New Zealand Crimes Act 1961, s. 66 (1) sets out complicity requirements in respect of the 'primary' principal offence. Complicity in incidental or 'collateral' offences is dealt with under s. 66 (2). The distinction and relationships between the two provisions has yet to be clearly settled. See G. Orchard, 'Parties to an Offence' (1988) *NZLJ* 151. Cf. the similar scheme of liability under the Canadian Criminal Code. ss. 21 (1) and 21 (2) for aiders and abettors; ss. 22 (1) and 22 (2) for counsellors and procurers. See below, n. 109.

[56] *Anderson and Morris* was cited in support of the proposition set out by Sir Robin Cooke.

[57] (1980) 143 CLR 108. Affirmed in *Mills* (1986) 61 ALJR 59. In *Britten and Eger* (1988) 36 A. Crim. R. 48, the South Australian Court of Criminal Appeal declined to follow the *Johns/Chan* contemplation formula in all situations, maintaining that the broad underlying basis of liability was one of 'authorisation' (50–1). Cases involving the open carrying of lethal weapons, as in *Chan*, should be seen as 'implicit authorisation' (51).

[58] Ibid. 118; citing *Russell*, 12th edn., 151.

The Doctrine of Common Purpose

Alluding to the parties' 'express or tacit' agreement to use force is superfluous, tending to lead the enquiry away from the current universal test of foresight. This can be seen occurring in the Court of Appeal case of *Slack*,[59] where, though acknowledging the general applicability of the *Maxwell* principle, the court held to the language of the parties' agreement — 'expressly or tacitly' — to act violently if necessary. It is true that evidence of an agreement or arrangement to use force is, so to speak, evidence of foresight of its use. But employing consensus terminology implies that an accessory who is aware of his partner's possible use of force, *contrary* to an express understanding, would not share in criminal responsibility for it. The cross-over point in judicial reasoning may be that a party who foresees yet dreads the possible or contingent use of violence will be *deemed* to have 'tacitly' agreed to it by virtue of continuing his association with the venture.[60] If this is so, it is following circuitous reasoning likely to guarantee continued confusion. In situations, such as in *Slack*, where the use of deadly force by another is contingent upon the need arising, the accessory can be said to have the *mens rea* of murder,[61] albeit conditional; he consents or assents to harm if necessary; indeed, he may want it to be used. This may be contrasted with the partner in crime who merely foresees the possibility of deadly force being used and who neither wants it nor consents to it.

The underlying philosophy of modern English decisions — whether common purpose or not — is culpability through conscious risk taking. Consensual or authorizational theories of liability are not readily compatible with this philosophy.[62] The language of 'mandate' is inappropriate; liability in common purposes cases turns on general *mens rea*[63] complicity principles.

Linked to the question of consent or foresight is that of the nature of the relationship between the doctrine of common purpose and principles of variation, particularly the objective probable consequence version. For

---

[59] [1989] 3 All ER 90. Similarly in *Wakely* [1990] Crim. LR 119 where Lord Lane CJ was critical of the trial judge's 'concentrating on foreseeability rather that tacit agreement or understanding', even though in his view the concepts might be 'practically indistinguishable'. But cf. *Sharp* [1987] 3 All ER 103.

[60] As suggested in *Chan* 'The criminal culpability lies in participating in the venture with that foresight'. Ibid. 175. Two hypothetical cases may be compared: (i) A and P agree to rob V and to use any force necessary; (ii) A and P agree to rob V but with no more than slight force. If in (ii) A knows of P's very violent propensities and fears the worst yet the robbery goes ahead during which V is killed by P, should A be convicted of complicity in V's murder? Is his culpability distinctly less than in case (i)?

[61] *Hancock and Shankland* [1986] AC 455.

[62] Canadian Criminal Code, s. 21 (2), has been interpreted to require a true common intention between the parties to carry out the unlawful purpose. Each party is then liable for any offence which was or should have been known by the defendant to have been a probable consequence of carrying out such common design. *Wong* (No. 2) (1978) 41 CCC (2d) 196; and see Rose, *Parties*, 66–7. And also see below, n. 109. Similarly, under Scottish law, liability appears to be based on what parties ought to have foreseen as a likely consequence of what was agreed; thus each 'may be convicted of an offence he neither desired nor contemplated. The test is a mixture of subjectivity and objectivity: what was actually agreed, and was the outcome objectively foreseeable?' Gordon, *Criminal Law*, 149–50. Cf. *Boyne* v. *HMA* 1980 SLT 56.

whether or not some form of consensus is necessary for complicity in respect of the criminal objective, the effects of principal variation from that objective (whether just foreseen or agreed to by the accessory) still require consideration.

4. COMMON PURPOSE AND VARIATION

As already seen, traditionally the terminology of common purpose has been invoked in cases where the secondary party has been an abettor and the principal has voluntarily departed from what the abettor agreed to or foresaw and committed an offence collateral to the parties' common primary purpose. The collateral offence will typically be fostered or facilitated by agreed conduct leading to commission of the primary offence, and usually of a more serious nature. Contrastingly, variation problems, rather than being concerned with whether an accessory should be responsible for a different or more serious offence than originally anticipated, instead centre on involuntary or voluntary changes in the subject-matter or victim of the parties' criminal objective, or on changes in the mode of performance of such an offence. Usually, as noted in *Variations in Performance*, questions of liability relating to these types of change have arisen where the secondary party was an accessory before the fact.

There is, however, nothing inherent in the nature of the paradigm common purpose problem of 'excessive' criminality that could not, circumstances permitting, manifest itself where there has been no common purpose and where the accessory is not present at the commission of the offence. For example,

A, a dealer in guns, knowing of *P*'s criminal plans, sells *P* a shotgun subsequently used in a robbery in which *A* has no part. If, in the course of the robbery, a resisting bank employee is shot dead by *P*, then *A*'s liability for the killing stands to be determined on the same principles as would have been the case if *A* had been part of a common purpose to rob and present at the offence.

Of course, both the common design to rob and[64] *A*'s presence would have evidential implications in establishing the necessary accessorial *mens rea*, but the ultimate substantive question of foresight would be the same.[65] In

---

[63] Also argued by Burchell and Hunt, *SA Criminal Law*, 431–2. Similarly Snyman, *Criminal Law*, 212–13. See also Ch. 3 n. 33 above.

[64] Common design or purpose will usually precede 'abetting', but it is not essential for an abettor may, without prior arrangement, join in and assist the already active principal; *Mohan v. R.* [1967] 2 AC 187. See R. C. Whiting, 'Joining In' (1986) 103 *SALJ* 38 and Ch. 3. n. 33, for discussion of SA case law and principles. Conversely, there may be a common purpose—a conspiracy—between *A* and *P* whereby *P* will execute the offence alone and unassisted by *A*. Here there is, in one sense, an accessory before the fact and a common purpose.

[65] See Ch. 2 (3) (4), for the effect of conspiracy on accessorial liability.

Maxwell the appellant was, effectively, both an 'abettor' to the offence of possessing explosive substances[66] and an 'accessory before the fact' to the second offence of placing a bomb on the targeted premises;[67] there was no suggestion by the House of Lords that liability for each separate count be determined on different principles.

By the same token, facts allowing, there may be a change of victim or subject-matter, or variation in the mode of performance, where all parties to the offence are present (executing the common purpose) which may be accidental, mistaken, or voluntary.[68] For example,

during the course of a burglary by *A* and *P* aimed at stealing only a particular bag of uncut diamonds, *P* deliberately helps himself to a handful of pearls, having already mistakenly disabled the wrong security guard by (contrary to prior arrangements) using a cosh instead of chloroform.

Determining the responsibility of *A* for each of *P*'s undesired actions will be subject to the same conceptual difficulties as experienced in respect of absent (and non-purposeful) accessories. Again, evidential inferences may differ, or operate only where the accessory is present at the offence's commission, but the substantive rules of variation should be common to all accessories — present or otherwise.

Whether or not Foster's complementary substantial variation and probable consequence theories are accepted, he expressly recognized that although most variation cases would involve accessories before the fact the rules had similar relevance to abetting.[69] This has been implicitly accepted from time to time by various modern authorities. In *Betts and Ridley*, for example, Foster was taken as relevant not only to both abettors and accessories, but also to the question of 'excessive' criminality which the Court of Criminal Appeal saw as a matter of mere variation in the 'manner of execution' of the primary criminal objective.[70] More recently, in *Bainbridge*, Lord Parker took Foster's substantial variation rule as consistent with and illustrative of the lack of any need for a secondary party

---

[66] Second count, [1978] 1 WLR 1350, at 1352.

[67] Ibid., first count. The count particulars of this offence are misleading; the report reveals that Maxwell had left the scene of the offence several minutes before the bomb was planted (1365). Their lordships used the expression 'aiding and abetting' throughout in a general sense; although Lord Scarman e.g. used the term 'accessory' at one point (1363).

[68] In cases such as *Saunders and Archer*, where there has been a miscarrying of the criminal plan, the presence or absence of the *principal* has been seen by some commentators (such as the code team in Law Commission Report 177, para. 9.30) as crucial to the question of accessorial liability: the principal's inactive presence at the miscarrying event converted the involuntary change into a voluntary one. The presence or absence of the *accessory* in similar circumstances would be irrelevant to liability for that turns on the characterizing of the *principal's* actions as voluntary or involuntary.

[69] *Crown Law*, 369, s. 2.

[70] (1930) 22 Cr. App. Rep. 148 at 155. The same classificatory exercise was carried out in *Appleby* (1940) 28 Cr. App. Rep. 1 at 6–8.

to know the insubstantial details of the offence that the principal ultimately committed.[71]

Categorization of issues according to the scope of the common purpose (where there is one), or whether the variation is substantial or not, fails to reveal the underlying theoretical similarities and dissimilarities between the two groups of problems. As some decisions suggest, there is a degree of appreciation that the problems sometimes overlap but not that two quite distinct poles of responsibility (and their own particular requirements) are involved. What has yet to be clearly articulated is that solutions to difficulties which, in one way or another, relate to the principal acting in some way not desired or foreseen by the accessory, are properly viewed as revolving around either causal or *mens rea* requirements, or both. In the case of common purpose, failure to separate these two elements is a legacy from earlier times when the doctrine of common purpose constituted a virtually indivisible amalgam of the *mens rea* and *actus reus* requirements of complicity for abettors.

Causation's role[72] and relevance (as well as that of *mens rea*) in resolving such difficulties is a question that has already surfaced in a sprinkling of appeal cases,[73] and most importantly in *Anderson and Morris* and *Reid*. In the former case, Lord Parker CJ for the Court of Criminal Appeal, dealing with the issue of an accessory's liability for manslaughter when the principal was convicted of murder, declared that there could be no accessorial liability for the killing because the fatal act was unauthorized and no part of the joint enterprise: a *mens rea* account of the accessory's lack of responsibility.[74] However, in concluding his judgment Lord Parker for good measure threw in an alternative, *obiter*,[75] explanation of the 'accessory's absence of liability:

There is nothing really illogical in such a result, in that it could well be said as a matter of common sense that . . . death resulted or was [wholly] caused by the [unauthorized] sudden actions of the adventurer who decided to kill and killed. Considered as a matter of causation there may well be an overwhelming supervening event which is of such a character that it will relegate into history matters which would otherwise be looked upon as causative factors.[76]

---

[71] (1960) 1 QB 129, at 134; noted with apparent approval by Lowery LCJ in *DPP for Northern Ireland* v. *Maxwell* (1978) 1 WLR 1350, at 1373. See also *Johns* v. *R.* (1980) 143 CLR 108, at 122.
[72] See Ch. 7, for consideration of alternative causal claims in connection with 'variation'.
[73] Cf. the early decisions in *Caton* (1874) 12 Cox 624 and *Duffy* (1830) 1 Lew. 194, 168 ER 1009.
[74] Purporting to follow *Smith* (1963) 1 WLR 1200 and *Betty* (1964) 48 Cr. App. Rep. 6. The exact nature of this is debatable; see below.
[75] Lord Parker began the paragraph after his reference to causation with 'Be that as it may' and then noted that the court would follow earlier authorities, such as *Smith*.
[76] [1966] 2 QB 110 at 120.

It may be that the concepts of 'substantial' variation and 'overwhelming supervening event' are close relatives, if not exactly the same thing; both aim to quantify the degree of deviation of action possible by the principal before freeing the accessory of any causal responsibility.

Subsequently, Lord Parker's remarks were taken up by the Court of Appeal to form part of the *ratio* in *Reid*. Here the fatal firing of a revolver by the principal, expected by the accessory to be used only to threaten the victim, was characterized by the Court of Appeal as no more than a 'mere unforeseen consequence of an unlawful act' of joint possession of the gun. The shooting was not 'an overwhelming supervening event' that freed the accessory of causal responsibility.[77] What these two cases failed to do was expressly to split the question before the court: was there both accessorial *mens rea* (or other fault element) and proof of a causal contribution from the accessory's actions? To restate the matter in fundamental terms: for complicity in homicide (as in any other offence) there must always be culpability and cause; in the absence of one or the other there can be no complicity; if there is a causal contribution from the accessory, then whether he is an accessory to murder or manslaughter turns on his own level of fault.

Overall, then, whether manifesting itself as a question of 'variation' or common purpose, accessorial liability for the principal's actions may be prevented by either lack of *mens rea* or causal requirements, or both. Clearer recognition of this offers an opportunity to resolve the English case law dispute over the appropriateness of convicting an accessory of manslaughter when the principal is guilty of murder or manslaughter by having gone beyond the 'common purpose'. The particular question is now considered.

5. Convicting the Errant Principal of Murder or Manslaughter and the Accessory of Manslaughter[78]

In England, over the last twenty years or so, two diverging bodies of case law have become established, each providing a different answer to the question of when, in cases of murder or manslaughter, a 'secondary party'

---

[77] (1968) 62 Cr. App. Rep. 109 at 112. See also *Penfold* (1979) 71 Cr. App. Rep. 4. The Court of Appeal's certified point of law of general public importance was: 'Where a person jointly with others takes part in a robbery during the course of which a killing takes place as a result of violence used by other parties to the robbery, is it necessary for the judge expressly to direct the jury that before they can convict of manslaughter they must be satisfied that the actions of the killer or killers were a consequence, albeit unforeseen, of the carrying out of the joint plan to rob and did not amount to supervening causative events wholly outside the scope of the agreed plan?' (12). The Court of Criminal Appeal decision in *Garforth* (1954) Crim. LR 936 appears to be one where the accessory's liability for manslaughter was through a *direct* causal contribution; thus making him a joint principal in one sense.

[78] See Ch. 4 for consideration of the general implications for the theory of derivativeness of differentials between principal and accessory liability.

should be convicted of manslaughter although the principal has acted outside the 'common purpose'. Judicial consideration of the issue has been handicapped by a combination of uncertainty over the relationship of the doctrine of common purpose and complicity's general *mens rea* requirements, together with confusion concerning the question's twin dimensions (*mens rea* and causal), compounded by lack of any (at least) tacit agreement over the most desirable penal policy to be pursued in such cases. The core question reduces to what, if anything, must the errant principal do to completely absolve the 'accessory' from any responsibility for the principal's homicidal actions?

The first significant decision in the cluster of relevant cases is *Smith*, where the principal was convicted of manslaughter by stabbing his victim in the course of a fight. Smith, the accessory, although aware of the principal's possession of the knife, denied being a party to any concerted action with its use. According to the Court of Criminal Appeal, the broad principle of liability was that 'anything which is within the ambit of the concerted arrangement is the responsibility of each party who chooses to enter into the criminal purpose'.[79] Awareness of the principal's possession and possible intended use of the knife made Smith a party to its use, but only for manslaughter as he lacked the necessary *mens rea* for murder.[80] The scope of the concerted action here was never set out by the court — nor did it explain how it was to be determined. As Smith was convicted of manslaughter it must be inferred that he did not contemplate the intended infliction of grievous bodily harm by the principal. In *Betty*,[81] a case with similar facts, counsel for the appellant advanced the argument that

> If the perpetrator of a fatal attack with a knife had malice aforethought, and therefore was guilty of murder, an accomplice who lacked such could not be convicted of even manslaughter as the perpetrator had gone beyond the scope of the concerted action.

Though 'attractive', Lord Parker CJ saw the court in *Smith* as having already rejected such a claim. The principal 'had not exceeded the bounds of the common purpose'. Here the concerted action was a 'knife attack' but one falling short of the use of a knife in deadly manner.[82] In effect, Lord Parker was maintaining that the accessory's responsibility was not erased by the principal acting beyond what the accessory foresaw, since foresight

---

[79] [1963] 1 WLR 1200 at 1207. Cf. *Spraggatt* [1960] Crim. LR 840 and *Murtagh and Kennedy* (1955) 39 Cr. App. Rep. 72. Why in the latter case was the driver's intention to run down the victim not such as to remove the action from the common purpose to drive close by? See *Betty* (1963) 48 Cr. App. Rep. 6.

[80] Arguably the ruling in *Smith* was overgenerous in suggesting that a party could not be an accessory to murder unless they 'intended' the principal to inflict at least serious harm; contemplation of the possibility of such action should be sufficient.

[81] (1963) 48 Cr. App. Rep. 6. The headnote is misleading, as acknowledged in *Anderson and Morris*.

[82] Ibid. at 10.

The Doctrine of Common Purpose

governs only the accessory's level of culpability and not the scope of the common purpose which determines whether the accessory is *completely* free of liability for the principal's fatal action. Arguably it is this element in the doctrine of common purpose which enables an accessory to be convicted of manslaughter because, whilst not having the culpability for murder, he was still in some way *causally* responsible for the fatal act. And in such cases the fault element for involuntary manslaughter is present — whether of the unlawful act or 'gross negligence' variety. According to *Smith* and *Betty*, once *any* use of a knife is contemplated by an accessory, manslaughter liability is inevitable as the death is always a possibility.

The Court of Criminal Appeal returned to the question three years later in *Anderson and Morris*.[83] In seeking a basis for liability the court accepted

> that if one of the adventurers goes beyond what has been tacitly agreed as part of the common enterprise, his co-adventurer is not liable for the consequences of the unauthorised act. [I]t is for the jury in every case to decide whether what was done was part of the joint enterprise, or went beyond it and was in fact unauthorised by the joint enterprise.[84]

In contrast with *Smith* and *Betty*, this and other parts[85] of the judgment may imply that an accessory will be free of *any* responsibility for a killing where the principal's murderous intent is not contemplated by the accessory. In addition to this *mens rea* account of the basis of an accessory's liability, Lord Parker, as already noted, invoked a causal explanation under which an 'overwhelming supervening event' will also free an accessory from any responsibility for the death. Quite what degree of principal deviation must occur to qualify as 'overwhelming' is not indicated. However, the implication that absence of cause necessarily means a complete absence of the homicide liability for 'accessories' must be correct. It is on this basis that the case law *may* be reconcilable.

When purporting to apply *Anderson*, the court in *Lovesey and Peterson* held that where a common design to inflict less than grievous bodily harm exists, and the principal 'goes beyond the scope of that design by using violence which is intended to cause grievous bodily harm, the others are not responsible'.[86] However, rather than ground this exclusion from all homicide liability on lack of causal attributability, the court appeared to base it on the absence of 'authority' to so act. This runs counter to *Smith*,

---

[83] [1966] 2 QB 110. As in *Smith*, a court of 5 judges.
[84] Ibid. at 118–19.
[85] Particularly at 120. The inconclusive state of the case law is not referred to in Law Commission Report 177, para. 9.26; the commentary begs the question exactly *what* is 'the effect of the cases' on the scope of common purpose? See Report ex. 28 (iv) which suggests that under the code provisions the accessory would not be liable for manslaughter as he did not intend to assist or encourage *that act* (see cl. 27 (1) (a)), but the accessory might still be a party to an assault. It is not obvious, though, how that clause would permit conviction for even an assault if the 'act' was not attributable to the 'accessory' for homicide purposes.
[86] [1970] 1 QB 352 at 356.

Betty, and possibly *Anderson and Morris* which arguably only supports a complete acquittal for homicide where there is no accessorial causal contribution.

The distinction between a 'mere unforeseen ... act' and an 'overwhelming supervening event' was expressly recognized by the Court of Appeal in *Reid*.[87] An act would be merely unforeseen — and therefore capable of convicting the accessory of manslaughter — if the joint enterprise had 'envisaged some degree of violence, albeit nothing more than causing fright' with 'offensive weapons such as revolvers or knives'.[88] This is consistent with *Smith* and *Betty*, and with the separable roles played by *mens rea* and causation.[89] However subsequently in *Dunbar*[90] the Court of Appeal expressly adopted the approach set out in *Anderson and Morris* and *Lovesey and Peterson*. Here it was accepted that where the defendant was a party to an agreement to inflict some harm less than grievous bodily harm, and the principal acted outside this design and intentionally inflicted fatal injuries, then the defendant was guilty of neither murder nor manslaughter. Yet, whilst following *Anderson* and *Lovesey* in excluding all homicide liability, rather than straightforwardly employing the language of authorization the Court of Appeal grounded potential complicity on what was either 'authorised' or contemplated; furthermore, no explicit reference is made to *Anderson*'s complementary causal explanation.

These vacillating judicial views leave three sizeable problems unresolved. 1. What role, if any, in limiting the 'accessory's' liability has the notion of authorized actions as distinct from foreseen actions? 2. How, or on what basis, can an inculpatory 'mere unforeseen ... act' be distinguished from the exculpating 'overwhelming supervening event'? 3. What relevance to liability, if any, has the carrying of weapons by the principal party?

(1) *Authorized or Foreseen Actions?*

This aspect of *mens rea* has already been considered; see *Agreement or Foresight?* above for the arguments and conclusions.

(2) *Unforeseen and 'Overwhelming Supervening Events'*

The second question partly entails a more general consideration of the role of cause and complicity, but for present purposes it may be suggested that

---

[87] (1976) 62 Cr. App. Rep. 109 at 112.

[88] Ibid. Unlike in *Smith* and *Betty*, the court in *Reid* drew no distinction, in effect, between the carrying of knives and firearms. *Reid* was cited with approval in *Tomkins* (1985) 2 NZLR 253 at 254–5.

[89] In *Penfold* (1979) 71 Cr. App. Rep. 4 the Court of Appeal again appeared to accept this distinction. See also the New Zealand Court of Appeal's review in *Tomkins* of the theoretical basis of manslaughter verdicts in complicity where a causal theory was advanced by the court's *amicus curiae* (at 255). *Chan Wing-Siu* raises the question of liability for murder only.

[90] [1988] Crim. LR 693. See also *Smith* [1988] Crim. LR 616 and *Barr* (1989) 88 Cr. App. Rep. 362.

the solution corresponds with that proposed for deliberate variation cases: was the principal acting uninfluenced and independently of the 'accessory's' assistance or encouragement? The questions and answers in variation and common purpose cases are the same, differing only in perspective and emphasis. In both situations the test seeks to answer the same central causal question: in what circumstances will the perpetrator be solely responsible for his actions? In variation issues the test of voluntariness and independence of the perpetrator's actions is, so to speak, 'tailor made' for complicity, whereas the 'overwhelming supervening event' formulation applied in common purpose situations has more obvious currency in certain non-complicity areas of causal attribution.

However, this leads to the possible contention that, in this context, rather than as an accessory to manslaughter, the 'accessory's' liability is better viewed as principal in nature, turning on general causal rules relevant to homicide. It may be no coincidence that Lord Parker's formulation of his causal principle in *Anderson and Morris* strongly resembles that set out in the general homicide case of *Smith*.[91] Moreover, in *Reid* Lawton LJ cited the non-complicity manslaughter case of *Larkin* in support of a manslaughter conviction.[92] Under general rules of causation an 'accessory's' action would be a cause of death if 'it made more than a negligible contribution to its occurrence'.[93] Lord Parker's formulation represents a causal principle most obviously applicable to *novus actus* circumstances — whether medical treatment or actions of a third party adventurer. The indirect relationship of the accessory's action and the cause of death raises problems of proximity. It is unclear just how far courts might be prepared to go in adopting this approach to convict a 'secondary party' of manslaughter. Some indication is provided by the Court of Appeal in *Reid* where it was emphasized that the appellant simply accompanying the armed principal to the victim's house, though 'grossly and utterly negligent', was not an adequate basis on which to convict him of manslaughter.[94] Instead, conviction properly rested on the unlawful joint possession with the perpetrator of the offensive weapons and the intention to use them for 'causing fright'.[95] Such reasoning circumvents complicity's basic culpability requirement of subjective foresight of the perpetrator's actions. This is more a consequence of manslaughter's wide and low sweep and, therefore, an issue of involuntary manslaughter's general legitimacy, rather than inadequacy of complicity doctrine.

---

[91] [1959] 2 QB 35 at 42–3. See Ch. 6 (5), and Ch. 4 (2) (5).
[92] (1976) 62 Cr. App. Rep. 109 at 112. *Larkin* (1943) 29 Cr. App. Rep. 18.
[93] Law Commission Report 177, cl. 17 (1) (*a*) restatement. However, the effect of cl. 17 (3), if enacted, might prevent incrimination via this route. See Report commentary para. 7.19.
[94] But cf. *Melvin* v. *HMA* 1984 SCCR 113 at 117.
[95] (1976) 62 Cr. App. Rep. 109 at 112. The court's slightly earlier formulation of the grounds of liability excluded the foresight of 'causing fright' and was based only on 'the unlawful and dangerous act of being in joint possession of offensive weapons' (at 112).

(3) Relevance of Weapons

The third outstanding question concerns whether possession of weapons involves evidential presumptions as to the parties' intentions or even substantive effects on liability. As with most other features relating to common purpose, here both case law and deducible theory are obscure. To return to the underlying issue: what conduct was agreed to or foreseen by the parties and were the principal's actions within the scope of this 'common design'? Where the parties, in order to achieve a particular common objective, anticipate the use of all necessary force to achieve such ends (or, in the time-honoured phrase beloved of generations of trial and appellate judges, where there is a 'resolution to resist all opposers')[96] then each party will be fully responsible for any level of violence perpetrated in pursuance of the common objective — even though not specifically foreseen. It is a form of complicity liability based on the 'blank cheque' given by each party to the others. Such a state of affairs may be inferred from the nature of the criminal objective and surrounding circumstances. Therefore if, for example, particular gold bullion is known to be always stored under the control of armed guards, it would be a virtually irresistible conclusion that killing a guard during the robbery was a possibility anticipated by all parties.

At a more particular level, several possibilities arise as to degrees of force or violence anticipated by parties. In cases where there is a common expectation of weaponless violence, the uncontemplated use of a weapon will not render other parties liable.[97] But this cannot be more than a prima-facie inference drawn to determine the level of violence contemplated by the accessory, for punches or kicks may be calculated to kill or severely injure.[98] If the accessory had knowledge of the principal's possession of the weapon actually used then there will obviously be a powerful implication that the possibility of such use was at least foreseen. But the accessory's knowledge of possession only provides an evidential inference of the necessary foresight of use. This point is recognized in most modern authorities including *Smith* and *Betty*.[99] However, if *any* sort of use is contemplated then *dicta* in *Reid* very closely approach laying down the rigid rule that where there is a joint venture involving the possession[100] of 'offensive weapons such as revolvers and knives', which 'envisaged some degree of violence, albeit nothing more

---

[96] e.g. *Tyler* (1835) 8 Car. & P. 616; 173 ER 643, and *Lovesey and Peterson* [1970] 1 QB 110.
[97] *Davies* v. *DPP* [1954] AC 378 at 401; *Caton* (1874) 12 Cox 624.
[98] Cf. *Williams and Blackwood* (1973) 21 WIR 329 at 340.
[99] See also *Skeet* (1866) 4 F. & F. 931, 176 ER 854; and Working Paper 43, 55, illustrations *d* and *e*.
[100] The judgment refers to 'joint possession' of weapons. It is difficult to see a principled distinction between one weapon carried with the knowledge of other parties and cases where each is equipped with a weapon; except that it might be said that the more heavily armed the group the stronger the presumption is of intended use. Cf. Law Commission Report 177, ex. 27 (v)

than causing fright, they will be guilty of [at least] manslaughter' because in such circumstances there is 'always a likelihood that, in the excitement and tensions of the occasion, one of them will use his weapon in some way which will cause death or serious injury'.[101] Effectively, because in such cases it is objectively obvious that harm is always likely, the parties will be *deemed* to have foreseen the risk of harm.

The approach in *Reid*, of turning strong evidential inferences into irresistible presumptions of foresight, was not adopted in *Penfold*. At one point the Court of Appeal firmly recognized the need for realism in inferring what the parties contemplated:

Robbers who burst into a house can hardly fail to contemplate the probable necessity of some degree of force to overcome or silence the occupants. While they may not desire to inflict any real harm they do agree, by implication, to put themselves under the dictates of any arising necessity.[102]

However, the court later confirmed the need for the jury to be 'satisfied that some real harm was contemplated' by the parties to be guilty of manslaughter.[103] Finally, though restricted to complicity in murder, the Privy Council observations in *Chan*[104] are pertinent. Here it was suggested that if a risk of killing or serious bodily harm 'has crossed the [accessory's] mind' it may still be foreseen as so remote a possibility as to be criminally 'negligible'. But, if the accessory 'knew that lethal weapons' were to be carried then it would be improper to accept any risk as 'negligible' except 'very rarely'.[105]

Quite how far courts *ought* to venture, in converting matters of evidence as to individual foresight into what amount to substantive rules and constructive forms of complicity, is an important element in the broader issue of desirable policy pursuits and the formulas best adopted for achieving them.[106] These matters are now considered.

6. COMMON PURPOSE AND POLICY OBJECTIVES

Reviewing the origins and operation of common purpose has raised two related issues: the function and continued use of the language of common

---

[101] (1976) 62 Cr. App. Rep. 109 at 112. Cf. the uncertainty in Scotland over whether certain similar rules are substantive or evidential. Gordon, *Criminal Law*, 161.

[102] (1979) 71 Cr. App. Rep. 4 at 8. No weapons were involved in this case.

[103] Ibid. at 12. Cf. *Sharp* [1987] 3 All ER 103, where not wishing to participate in a robbery in which he knew weapons might be used did not prevent the defendant's conviction for manslaughter.

[104] [1985] 1 AC 168; see Ch. 6 (2).

[105] [1985] 1 AC 179. Neither *Chan* nor other authorities make clear whether the standard of foresight for the *possession* of weapons must be higher than the perceived likelihood (a mere possibility) that an offence might take place. *Chan*, along with other cases, refers to 'knowledge' that weapons were to be carried. Cf. *Britten and Eger* (1988) 36 A. Crim. R. 48 at 51 and *Wakely* [1990] Crim. LR 119.

[106] See Ch. 6 (7).

purpose, and whether the fault level for offences collateral to the main objective or primary offence of the criminal association is, and should be, less than it would be if it were the primary objective.

The doctrine and language of common purpose have in the past facilitated, if not actually generated, much confusion over quite what mental culpability accessories needed to have for the primary criminal objective in any joint enterprise. It has also served to obscure the nature or basis of liability for collateral offences. Common purpose terminology has been instrumental in suggesting that express or implicit consent or agreement between the parties is the basis of liability. However true that may formerly have been, it is probably no longer the case in English law. Consequently, employment of the language of consensus, rather than foresight, is outmoded, misleading, and confusing. Recognition of this would offer a more promising starting-point for resolving the overlapping cluster of problems concerning the accessory's responsibility for either variational or collateral action. Not only is there 'no magic'[107] in the doctrine of common purpose, it is an historical relic whose continued, albeit half-hearted, employment is an easily avoided nuisance in an area of the criminal law of considerable inherent complexity.

As has been seen, paradoxically, the doctrine of common purpose has played host to two features, one of which operates to expand the ambit of complicity whilst the other acts to restrict liability. This latter effect follows from the consensual implications of the very notion of a joint venture and runs strongly counter to the subjectively perceived risk rationale established in *Maxwell* and *Bainbridge*. The opposite effect would (theoretically) follow from open adoption of some form of constructive or imputed liability for collateral offences, along the lines of the objectively foreseeable consequence rule. Although clearly[108] not the current position in English law, the approach's strong appeal is evidenced by its place in many jurisdictions including Canada,[109] a number of American states,[110] and some Australian

---

[107] Burchell and Hunt, *SA Criminal Law*, 430.

[108] Cf. Lanham [1980] 4 *Crim. LJ* 78 at 83–5.

[109] See the Canadian Criminal Code ss. 21 (2) and 22 (2) and Rose, *Parties*, 73–8 and 139–44. The test of objective probability has been found to be contrary to 'principles of fundamental justice' under s. 7 of the Canadian Charter of Rights and Freedoms (1982). In place of an objective standard a *subjective* one has to be substituted. *Logan* (1988) 46 CCC (3d) 354. The differential still survives in a greatly reduced degree in that the principal criminal objective must be assisted or encouraged purposefully, whereas the collateral offence need only be foreseen as probable.

[110] See e.g. *US* v. *Clayborne* 509 F. 2d 473 (1974) and *Johnson* v. *US* 386 A. 2d 710 (1978). Although varying in their formulations, those states with code provisions incorporating objective tests for collateral liability include Arkansas s. 41–303, Iowa s. 703.2, Kansas s. 21–3205, and Wisconsin s. 939.05 (2) (c); all of which run counter to the MPC s. 2.06 (3) (1962) requiring the same mental culpability for collateral offences as for primary ones. See the rejection of such liability in the code commentary. TD 1 (1953), 26, and revised commentary (1985) 311–13.

codes.[111] Such provisions involve a consciously constructed differential in respect of the necessary level of culpability for an offence, determined by whether it was primary or collateral to the parties' complicity.

The supporting penal philosophy for this variety of constructive liability is, like felony-murder[112] or involuntary manslaughter, one of the qualifying criminality of the primary objective being used to impute to the defendant responsibility for another (usually more serious) collateral offence. And, as in other forms of constructive liability, it constitutes an exception or qualification to the standard basis governing (complicitous) imputability. This commonality of reasoning follows through into the practical justifying grounds for the different varieties of constructive responsibility. At its broadest, it is aimed at denying actors (in certain criminal offences) the power to control the extent of their criminality by their own narrow criminal objectives or perceptions of the risks entailed in the venture. Within limits, engaging in criminal activity is made an additionally hazardous occupation; a particular manifestation of chance[113] which operates in the criminal law against the secondary actor to swell his overall liability. In complicity's case the obvious and sometimes expressed[114] policy is to deter people from forming criminal alliances, most particularly 'with unreliable psychopaths, or from taking part in any enterprise in which weapons are carried'.[115] Or, with greater Holmesian felicity: to 'throw on the actor the peril, not only of the consequences foreseen by him, but also of consequences... predicted by common experience'.[116] Additionally, it might be maintained that those participating in criminal combinations will, because of their responsibility for the wayward behaviour of co-participants, exercise greater restraint or supervision over their conduct. Moreover, it can be fairly claimed that, besides this negligence-based culpability, the accessory will have, in some sense, increased the likelihood of the collateral offence by his earlier involvement.

Against these legitimate grounds for supporting some form of constructive collateral liability, a stronger opposing case can be made out favouring the (probable) current English position. First, the general use of (for instance) Foster's probable consequence principle would mark a double

---

[111] See Gillies, *Criminal Complicity*, 109–20 and Lanham, 'Accomplices and Constructive Liability'. During the 1950s SA law moved from a generally objective standard of liability to a generally subjectively based one. See Rabie (1971) 88 SALJ 227 and Burchell and Hunt, *SA Criminal Law*, 430–6. But cf. e.g. *S. v. Nhiri* 1976 (2) SA 789 (RAD), and Whiting (1986) 103 SALJ 38, on the causal issues thrown up by resort to common purpose reasoning in most killings.

[112] Cf. the special evidential provisions in some US state codes where felony-murder exists, under which it is a defence to complicity in felony-murder if (broadly) the accessory could not in the circumstances have reasonably foreseen the fatal attack. This provision puts liability on a negligence basis subject to the reversal of onus of proof. See the states listed by Robinson, 'Imputed Criminal Liability', 667.

[113] See Ch. 3 for the considerable potential of the role of chance in complicity.

[114] e.g. Pollock CB in *Skeet*, and Lord Alverstone in *Rubens* (cit. n. 26).

[115] Gordon, *Criminal Law*, 150.

[116] O. W. Holmes, *The Common Law* (1881), 59. The original sense of the extract has been modified to fit the context.

departure from usual complicity culpability requirements under English law. For example, A and P agreed to steal the contents of a coin-operated gas meter by P carefully levering the appropriate part open with a jemmy while A remains outside keeping watch. Failing to open the meter in the agreed way, P batters it apart with the jemmy and at the same time ruptures the gas pipe. Predictably, the escaped gas later explodes causing extensive damage to the building and injuries to the occupants. To make A liable for criminal damage to the building as well as burglary would involve responsibility for the unforeseen (but probable) actions of P without satisfying usual *mens rea* and other complicity demands. Of course, the extent of derogation from standard complicity requirements and its practical effect on the convictability of an accessory will turn on the knowledge or information imputed to the accessory because he *ought* to have been aware of it. If, say, A's chosen partner in crime, P, is a kleptomaniac with a particular weakness for jewellery, would A be a party to theft from a house jointly visited for the purpose of killing or harming the owner?[117] Arguably P's strong susceptibilities make his action more foreseeable, but if the test were one where only the nature of the joint offence dictates what would be a probable consequence, and important subsidiary factors including the propensities of parties are ignored, then the practical effect of the objective test would be likely to be far less than might at first appear.[118] Furthermore, in most situations where the evidence is strong enough to support the conclusion that what occurred was an objectively foreseeable consequence, it will be equally so to the accessory — or at least a court would be likely to infer this.

Beyond these arguments, there is the objection that the (re)recognition of a probable consequence basis of liability would be at odds with the steady movement towards subjectivizing criminal liability (outside regulatory offences), particularly illustrated by the abolition of felony-murder, and by other efforts to restrict the role of chance and imputed culpability, such as proposals for abolition of involuntary manslaughter and its replacement by a subjectively-based form of homicide.[119] Moreover, it is arguable that for the various reasons considered in earlier chapters examining the *mens rea* of complicity, the boundaries of secondary liability have expanded in recent times to take in the reckless and disinterested accessory. This being so, recognition of subjectively foreseeable risk liability acting as the substantive springboard[120] for objectively foreseeable risk liability would need especially strong justifying grounds.

[117] Assuming that the offences are *not* of the same 'type'.
[118] This is something not clear from Foster's test, nor from Stephen's version of it. Here the theft is probable but not 'natural' in any sense of occurring in the normal course of events.
[119] e.g. the Criminal Law Review Committee, 14th Report, paras. 88–94.
[120] The Canadian Law Reform Commission Report 31 (1987) proposals concerning complicity preserve the notion of qualifying or 'springboard' criminality in that the new offence of 'furthering' requires purposeful action but the furtherer will also be liable for 'any crime which he knows is a probable consequence of such agreement or furthering': s. 4 (6) (c).

III

Exclusion, Limitation, and Withdrawal

Although both *actus reus* and *mens rea* demands have been met, the presence of other pertinent factors may operate to exclude or limit the 'accessory's' liability.

Chapter 9 considers three ways or techniques for excluding or limiting complicity: through construing the offence's enacting statute as excluding inevitable incidental participation; on the grounds of the 'accessory's' law enforcement motives for acting; and possible limitations against multiple offence complicity based on a single complicitous act.

Chapter 10 examines the applicability of general defences to secondary offenders and the rationale and requirements of the special defence of withdrawal.

9

Exclusion and Limitation of Complicity

Certain circumstances or features external to secondary liability's general principles may operate to exclude or limit its reach. Because of the presence of such circumstances or special features, an 'accessory', who otherwise satisfies complicity requirements, will be free of complicity liability. Two distinct categories of exempting circumstances are identifiable. The first rests on statutory construction excluding from incrimination the inevitable incidental involvement of a secondary party demanded by the definition of specific offences. The second grants exemption on the basis of the 'accessory's' laudable law enforcement motivation. However, the full scope of these excluding conditions and the policy rationale of each resist easy or confident restatement. A third, but unrelated, limitation issue concerns an accessory's potential liability for a whole series of offences carried out with assistance derived from a single complicitous act.

1. Inevitable Incidental Participation

The enactment of any crime implicitly carries the potential for secondary liability in the offence. As already seen, this presumption holds true even where definitional requirements for a principal specify characteristics or a status not necessarily possessed by a secondary party.[1] Moreover, while the nature of most crimes is such that the willing and informed involvement of another party is always a possibility, it will not be a necessary ingredient of the offence's commission. However, some crimes necessarily entail the participation of more than one principal party or perpetrator—as is so, for example, in conspiracy and offences under the Public Order Act. Distinguishable from such offences are other forms of multi-party liability where the necessary role performed by one participant is passive, supportive, or secondary to that of the perpetrator. In these cases courts

[1] Cf. Model Penal Code, s. 2.06 (5): 'A person who is legally incapable of committing a particular offence himself may be guilty thereof if it is committed by the conduct of another person for which he is legally accountable, unless such liability is inconsistent with the purpose of the provision establishing his incapacity.'

have, on rare occasions, construed the underlying legislative intent as limiting criminality to the principal actor and excluding from liability any inevitable secondary participant.

As a matter of principle and practice, English courts have eschewed recognizing a general rule of statutory construction that excludes complicity liability where such conduct is inevitably incidental to an offence's commission. Consequently, for example, a seller's infringement of legislation designed to regulate sales has been construed as also permitting conviction of the criminally aware purchaser/accessory.[2] Rather than adopting a general exclusionary principle, English courts have based any accessorial exemption on the far narrower[3] grounds that the relevant legislative policy was aimed at protecting a class of participants (or 'victims') vulnerable to exploitation or abuse. And even here case law demonstrates a very limited conception of a 'victim', with the late nineteenth-century decision of *Tyrrell*[4] offering the only unequivocal recognition of such a rule of statutory interpretation. *Tyrrell* declared a girl under 16 incapable of complicity in her own unlawful consensual sexual intercourse, as it was not 'intended that the girls for whose protection it was passed should be punishable' for offences committed against them.[5] Furthermore, as a matter of practicality, it is clear that holding 'victims' liable for such offences would render conviction of principal offenders particularly difficult because of the victim's natural reluctance to furnish self-incriminating evidence.[6]

The tight limits and uncertainty of the concept of complicity-free

---

[2] *Fairburn v. Evans* [1916] 1 KB 218 and *Sayce v. Coupe* [1953] 1 QB 1 where the purchaser unsuccessfully expressly claimed that the statutory provision should be construed as restricted to the seller as the nature of a sale was fundamentally different from a purchase. The position of employees selling for an employer has produced conflicting authorities on whether the employee is to be treated as a principal or accessory. Cf. *Hotchkins v. Hindmarsh* [1891] 2 QB 181 and *Caldwell v. Bethell* [1913] 1 KB 119, with *Williamson v. Norris* [1898] 1 QB 7. In relation to the disposition by a thief to a handler making the thief an accessory to handling, see *Carter Patersons Ltd. v. Wessel* [1947] KB 849.

[3] While all 'victims' are necessarily incidental 'accessories', all necessarily incidental accessories are not 'victims'.

[4] [1894] 1 QB 710. The notion of excluding 'victims' from complicity was employed (arguably inappropriately) in *Whitehouse* where it was decided that a 15-year-old girl may not be an accessory to another's incestuous sexual intercourse with her. Rather than an offence against the person it could be maintained that incest is founded on a combination of moral repugnance and eugenic worries. Therefore the decision ought to have rested solely on ordinary statutory interpretation. Cf. Williams, *Textbook*, 366. However, the element of possible long-term mental injury inflicted by such experiences is also a further basis for criminalizing the practice and excluding liability of the victim 'accessory'. Earlier incest decisions, where the status of the girl has needed determination for evidential purposes, suggest potential complicity liability. See *Brown* (1910) 6 Cr. App. Rep. 24 and *Draper* (1929) 21 Cr. App. Rep. 147.

[5] [1984] 1 QB 710 at 712, per Lord Coleridge CJ. See to the contrary the modern abduction case of *Preston* [1962] Tas. SR 141 construing s. 3 of the Tasmanian Criminal Code Act 1924, discussed by Gillies, *Criminal Complicity*, 161.

[6] Cf. Matthew J. [1894] 1 QB 710, 712. One possible procedural response to such objections is to stay proceedings against the 'victim'.

'victims' are indistinctly illustrated by a thin scattering of inconclusive case law. For instance, while in one sense a 'victim', a woman who knowingly submits to an unlawful abortion has still been held potentially liable for complicity in the offence.[7] Much the same view has been taken by courts in relation to miscellaneous unnatural offences.[8] As a body, these cases are not easily translatable into any coherent principle and present several questions. Why should any *special* rule of statutory construction be adopted? If there is justification, should a wide 'inevitably incidental' approach be followed, or something more specific, such as the 'victim' rule? Or should the vagaries of judicial reading of legislative objectives give way to the certainties of express exempting provisions?

Clearly complicity should be excluded where incrimination of a secondary actor is antithetical to or would undermine penal policies embodied in any particular substantive offence. But not all necessarily incidental secondary behaviour is hostile to the policy considerations responsible for enactment of the substantive offence involved. For example:

Should a woman be deemed an accomplice when an abortion is performed upon her? Should... the purchaser [be] an accomplice in the unlawful sale, the unmarried party to a bigamous marriage an accomplice of the bigamist, the bribe-giver an accomplice of the taker?[9]

These dissimilar situations encompass 'conflicting policies and strategies'[10] because of the frequently disputable quality of the secondary party's actions:[11] are they criminally blameworthy and of the same unacceptable nature as the principal's behaviour? Moreover, will successful prosecution of the principal be inhibited or made less likely by criminalizing the secondary role and so introducing additional evidential problems of corroboration in some situations or unwillingness to risk self-incrimination? This difficult combination of uncertain policy objectives incorporated in a diverse range of substantive offences and their applicability to inevitable

---

[7] See *Sockett* (1908) 1 Cr. App. Rep. 39, 101; and *Price* (1968) 52 Cr. App. Rep. 295, concerning status for evidential purposes.

[8] Cf. *Baskerville* [1916] 2 KB 658; *Tate* (1908) 1 Cr. App. Rep. 39 with *Tatam* (1921) 15 Cr. App. Rep. 132, and *Cratchley* (1913) 9 Cr. App. Rep. 232. See Smith and Hogan, *Criminal Law*, 473 for consideration of the latter two decisions.

[9] Commentary on Model Penal Code TD 1 (1953), 35–6; and revised commentary (1985), 323–5.

[10] Ibid. *Quaere*, the position of third parties who encourage or facilitate the victim's actions?

[11] Compared with English decisions, US case law generally shows a markedly more generous attitude towards exempting necessarily incidental secondary parties. For instance, see *US* v. *Farrar* 281 US 624 (1930) and *State* v. *Hayes* 351 NW 2d 654 (1984) — purchasers not accessories to illegal sales; and *People* v. *Vedder* 98 NY 630 (1885) — a woman not an accessory to her own abortion. For modern state code provisions, see below. The Canadian position rejecting necessary liability in the case of illegal sales is represented by a strong judgment in *Ex p. Barker* (1891) 30 NBR 406, 413–14, followed e.g. in *Evans* v. *Pesce and Attorney-General for Alberta* [1970] 3 CCC 61.

secondary participation, coupled with questions of enforcement strategy, has led to pronounced differences of approach in reform or codification measures, in both English and American jurisdictions. Taken together these various proposals provide a review of the main options open in dealing with the issue.

The most simplistic and least satisfactory approach would be to leave resolution of the matter to the general rules of statutory interpretation, a position probably close to that presently occupied by English law. The ill-defined and uncertain scope of these general rules (and especially the so-called 'mischief rule')[12] renders them a less than acceptable means of limiting complicity. More realistically, the real choice lies between some formulation of the 'victim' rule and the broader based 'inevitably incidental' exclusion test, under which there would be no complicity liability unless in the relevant case there had been legislative 'opting in'. Complicity immunity following the former 'victim' approach is recognized in the American Proposed New Federal Criminal Code (1971)[13] and the Law Commission Draft Criminal Code Bill (1989).[14] In effect, these provisions are specially articulated rules of statutory interpretation. The operating width of such proposals still turns largely on how courts choose to interpret the 'purpose of an enactment' and 'victim';[15] for instance, would it be sufficient if one of a cluster of underlying legislative purposes was protective of the 'victim' class? Is a woman who permits an unlawful abortion on herself a 'victim' the protection of whose personal welfare was part of the statutory purpose of the principal offence?[16] Borderline cases, such as this, could without resort

[12] See e.g. Cross, *Statutory Interpretation*.

[13] National Commission on Reform of Federal Criminal Laws, Final Report (1971), s. 401 (1). Wider exempting provisions were rejected on the grounds that 'they may impose too great a limitation on all Federal regulatory legislation, which is frequently enacted without careful regard for principles of criminal liability. Under applicable Federal case law it may be expected that those criteria will be taken into account'. See also Working Papers (1970), 1, 158.

[14] Cl. 27 (7): 'Where the purpose of an enactment creating an offence is the protection of a class of persons no member of that class who is a victim of such an offence can be guilty of that offence as an accessory'. *Quaere* could, say, a 15-year-old girl be liable as a *principal* offender to unlawful sexual intercourse (under cl. 26 (1) (*c*)) if she procured a lunatic to perform the act? The same point can also be made in respect of the Model Penal Code provisions: s. 2.06 (2) (*a*), 2.06 (5), and 2.06 (*a*) and (*b*). Note also the Criminal Law Revision Committee 15th Report (1984) Cmnd. 9213. Similar treatment in the Code for 'victims' is provided in the cases of incitement, cl. 47 (3), and conspiracy, cl. 48 (4); see commentary para. 13.17. In respect of conspiracy, s. 2 (1) of the Criminal Law Act 1977 already sets out such a rule; discussed by Williams, *Textbook*, 434–5. Parallel provisions are found in the Model Penal Code s. 5.04 (1) (*a*).

[15] In relation to 'victims', Law Commission Report 177 maintains: 'The principle, although expressed as a generalisation, will be of very narrow application if the word "victim" is understood as we intend. A person upon whose body a sexual offence is committed is plainly a "victim" to that offence. Not so, as we understand the word, a factory worker who happens to be injured by an unfenced dangerous machine; the failure to fence, although against the interests of the group of which the worker is a member, is not directed against that worker as a "victim"' (para. 9.39).

[16] Cf. Smith and Hogan, *Criminal law*, 159 and Williams, *Textbook*, 367 on the debatable significance of *Sockett* (see n. 7). Although having no general statutory provision dealing with

to perverse judicial interpretation quite easily be drawn in under the 'victim' rule.

However, even granting the most liberal and imaginative efforts of judicial creativity, many examples of inevitably incidental secondary conduct could never be regarded as within the 'victim' category. Therefore, the question arises how, for example, illegal sales, spectators at obscene or other[17] unlawful events, unmarried bigamy partners, ransom payers, bribe givers, or a 'tippee' receiving 'insider' information[18] should be treated. Arguably,[19] most, if not all, of these cases are appropriate for complicity exemption. Whether or not they should be requires some determining mechanism. What is most acceptable is partly governed by the general view taken of complicity where secondary conduct is necessarily incidental. Claims that such liability breaches the 'rule that a criminal offence should not be created by implication'[20] are misleading as they ignore the need in all cases for satisfaction of standard complicity requirements. More germane is the machinery for adjudication, which may be formal legislative procedures or the informal medium of prosecutorial discretion. The ideal process of systematic legislative sifting out or deselection of socially appropriate cases seems an unrealistic proposition unless carried out in the context of a *de novo* codification programme. Blanket exemption proposals for inevitably incidental secondary participation (subject to express exceptions), favoured by the Model Penal Code[21] and in Law Commission Working Paper 43,[22] are also somewhat problematic. Only if it is believed that reliance on prosecutorial discretion would risk 'anarchical diversity',[23] and that the overwhelming bulk of likely active 'inevitably incidental' situations merit exemption, could a general exclusionary provision be justified. The existence of both of these supporting conditions must be doubted.[24] Consequently, the least unsatisfactory approach, short of wholesale

---

complicity and inevitably incidental participation, the Wisconsin penal code carries a special provision preventing prosecution of women as accessories to their own abortions: Wis. Stat. Ann. s. 940.13.

[17] *Wilcox v. Jeffery* [1951] 1 All ER 464.

[18] Company Securities (Insider Dealing) Act 1985.

[19] See e.g. the Model Penal Code commentary TD 1 (1953), 35–7; and Law Commission Working Paper 43, 67–9. Cf. Law Commission Report 177, para 9.40; and Proposed New Federal Criminal Code, Working Papers (1970), 1, 158.

[20] Working Paper 43, 69.

[21] S. 2.06 (6) (*b*). Followed in many state code reformulations, e.g. Alabama Code s. 13A–2–24 (1)–(2); Maine Rev. Stat. Ann. tit. 17-A, s. 57 (5) (A)–(B); NJ Stat. Ann. s. 2C: 2-6 (*e*) (1)–(2).

[22] Expressly based on Model Penal Code proposition 8: 'A person does not become an accessory to an offence if the offence is so defined that his conduct in it is inevitably incidental to its commission and such conduct is not expressly penalised'.

[23] Model Penal Code, commentary TD 1 (1953), 36 and revised commentary (1985), 325.

[24] The conclusion also reached in Law Commission Report 177, commentary para 9.40; and see also Proposed New Federal Criminal Code, Working Papers (1970), 1, 158.

criminal code re-evaluation and reform, is piecemeal identification and exclusion of particular cases where policy dictates clearly support such a course.

2. Secondary Participation Motivated by Law Enforcement Objectives

On some occasions an apparent accessory[25] may have acted for law enforcement reasons, such as to furnish evidence capable of convicting the principal offender. Almost invariably the party will be either a police officer or some other person working in collaboration with the authorities.[26] Involvement of this nature raises two issues: the effect on the entrapped party's liability and, secondly, the effect on responsibility of the 'accessory'. In English law, entrapment or instigation by a law enforcement agent offers the entrapped party no defence.[27] The position of the entrapper or agent is rather less certain. While in some circumstances a defence is judicially recognized,[28] neither its scope nor its rationale is authoritatively settled.

English case law probably draws the boundary between permissible and impermissible (unlawful) participation at the point where assistance or aid crosses over into instigation. If the criminal venture is unlikely to have occurred but for the agent's encouragement, he will have no defence,[29] unless his involvement only affected matters of detail, such as the timing of the offence.[30] It is where the offence is *initially* instigated by the agent that courts are most likely to view his participation as beyond immunity, for such action will provide the most cogent evidence that the offence would not have occurred without the agent's activities. As a judicial rule of thumb,

---

[25] The issue may, of course, also arise in relation to principals, either for substantive or inchoate liability. Cf. *Clarke* (1984) 80 Cr. App. Rep. 344. But there are matters peculiar or of particular relevance to accessories that merit its treatment as a special, rather than a general defence. The unwillingness of courts to grant immunity to participants is probably greatest when they are principals: *Birtles* (1969) 53 Cr. App. Rep. 469 and *Clarke* (1984) citing *dicta* from *Birtles*.

[26] It appears likely that the position of police or similar agents is no different from the crusading private citizen acting alone on his own initiative. The defendant in *Smith* [1960] 2 QB 423 *instigated* an offence under the Prevention of Corruption Act 1906 with the object of exposing an alleged corrupt mayor. His claimed defence of law enforcement motivation would have failed even if he had been an 'authorised' police agent. See below, and *Clarke* where the Court of Appeal did not appear to tie the defence to 'authorised' actions thereby putting the police and ordinary citizens on the same footing in respect of *non*-instigatory involvement; similarly, Law Commission Working Paper 43, and Report 177.

[27] See *Sang* [1980] AC 402 and case law on s. 78 of the Police and Criminal Evidence Act 1984; note also the discussion in Law Commission Report 83 (1977).

[28] Most relevant case law has dealt with the issue obliquely in the course of ruling on the 'accessory's' status for evidential purposes. But this was not true e.g. in *Clarke* (1984) 80 Cr. App. Rep. 344.

[29] *Sang* [1980] AC 402; *Mealey* (1974) 60 Cr. App. Rep. 59.

[30] *McEvilly* (1973) 60 Cr. App. Rep. 150.

the agent's role will not be seen as crucial[31] when the enterprise joined by the agent is already set up or 'laid on'.[32]

The incentive to mark out reasonably precise limits to the defence is inhibited by the conflict between the patent benefits to law enforcement of using undercover agents and the equally manifest risks entailed in permitting such authorities a free hand in the methods used to achieve desirable ends. Discrediting the criminal justice system and promoting the appearance of individual injustice[33] against entrapped parties are serious dangers which courts are naturally anxious to avoid. These legitimate concerns largely explain the cardinal distinction laid down between *unlawful* initiated action and *lawful* assisted or sustained criminality.[34] As already seen,[35] under general principles motive is irrelevant to complicity liability. In the present context the role performed by the laudable motive of law enforcement is not so much what it reveals of the accessory's disposition but rather to indicate the acceptability of the actions directed towards the socially desirable goal of incriminating criminally disposed parties. Therefore, paying an agent a large sum of money to act with and inform on his criminal associates will not exclude eligibility for exemption, even if the agent was originally a 'genuine' accomplice.

A final unresolved aspect of the defence relates to the range of qualifying objectives. It is probably permissible to act not only to prevent the commission of the offence, but also to 'nullify' or neutralize its effect.[36]

---

[31] The test's logic is suspect in that the agent's role may be crucial without being initiatory in so far as he supplies vital and scarce equipment or skills. This apparent illogicality suggests the importance of other broader reasons for exculpating agents, see below.

[32] *Birtles* (1969) 53 Cr. App. Rep. 469; *McCann* (1971) 56 Cr. App. Rep. 359 and *Clarke* (1984) 80 Cr. App. Rep. 344. An offence may qualify as already 'laid on' when the entrapped principal is instigated to commit a particular offence after being suspected of having carried out a series of similar types of offence. Cf. *Marsh* v. *Johnston* [1959] Crim. LR 444, cited by Smith and Hogan, *Criminal Law*, 161.

[33] A theoretically parallel issue arises in relation to innocent agents working for the authorities where the question is whether the duped principal is convictable. Case law is divided: see *Bannen* 1844 1 Car. & K. 295 and *Valler* (1844) 1 Cox 84, both convicting the principal; and *Eggington* (1801) 2 Leach 913 and *Johnson* (1841) Car. & M. 218, both for acquittal. Law Commission Working Paper 43, citing *Johnson* and because conviction 'would seem unreal', proposed exemption from innocent agency liability of cases where the 'innocent agent acts with the purpose of preventing the commission of the offence or of nullifying its effects' (proposition 3 and commentary 15–17).

[34] It is certainly maintainable that the *moral* distinction is not by any means always clear cut; e.g. where the wavering principal seeks advice as to whether he should continue with the criminal venture. The distinction is implicit in both Law Commission Working Paper 43, proposition 7, and in Law Commission Report 177, cl. 27 (6) (*a*) and (*b*): 'A person is not guilty of an offence as an accessory by reason of anything he does — (*a*) with the purpose of preventing the commission of the offence; or (*b*) with the purpose of avoiding or limiting any harmful consequences of the offence and without the purpose of furthering its commission'. However, cl. 45 (*c*)'s preservation of 'common law' excuses or justifications could have the effect of not ruling out exemption for complicity in initiated acts.

[35] See Ch. 5.

[36] *Clarke* (cit. n. 28): 'Conduct which is overall calculated and intended not to further but to frustrate the ultimate result of the crime' such as planning to reveal the hiding place of stolen

However, it may be that a secondary party acts with the purpose of *limiting* harmful consequences rather than completely eliminating them.[37] This will occur, for instance, where there is an intention to allow a crime to be carried through to its conclusion, including permitting low level violence and harm, but with the objective of thwarting more serious harmful consequences. Actions of this nature are a tempting and arguably proper generic development of the defence.[38] Yet placing workable limitations on such use is problematic, with the defence being underwritten by something resembling a balancing of harms calculation: is any advantage to law enforcement likely to be gained greater or less than the additional risks generated by legitimizing the agent's assistance? Moreover, a defence of limited mitigatory effects carries the potential to subvert general *mens rea* requirements. For example, A might have sold P plastic explosives knowing they were to be used for safebreaking. Why should A not plead as a defence that he was motivated by the desire to stop P using dynamite which A knew was much more likely to cause greater damage to buildings and imperil the lives of others? He has satisfied general complicity requirements but he was at the same time acting partly to limit harmful consequences.

3. Limitations on Complicity in Subsequent Offences

The overall question considered here is not an accessory's potential liability for a series of offences carried out beyond that initially counselled or assisted, but the chances of *unfair* or inappropriate incrimination. Unfairness to the accessory could be said to occur if some dilution in standard complicity culpability requirements were permitted for subsequent offences. However, even if this is not the case, conviction for later offences may be seen as inappropriate in the sense that the linkage between initial complicitous actions and (far) later offences wears the appearance of being too tenuous or remote; although factually active, the original complicity and criminality should be regarded as spent.

Taking an extreme illustration, it is possible that a single act of complicity may set up a principal offender for a lengthy career in crime. When

---

goods. *Quaere* whether irreversible damage or harm is permissible? It has been suggested that it is the police's 'duty' to mitigate the consequences of the principal offence: *Birtles* cited in *Clarke*. Law Commission Working Paper 43 refers to an agent acting with the purpose of 'nullifying' the offence's effects (proposition 7). Report 177 refers to 'avoiding or limiting any harmful consequences', cl. 27 (6) (*b*).

[37] Law Commission Report 177, cl. 27 (6) (*b*) and commentary paras. 9.33–5.
[38] Working Paper 43, proposition 7, would not cover it, but Report 177, cl. 27 (6) (*b*), would; thus providing a defence in cases such as *Gillick*. The conduct in *Fretwell* would not appear to qualify as the defendant's purpose in supplying the abortifacient was to prevent V committing suicide, not to limit or avoid an abortion's harmful consequences. Fretwell chose to facilitate abortion in preference to risking V's suicide.

eventually apprehended, will, say, his original supplier or outfitter be at risk of conviction for complicity in possibly hundreds of offences perpetrated by the active principal? More concretely, supposing A equips P, a young safebreaker just starting up in the profession, with special equipment, knowing full well its likely use, will A be an accessory to all of P's subsequent safebreakings carried out with the equipment? In arriving at a conclusion several possible factors may preclude further liability; some of which are inherent in complicity's positive requirements or of special relevance to them, while others are extrinsic and of application to criminal liability generally. Beyond the particular defence of withdrawal, the former group includes absence of necessary *mens rea*, lack of causal effect, the presence of an express stipulation as to the victim or subject-matter, and, possibly, a special limiting principle. Coming within the latter group, are general judicial discretionary powers to terminate unfair or oppressive proceedings, and sentencing conventions in respect of multiple charges or convictions.

(1) Mens rea

The *Bainbridge* formula places no limitations on liability for subsequent offences of the same type committed using the means supplied for the initial offence. In *Maxwell*, Lowry LCJ observed:[39]

Interesting hypothetical problems can be posed if, for example, one person supplies to another house-breaking implements or weapons which are used — and perhaps used repeatedly — by the person supplied or by a third person, either immediately or months or years later. Such questions must, we think, be solved by asking whether the crime actually committed is fairly described as the crime or one of a number of crimes within the contemplation of the accomplice. They are typical of the kind of problem which may be encountered in the application of any principle of the common law which while requiring to be soundly based, can only proceed from one instance to another.

In other words, *mens rea* requirements for subsequent offences are just the same as those for the initial one. Consequently, the more specific the foresight of 'essential matters' needed, the less chance there is of further offences coming within such required contemplation.[40] Additionally, the accessory needs to believe that there was more than a 'negligible' risk of such further offences being committed.[41] Therefore the accessory's mental culpability or fault in respect of any subsequent offences will be no less than necessary for the original offence, and, in this sense, no less 'fair'.

---

[39] [1978] 1 WLR 1350 at 1375.
[40] See Ch. 6 (1) (3) and (4).
[41] See Ch. 6 (2).

(2) Causation

Though the contrary is imaginable, a single act of encouragement is unlikely to carry through to later crimes. Therefore in respect of causal contribution[42] the issue will almost inevitably be confined to the provision of the *means* to commit the initial offence — whether in the form of equipment or information. Clearly in cases of equipment or information the causal potency of the original complicity may, depending on the circumstances, survive almost indefinitely.

(3) Express Limitations

A principal's non-compliance with any restriction imposed by an accomplice on the use to which his assistance might be put will, in general, be ineffective in preventing undesired but foreseen liability. This will be true for subsequent offences as well. The possible exceptional position under English case law of specified victims or objects should also have similar relevance to further offences.[43]

(4) Judicial Discretion in Respect of Criminal Proceedings

Conceivably, cases could arise where the presence of some factor makes an accessory's conviction for subsequent offences unfair — for example, if the accessory reasonably believed his assistance had become valueless. In such situations the court may feel minded to 'decline to hear proceedings on the ground that they are oppressive and [or] an abuse of the process of the court'.[44] So far this power has been confined to *res judicata* problems, but it has arguable potential use in relation to complicity. One modern decision of possible broad parallel relevance is the Trade Descriptions Act case of *Thomson Holidays Ltd.*[45] which raised issues analogous to those in complicity: whether a single act (or group of actions) may incur successive and separate liability; and the possible importance of the reasonableness of the defendants' inaction. The appeal in *Thomson Holidays Ltd.* against conviction for a travel brochure misdescription rested on two grounds: first, the same misdescription in other copies of the brochure could not support a second prosecution and conviction — a plea of *autrefois convict*; secondly, the further prosecution was an abuse of process and should be disallowed under the court's discretion. In response, the prosecution contended that while the defendants probably could not have prevented all potential

---

[42] See Ch. 3.
[43] See Chs. 7 and 8.
[44] Per Lord Parker CJ in *Mills v. Cooper* [1967] 2 QB 459 at 467. Cited by Lord Salmon in *DPP v. Humphrys* [1977] AC 1. See also *dicta* of Lords Reid, Devlin, and Pearce in *Connelly v. DPP* [1964] AC 1254.
[45] [1974] 1 QB 592.

customers reading the brochure's misdescription they could still have 'done their best; [but] they did nothing'.[46] Although this was accepted by the Court of Appeal as having 'some force', it rested its decision on the safer grounds of statutory construction:

[The provision] itself envisages that more than one prosecution may be brought . . . in respect of the same course of conduct [therefore, the second prosecution] cannot be said to be either an abuse of process or oppressive.[47]

(5) Limitation of Punishment

Punishment of principal offenders for multiple convictions is governed by a range of sentencing conventions of varying degrees of clarity and weight. In settling whether a multiple offender shall be subject to concurrent or consecutive sentences for several offences, two major (though indistinct) limiting principles operate: the 'one-transaction rule' and the 'totality principle'.[48] If the defendant's criminality flows from a single transaction or incident (or even a cluster of incidents closely related in time and nature) then the expectation is of concurrent sentences. The 'totality principle' seeks to ensure that the 'totality of criminal behaviour' is properly reflected in the aggregate sentence arrived at through principles relating to consecutive sentences; to determine that in the circumstances the aggregate sentence is 'just and appropriate'. These separate notions of a single source or occasion of criminal behaviour and the almost impressionistic assessment of what is 'just and appropriate' would seem to have arguable relevance to the sentencing of a multiple offence accessory.

(6) A Direct Limitation Rule

Law Commission Working Paper 43 suggested it was 'wrong' to subject an accessory to a series of convictions following a single act of complicity. Rather, it was 'just to regard' an accessory as having 'in effect committed only one wrongful act'. To deal with this a special defence of *autrefois convict* was proposed:

Where a principal is helped in the commission of more than one offence by a single act of help, the accessory who afforded that help shall not, after having been convicted of one or more of such offences, be convicted of another of such offences of equal or lesser gravity.[49]

---

[46] [1974] 1 QB 592 at 598.
[47] Ibid. See also *Riebold* [1965] 1 All ER 653, and *Moxon-Tritsch* [1988] Crim. LR 46. Generally, R. Pattenden, *Judicial Discretion and Criminal Litigation* (1990), ch. 2, and 'The Power of the Courts to Stay a Criminal Prosecution' [1985] Crim. LR 174.
[48] D. A. Thomas, *Principles of Sentencing* (1979), ch. 2; and A. J. Ashworth, *Sentencing and Penal Policy* (1983), ch. 6.
[49] Proposition 10, and commentary 75–7.

Exclusion and Limitation of Complicity

Under this provision, an accessory could still be charged with complicity in a long series of offences provided the prosecution of all such offences takes place on the same occasion. But further crimes carried out by the original principal could not be attributed to the accessory. Therefore, if A supplies P with enough explosives for twenty safebreakings and A is apprehended and convicted after three have been committed, but P (still at large) goes on to complete his full quota of twenty, then A could not later be convicted of complicity in the seventeen offences. Bearing in mind the constructional difficulties likely to be encountered with such a proposal,[50] the earlier limiting factors already considered and the potential availability of a withdrawal defence, it must be very doubtful whether specific provisions governing complicity in subsequent offences are warranted.[51]

---

[50] Settling the meaning of a 'single act' might prove difficult. In the safebreaking example, suppose A delivered the explosives in two instalments before the first offence was committed, would they be regarded as a 'single act'? What if the second instalment had been delivered after the third safebreaking? As for the 'gravity' of an offence, would its meaning be free of the sort of difficulties associated with 'type'? In addition to formal classification, would particular circumstances be a determinant of 'gravity'? Would e.g. a robbery involving £100 and another for £100,000 be seen as of 'equal gravity'? Similarly a robbery in which the victim is roughly jostled and one where he is severely beaten.

[51] No reference occurs to proposition 10 in Law Commission Report 177.

10

General Defences and Withdrawal

1. General Defences

The effects of certain complete and partial defences on the principal–accessory relationship have already been reviewed from the standpoint of compatibility with complicity's derivative structure.[1] Here the question addressed is the extent of the potential relevance and availability of general defences to accessories. Beyond 'defences' relating to absence of necessary *mens rea* or *actus reus* elements, general defences[2] should have *broadly similar* applicability to secondary parties as to principals. This would seem to follow from the justification or excuse basis underlying defences having equal potential relevance to any participant, whether principal or secondary. But such logic may not hold true in all cases and for every defence. In particular, the distinctiveness between accessory and principal *mens rea* requirements may lead to modifications in defence qualifying conditions.[3]

Intoxication is one defence where such differences might be significant. In the case of secondary parties, the *Majewski*[4] distinction between crimes of 'specific intent' and 'basic intent' may not be recognized, with even offences of 'basic intent' requiring the standard level of subjective foresight necessary for accessories. Therefore, in offences of 'basic intent', such as rape,[5]

---

[1] See Ch. 4.

[2] e.g. self-defence or prevention of an offence under the Criminal Law Act 1967 (s. 3 (1) expressly refers to 'effecting or assisting' in lawful arrest), duress, insanity, and intoxication. In the severely limited supporting case law, the position of duress is the most thoroughly aired. See *Howe* [1987] 1 All ER 771 and authorities cited.

[3] Between 1976 and 1987 English law recognized that duress could be a defence to murder for secondary but not principal parties. See *Lynch* v. *DPP for Northern Ireland* [1975] AC 653; *Abbott* [1977] AC 755; and *Howe* [1987] All ER 771. Rather than any doctrinal wrangle over the distinction between principal and secondary parties in relation to duress, the disagreement centred around whether the defence should be available for murder for *any* participant. The temporary distinction was largely a consequence of two factors: the accident of the particular composition of the judicial bodies on each occasion; and the fact that *Lynch* was only called upon to decide the position of secondary parties (abettors). On the anomalous results which could follow from making the defence available to secondary parties in murder, but not to principals, see J. C. Smith [1974] Crim. LR 349 and [1976] Crim. LR 564.

[4] [1977] AC 142. See Smith and Hogan, *Criminal Law*, 211–15.

[5] [1977] AC 142. *Cogan* suggests otherwise: 'The drink [the perpetrator] had seems to have

although the perpetrator is convictable despite being too inebriated to have perceived or foreseen what he otherwise would have if sober, liability of an equally intoxicated accessory[6] would still be subject to satisfaction of normal subjective complicity demands.[7] Although less than completely compelling,[8] this distinction might be justified on the grounds that abandoning an accessory's more complex and extensive *mens rea* requirements[9] would mark an even greater departure from standard fault demands than is the case under *Majewski* for principal offenders.

Another possible defence distinction between parties involves those defences incorporating objective elements.[10] If the principal is convictable on the basis of unreasonably misunderstanding the reality of a situation or acting unreasonably, for example, in self-defence, it may be that an accessory is subject to a higher fault requirement—liability being conditional upon actual awareness of the true position ('essential matters'[11] of the offence).

2. Withdrawal

(1) Preliminary Issues

There is often a period of time between when *potentially* complicitous behaviour occurs and when liability crystallizes by performance of the principal offence. This, so to speak, pre-inculpatory interlude offers 'accessories' the opportunity to recant and withdraw from the enterprise. Although the common law has long[12] accepted that in certain circumstances such a withdrawal[13] prevents the incurring of secondary liability, the

---

been a reason, if not the only one, for mistaking her sobs and distress for consent.' ([1975] 2 All ER 1059, 1061.) If the Court of Appeal had employed the notion of 'basic intent' the perpetrator ought to have been convicted.

[6] It was accepted in *Clarkson* [1971] 3 All ER 344, 347, that a passive witness to rape would escape complicity liability if because of intoxication he failed to perceive that his presence encouraged the perpetrator. Cf. *Kearon* [1955] Crim. LR 183; *Waterfield* (1974) 18 CCC (2d) 140; *Chapin* (1978) 41 CCC (2d) 300; and *Fraser* (1984) 13 CCC (3d) 292, requiring standard complicity culpability for offences of 'basic intent' when the accessory is intoxicated.

[7] See Dennis, 'The Mental Element', 51, for an alternative interpretation of *Clarkson*.

[8] Cf. the culpability differential between accessories and principals in respect of offences based on objective fault or strict liability; see Ch. 6 (5) and (6).

[9] In so far as the accessory's *mens rea* relates to his own and the principal's actions he must intend his actions, be aware of their ability to assist or encourage, and foresee with prescribed particularity the principal's possible offence.

[10] e.g. self-defence and intervention to prevent an offence.

[11] See Ch. 6 (1).

[12] At least from *Saunders and Archer* (1576) 2 Plowd. 473, 476. And *Co. Inst.* iii. 51; Hale, PC i. 436, 618.

[13] Case law and codes adopt no uniform term. Other than 'withdrawal', use is sometimes made of 'renunciation', 'abandonment', and 'countermand'. The aptness of different terms varies with the context, although 'withdrawal' is probably the most flexible.

necessary qualifying conditions lack anything approaching adequate judicial expression. It is a state of affairs in good measure attributable to confusion over the 'defence's' status or nature, allied to absence of agreement in respect of its justifying rationale. Clarification of these two preliminary matters needs to precede any attempt at sifting case law for the qualifying requirements of legally effective withdrawal.

(a) *Claims of No* Actus Reus *and Defences* Confusion over withdrawal's exculpatory nature, apparent in some case law,[14] often stems from a failure to distinguish what may be a simple assertion of no *actus reus* from a true defence claim.[15] An accessory's liability is contingent upon having aided, abetted, counselled, or procured the principal offence's commission. If before commission these prior actions, with the potential to aid, abet, counsel, or procure, are erased or neutralized, then there can be no complicity for there will be no accessorial *actus reus* at the critical time when the principal offence is carried out. This obvious, but frequently overlooked, consideration is especially apparent when complicity's causal[16] structure is borne in mind: if the 'accessory's' causal contribution, whether encouragement or assistance, is effectively countermanded or rendered valueless before the principal offence is carried out, it cannot have affected the occurrence of such an offence. Therefore, coherent discussion of a 'defence' of withdrawal must proceed on the basis of recognizing some means of exculpation beyond a claim of no *actus reus* — even though he has participated in the offence's commission the 'accessory' should, because of certain features in his behaviour, be excluded from liability.[17]

[14] e.g. *Croft* [1944] KB 295, 'he expressly countermanded or revoked [his complicity and] never said anything . . . which could have removed from her mind the effect of counsel' (298). In *MacNeil* v. *HMA* 1986 SCCR 288, the court denied the existence of a 'defence of dissociation' yet appeared to accept that liability could be avoided by taking 'steps to prevent [the offence's] completion'. No indication is given as to the nature of such steps.

[15] *People* v. *Ortiz* 219 P. 1024 (1973) at 1027: 'not only must he have acted in time, and done everything practicable to prevent the [offence], but [the offence] if it takes place must be imputable to some independent cause'. And in *Menniti* [1985] 1 Qd. R. 520 when considering the Queensland and Western Australian Criminal Codes.

[16] '[W]hat must be done in criminal matters involving participation . . . to breach the chain of causation and responsibility . . . must depend upon the circumstances of each case': Sloane JD in *Whitehouse* [1941] 1 WWR, 112, 116.

[17] In English law withdrawal is no defence to inchoate liability, although it may affect sentence (cf. M. Wasik, 'Abandoning Criminal Intent' [1980] Crim. LR 785, 793). Nor has there been much support for a change in the law to make it a defence in these cases. See Law Commission Report 102 (1980). The position of inchoate offences is clearly logically distinct from secondary liability: in the former case withdrawal may necessarily only occur *after* the incurring of liability; for complicity, withdrawal relates to actions *before* secondary liability crystallizes by commission of the principal offence. However, despite this logical distinction the Model Penal Code and many jurisdictions incorporate withdrawal provisions for inchoate offences based on broadly similar rationales to those put forward for complicity; the cogency of each varies with the individual inchoate offence. Cf. D. L. Rotenberg, 'Withdrawal as a Defense to Relational Crimes' (1962) *Wis. LR* 596, and Model Penal Code TD 10 (1960), 73. The Model Penal Code provisions (followed in the majority of state code revisions, see

(b) Justifying Rationale of a Withdrawal Defence[18] Clearly, the qualifying conditions of a withdrawal defence are (or should be) shaped by its justifying rationale(s). As is often true of policy questions, the justifying basis of withdrawal is open to dispute. Two broad types of justification may be offered: one focusing on the power of a withdrawal defence to act as an incentive for 'accessories' to think again; the other looking to withdrawal as cogent evidence of the 'accessory's' substantially diminished culpability or dangerousness.

An incentive rationale rests on the belief that providing the means by which an 'accessory' can legally extricate himself from a criminal enterprise increases the likelihood of a party doing so, thus decreasing the risk of the substantive offence occuring.[19] The most compelling ground for scepticism[20] over such reasoning is the necessary assumption that the actor will be aware of the defence and thus capable of being influenced by it. However, once such a defence is clearly established in any social culture, the weight of this counter-argument declines. Therefore, whilst the force of an incentive rationale is far from irresistible, it is not wholly discredited, with some cases possible where the defence might encourage a less than tenaciously committed party to abandon his criminal venture.[21]

Rather than reducing the chances of the principal offence, the second type of justification of a withdrawal defence is its ability to demonstrate the actor's reduced criminal fault in the particular case. Abandonment can serve as evidence of either irresolute purpose or a complete change of heart. Or, prognostically, he may be perceived as someone with fewer socially dangerous tendencies. Either way, the actor because of his withdrawal may be viewed as less deserving of punishment, or, deserving less punishment.[22]

Robinson, *Criminal Law Defenses*, ch. 3, s. 81) differ from the complicity requirements in two crucial respects: the defendant must have prevented the substantive criminal offence taking place 'under circumstances manifesting a complete and voluntary renunciation of his criminal purpose', s. 5.01 (4). For the meaning of 'complete and voluntary', see below.

[18] Classifying the withdrawal defence as either 'justificatory' or 'excusatory' (Ch. 4) is problematic. An incentive account of the defence is distinctly justificatory in nature in so far as withdrawing actions and their potential ability to prevent the substantive offence are socially desirable. The alternative of using withdrawal as an indicator of greatly diminished culpability or reduced future dangerousness is more excusatory. Because of the relative weakness of each of these explanations the defence may perhaps be better theoretically accounted for as an illustration of the 'conduct rule'–'decision rule' distinction: a withdrawal being a 'decision rule' addressed to the officials (judges) rather than a 'conduct rule' addressed to the public. See M. Dan-Cohen, 'Decision Rules and Conduct Rules: An Acoustic Separation in Criminal Law' (1984) 97 *HLR* 625.

[19] See e.g. Law Commission Working Paper 43, 71–2; Working Paper 50, para. 141; Model Penal Code, TD 1 (1953), 37–8, and TD 10 (1960), 72.

[20] More generally, note Fletcher, *Rethinking Criminal Law*, 186.

[21] He may still be liable for incitement or conspiracy, but not always so. Cf. *Bainbridge* type circumstances where there is neither incitement nor conspiracy.

[22] See *Sheckles v. State* 501 NE 2d 1053 (1986). This holds true whether punishment is premised on utilitarian reformist or retributive principles. Cf. A. Katz, 'Dangerousness: A Theoretical Reconstruction of the Criminal Law, Part I' (1970) 19 *Buffalo LR* 1; and

As will be seen, in practice withdrawal defences implicitly incorporate at least an inducement or risk of crime reduction rationale, and in many jurisdictions the relevance of the second, more subjective, group of features also shows up in the defence's qualifying conditions — most particularly where 'voluntariness' or motive is an essential factor.

(2) Forms of Withdrawal

(a) Theoretical and Practical Possibilities Strictly, consistency with general criminal law principles is hostile to the granting of any defence of withdrawal. Where a principal party sets off a train of events leading to the occurrence of an offence, fruitless efforts to reverse the process will not exonerate. For a principal there will almost never be an opportunity for him to change his mind between acting and before liability is fixed. Even when the intended criminal harm might be seen, for all reasonable purposes, as reversible (such as where stolen goods are returned before the owner is aware of the theft) the fact of the offence's commission cannot be erased, though there may be mitigation of sentence.

But whilst rare, situations are imaginable in cases of principal liability where there is an interlude between an initial action and eventual complete criminal liability. For instance, in a fit of pique P pushed a heavy beer barrel down a narrow steep alley with the intention of knocking down V who was coming up the alley. Gripped by almost instant remorse, P shouts a warning to V to jump clear of the speeding barrel. Reacting too slowly, V is hit and injured. Despite his efforts, P will be liable for injuring V based on his initial and indelible fault or culpability. Further comparative examples illustrate complicity's special position

> (a) A, intent upon destroying a military installation and killing its occupants, incites impressionable P to plant a bomb.
> (b) As in (a), but P is used as an innocent agent to plant the bomb.
> (c) Instead of using another party, A plants the bomb himself.

In each situation an explosion occurs with fatal consequences but only after A had changed his mind and desperately sought to retrieve the bomb. In variants (b)[23] and (c)[24] A would have no defence for the offences involved; but A's actions might constitute a legally effective withdrawal in situation

---

G. Strong, 'Fault, Threat and the Predicates of Criminal Liability' (1980) *Wis. LR* 441; and P. R. Hoeber, 'The Abandonment Defense to Criminal Attempt and Other Problems of Temporal Individuation' (1986) 74 *Cal. LR* 377.

[23] Under the doctrine of innocent agency A's liability is *generally* subject to the rules affecting principal liability; see Ch. 4 and cf. *White and Ridley* (1978) 140 CLR 342, which contains conflicting judgments on the point.

[24] Generally, G. Marston, 'Contemporaneity of Act and Intention' (1970) 86 *LQR* 208; and see *Jakeman* (1983) 76 Cr. App. Rep. 223.

(a). Although policy reasons underlying a withdrawal defence in complicity[25] also have some relevance to principals in certain limited circumstances, the obvious practical difficulties and dangers entailed in catering for a few remote examples rules out a withdrawal defence for perpetrators.

As suggested, the qualifying conditions for a defence of withdrawal in complicity should largely be determined by the policy objectives already identified: producing conditions which further, or are at least not inconsistent with, such policies. Consequently in settling qualifying conditions the nature of the accessory's complicity will be influential. Material assistance and encouragement are likely to demand different withdrawal measures if there is to be a reduction in the likelihood of the offence's occurrence. Yet if either a diminished culpability or dangerousness of character justifying rationale is employed, then the recanting accessory's patent ineptitude would be less likely to preclude entitlement to the defence. Of the potential range of effective withdrawal measures, the most demanding would require an accessory to have attempted to prevent the *offence*; the least demanding might require an attempt to communicate notice of withdrawal to the principal. Possible actions between these two extremes include the accessory attempting directly to neutralize his previous actions by recovering materials provided or by retracting encouragement; or indirectly, by informing the police or the intended victim.

A final preliminary question on theoretically possible forms of withdrawal is whether the law should[26] require, at least, withdrawal which is actually communicated, either to the principal or to a law enforcement agency. Should an accessory who has taken extraordinary but ultimately fruitless measures to locate the principal be denied the defence? Again, the answer turns largely on the justifying basis of withdrawal. In so far as the defence's rationale depends on the accessory's demonstrated reduced culpability or dangerousness, then whether successful or not in reaching the principal the defence should be open to a party who has attempted (or taken reasonable steps) to withdraw. However, if greater prominence is given to an *actual* risk-reducing justification for the defence, a reasonable level of effectiveness in the accessory's efforts would naturally start with having

---

[25] And for inchoate liability, see below. On the possibility of the use of the defence beyond complicity and inchoate offences see D. G. Moriarty, 'Extending the Defense of Renunciation' (1989) 62 Temp. LR 1.

[26] English case law does not expressly cover the point but, by implication, suggests communicated countermand is necessary. The court in *Becerra* (1976) 62 Cr. App. Rep. 212 spoke of 'communication'; similarly in *Whitefield*: 'If [the accessory's] participation is confined to advice or encouragement he must at least communicate his change of mind to the other' (40). Stephen refers to the principal having 'notice' of the countermand, adding that it 'may be doubted whether [withdrawal] would extend to the case of a man who did his best to countermand his advice, but failed, as by an accident in the course of post etc.': *Digest*, art. 42, illustration, n. 1. American case law supports the need for effective communication; e.g. *People* v. *Rybka* 158 NE 2d 17 (1959) and *State* v. *Guptill* 481 A. 2d 772 (1984). Cf. the equivocal Australian decision in *White* v. *Ridley* (1978) 140 CLR 342.

successfully communicated his withdrawal. Of course, unfairness may result where the accessory has taken what would normally be effective action to communicate withdrawal, but, because of some unforeseeable event, the communication never reaches its destination.[27]

(*b*) *Case law* According to the Court of Appeal[28] in *Becerra and Cooper*:

Where practicable and reasonable there must be timely communication of the intention to abandon the common purpose from those who wish to dissociate themselves from the contemplated crime and those who desire to continue in it. What is timely communication must be determined by the facts of each case but where practicable and reasonable it ought to be such communication, verbal or otherwise, that will serve unequivocal notice [of intention to withdraw].

What will constitute 'unequivocal notice'?[29] Must express notice of withdrawal be given or will it be sufficient if the accessory's abandonment of the enterprise is obvious from his conduct? Although a few earlier authorities may suggest that actions *implying* withdrawal could be sufficient,[30] the weight of case law requires express notice[31] or, at least, more than failure to fulfil a promise to assist.[32] By qualifying its reference to 'unequivocal notice' with 'where practicable and reasonable', *Becerra* itself implicitly recognizes other ways by which an accessory might be entitled to

---

[27] Law Commission Report 177, cl. 27 (8), may, in this respect, be wider than the current law by permitting withdrawal either if the accessory has 'countermanded his encouragement' (27 (8) (*a*)) or by taking 'reasonable steps' (27 (8) (*b*)) which does not necessarily entail effective communication. The 'Scrutiny Group' examining the complicity proposals in Law Commission Report 143 argued for withdrawal to be a matter for mitigation of sentence only. The Model Penal Code (s. 2.06 (6) (*c*)), is equivocal in that it requires that the accessory 'terminates his complicity', which may imply communication, and gives 'Timely warning to the law enforcement authorities or otherwise makes proper effort . . . '. 'Timely warning' strongly implies communication; the alternative of 'proper effort' does not. Commentary on TD 1 (1953) (and in the 1985 revision, 326) supports a general need to communicate interpretation. This is also true of the 'Study Draft' revised US Federal Criminal Code in that the accessory must take actions 'which substantially reduced the likelihood' of the offence's commission (s. 401 (3)). However, the 'Final Draft' (1971) included no express withdrawal provisions for complicity. The 'Report of the Committee on the Judiciary United States Senate' on the 'Criminal Code Reform Act of 1979' (1980) briefly notes that the committee did not favour codification of the 'doctrine of withdrawal' and 'intends the issue to be left for further development by the Federal courts' (78).

[28] Quoting a passage from the Canadian decision of *Whitehouse* [1941] 1 WWR 112 at 115–16.

[29] The Court of Criminal Appeal in *Fletcher and Zimnowodski* [1962] Crim. LR 551 spoke of the need for 'unqualified' withdrawal. Cf. *Miller and Cockriell* (1976) 31 CCC (2d) 170: 'timely and reasonable unequivocal notice', following *Whitehouse*; and similarly *Saylor* [1963] QWN 14.

[30] Cf. *Hyde* (1672) Hale, *PC* i. 537, and Foster, *Crown Law*, 354; *Edmeads* (1828) 3 Car. & P. 389, 172 ER 469; *Young* (1838) 8 Car. & P. 644, 173 ER 655.

[31] e.g. *Saunders and Archer* (cit. n. 12), and *Croft* [1944] KB 295: 'An accessory . . . must establish that he expressly countermanded or revoked the advising, counselling, procuring, or abetting which he had previously given'. Similarly *Reismann* v. *US* 409 F. 2d 789 (1969) at 793.

[32] *Goodspeed* (1911) 6 Cr. App. Rep. 133.

General Defences and Withdrawal

the defence. Whether basing withdrawal on an inducement or reduced culpability rationale, other equally effective methods should qualify, such as warning law enforcement authorities[33] or the projected victim.

Even though an accessory has served 'unequivocal notice' of withdrawal on the principal, or has clearly signalled his dissociation from the enterprise in some other acceptable way, it is far from certain when this alone will be sufficient. English courts[34] have, on the whole, demonstrated a marked reluctance to find that an accessory has legally withdrawn, even in situations where, on the evidence, actions appear to have satisfied qualifying criteria set down in the particular case. This is true, for instance, in *Becerra*, and *Fletcher*.

In the former case, the defendants were disturbed by X during the course of a burglary, whereupon Cooper fatally attacked X with a knife provided earlier by Becerra. Becerra claimed to have effectively withdrawn from the common purpose of burglary before the stabbing by telling Cooper 'come on, let's go', and then immediately quitting the premises. Unequivocal as such notice might appear, the Court of Appeal had no doubt that in the circumstances the manner of withdrawal would have to be 'vastly different and vastly more effective'.[35] Similarly, in *Fletcher*, in attempting to extricate himself from an agreement to carry out arson the accessory had told the principal 'Don't do it' or 'Don't be a fool'. In response the Court of Criminal Appeal accepted:

It was true as had been argued on his behalf that a conspirator could withdraw without taking an action to restrain his co-conspirators physically. However, the withdrawal must be unqualified and the evidence was too vague to show an unqualified withdrawal from the common design.

Again, as in *Becerra*, it is difficult to fathom quite what further evidence and conduct the court had in mind. Contrastingly, the burglary case of *Whitefield*[36] shows a greater willingness by the Court of Appeal to recognize 'unequivocal notice' as a sufficient basis for withdrawal.[37]

Although no more than hinted at in *Becerra*, implicit in the defence appears to be a proportionality or relational condition whereby the greater the accessory's involvement in an enterprise the more substantial the effort needed to remove himself from liability. This is broadly responsible for the probable distinction between cases of encouragement and those where

---

[33] Cf. Model Penal Code, s. 2.06 (6) (ii).
[34] See also e.g. *Malcolm* [1951] NZLR 470; *Joyce* [1968] NZLR 1070, 1074, and 1079; *White and Ridley* (1978) 140 CLR 342 (fully discussed by Lanham, 'Accomplices and Withdrawal', 576–9, 582–4) and *Menniti* [1985] 1 Qd. R. 520.
[35] (1976) 62 Cr. App. Rep. 212, 219. The court declined to say whether the only effective withdrawal would have been Becerra's physical intervention. Cf. *S. v. Ndebu* 1986 (2) 133 SA, considering English case law including *Becerra*.
[36] (1984) 79 Cr. App. Rep. 36.
[37] And cf. *Eddy* v. *Niman* [1981] Crim. LR 502.

material assistance has been supplied. It is also a difference which follows from employing either main type of justifying rationale already suggested for withdrawal.[38] Moreover, if the supplier of material assistance were able to free himself from liability by no more than genuine notice of dissociation, then the accessory in circumstances such as *Bainbridge* could avoid incrimination by issuing such notice at or after the time when aid was provided.[39] Additionally, cases similar to *Fretwell* would, presumably, be open to solution in this way if the supplier (of the abortifacient) has indicated the materials were unwillingly provided.

Whilst withdrawal from situations where material aid has been furnished is implicitly recognized by English case law,[40] quite how much more than an express countermand is necessary lacks authority. A possibly important difference may exist between renunciatory action directly aimed at neutralizing or recovering the assistance given, and attempts to prevent the offence occurring. Withdrawing simple encouragement is, in theory, clearly distinguishable from attempting[41] to dissuade the principal from committing an offence, although it may often amount to the same. Consistency with cases of encouragement, where one variety of exculpatory requirement is (in effect) trying to take back or erase the effects of encouragement from the principal's mind, would suggest that for material aid the accessory could withdraw by acting in a similar fashion. Therefore, an attempt to recover previously provided assistance ought to qualify as withdrawal even though carried out *solely* to end the accessory's involvement and not necessarily with a 'view to preventing [the offence's] commission'.[42] For example, if A

---

[38] Law Commission Working Paper 43 proposed that whatever the mode of complicity it would be sufficient if the accessory 'Communicates his withdrawal to the Principal' (proposition 9).

[39] Nor would there be alternative liability for incitement or conspiracy.

[40] In *Croft* and *Becerra* the accessory both encouraged and provided material assistance.

[41] In *Grundy* [1977] Crim. LR 543 the assistance was information which facilitated the principal offence. The accessory did more than dissociate himself from the offence: he attempted to dissuade the principal from committing the offence.

[42] Law Commission Report 177, cl. 27 (8), provides: 'A person who has encouraged the commission of an offence is not guilty as an accessory if before its commission — (a) he countermanded his encouragement with a view to preventing its commission; or (b) he took all reasonable steps to prevent its commission.' Unlike in Report 143, the defence is limited to cases of encouragement because of the 'unclear state of authorities and of some lingering disquiet expressed on consultation' (paras. 9.41–2). Unclear as the authorities are, in the case of encouragement the authorities do not appear to restrict an accessory to withdrawal 'with a view to preventing' the offence. Rather, withdrawal motivated by a desire to be no part of the venture seems to be sufficient. Like Report 177, the Model Penal Code proposals also require the accessory's actions to be aimed at preventing the offence's commission, s. 2.06 (6) (c) (ii). Elaborate and nuanced provisions are set out in the First Criminal Law Commissioners' 7th (1843) and the Second Commissioners' 2nd (1846) criminal codes. For abettors, actual abandonment without leaving in the minds of others 'any reasonable expectation . . . of support' was sufficient — close to a plea of no *actus reus* (arts. 9 and 7). A 'procurer or promoter' must countermand and 'use his utmost endeavour to prevent' the offence (arts. 12 and 9). Under the 1843 code (art. 18) 'several persons assembled together' with a 'common design' were able to withdraw effectively by abandoning the design and 'withdrawing from the further prosecution thereof'. However, the 1846 code (art. 14) also demanded the accessory 'use his utmost endeavour' to prevent the offence. Unfortunately the reasoning behind these carefully drawn distinctions is not revealed.

has lent P a revolver for use in a robbery, but, after reflection on the risks of such an enterprise to his family's good name, A attempts to withdraw by unsuccessfully trying to recover his revolver, he will not be entitled to the defence if his actions must be aimed at preventing the offence. This would be equally true whatever A did and however reasonable it might otherwise seem, unless he acted with a view to preventing the offence.[43]

Limiting exculpatory behaviour to actions directed at preventing the offence could be seen as incorporating into the defence a form of penalty against the accessory for his initial voluntary[44] involvement, or a charge for the concession of granting the defence. In practical terms, such a condition forces a withdrawing accessory into either warning the targeted victim or law enforcement authorities of the planned offence — both of which approaches with their risks of exposure might prove unattractive to repentant accessories. However, despite this, it might be thought that only where withdrawing actions are directed at preventing the offence is the chance of thwarting the principal sufficiently meritorious[45] to warrant excusing the accessory. Such calculations are of a very fine order and necessarily highly speculative. Furthermore, it is certainly arguable that legitimate concerns over an accessory properly *earning* his exemption (at least in respect of his *form* of withdrawal) are adequately met by requiring that he took 'all reasonable steps'[46] or 'makes proper effort'[47] to withdraw.[48] Depending on the circumstances, there may be no option for withdrawal other than by directly or indirectly attempting to prevent the offence's commission. This would be true of the provision of useful information.[49] General use of a reasonableness test carries the flexibility to

---

[43] As under the Model Penal Code, s. 2.06 (6) (*c*).

[44] Cf. the operation of a penalty notion in duress which disqualifies prior criminal associates from pleading the defence. For English case law, see Smith and Hogan, *Criminal Law*, 237–8; and restatement in Law Commission Report 177, cl. 42 (5).

[45] Whether in terms of showing less culpability or fault on the accessory's part, or offering evidence of a less dangerous or criminal disposition.

[46] Law Commission Report 177, cl. 27 (8) (*b*), but limited to the accessory aiming to prevent the offence. The trial judge in *Becerra* employed such a test, but the Court of Appeal expressly declined to give a view on whether this was a universally applicable standard ((1976) 62 Cr. App. Rep. 212, 219). Similar caution is found in *Whitehouse* [1941] 1 WWR 112, 116.

[47] Model Penal Code, s. 2.06 (6) (*c*), but limited to the accessory aiming to prevent the offence.

[48] The position of an accessory in such situations might be compared with two other forms of liability: first, complicity through omission where the accessory has some power or right to control the principal or materials in his possession; secondly, 'supervening fault' liability, as in *Miller* [1983] 2 AC 161 (restatement in Law Commission Report 177, cl. 23). In the former case, to be free of liability the 'accessory' must probably take (*quaere*, reasonable) measures to assert his authority with the purpose of either recovering possession of property/premises or dissuading the principal from criminal activity (see Ch. 2 (3) (3)). The relevant case law does not require the 'accessory' owner/controller to act with the objective of preventing the offence. Although that would usually be the inevitable effect, it need not be his *reason* for acting. Supervening fault liability, though principal in nature, raises a *roughly* parallel issue of offence-harm prevention measures. Here the actor may incriminate himself by failing to do what would be reasonable in the dangerous situation he has created.

[49] *Grundy*, and cf. *Barton* [1976] Crim. LR 514 where the defendant had performed in an obscene film, it was held that he was an 'abettor' of the 'continuing' offence of others

achieve an appropriate correlation between the nature and particular circumstances of the complicity and the type of countermanding action which should exempt the accessory.

(3) Must Withdrawal be 'Timely'?

A factor likely to have an important bearing on any judgment whether the accessory has taken 'all reasonable steps' or made 'proper effort' is the timeliness of his actions. Both case law[50] and code[51] provisions explicitly recognize the relevance of the time factor. The closer the withdrawing action to the principal offence the less realistic is the possibility of the offence not occurring.[52] This is true in cases where the accessory's counter-actions are directed at the principal, for the further the criminal venture has progressed the smaller the likelihood of turning back. Timing will be even more critical in cases where the method of withdrawal involves warning law enforcement authorities or the victim.

Besides being obviously relevant to the offence-prevention rationale of the defence, timeliness could also be taken as evidence of the genuineness or voluntariness of withdrawal. Whether or not any formulation of the defence requires specific reference to the withdrawal being 'timely' is debatable. By implication, a 'reasonable steps' or 'proper effort' test embraces all pertinent factors including timeliness. Rather than substantive, the issue is essentially a matter of drafting[53] or judicial preference, although explicit inclusion of a timeliness requirement helps clarify the point and enhance chances of consistency.

possessing the film with intent to publish it. The Court of Appeal thought it 'right in principle' that the defendant continued to abet the offence until he 'dissociated' himself from it. No indication was offered as to how this could be achieved. The defendant had no civil entitlement to take possession of the film, therefore presumably informing the authorities was the only serious possibility for withdrawal.

[50] The reference in *Whitehouse* to 'timely communication' (adopted in *Becerra*) is qualified by 'where practicable and reasonable' (115) which probably means the defence will not be available without timely action in any situation. This was the construction given in *Wagner* (1979) 8 BCLR 258. See also *Miller and Cockriell* (1976) 31 CCC (2d) 417; *White v. Ridley*; Hale, *PC* i. 618.

[51] Law Commission Working Paper 43, proposition 9; Model Penal Code, s. 2.06 (6) (c) (ii). Some US state codes set out detailed requirements: for Arizona a 'warning to law enforcement authorities is not timely within the meaning of this section unless the authorities reasonably acting upon the warning, would have the opportunity to prevent the conduct or result': Rev. Stat. Ann. para. 13–1005 (D).

[52] Withdrawal must occur 'before the act with which he is charged is in the process of consummation or has become so inevitable that it cannot reasonably be stayed': *People v. Brown* 186 NE 2d 321, 324 (1962); similarly, *Comm. v. Mangula* 322 NE 2d 177, *Comm. v. Lee* 399 A. 2d 104 (1979), and *State v. Pyle* 476 NE 2d 124 (1985).

[53] Law Commission Report 177, cl. 27 (8) (*a*) does not include any reference to timeliness or 'reasonable steps'. Under cl. 27 (8) (*a*) it would be possible effectively to withdraw if the accessory countermands encouragement at any point up to the commission of the offence even though its potential affect on the principal may be much less if very close to his actions. Under Report 143, cl. 31 (9), 'reasonable steps' covered all forms of withdrawal including countermanding encouragement.

(4) Motivation for Withdrawal

A final feature common to some jurisdictions is the distinction drawn between withdrawal motivated by the pangs of conscience and that prompted by less creditable reasons, such as fear of apprehension. The difference is well encapsulated in almost biblical terms by *Weaver v. State*:[54] 'whether he was frightened by the approach of the officers or deterred by the voice of conscience and repented of his wicked intentions'. A 'voluntary and complete' withdrawal condition appears in a few American state code reformulations.[55] Amongst the first to incorporate such a demand was the frequently innovatory New York penal code[56] which provides:

A renunciation is not 'voluntary and complete' . . . if it is motivated in whole or in part by (a) a belief that circumstances exist which increase the probability of detection or apprehension of the defendant or another participant in the criminal enterprise, or which render more difficult the accomplishment of the criminal purpose, or (b) a decision to postpone the criminal conduct until another time or to transfer the criminal effort to another victim or another but similar objective.

English authorities on withdrawal offer no direct[57] allusion to the issue, and consequently it is impossible to predict how a future court might respond if confronted with the question of the relevance of motivation.[58] However, as with the problem of what *form* withdrawal should take, here also the solution must turn substantially on the defence's general rationale(s). If an

---

[54] 42 SE 745 (1902) at 747, made in respect of attempt.

[55] Most states with inchoate offence withdrawal provisions include a 'voluntary and complete' element though not for their complicity provision. The basis of the distinction is unclear but may rest on the view that for inchoate offences the defendant, having already incurred liability before withdrawal, must do more than an accessory and with a purer motive to earn his exculpation. This may also explain the requirement that inchoate offenders must prevent the substantive offence occurring (Model Penal Code, s. 5.01 (4)).

[56] Originally enacted in 1965, formerly s. 35.45, now s. 40.10; see *People* v. *Gilmore* 134 AD 2d 653 (1987). See also e.g. earlier similar provisions in the Connecticut Penal Code (1958 Rev) s. 53a-10. Some codes, such as Indiana (s. 35-41-3-10), stipulate 'voluntary' withdrawal without further elaboration. In Indiana's case this has been (generously) construed to mean a 'change of heart, desertion of criminal purpose, change of behaviour, or rising revulsion for the harm intended': *Pyle* v. *State* 476 NE 2d 124 (1985) at 126, and *Peak* v. *State* 520 NE 2d 465 (1988) at 467.

[57] Use of the term 'repent' from *Saunders and Archer* onwards (also Hale, PC i. 618 and Hawkins, PC ii, ch. 29, s. 16) is inconclusive on whether true moral repentance is necessary. In *Becerra* the trial judge appeared to use 'repent' as no more than a synonym for 'countermand' (1976) 62 Cr. App. Rep. 212 at 219. In *Whitehouse* use is made of the expression 'genuine repentance' [1941] 1 WWR 112 at 116. Law Commission Working Paper 43, proposition 9, refers to an accessory who 'genuinely withdraws'; but the commentary implies 'genuinely' means 'real' or 'actual' rather than anything related to motivation (71–3).

[58] Touching on the question of voluntariness in a literal sense is the effect of arrest on an accessory's liability for later offences committed by associates. Where the accessory's detention is unknown to the principal(s) then the accessory's liability remains unaffected, for previous encouragement or material assistance continues. *Johnson and Jones* (1841) C. & M. 218, 174 ER 479. If the principal is aware of his accessory's arrest the effects of prior encouragement will probably be terminated (*Jackson* (1673) Hale, PC i. 464) but material assistance may still retain its potency to incriminate. Effective encouragement or assistance can be rendered by fresh accessorial action *after* arrest. *Craig and Bentley, The Times* 10 December 1952.

incentive/crime-prevention justification is adopted, it is arguable that stipulations as to acceptable motives might inhibit the possible appeal of withdrawal to an equivocating accessory. But if a party is prompted to abandon the venture because of encountering unexpected difficulties or increased fears of detection, how much further incentive will be needed? And, as already suggested, it has to be assumed that accessories are well apprised of the defence's qualifying conditions for the disincentive as well as inducement claim to enjoy credibility. Taking the alternative or complementary view of withdrawal as an indicator of the lack of (or diminished) culpability, or future social dangerousness, would more clearly point to the necessity of distinguishing true repenters from opportunist or inveterate sinners.

However, whilst for reasons such as these, discriminatory provisions, on the lines of the New York code have considerable logical attraction, they suffer from two types of difficulty: determination of *what* motives are to qualify or disqualify and how reliably they could be discerned by a court.

Illustrative of the type of problem involved in settling what behaviour manifests acceptable motivation is where a party abandons an anticipated peaceful criminal enterprise after discovering that his confederates intend to use violence to accomplish the same criminal objective,[59] as in *Becerra*. Is such a motive an acceptable basis for the defence? The actor's repugnance at the means to be employed is laudable, but is he no longer a fitting subject for punishment, or does he still deserve at least a mitigated sentence? As for proof of motive, how easily can an initial lack of firm criminal resolve be distinguished from a change of heart brought on by an unexpected turn of events increasing the chances of apprehension[60] or decreasing those of successfully completing the offence? Yet despite such problems involved in identifying and establishing appropriate (dis)qualifying motives, some discrimination of the sort practised by the New York code is desirable. Without such distinctions patently undeserving examples of excused liability are imaginable,[61] where withdrawal will neither be encouraged by the promise of a defence nor will the accessory have adequately demonstrated a significantly reduced disposition towards criminal activity.[62]

---

[59] Cf. *Wagner* (1979) 8 BCLR 258 at 260 and *Henderson* (1949) 2 DLR 121 at 139. By implication in *Barnard* (1979) 70 Cr. App. Rep. 28 at 33, the Court of Appeal did not rule out the possibility of withdrawal when the accessory was motivated by the belief that the material object of the crime had been relocated to other premises — so making the crime more difficult or impossible.

[60] Was the increased fear of apprehension also a reason for withdrawal in *Becerra*? American jurisdictions deal with the issue by generally making withdrawal an affirmative defence, thus casting on the defendant the burden (a preponderance of the evidence standard) of establishing his motivation for acting. See case law and code provisions cited by Robinson, *Criminal Defenses*, s. 81 (a), 349–50. English authorities provide no clear indication on the question whether the defendant must do more than offer sufficient evidence to raise the issue. Law Commission, Working Paper 43, without directly considering the point, refers to the defendant *establishing* the defence (73).

[61] e.g. having organized a bank robbery, A withdraws without giving his true reasons on learning that the police have been tipped off.

[62] Although perhaps it could be said culpability was less for *that* offence.

Bibliography

Alldridge, P., 'The Coherence of Defences' [1983] Crim. LR 665.
—— 'The Doctrine of Innocent Agency' (1990/1) Crim. L. Forum (forthcoming).
American Law Institute, Model Penal Code (1962) and commentaries (1953–85).
American National Commission on Reform of Federal Criminal Law, Study Draft (1970).
—— Working Papers (1971).
—— Final Report: Proposed New Federal Criminal Code (1971).
—— Report of the Committee on the Judiciary United States Senate: Criminal Code Reform Act of 1979 (1980).
Anscombe, G. E. M., 'Causality and Determination', in E. Sosa, ed., *Causation and Conditionals* (Oxford, 1975), 63.
Ashworth, A. J., 'Transferred Malice and Punishment for Unforeseen Consequences', in P. R. Glazebrook, ed., *Reshaping the Criminal Law: Essays in honour of Glanville Williams* (London, 1978), 77.
—— 'The Elasticity of Mens Rea', in C. F. H. Tapper, ed., *Crime Proof and Punishment: Essays in honour of Sir Rupert Cross* (London, 1981), 45.
—— *Sentencing and Penal Policy* (London, 1983).
—— 'Sharpening the Subjective Element in Criminal Liability', in R. A. Duff and N. Simmonds, eds., *Philosophy and the Criminal Law* (Wiesbaden, 1984), 79.
—— 'The Draft Code, Complicity and Inchoate Offences' [1986] Crim. LR 303.
—— 'Belief, Intent, and Criminal Liability', in J. S. Bell and J. M. Eekelaar (eds). *Oxford Essays in Jurisprudence: Third Series* (Oxford, 1987), 1.
—— 'Defining Criminal Offences without Harm', in P. F. Smith, ed., *Criminal Law: Essays in honour of J. C. Smith* (London, 1987), 7.
—— 'Criminal Attempts and the Role of Resulting Harm under the Code and in Common Law' (1988) 19 *Rut. LJ* 725.
—— 'The Scope of Criminal Liability for Omissions' (1989) 105 *LQR* 424.
Attenborough, F. L., ed. and trans., *The Laws of the Earliest English Kings* (Cambridge, 1922).
Austin, J., *Lectures on Jurisprudence*, 4th edn. (London, 1879).
Austin, J. L., 'A Plea for Excuses' (1956–7) 57 *Proceedings of the Aristotelian Society* 1, reproduced in A. R. White, ed., *The Philosophy of Action* (Oxford, 1968), 19.
Becker, L. C., 'Criminal Attempts and the Theory of the Law of Crimes' (1974) 3 *Phil. and Pub. Aff.* 262.
Bein, D., 'Recent Developments in Israeli Criminal Law' (1977) 12 *Is. LR* 180.
Bentham, J., *An Introduction to the Principles of Morals and Legislation* (1789), ed. J. H. Burns and H. L. A. Hart (London, 1982).
Benyon, H., 'Causation, Omissions and Complicity' [1987] Crim. LR 539.
Binavince, E. S., 'The Ethical Foundations of Criminal Liability' (1964) 33 *Ford. LR* 1.
Blackstone, W., *Commentaries on the Laws of England* (Oxford, 1767).

Bracton on the Laws and Customs of England, trans. S. E. Thorne (Cambridge, Mass., 1968).
Burchell, E. M., and Hunt, P. M. A., *South African Criminal Law and Procedure*, 2nd edn. (Cape Town, 1983).
Buxton, R. J., 'Complicity in the Criminal Code' (1969) 85 *LQR* 252.
—— 'Complicity and the Law Commission' [1973] Crim. LR 223.
—— 'The Extent of Criminal Complicity' (1979) 42 *MLR* 315.
Campbell, K., 'Offence and Defence', in I. H. Dennis, ed., *Criminal Law and Justice* (London, 1987), 73.
Canada, Law Reform Commission, Working Paper 45, *Secondary Liability: Participation in Crime and Inchoate Offences* (1985).
—— Report 31, *Recodifying Criminal Law* (1987).
Carpenter, C., 'Should the Court Aid and Abet the Unintending Accomplice: The Status of Complicity in California' (1984) 24 Santa Carla LR 343.
Charen, S. C., and Colangelo, J. P., 'The Proposed New Federal Criminal Code' (1976) *An. Survey of Am. Law* 313.
Chitty, J., *A Treatise on the Criminal Law* (London, 1816).
Crabtree, J. H., 'Accessory Liability: Acquittal of Principal' (1984) 15 Memphis SULR 87.
Criminal Code Bill Commission Report (1879).
Criminal Law Commissioners' Reports (1834–49).
Criminal Law Revision Committee, 11th Report, *Evidence* (1972), Cmnd. 4991.
—— 14th Report, *Offences Against the Person* (1980), Cmd. 7844.
—— *Working Paper on Sexual Offences* (1980).
—— 16th Report, *Prostitution in the Street* (1984), Cmnd. 9329.
Cross, R., 'Duress and Aiding and Abetting' (1952) 69 *LQR* 354.
—— 'The Reports of the Criminal Law Commissioners (1833–1849)', in P. R. Glazebrook, ed., *Reshaping the Criminal Law: Essays in honour of Glanville Williams* (London, 1978), 5.
—— *The English Sentencing System*, 3rd edn. by A. J. Ashworth (London, 1981), 152.
—— *Evidence*, 6th edn. by C. F. H. Tapper (London, 1985).
—— *Statutory Interpretation*, 2nd edn. by J. Bell and G. Engle (London, 1987).
Dan-Cohen, M., 'Decision Rules and Conduct Rules: An Acoustic Separation in Criminal Law' (1984) 97 *HLR* 625.
Davis, M., 'Why Attempts Deserve Less Punishment than Complete Crimes' (1986) 5 *Law and Phil.* 1.
Dawkins, K. E., 'Parties, conspiracies and attempts' (1990) 20 VUWLR Monograph 117.
Dennis, I. H., 'The Mental Element for Accessories', in P. F. Smith, ed., *Criminal Law: Essays in honour of J. C. Smith* (London, 1987), 40.
—— 'Intention and Complicity: A Reply' [1988] Crim. LR 649; [1989] Crim. LR 168.
Devlin, J., 'Criminal Responsibility and Punishment' [1954] Crim. LR 661, 666–7.
Doherty, P., 'A New Crime: Criminal Facilitation' (1971) 18 Loyola LR 103.
Downer, L. J., ed. and trans., *Leges Henrici Primi* (1972).
Dray, W. H., 'Causal Judgment in Attributive and Explanatory Contexts' (1986) 49 *Law and Contemp. Probs.* 13.

Dressler, J., 'New Thoughts about the Concept of Justification in the Criminal Law: A Critique of Fletcher's Thinking and Re-thinking' (1984) 32 *UCLA LR* 61.
—— 'Reassessing the Theoretical Underpinnings of Accomplice Liability: New Solutions to an Old Problem' (1985) 37 *Hastings LJ* 91.
—— 'Provocation: Partial Justification or Partial Excuse?' (1988) 51 MLR 467.
Duff, R. A., 'Can I help you?' (1990) 10 LS 165.
East, E. H., *A Treatise of the Pleas of the Crown* (London, 1803).
Edwards, J. L. J., *Mens Rea in Statutory Offences* (London, 1955).
Eser, A., 'Justification and Excuse' (1976) 24 *Am. J. Comp. L.* 621.
Feinberg, J., 'Causing Voluntary Actions', *Doing and Deserving* (Princeton, 1970), ch. 7.
—— *Harm to Others* (New York, 1984).
Fletcher, G. P., 'The Individualisation of Excusing Conditions' (1974) 47 *S. Cal. LR* 1296.
—— *Rethinking Criminal Law* (Boston, 1978).
Foster, M., *A Report on Crown Cases and Discourses on the Crown Law* (London, 1762 edn.).
Gasking, D., 'Causation and Recipes' (1955) 64 *Mind* 479.
Gillies, P., *The Law of Criminal Complicity* (Sydney, 1980).
Gordon, G. H., *The Criminal Law of Scotland*, 2nd edn. (Edinburgh, 1978).
Greenawalt, K., 'The Perplexing Borders of Justification and Excuse' (1984) 84 *Col. L. Rev.* 1897.
—— 'Distinguishing Justifications from Excuses' (1986) 49 *Law and Contemp. Probs.* 89.
—— 'A Vice of its Virtues' (1988) 19 *Rut. LJ* 929.
Griew, E., 'Consistency, Communication and Codification: Reflections on Two Mens Rea Words', in P. R. Glazebrook, ed., *Reshaping the Criminal Law: Essays in honour of Glanville Williams* (London, 1978), 72.
—— 'Dishonesty: The Objections to Feely and Ghosh' [1985] Crim. LR 341.
—— *The Theft Acts 1968 and 1978*, 5th edn. (London, 1986).
—— 'It Must Have Been One of Them' [1989] Crim. LR 129.
Gross, H., *A Theory of Criminal Justice* (New York, 1979).
Gur-Ayre, M., 'A Theory of Complicity: Comment', in R. Gavison, ed., *Issues in Contemporary Legal Philosophy: The Influence of H. L. A. Hart* (Oxford, 1987).
Hale, M., *The History of the Pleas of the Crown* (London, 1736).
Hall, J., *General Principles of Criminal Law*, 2nd edn. (Indianapolis, 1960).
—— 'American Penal Law viz à viz German Penal Theory', in *Law, Social Science and Criminal Theory* (Littleton, Col., 1982), 165.
Hart, H. L. A., *Punishment and Responsibility* (Oxford, 1968).
—— and Honoré, T., *Causation in the Law,* 1st edn. (1959), 2nd edn. (Oxford, 1985).
Hassett, P., 'Absolutism in Causation' (1987) 38 *Syr. LR* 683.
Hawkins, W., *A Treatise of the Pleas of the Crown*, 8th edn. by J. Curwood (London, 1824).
Hobbes, T., *Leviathan* (London, 1651).
Hoeber, P. R., 'The Abandonment Defense to Criminal Attempt and Other Problems of Temporal Individuation' (1986) 74 Cal. L. Rev. 377.
Holdsworth, W., *A History of English Law* (London, 1922).

Holmes, O. W., *The Common Law* (London, 1881).
Horowitz, D. L., 'Justification and Excuse in the Program of the Criminal Law' (1986) 49 *Law and Contemp. Probs.* 109.
Husak, D. N., 'Justifications and the Criminal Liability of Accessories' (1989) 80 J Crim. L and Crim. 491.
Kadish, S. H., 'Complicity, Cause and Blame: A Study in the Interpretation of Doctrine' (1985) 73 *Cal. L. Rev.* 324.
—— *Blame and Punishment* (New York, 1987).
—— 'Excusing Crime' (1987) 75 *Cal. LR* 257.
Karp, D. J., 'Causation in the Model Penal Code' (1978) 78 *Col. LR* 1249.
Katz, A., 'Dangerousness: A Theoretical Reconstruction of the Criminal Law, Part I' (1970) 19 *Buffalo LR* 1.
Kelly, R. D., 'Social Host's Criminal Liability' (1986) 39 *Okl. LR* 689.
Kenny, C. S., *Outlines of Criminal Law*, 1st edn. (Cambridge, 1902); ed. J. W. C. Turner (Cambridge, 1952–66).
Kling, L., 'Constitutionalizing The Death Penalty for Accomplices to Felony Murder' (1988) 26 Am. Crim. LR 463.
La Fave, W. R., and Scott, A. W., *Criminal Law* (St Paul, Minn., 1986).
Lanham, D., 'Accomplices and Constructive Liability' (1980) 4 *Crim. LJ* 78.
—— 'Accomplices and Transferred Malice' (1980) 96 *LQR* 110.
—— 'Accomplices, Principals and Causation' (1980) 12 *Mel. ULR* 490.
—— 'Complicity, Concert and Conspiracy' (1980) 4 *Crim. LJ* 276.
—— 'Accomplices and Withdrawal' (1981) 97 *LQR* 575.
—— 'Drivers, Control and Accomplices' [1982] Crim. LR 419.
—— 'Limitations on Accomplice Liability' (1982) 6 *Crim. LJ* 306.
Law Commission Working Paper 43, *Parties, Complicity and Liability for the Act of Another* (1972).
—— Working Paper 50, *Inchoate Offences, Conspiracy, Attempt and Incitement* (1973).
—— Report 83, *Defences of General Application* (1977).
—— Report 102, *Attempt, and Impossibility in Relation to Attempt, Conspiracy and Incitement* (1980).
—— Report 143, *Criminal Law: Codification of the Criminal Law: A Report to the Law Commission* (1985).
—— Working Paper 104, *Conspiracy to Defraud* (1987).
—— Report 177, *Criminal Law: A Criminal Code for England and Wales* (1989).
Lucas, J. R., *On Justice* (Oxford, 1980).
McAuley, F., 'Anticipating the Past' (1987) 50 *MLR*.
Mackie, J. L., *The Cement of the Universe* (Oxford, 1980).
Mandil, D. M., 'Chance, Freedom and Criminal Liability' (1987) *Col. LR* 125.
Marston, G., 'Contemporaneity of Act and Intention' (1970) 86 *LQR* 208.
Matzukis, N. A., 'The Nature and Scope of Common Purpose' (1988) 2 SACJ 226.
Milsom, S. F. C., *Historical Foundations of the Common Law* (London, 1969).
Moore, M. S., 'Causation and the Excuses' (1985) 73 *Cal. L. Rev.* 1091.
Moriarty, D. G., 'Extending the Defense of Renunciation' (1989) 62 Temp. LR 1.
Mueller, G. O. W., 'Causing Criminal Harm', in id., ed., *Essays in Criminal Science* (1961), 169.
Nagel, T., 'Moral Luck' (1976) 50 *Proc. of the Aristotelian Soc.* supp. 137.

Nichols, F. M., ed. and trans., *Britton* (Oxford, 1865).
Orchard, G., 'Parties to an Offence: The Function of s. 66 (2) of the Crimes Act' [1988] NZLJ 151.
O'Regan, R. S., 'Complicity and the Defence of Timely Countermand or Withdrawal under the Griffith Code' (1986) 10 *Crim. LJ* 236.
Pattenden, R., 'The Power of the Courts to Stay a Criminal Prosecution' [1985] Crim. LR 174.
—— *Judicial Discretion and Criminal Litigation* (Oxford, 1990).
Perkins, R. M., and Boyce, R. N., *Criminal Law*, 3rd edn. (Mineola, NY, 1982).
Pollock, F., and Maitland, F. W., *The History of English Law before the Time of Edward I*, 2nd edn. (Cambridge, 1898).
Proceedings before the Justices of the Peace in the XIVth and XVth century, ed. B. H. Putnam (1938).
Radzinowicz, L., *A History of English Criminal Law and its Administration from 1750* (London, 1948–).
Robertson, A. J., ed. and trans., *The Laws of the Kings of England from Edmund to Henry I* (Cambridge, 1925).
Robinson, P. H., 'A Theory of Justification: Societal Harm as a Prerequisite for Criminal Liability' (1975) 23 *UCLA LR* 266.
—— 'Criminal Law Defenses: A Systematic Analysis' (1982) 82 *Col. LR* 199.
—— 'Element Analysis in Defining Criminal Liability: The Model Penal Code and Beyond' (1983) 35 *Stan. LR* 681.
—— *Criminal Law Defenses* (St Paul, Minn., 1984).
—— 'Imputed Criminal Liability' (1984) 93 *YLJ* 609.
Rogers, P., 'The Waltham Blacks and the Black Act' (1974) 17 *Hist. Jo.*, 465.
Rose, V. G., *Parties to an Offence* (Agincourt, Ont., 1982).
Rosenthal, J. L., 'Aiding and Abetting Liability for Civil Violations of RICO' (1988) 61 Temp. LR 1481.
Rotenberg, D. L., 'Withdrawal as a Defense to Relational Crimes' (1962) *Wis. LR* 596.
Roxin, C., *Täterschaft und Tatherrschaft*, 4th edn. (Hamburg, 1984).
Russell on Crime, 3rd edn. (London, 1843) and 4th edn. (1865) by C. S. Greaves; 5th edn. (1877) by S. Prentice; 10th–12th edns. (1950–64) by J. W. C. Turner.
Sayre, F. B., 'Criminal Responsibility for the Acts of Another' (1930) 43 *HLR* 689.
Schreiber, H. L., 'Problems of Justification and Excuse in the Setting of Accessorial Conduct' (1986) *Brig. Young ULR* 611.
Schulhofer, S. J., 'Harm and Punishment: A Critique of Emphasis on the Results of Conduct in the Criminal Law' (1974) 122 *U. Pa. LR* 1497.
Smith, J. C., 'The Element of Chance in Criminal Liability' [1971] Crim. LR 63.
—— 'Aid, Abet, Counsel, or Procure', in P. R. Glazebrook, ed., *Reshaping the Criminal Law: Essays in honour of Glanville Williams* (London, 1978), 120.
—— 'Reform of the Law of Offences Against the Person' [1978] *CLP* 15.
—— 'Secondary Participation and Inchoate Offences', in C. F. H. Tapper, ed., *Crime, Proof and Punishment: Essays in honour of Sir Rupert Cross* (1981), 21.
—— *Justification and Excuse in the Criminal Law* (London, 1989).
—— *The Law of Theft*, 6th edn. (London, 1989).
—— and Hogan, B., *Criminal Law*, 6th edn. (London, 1988).
Snyman, C. R., *Criminal Law* (Durban, 1984).

Sobel, N. R., 'The Anticipatory Offences in the New Penal Law: Solicitation, Conspiracy, Attempt and Facilitation' (1966) 32 *Brooklyn LR* 257.
Spencer, J. R., 'Trying to Help Another Person Commit a Crime', in P. F. Smith, ed., *Criminal Law: Essays in honour of J. C. Smith* (1987), 148.
Stephen, J. F., *Digest of the Criminal Law*, 3rd edn. (London, 1883).
—— *History of the Criminal Law of England* (London, 1883).
Stokes, W., *Anglo-Indian Codes* (Oxford, 1887).
Strong, G., 'Fault, Threat and the Predicates of Criminal Liability' (1980) *Wis. LR* 441.
Stroud, D. A., *Mens Rea* (London, 1914).
Sullivan, G. R., 'Intent, Purpose and Complicity' [1988] Crim. LR 641; [1989] Crim. LR 166.
Taylor, R. D., 'Complicity and Excuses' [1983] Crim. LR 656.
Thomas, D. A., *Principles of Sentencing* (London, 1979).
Thompson, E. P., *Whigs and Hunters* (London, 1975).
Unterhalter, D., 'The Doctrine of Common Purpose: What Makes One Person Liable for the Acts of Another?' (1988) 105 SALJ 671.
Vangel, J. T., 'A Complicity-Doctrine Approach to Section 10 (b) Aiding and Abetting Civil Damages Actions' (1989) 89 Col. LR 180.
Wasik, M., 'Abandoning Criminal Intent' [1980] Crim. LR 785.
Weinert, H. R., 'Social Hosts and Drunken Drivers: A Duty to Intervene?' (1985) 133 *U. Penn. LR* 867.
Westerfield, L., 'The Mens Rea Requirement of Accomplice Liability in American Criminal Law: Knowledge or Intent' (1980) 51 *Miss. LJ* 155.
White, A., 'The Scope of Accomplice Liability under Section 18 USC section 2 (b)' (1981) 31 *Case West RL Rev.* 386.
Williams, G. L., *Criminal Law: The General Part*, 2nd edn. (London, 1961).
—— 'Offences and Defences' (1982) 2 *LS* 233.
—— 'The Theory of Excuses' [1982] Crim. LR 732.
—— 'Convictions and Fair Labelling' (1983) 42 *CLJ* 85.
—— *Textbook of Criminal Law* (London, 1983).
—— 'What Should the Code Do about Omissions?' (1987) 7 *LS* 92.
—— '*Finis* for *Novus Actus*? (1989) *CLJ* 391.
—— 'Which of You Did it?' (1989) 52 *MLR* 179.
—— 'Complicity, Purpose and the Draft Code' [1990] Crim. LR 4 and 98.
Winfield, P. H., *History of Conspiracy and Abuse of Legal Procedure* (Cambridge, 1921).
Wright, R. S., *Law of Criminal Conspiracies and Agreements* (London, 1873).

Index

abortion
  accessory, mental culpability of 187
  party to procuring 146
  'victim', complicity of 240
accessory
  acquittal of principal, conviction after 113
  actus reus 5
  see also *actus reus*
  after the fact 7, 22
  agent of, perpetrator as 6
  at the fact 23–4, 111
  before the fact
    abettors distinguished 128
    participation, degree of 22
    principal
      convicted and sentenced after 25, 111–12
      greater liability than, not having 117, 127–9
      second degree, in 33
  broad theory of liability 120 n.
  cause, proof of 61
  common purpose, see common purpose
  consent or knowledge of principal, acting without 74
  de minimis principle 86
  delimitation of liability 206
  different level of criminality to that of principal, liable for 127–34
  essential matters, knowledge of
    belief, knowledge extending to 169–70, 183
    'blank cheque' principle 167–70, 194
    case law 161–9
    categorization, not dependent on 165
    contemplation test 166–7, 175
    essential matters, meaning 162–3
    generally 13–14
    large criminal organization, membership of 170
    modern *mens rea* formula 160–2
    particular crime theory 167
    principal offender, state of mind of 178
    specificity, problem with 171–2
    suspicion distinguished 163 n., 169
    theoretical implication 169–72
    type test of specificity 163–8
  foresight of offence occurring 13–14, 166, 170–2
  German law of 81
  harm
    criminally wrong, existence of 123
    perpetrator lacking criminal fault,
      where 118–20
    requirement of 114–18
  infanticide cases, in 132
  knowledge of assisting or encouraging principal
    American cases 142–3
    assent to criminal venture, not requiring 150–3
    English case law 143–50
    facilitation offences 157–60
    foreseeing principal action 153
    Gillick case 147–9
    indifference, effect of 144
    intention of 141
    problem of 141–3
    purpose, not requiring 150–3
    unlawful sexual intercourse, aiding and abetting 147–9
  law enforcement objectives, actions motivated by 15, 243–5
  manslaughter, to 186–9
  mens rea
    causal element 195
    conclusions as to 194–6
    elements of 139
    essential matters, knowledge of, see essential matters, knowledge of, *above*
    indifference 159
    knowledge of assisting or encouraging principal, see knowledge of assisting or encouraging principal, *above*
    normative issue of 154
    presence, effect of 155
    principal offence, see principal offence, *below*
    principal offender, *mens rea* of 177–9
    procuring, state of mind as to 155
    proper level of 154–5
    purposefulness, introducing 196
    purposive standards 159–60
    transaction, in context of 155–6
  multiple subsequent offences, incrimination for 15
  outcome of action, attitude to 12
  participation by 6
  positive action, liability without 34
    see also inaction
  presence at offence 25–6
  principal in second degree, as 23–4
  principal offence
    accessorial liability without, justification of 134

accessory (cont.):
  attitude to 13, 142, 149–50, 194
  circumstances and consequences, knowledge of
    essential matters, of 183
    foresight, appropriate level of 183–4
    generally 179–80
    meaning 180–3
    more than one level of 184
    need for 180
    negligence, offences of 180, 189
    recklessness 181, 184–5
    specific *mens rea*, offences requiring 180
  essential matters, knowledge of, *see* essential matters, knowledge of, *above*
  gravity, effect of 157
  interest in outcome of 142
  knowledge of 139
  negligence, of
    abortion cases 187
    acting dangerously 188
    circumstances or consequences, knowledge of 180, 189
    conduct offences 185
    consequence offences 185
    dangerous driving cases 189
    participants, designation of causal roles to 190
    principal of parallelism 186
    unlawful homicide, unintended consequence of 185–90
  occurrence, perceived likelihood of
    common purpose cases, in 175–6
    high level of 174
    jury, function of 176–7
    knowledge, requirement of 173
    primary objective, in course of carrying out 174–5
    'probable' or 'possible' 175
    purposeful identification with 173
    where required 173
  requirement of 94, 110–12, 114, 118
  see also principal offence
principal offender
  action, foresight of 153–4
  complete defence, having 120–4
  see also defences
  conviction of, 22–3
  criminal fault, lacking 118–20, 130
  different level of criminality, liable for 127–33
  innocence of, *see also* innocent agency, doctrine of
    acquittal after conviction of accessory 113
    duress, acquittal on grounds of 116
    effect of 114–16
    liability of accessory, derivation of 117
    rape, belief in consent of victim 116
  joint indictment with 113
  mens rea, accessory's knowledge of
    assistance, where provided 178
    common purpose cases, in 179
    instigation, in case of 178
    liability, affecting 178
    no *mens rea*, where 179
  non-conviction of 112
  not criminally liable, where 114–20
  not charged, where 115–16
  perception of 139
  semi-innocent 130–3
  variation in performance by, *see* principal offender
provocation, plea of 132
punishment 72–3, 90
renunciation by 15
strict liability offences, *see* strict liability offences
suicide, to 146
use of term 1 n.
victim of crime, as 15, 239–42
withdrawal by, *see* withdrawal
accident
  transferred malice, doctrine of 198–9
  variation by principal due to 198
accomplice
  subsequent offence, limitation as to 247
  use of term 1 n.
actor
  actus reus, substantial part in bringing about 157–8
  perpetrator, *mens rea* greater than 128–9
  use of term 2 n.
actus reus
  accessory, of 5
  common purpose as 63
  causation, *see* causation
  direct or immediate cause of 28
  fault requirements, fulfilling 29
  innocent agency, *see* innocent agency, doctrine of
  joint activity 28–9
  mens rea level, trading off 158
  proximate concern with 27
  rape, of 36
  substantial role in bringing about 157–8
  withdrawal, effect of 252
advice, meaning 34 n.
affray, presence at scene of 36
agency
  civil law of 74
  commercial considerations 76
  complicity compared

Index

consent 74
  dissimilarities 75–6
  ostensible or apparent authority 75
  ratification 75
  reversal of roles 75
consensus, importance of 74
control, notion of 75
hegemony theory 75
innocent, doctrine of, *see* innocent agency, doctrine of
primitive civil law notions of 6
principal
  control or dominance of 75
  innocent agency, in, *see* innocent agency, doctrine of
  semi-innocent 130–3
  voluntary or involuntary action 68–9
aiding, abetting, counselling or procuring
  degrees of 33–4
  literal construction 32–3
  matter of fact, as 35
  meaning 30–4
  presence or absence, indicating 32
  statutory provisions 31–3, 213 n.
aiding and abetting
  agreement in 218
  essential matters, knowledge of, *see* accessory
  mens rea 144
  teminology, use of 161 n.
assault and battery, personal action, by 108
attempt
  complicity charge, acting with 10
  complicity in 53–4
  inchoate offences, as 9
  proximity, problems of 4
  sentence, equality of 72 n.
autrefois convict 247–8

benefit of clergy 23–4
bigamy, procuring 114–15
buggery, complicity in 115–16
burglary, personal action, by 107

causation
  analysis of, generally 19
  'cause'
    accessory causing principal's action 67
    agent, voluntary or involuntary action of 68–70
    assumed 87–8
    case law, alternative interpretations of 69
    common speech, in 69
    deliberate human act thesis 66–72, 78, 81
    directness or immediacy of 80–2
    factual 66
    foreseen intervening act 70
    interpersonal transactions, in relation to 67–8, 83
    meaning 66–70, 78
    proximity, determining 66
    voluntary human action 66–70, 78, 81
  common purpose, *see* common purpose
  complicity, role in
    accessory, instigation of 56–7
    actus reus, immediate cause of 80–2
    case law, paucity of 63–4, 88
    causal contribution of accessory 56, 79–82
    de minimis principle 86
    encouragement, *see* encouragement
    minimum 82–5
    proof of 86–8
    sina qua non notion 82–4
    substantiality 86–8
    variation of actions 82–3
  cause, meaning 66–73
    see also 'cause', *above*
  common purpose, principal's actions going beyond 56
  counselling 59–60
  coverage, narrow 90
  criminal responsibility, choice and chance in 64–6
  English case law 55–60
  foreign authorities 61–2
  institutional authorities 61
  intended actions, limited to 67
  principals and accessories, causal distinction of 79–82
  procuring, in respect of 55, 58–9
  rationale 78
  theoretical possibilities 64
  conspiracy, in respect of 51
  harm, role of 70–1
  innocent agency, in, *see* innocent agency, doctrine of
  mere presence, where 38–9
  omission, in respect of 44
  subsequent offences, in respect of 247
  voluntary human action, role of 68–70
cause and control theories 6, 7
'causing' offences
  complicity, as development of 125
  external elements of 125
  innocent agency, resemblance to 125–6
  liability, extent of 126
  principal, punishable as 124
  statutory development of 124–7
chance
  criminal responsibility, in 64–6
  principal liability, in fixing 83
collateral offences, liability for 209–10

272 Index

common law
  derivative form of complicity 3, 133
  innocent agency, recognition of 12, 95
    see also innocent agency, doctrine of
  liability, development of 89–90
  participation in crime, evolved approach to 89–90
common purpose
  actions going beyond 56, 226–8
  actus reus of accessory, as 63
  agreement
    express or tacit 218, 221
    going beyond 219–21
    limitation of accessorial liability by 218–19
  agreement in conspiracy compared 53, 218
  basis of 203
  case law 49
  collateral offences, liability for 209–10
  constructive liability 211, 233–4
  contemplation, reference to 219–20
  convicting accessory of manslaughter where principal convicted of murder, see manslaughter
  doctrine of
    function and nature of 209, 231–2
    generally 14–15
    mental culpability, confusion as to 232
    relevance of 63
    standard formulation of 209
  existence and operation of 63
  felony–murder rule 214–18
  foresight 218–22
  modern case law issues 214–18
  murder, in context of 215–17
  nineteenth century and earlier developments 210–24
  perceived likelihood of occurrence of offence 175–6
  poaching, shooting in course of 215
  policy objectives 231–4
  principal's state of mind, accessory's knowledge of 179
  scope, categorization of issues according to 224
  statutory proposals 212–13
  terminology of 209, 218, 231–2
  variations in performance, relationship with 197–8, 221–5
complicitous behaviour, modes of
  absence or presence, on basis of 32–3
  aid, abet, counsel or procure, meaning 30–4
  generally 26–7
  inaction 34–47
    see also inaction
  principal offender, see principal

complicity
  agency compared, see agency
  Canadian Law Reform Commission proposals 91
  causation, role of, see causation
  consent, no requirement of 74
  conspiracy, features shared with 47
  defences, see defences
  dependent or derivative structure, nature and extent of 11
  derivative form, development and adoption of 3
  derivative nature, see derivative nature of complicity
  exemption from liability for, see exemption from liability
  felonies, see felonies
  function of 1
  inaction, through 34–47
    see also inaction
  inchoate liability, as parent of 9
  liability elements 1
  limitations of liability for, see limitation of liability
  materials, supply of 92–3
  mental requirement 12–15
    see also *mens rea*
  modes of 20 *et seq*
  motive, immateriality of 145, 151
  offence, carrying out 77
  old laws of 2 n.
  omission to exercise right, grounded on 10, 11
  plot device, as 2
  principal liability, relationship with 4, 5
  punishment, see punishment
  scope of 10, 19, 92–3
  strict liability offences, in, see strict liability offences
  suicide, in 57
  superstructure of rules 4
  theories of 4–7
  use of term 1 n.
  wrongfulness, degree of 119–20
conspiracy
  agreement, requirement of 47
  auxiliary mode of complicity, as agreement and *actus reus/mens rea* requirements 52–3
    American law 49–54
    English authority as to 48–9
    generally 11
    'Pinkerton doctrine' 49, 51–2
    shared features and functions 47
  behaviour sufficient to make person party to 50–1
  boundaries 48
  causation requirements 51

Index

common objective, offences in furtherance of 50
common purpose compared 53, 218
complicity charge, supporting 9
complicity in 54
English Draft Code, under 50
inchoate offence, as 9, 47
overlap with complicity 118
principal liability in 51
contraceptive advice
  unlawful sexual intercourse, aiding and abetting 147–9
control, omission to exercise right 10, 11
counselling
  causal connection 59–60
  ordinary meaning of 60
  see also aiding, abetting, counselling or procuring
crime
  reasonable force, prevention by 152–3
  thwarting by witholding property 152
criminal activity
  designation, basis for 119
  explicit approval of 76
  uncommunicated encouragement of 76
criminal liability
  causal connection between action and proscribed harm, resting on 3
  civil obligations, in course of satisfying 151–2
  elements 1
  uncontrollable and unpredictable behaviour of another, turning on 65
criminal responsibility
  choice and chance in 64–6
  harm, linked to 70–1
  mental culpability 119
criminality
  appropriate limits of 4

defences
  coercion 122
  excusatory 120
    meaning 121–2
  general 15–16, 250–1
  incapacity 122–3
  inevitable incidental participation 238–43
  intoxication 250–1
  justificatory 120–1
  law enforcement objectives, secondary participation motivated by 15, 243–5
  perpetrator having 120–4
  provocation 132
  withdrawal, see withdrawal
derivative nature of complicity
  criminal behaviour, requirement of 94
  departure from 134
  evolution of 133
  function of 73
  generally 11, 12, 89, 94–5
  historical development 133
  innocent agency, see innocent agency, doctrine of
  prominent element, as 73
  quality of 73
  trigger, operation of 73–4
diminished responsibility, reduction of liability 131
doctor, unlawful sexual intercourse, aiding and abetting 147–9
driving offences
  control or possession, omissions relating to 40–1
  negligence, offence of 189
  perpetrator, finding of no fault by 123–4
  personal action, requiring 108
  procuring 58

employment, control, failure to exercise 41–2
encouragement
  accessory's knowledge of, see mental culpability in complicity
  aiding and abetting, whether amounting to 36–7
  communication of 77
  deliberate and unintentional deviation, distinction between 200 n.
  liability, accounting for 84
  minimum requirement for complicity, as 36
  more than one party, by 85
  offence already settled, where 85
  purposive state of mind, entailing 155
  withdrawal of 255, 257–8
equivalence theories
  principal criminality, replicating 5
  variable level of culpability 5
evidence, principal and accessory, different for 112–13
exemption from liability
  inevitable incidental participation, for 238–43
  law enforcement objectives, secondary participation motivated by 15, 243–5
  passive, supporting or secondary role 238
  penal policies, where incrimination undermining 240
  victims, of 239–42
explosives offences, essential matters, accessory's knowledge of 164–5

facilitation offences
  criminal, American offence of 158

facilitation offences (*cont.*):
    explicit twin bases of 159
    purposive standard with 159–60
    substantial role in 157–8
felonies
    abolition 24
    benefit of clergy 23–4
    participation, separate levels of 20, 22–3
felony–murder rule 214–18

grievous bodily harm, common design, violence going beyond 227

harm
    inchoate liability, lack of 71
    intangible 71
    perpetrator lacking criminal fault, where 118–20
    principal offence, or 114–18
    punishment, and 71–2, 91
    responsibility, linked to 70–1
homicide
    collateral liability for 210
    constructive 214
    convicting accessory of manslaughter where principal convicted of murder, *see* manslaughter
    diminished responsibility, plea of 131
    unintended consequence of 185–90

illegal functions, presence at 10
inaction
    causal connections 38–9
    complicity, association with 34
    control, omission to exercise as complicity
        acceptable form of criminality, whether 45
        basis and scope of 39
        causation 44
        courts, recognition by 46
        duty, performance as 39–40, 42
        employment situations, in 41–2
        hypothetical cases 46
        licensee, by 42–3
        moral responsibility 45
        motor vehicles, in relation to 40–1
        personal harm, risk of 47
        principal liability, comparison with 43
        relationship with parties 47
        risk potential, production of 44–5
        theoretical legitimacy 43–7
    criminal activity, abstaining from preventing 35
    encouragement of principal, requirement of 36–7
    legal duty, failure to perform 34
    minimal qualifying activity 35
    non-intervention, entitlement of 38
    presence as basis for complicity 35–9
    public performance, presence at 36–8
    right, failure to exercise or assert 34
inchoate liability
    autonomous nature of 9
    communication of encouragement 77
    complicity in offences of 53–4
    creation of 8–10
    formal punishment provisions 72
    harm, lack of 71
    nature of criminality represented by 72
    preliminary premises 76–7
    punishment 77
    rationale of 77
    reassessment and restructuring of complicity, drawing into 93
    responsibility for 72
    specific offences, linked to 171
incitement
    complicity in 54
    inchoate offence, as 9
    overlap with complicity 118
indirect participation, criminal nature of 2
infanticide
    accessory in 132
    reduction of liability for 131
innocent agency
    actions and results, attributing 101–2
    borderline cases 102
    'causing' action
        authorities, agent being agent of 104–5
        basis for 103–5, 125–6
        conduct offences, in 106
        human agency, use of 105–6
        immediate cause, identification with 105
        limitation on use of doctrine 104
        personally performed actions, offences implicitly requiring 107–10
        prescribed qualities or status, perpetrators needing 106–7
        principal, what is attributed to 103, 105–10
        rape 106–9
        requirement of 103
        resemblance to 125
    incapable perpetrator, where 123
    insanity, innocence in form of 100 n., 105
    manipulation or control
        responsibility, attribution of 109
        whether of the essence 102 n.
    morally guilty party, whether appropriate to incriminate 98–9
    'non-proxyable' act 107–8
    novus actus interveniens, effect of 100–1
    principal, mental culpability of
        actions towards agent, as to 97–8
        complicity, extension of 117–18

Index

general causal principles, use of 103
generally 96
intention to cause actions 97–103
nature of agent's innocence, awareness of 97
negligence or recklessness, crimes requiring 98
no criminal liability, having 114–20
recognition by common law 12, 95
restriction of scope 98–9
scope, extension of 116–17
'shield cases' 99–100
'shoot back' cases, in 99–101
simplicity of 95–6
intoxication, defence, as 250–1

law enforcement objectives, secondary participation motivated by 15, 243–5
liability, generally
　constructive 211
　derivative quality of 19
　primary or secondary 27–8
licensee, inaction by 42–3
limitation of liability
　autrefois convict 247–8
　express 247
　judicial discretion 247–8
　subsequent offences by principal
　　causation 247
　　generally 245–6
　　Law Commission proposals 248–9
　　mens rea 246
　　restriction by accomplice 247

manslaughter
　abortion, *see* abortion
　accessory, mental culpability of 186–9
　conviction of accessory where principal convicted of murder
　　basis for liability 227
　　case law 225–8
　　common purpose, not acting beyond 226–7
　　fault element 227
　　overwhelming supervening event 228–9
　　unforseen act 228–9
　　weapons, relevance of 230–1
　intentionally assisting or encouraging 189
　perpetrator excused for lacking fault, where 123
mens rea
　accessory, of, *see* accessory
　actus reus level, trading off 158
　aiding and abetting, required for 144
　coincidence of purpose 141
　collateral offences, in relation to 209–10
　see also common purpose

commercial purpose, carrying out 150–1, 153–6
complexity of 139
complicity, of, generally 145
different levels of 128, 131
intoxication, effects of 250–1
principal, of
　accessory's knowledge of 139, 177–9
　essential matters, knowledge of 162
　innocent agency, *see* innocent agency, doctrine of
　subsequent offences, in respect of 246
mental culpability, see *mens rea*
misdemeanour, participants as principals 20
mistake, variation by principal due to 198–200
motivation for withdrawal 261–2
motive, complicity, immaterial to 145, 151
motor vehicles, control or possession, omissions relating to 40–1
multi-party liability 238
murder, *see* homicide

negligence, offences of
　abortion cases 187
　acting dangerously 188
　circumstances or consequences, knowledge of 180, 189
　conduct offences 185
　consequence offences 185
　dangerous driving cases 189
　participants, designation of causal roles to 190
　principle of parallelism 186
　unlawful homicide, unintended consequence of 185–90

parallel liability theories
　diminishing appeal of 5
　similar culpability levels, demanding 5
　variable level of culpability 5
participation
　evidence of complicity, as 6
　evolved approach to 89
　felonies, in 20
　inevitable incidental 238–43
　law enforcement objectives, motivated by 15, 243–5
　precise roles in 27–8
　primary or secondary 27–8
　principal, requirement of 238
perpetrator
　agent of accessory, as 6
　complete defence, having 120–4
　criminal fault, lacking 118–20
　liability, free of 114–18
　semi-innocent 130–3
　use of term 2n.

perpetrator (cont.):
  'Pinkerton doctrine' 49
possession offences, presence 36
presence
  affray, at scene of 36
  aiding and abetting indicating 32
  encouragement by 36–8
  hundreds of people, of 39
  inactive 34–9
  mens rea, effect on 155
  modes or complicity, delimiting 32–3
  necessary assistance, to render 36
  no particular act, finding of 35–6
  non-intervention, entitlement of 38
  offence, at 25–6
  possession offences, in 36
  public performance offence, at 36–7
  rape, at 141
principal offence
  accessory
    attitude of 13, 142, 149–50
    circumstances and consequences, knowledge of 179–85
    knowledge of 139, 141–60
      see also accessory
    negligence, offences of 180, 185–90
    perceived likelihood of occurrence 173–7
    repeated 15
  requirement of
    evidence 112–13
    generally 94
    harm, of 114–18
    historically 110–12, 118
principal offender
  accessory, position of, *see* accessory
  acquittal of 113
  actus reus see *actus reus*
  agency, in, *see* agency
  conviction before accessorial liability proved 22–3, 110–11
  deviation by, *see* variation in performance from that contemplated, *below*
  encouragement of, *see* encouragement
  essential matters, knowledge of 162
  expressed limited authority of 202–3
  joint 27–30, 80 n.
  mental culpability, see *mens rea*
  misdemeanours, in 20
  non-conviction of 112
  person being 27–30
  primary or secondary liability 27–8
  secondary party, joint indictment with 113
  treason, in 21
  use of term 2 n.
  variation in performance from that contemplated
    accidental 198–200

common purpose, relationship with 197–8, 221–5
complementary causal analysis 207
complexity of 198
deliberate
  accessorial liability, preventing 200
  causal independence 203–8
  current English law 205–6
  expressed limited authority 202–3
  independence of principal 203–8
  scope for 200
  substantial, of 201–2, 223, 225
  mens rea account of 207
  mistaken 198–200
  voluntary and causally independent 203–8
prize fight, presence at 36–7, 85
procuring
  causal connection 55, 57–9
  complicity, as 118
  construction of 58
  endeavour, production by 59, 67 n.
  manipulative or controlling nature of 58
  purposive state of mind, entailing 155
  voluntary response, triggering 69
  see also aiding, abetting, counselling or procuring
property
  use of force in retrieving 153
  withholding to prevent commission of offence 152
provocation, plea of 132
public performance offence, presence at 36, 85
punishment
  accessories, of 72–3, 90
  equality of
    inchoate offences compared 77
    prominent element of 73
  harm, linked to 71–2, 91
  inchoate offences, of 72
  multiple convictions, for, limitation 248
  proper rationale of 91–2

rape
  innocent agent, through 106–9
  intoxication, effect of 250–1
  positive *actus reus* 36
  presence and encouragement at 141
  principal liability, limitation of 110
secondary party
  manslaughter, convicted of, *see* manslaughter
  self-incrimination 240
  use of term 1 n.
  victim as 15, 239–42
  see also accessory
sexual offences

aiding and abetting, *Gillick* case, 147–9
  personal action, requiring 106, 108
'shoot back' cases 99–101
'shield cases' 99–100
strict liability offences
  complicity in 191–3
  degree of criminality 43
  essential circumstances, accessory's
      knowledge of 191
  general suspicion of 191–2
  social objectives behind 192
  universal culpability standard 5
suicide
  accessory to 146
  complicity in 57

transferred malice, doctrine of 198–9
treason, participants as principals 21

unlawful sexual intercourse
  aiding and abetting, *Gillick* case 147–9
  complicity of victim in 239

vicarious liability
  function of 193
  selective form of complicity, as 193

statutory construction, as 8
victim of crime, accessory, as 15, 239–42

withdrawal
  actus reus, no 252
  classification of defence 253 n.
  effect of 251–2
  effective measure 255
  encouragement, of 255, 257–8
  forms of
    case law 256–60
    theoretical 254–6
  fruitless 254–5
  generally 15–16
  material aid, of 258–9
  motivation for 261–2
  opportunity of 251
  preliminary issues 251–4
  preventing commission of offence 259
  qualifying conditions 253, 255
  rationale, justifying 253, 258
  reasonableness test 259
  timely 260
  unequivocal notice of 256–7
  voluntary and complete 261
  warning 259